Mass Education and the Limits of
State Building, c.1870–1930

Also by Laurence Brockliss

CALVET'S WEB: Enlightenment and Republic of Letters in Eighteenth-Century France

FRENCH HIGHER EDUCATION IN THE SEVENTEENTH AND EIGHTEENTH CENTURIES

MAGDALEN COLLEGE OXFORD: A Cultural History

ADVANCING WITH THE ARMY: Medicine, the Professions and Social Mobility in the British Isles 1790–1850 (*with M. Moss, M. Ackroyd, J. Stevenson and K. Retford*)

MAGDALEN COLLEGE AND THE CROWN (*with Gerald Harris and Angus Macintyre*)

THE MEDICAL WORLD OF EARLY MODERN FRANCE (*with Colin Jones*)

NELSON'S SURGEON: William Beatty, Naval Medicine and the Battle of Trafalgar (*with Michael Moss and John Cardwell*)

CHILDHOOD AND VIOLENCE FROM THE BRONZE AGE TO THE PRESENT (*co-edited with Heather Montgomery*)

RICHELIEU AND HIS AGE (*co-edited with Joseph Bergin*)

A UNION OF MULTIPLE IDENTITIES: The British Isles, c.1750–c.1850 (*co-edited with David Eastwood*)

THE WORLD OF THE FAVOURITE, 1550–1650 (*co-edited with J.H. Elliott*)

Mass Education and the Limits of State Building, c.1870–1930

Edited by

Laurence Brockliss
Professor of Early Modern French History, Magdalen College, Oxford, UK

and

Nicola Sheldon
Academic Research Fellow, Institute of Historical Research, University of London, UK

First published 2012 by
PALGRAVE MACMILLAN

Palgrave Macmillan in the UK is an imprint of Macmillan Publishers Limited,
registered in England, company number 785998, of Houndmills, Basingstoke,
Hampshire RG21 6XS.

Palgrave Macmillan in the US is a division of St Martin's Press LLC,
175 Fifth Avenue, New York, NY 10010.

Palgrave Macmillan is the global academic imprint of the above companies
and has companies and representatives throughout the world.

Palgrave® and Macmillan® are registered trademarks in the United States,
the United Kingdom, Europe and other countries

ISBN: 978–0–230–27350–4

This book is printed on paper suitable for recycling and made from fully
managed and sustained forest sources. Logging, pulping and manufacturing
processes are expected to conform to the environmental regulations of the
country of origin.

A catalogue record for this book is available from the British Library.

A catalog record for this book is available from the Library of Congress.

10 9 8 7 6 5 4 3 2 1
21 20 19 18 17 16 15 14 13 12

Printed and bound in Great Britain by
CPI Antony Rowe, Chippenham and Eastbourne

Contents

Part III The Wider World

Part IV The Colonial Empires

Preface and Acknowledgements

This book began as a seminar series organised by the Oxford University Centre for the History of Childhood in the academic year 2007–08. The Centre for the History of Childhood, the only such centre in the United Kingdom, promotes the historical study of aspects of childhood and child development that are of particular concern to policy makers and childcare professionals (teachers, social workers, psychiatrists, paediatricians, and so on) today. For the year 2007–08, the Centre took as its theme 'Children as Citizens' and explored the different ways from the Greeks to the present in which children and young people were turned into socialised and productive adults. In the course of the year, it became apparent that the most interesting period in the long history of citizenship training was the decades before and after the turn of twentieth century when states all round the world came to accept that the key instrument of acculturation should be henceforth institutionalised education. As a result, it was decided to hold a colloquium entitled 'Citizenship, Modernisation and Nationhood: The Cultural Role of Mass Education 1870–1930' under the auspices of the Centre in September 2009, in which leading national experts on the development of systems of mass education were invited to discuss the experience of individual countries in a comparative framework.

The colloquium debated the coming of mass education under a series of headings, but the one that struck a universal chord among the participants and took us furthest away from received accounts was the gap between intention and achievement. Wherever the state and whatever its level of economic development and national cohesion, there was absence of fit between the state's heroic aims and the reality on the ground, when we drilled down to the bedrock of classroom reality. In presenting the fruits of the colloquium to a wider audience in the form of a book, the editors concluded it was essential that the limitations of the mass educational experiment should be made clear in the title. Nine of the papers presented at the colloquium appear in this book, but in a heavily reworked form in the light of our deliberations. Two more have been specifically commissioned in order to ensure as complete coverage as possible in a volume that takes the world for its province but is inevitably constrained by space to reduce a rich and complex narrative to the experience of a selected sample of states.

It is to the contributors to this volume that the editors are first beholden. As every attempt has been made to make this a readable and coherent book, albeit one comprising individual voices, the contributors have been continually asked to hone their chapters to ensure they combine succinctness and clarity. The contributors have responded to the editors' blandishments with good humour and alacrity and have allowed the book to proceed on schedule. Secondly, the editors must thank Magdalen College, Oxford. Without the generosity of the Fellows at the college, who financed the initial colloquium, the book could never have seen the light of day. At a time when British universities have very limited resources to fund academic conferences and when the Grant Giving Bodies of the United Kingdom are overwhelmed with requests for support, historians in this country are fortunate that Oxbridge colleges with their substantial, but certainly not limitless, endowments, are frequently ready to step into the breach and allow international meetings of scholars to continue. And, finally, thanks must be conveyed to Palgrave Macmillan for agreeing to make this volume part of their list. Michael Strang has since left the publishing house, but initially it was under his enthusiastic but critical eye that the book took shape. More recently, the book has been steered into port by Ruth Ireland. The editors wish to thank her and her very capable team for the essential part that they have played in the realisation of this volume, and only hope that its readers will believe that its contents merit the care that they have lavished on its production.

Contributors

Ellen L. Berg, University of Maryland

Laurence Brockliss, Magdalen College, Oxford University

Gunilla Budde, University of Oldenburg

Jean-François Chanet, University of Paris (Sorbonne)

Nazan Cicek, University of Ankara

S. E. Duff, Birkbeck College, London

Ben Eklof, University of Indiana

Maria Cristina Soares de Gouvea, University of Minas Gerais, Brazil

Heather Ellis, Humboldt University, Berlin

Nita Kumar, Claremont McKenna College, California

Deirdre Raftery, University College, Dublin

Martina Relihan, University College, Dublin

Alessandra Frota Schueller, Rio de Janeiro State University

Nicola Sheldon, Institute of Historical Research, London

Susannah Wright, Oxford Brookes University

Note on Timelines and Glossaries

At the end of each chapter before the references, there is a short timeline and glossary of ambiguous or unfamiliar terms used in the course of the chapter. These terms, when used for the first time in the chapter, are prefaced with an asterisk.

General Introduction

Laurence Brockliss and Nicola Sheldon

Systems of formal education have existed in all sophisticated pre-industrial societies for at least 4000 years. These educational systems primarily trained up a small
but powerful priestly, scholarly or citizen cadre who either constituted the ruling elite or acted as its administrative arm and provided its ideological support.
Admission to the system could be closed or relatively open, but the proportion
of the population that would have experienced a long and continuous period
of formal schooling before the modern era would have been always very small
(perhaps 2 to 3 per cent). While the ability to read if not write was quite widely
diffused in some ancient and medieval societies, it is only in the last 500 years
that schooling has come to be regarded as a priority for the majority of the rural
and urban population.[1]

The idea that formal education should be imparted to everyone seems to have
received state support for the first time in late fourteenth-century China when the
idea was promoted by the incoming Ming as a way of maximising the Confucian
belief in human goodness and ensuring universal harmony. But enthusiasm soon
waned, and the Manchu dynasty that came to power in the mid-seventeenth
century left the provision of schools for the poor in the remainder of the imperial period primarily to private initiative.[2] In the interim, a more powerful and
permanent stimulus for the promotion of compulsory schooling had emerged in
Europe as a result of the division of Christendom into warring camps. In the first
years of the Reformation, Luther and other religious reformers called on the city
administrators and princes to establish schooling for all (both boys and girls), so
that everyone would be able to develop their individual calling.[3] Towards the end
of the sixteenth century, elementary education also began to be fostered by the
reformers' confessional opponents, anxious to secure the religious allegiance of
the young by giving them access to suitable devotional literature.[4] Yet even then
progress was slow. It was only in the second half of the eighteenth century, when
governments were persuaded by the wealth-creating theories of the *philosophes*
that there might be material as well as spiritual benefits from schooling the poor,
that the first systems of state-wide elementary education were promulgated –
particularly in the Kingdom of Prussia and the Austrian Empire.[5] And only in the

1

nineteenth century, as Europe escaped from its pre-industrial past, were universal systems successfully constructed.

In the course of the nineteenth and early twentieth centuries, virtually every European state instituted or tried to institute a nationwide system of elementary education for boys and girls of between six and eight years duration that was eventually, if not usually initially, compulsory and free. After Prussia in 1763, the first to do so was Denmark in 1814; in Western Europe, the last country to make schooling compulsory was Belgium a hundred years later. Before 1870, setting up the system on the ground proved difficult, especially for the countries on the continent that had fewer resources at their disposal. Portugal had legislated for a national system in the late 1830s and again in 1844 but only 13 per cent of its school-age children were receiving formal tuition on the eve of the Franco-Prussian war.[6] In the next 50 years, however, states proved much more adept at getting the young into the classroom, and even in a country as vast, populous and agrarian as the Russian Empire, where schooling was never compulsory, virtually half of children between the ages of eight and eleven were in school on the eve of the First World War.[7]

By then, state-supervised systems of elementary education were being set up in many other parts of the world as well, with varying degrees of success. In the Americas, the new nations that had replaced the former European colonies were as quick to promote universal systems as their erstwhile mother countries (and sometimes quicker). The northern half of the United States developed successful compulsory school systems in the years 1830–60; the southern states followed after the Civil War;[8] while Brazil and Peru had erected a system, albeit on paper, as early as 1834 and 1850.[9] State systems too were enacted in the regions of the world that were still or newly under white European control: Ontario, for instance, created a system of free, though not yet compulsory, schooling in 1852; Victoria, the first Australian state to take the plunge, did it 20 years later.[10] But the most impressive leap forward came in Japan, a hitherto isolated Asian power, which in the mid-nineteenth century was threatened by European domination for the first time. Japan developed a system of national elementary education almost immediately after the Meiji Restoration in 1868, and later spread the initiative to its own colonies.[11] Even China, just as threatened but much more reluctant to imitate the West, showed some interest in mass education. Little was achieved under the last emperors but the Nationalists, who came to power in 1912, were seriously considering developing popular schooling in the short space of time they were in control before their rule collapsed in the mid-1930s.[12]

The systems set up prior to 1930 were principally intended to provide the children of the masses with a basic education. Before the end of the First World War, the schools were not seen as significant agents of social mobility, except in the United States. As a result, they were largely separate from the systems of higher or secondary and tertiary education that trained the sons (and to a small extent, from the turn of the twentieth century, the daughters) of the elite for the growing number of professional careers that were engendered in an industrialising society. Indeed, it was only really in the years following the Second World War that most states around the world fully accepted the idea that schooling at every level might be a vehicle for identifying and fostering individual capacity and potential, and so serve to promote meritocracy. By then, the establishment of universal systems of education had ceased to be controversial. The myriad of states which emerged from post-war decolonisation moved immediately to introduce mass schooling (if none already existed), and the value of formal education was recognised by regimes of every stripe. By 1980, UNESCO estimated that 68 per cent of children of primary school age (girls and boys) in the developing world were enrolled in school.[13] Hostility to the development by parents, employers, religious leaders and taxpayers – factors that had played a part in the slow spread of mass education on the ground in nineteenth-century Europe – had disappeared in all but the most conservative societies such as Afghanistan.

The focus of the present volume is the period 1870 to 1930 when compulsory systems of elementary education were instituted with greater or lesser degrees of success in many parts of the world, but when the systems offered pupils limited opportunities to continue full-time study after their early teens. Through a series of country-specific essays, it aims to deepen our general understanding of why and how these first systems were set up and how they operated. As such, it is intended as a historical contribution to a debate that was begun in the middle of the twentieth century by sociologists, who saw mass education as a key component of modernisation. Initially sociologists saw mass education as a simple consequence of industrialisation. According to the American functionalist, Talcott Parsons, not only was institutionalised education needed to create a sense of commonality in an industrial world where traditional ties had broken down, but it was an essential element in maximising efficiency by identifying the strengths and weaknesses of future members of the workforce and ensuring individuals were slotted into the right career and given the necessary training.[14] In the last decades of the twentieth century, however, both British and American sociologists largely abandoned an economic interpretation of the development on the grounds that the timing of the establishment of national systems of education bore little relation to the pattern of industrialisation. The states that led the way in mass education were usually economically backward, like Denmark and Prussia, while Britain, the first country to industrialise, towards the rear. Instead, a group of Stanford sociologists in the 1980s and early 1990s preferred to attribute the establishment of systems of mass education to the need of the nineteenth-century nation state, especially in its liberal form, to gain the positive endorsement of its citizens/ subjects. The chronological differential in turn was explained by relative levels of cultural homogeneity. Weaker states, ethnically and religiously divided, logically created national systems before stronger ones with a secure national identity.[15] The British educational sociologist, Andy Green, in a study of England, France, Prussia and the United States published in 1990, largely concurred but placed greater emphasis on the role of class in explaining the phenomenon.[16] On the one hand, he accepted the argument of Margaret Archer, put forward 10 years before, that universal education was an instrument to disseminate and consolidate the values of the rising bourgeoisie.[17] On the other, he followed Gramsci in seeing the state as being above class conflict in important respects. To maintain stability, the state had to enforce class hegemony in a way that brought comfort to other competitive groups, so that mass education could be viewed as a working-class and not just a bourgeois desideratum: it created compliant citizens but also offered the tools of empowerment, so its introduction was connected to the balance of social forces in a country.

Since the early 1990s, sociologists have largely lost interest in understanding the rise of mass educational systems. To the extent their development had been connected with the needs of the emerging nation-state to create a patriotic citizenry, they quickly lost their allure as agents of modernisation in the post-modern age of globalisation, mass migration and the celebration of cultural difference. The field has thus been left open to the historian. National histories of the development of mass education have been written since the beginning of the twentieth century, if not before, and in the past 25 years have become ever more specific and detailed, so that few countries in the world now lack their national narrative.[18] Many, moreover, are of a high calibre and have made important nation-specific contributions to an understanding of the role of education in nation building.[19] So far, though, historians have made little attempt to build an overview of the phenomenon that could interrogate and refine others' insights. In fact, there is only one historical rather than sociological study in English that offers a broader account of the development of systems of education in the modern world – a collection of essays put together by J. A. Mangan and published in 1988.[20] This, however, limits its area of enquiry to the British Isles and the white dominions, its focus is on secondary as much as elementary education, and the chronological parameters are hazy.[21]

It is our hope that the present volume of essays will fill the gap for English-speaking readers interested in the early period of mass education when states primarily concentrated on creating a system of universal but relatively closed schooling. The book aims to provide the first comprehensive and coherent overview of this worldwide phenomenon in English or any other language. It does this in four ways. First, its range is extensive. Although space precludes chapters on every state that began to develop a system of mass education in the decades before the First World War, its vision can claim to be global. In its scope, it embraces not just Britain, Europe and the United States, but parts of the world hitherto largely ignored in the English language literature: Latin America, the Near East, South Asia and South Africa. Secondly, the chapters are authoritative. Authored by a mix of young and established scholars, many of them natives of the state that they are examining, the chapters provide an expert account of the current state of research.[22] Thirdly, all the essays have a specific period focus that starts about 1870 and extends into the 1920s and 1930s. Historians of education, like historians of Europe generally, tend to treat 1914 as a watershed. This is understandable, and in the field of education, as in many other areas, the First World War was a defining moment. There can be no doubt that after the war, much rethinking went on in Europe about the purpose and organisation of mass education. Hitherto the new elementary systems of education attended by the mass of the population had had a limited connection with the existing networks of secondary and tertiary education that principally served to educate and replicate the elite. The burning post-war question, in the light of the slaughter of millions of ordinary people and a growing belief that education should be an instrument of social mobility, was how the two systems might be better integrated. For all the consequent discussion, however, the events of 1914–1918 often did not materially alter Europe's two-tiered educational system in subsequent decades. The changes that the establishment of the Soviet Union brought to education in the former Russian Empire, for instance, were not replicated in England or France. In those parts of the world hardly touched by the war, moreover, educational change had its own internal dynamic. In the United States, mass education had already begun to be an instrument of meritocracy at the turn of the twentieth century; in Brazil, even the effective establishment of universal schooling had to await the collapse of the republic in 1930. Therefore, any attempt to provide a global overview of the first, non-meritocratic stage of mass education must extend its vision into the interwar years.

Fourthly, and most importantly, the volume aims to get beyond the simple description of the mass systems that were erected and the educational rhetoric that justified and sustained them. These questions cannot of course be ignored. In order for fresh light to be thrown on the factors that brought the systems into being, there is an evident need for detailed analyses of the elementary school curriculum. But educational systems do not simply come into being by state decree and carry out their state-imparted task until directed otherwise. How systems actually work and what they actually achieve is determined by factors that are frequently outside the state's control. Once given form in legislation, they are never set in aspic. In particular, they are shaped by their stakeholders (to use a modern term), whose attitude to the system in question may be far removed from that of its initial creators. Yet this is an aspect of the development of universal schooling completely ignored by the social scientists. Interested primarily in modelling its cause, they have shown no interest at all in its effective achievements. It need hardly be said, however, that the sources for a 'stakeholder' approach are not as readily available as those for a traditional top-down survey. Children's 'voices' are particularly difficult to hear. As a result, the extent to which individual authors in this volume have been able to capture the 'user' experience depends very much on the degree to which the recollections of teachers and pupils, for example, have been systematically collected and housed in a public archive.[23]

This book consists of 11 chapters divided into four parts. The first part deals with the British Isles, the second with continental Europe, the third with the independent states of the rest of the world and the fourth with colonial territories. Apart from the two contributions which are devoted to England, each chapter charts the development of mass education in a particular country. To prevent the book being a collection of individual case studies, each part is introduced by a short section which provides an overview of the development of mass education throughout the region under consideration. The chapters that follow then put flesh on this skeleton by offering a detailed analysis of the experience of specific states selected for their contrasting demographic, economic and cultural profiles. A synopsis of these individual chapters is provided in the introductory sections.

The picture that emerges from these 11 chapters takes our understanding of the development of mass education to a new level. As we have seen, sociologists in the last 20 years have placed great emphasis on the role of institutionalised education as an agent of national cohesion. The chapters in this book certainly confirm that this was an important element in the establishment of a network of state schools, but it is also clear that the rationale behind their creation was far more complex. Systems of mass education were not necessarily set up primarily to promote national cohesion. The extent to which this was the case depended very much on the degree of national cohesion that already existed. This then did not just affect the timing of the development, as the sociologists have suggested, but also its raison d'être. States that were linguistically, ethnically and religiously divided, especially new states or states with large immigrant populations, like the United States, definitely saw state education as a means of inculcating a common culture. Long-established political entities, such as Britain, on the other hand, were less interested in the role education could play in stimulating a common identity than in promoting the bourgeois values of cleanliness, politeness, sobriety and godliness. Compulsory elementary education was definitely used to promote attachment to the British Empire, but it was principally seen as a means of 'civilising' the working-classes and improving law and order. In most countries, furthermore, mass education was also usually intended to be an instrument of political education in an age that saw the establishment of democratic systems of government in most European states and the parts of the world that had European settlers. Universal schooling was intended to ensure that the newly enfranchised used their vote 'wisely' and did not threaten the social and economic status quo. Indeed, in the German classroom, pupils were specifically taught to abhor socialism as the spawn of the devil. *Pace* recent sociologists, too, there were frequently economic motives for introducing systems of mass education: legislators in countries as diverse as Britain and Brazil expected major material benefits to flow from forcing children into the classroom.

On the other hand, the chapters equally suggest that it is far too simple to see the introduction of mass education as a bourgeois capitalist plot to keep the masses in their place. What is evident is that in the most democratic states, there was an increasing recognition as the period wore on that the state educational system should develop individual potential as well as promote the collective good. Bright children should be given the opportunity to rise up the social ladder, albeit in small numbers. If it was only in the United States that secondary education was automatically open to all, most economically developed countries around the globe paid, at the very least, lip service to the concept of educational meritocracy by the 1930s. Even considered from the top down, the systems of mass education, once constructed, were always being adjusted. In the early twentieth century, national governments were continually forced to rethink and extend the state's educational provision as they came under pressure from groups in society with more radical educational agendas: organised labour and its political representatives, a newly emergent and energised teaching profession, the first generation of child psychologists[24] and even many educational bureaucrats. In particular, the number of years that should be spent in school and the scope of the curriculum and its method of its delivery were the subject of intense and constant debate. Once institutionalised education had been accepted by the state as a power for good, moreover, its role was quickly extended. By the turn of the twentieth century, in many parts of northern Europe, schools became the forum for monitoring and improving children's physical as well as moral development. The school nurse and the dinner lady joined the burgeoning educational establishment.

The book also makes clear how difficult it was to set up working systems of mass education, a point frequently overlooked not just by sociologists but even by historians too often content to describe the key pieces of legislation rather than burrow beneath the surface. Good intentions were never enough. Britain was committed to extending what were perceived to be the benefits of a formal western education to the native peoples in its many colonies.[25] Yet, as its sad performance in India shows, the Westminster government was never willing to commit the necessary resources itself or raise the money in India. Educating Indians, admittedly a tougher proposition given the size of the population, was never as important as schooling Britons. The task was therefore left to the missionary societies throughout the period, despite the fact that the limitations of the voluntarist approach had been the catalyst for setting up a national system in Britain itself.[26] Even governments willing to fund mass education were stymied in their progress unless the national economy was sufficiently developed. There were many calls on the national budget and in poor countries the education department was starved of the funds it needed to build schools and train and pay teachers. This situation was particularly dire where the state was populous and educational provision had been historically sparse. The Ottoman Empire, for instance, for all its commitment to Westernisation in the last decades of its existence, never succeeded in getting its plans for a state system of education beyond the drawing board. It was left to its much smaller Turkish successor state to lay the foundations of a national network.

A lack of money however was not the only handicap. The elite was not always united in its views of the value of universal schooling. In agricultural Brazil, for example, the liberals who ran the republican state at the centre strongly supported the creation of state-run schools. Putting this into effect under the federal constitution, on the other hand, was left to the provincial elites – the great landowners effectively – and they had no interest in the creation of an educated workforce. This was chiefly because the black majority were considered to be second-class citizens throughout the period under review, a legacy of the fact that Brazil had been a slave society until the very eve of the republic's foundation. Racial prejudice equally explains the failure to establish equitable systems of universal education in other parts of the world. In the southern United States, educational provision was segregated and the negroes' schools deliberately underfunded. In South Africa no attempt was made to establish a universal system at all, and the education of the country's majority black population left again to the charitable efforts of the missionary societies.

Furthermore, the eventual successful imposition of universal schooling was usually achieved at a price. As the essays in this volume repeatedly stress, one of the most important but again overlooked elements in the establishment of systems of mass education in most parts of the Christian world is the compromise that the state had to make with the forces of religion. Most Christian states in the second half of the nineteenth century were either religiously divided or suspicious of the power that one or more of the churches within their borders exerted over its flock. In setting up a national educational system, the state usually aimed to create a space where all children might mix together free from the incubus of confessionalism. In many cases, it was hoped religion could be taken out of the classroom altogether. This ambition was seldom achieved due entirely to the intransigence virtually everywhere of the churches, especially the Catholic Church. The papacy, backed up by the local episcopate, made it clear that Catholic parents should send their children to Catholic schools: there should be no pussyfooting with secular or even non-denominational schooling. As the democratic state could hardly stop the Catholics, or any other denomination, from running their own schools, it had two alternatives. Sometimes, it allowed Catholics to have their own network of schools but denied them funding. Usually, it threw in the towel and allowed state schools to become confessionalised: in Germany, for instance, despite Bismarck's *Kulturkampf,* the state provided a separate network of schools for Protestants and Catholics. Sometimes this happened by default. In Ireland when a national network of schools was set up in the 1830s, it was intended to be non-denominational and heal the confessional divide; as the schools were established by local initiative, however, they were normally erected in the heart of a confessional community and were denominationally exclusive. Even in the few states where the Catholics did not obey the command of their priests, Catholic parents ensured that the state's schools did not threaten their children's religious loyalties. In the United States, immigrant parents wanted their children to be educated alongside other white Americans but they were unhappy with the traditional Protestant tone of the state elementary school and successfully fought to remove it. There were few parts of the Christian world therefore in which a national system of education was set up where all children were subjected to a common schooling or the form of schooling preferred by the ruling elite. Only in France in the last decades of the nineteenth century was the state able to set up a secular and universal system of elementary education without kowtowing to either the Catholic majority or the Calvinist minority church. But in France the Catholic teaching orders were banned and the Church lacked funds, so the Catholic hierarchy had no means of setting up an alternative network of schools for the children of the poor.

It was one thing, moreover, for a system to be set up, however imperfect. It was another to get parents to treat it with respect. Once a working system was in place, it was a long time before all children of school age were successfully immured in the classroom. In 1870, the new German Empire had the most developed system of state education in Europe but it took a further 30 years to wipe out large scale truancy. Working-class parents did not see the point of years of education and wanted their children contributing to the household economy as soon as possible. Employers, even many bureaucrats, were happy to fit in with their desires. Parents too who *could* see the value of education did not necessarily subscribe to the vision of its establishment promoters. At the turn of the twentieth century, the Russian Empire, behind its European rivals in many areas, made great strides to catch up in the provision of elementary schooling. The advocates of universal education wanted to use the school to entice peasant children into the towns to further the cause of industrialisation: in the higher grades they were to be deliberately introduced to an exotic world beyond the village. Their peasant parents, however, would have none of this. They were content that their children should learn to read and write on the grounds that smallholders and farm labourers needed these skills to ensure they could deal on equal terms with officialdom and greedy landlords. But the peasants did not want the children to leave the village, so took them out of school before they could be subjected to the siren song of the town.

There is no reason either to assume that once confined in the classroom for the optimum number of years school children picked up the cultural messages that the teachers directly or indirectly were seeking to impart. Evaluating success in this area is extremely difficult. But there is a considerable amount of anecdotal literature based on childhood reminiscences to suggest that schools had limited success in 'civilising' their charges or that success was short-lived. In the German classroom children might be taught the evils of socialism, yet this in no way discouraged them as adults from voting for the socialist party (the SPD). There is even evidence that universal schooling could become the starting point for a counter culture. The offshore Chinese island of Taiwan became a Japanese colony in 1895. The Japanese set about educating the Taiwanese in the superiority of all things Japanese and the benefits that would accrue from being part of the Japanese Empire. However, far from turning the Taiwanese into good Japanese subjects, teaching them to read and write encouraged the development of a sense of Taiwanese nationhood for the first time.[27]

It is the degree to which national systems of elementary education seem to have escaped from the hands of their creators in this first period of universal schooling which explains the title of this book. Although always presented as one of the key elements of modernisation and the first significant step on the road from the warfare to the welfare state, what a detailed examination of the classroom reality reveals is the limits of nation building. Badgered and harassed by educational radicals, stymied by financial exigency, forced to come to terms with confessionalism, and diverted from its purpose by parental indifference or cunning, the state in the late-nineteenth and early-twentieth centuries could seldom keep a tight rein over its creation. This is not to say that in building systems of national education, however incomplete, states had not greatly extended their authority over their citizen-subjects. In the most affluent parts of the European world (and in Japan and its colonies), parents came to accept that children had to spend seven or eight years of their life in a classroom. Through political concessions to both conservative and radical forces, working national systems were created that came to command widespread acceptance and could largely survive the First World War. What this book seeks to point up is the amount of agency that the stakeholders (parents, children and teachers) always retained, even in systems largely set up to establish deferential, law-abiding, economically productive and patriotic adults. That this should be the case is scarcely an earth-shattering conclusion. The social service state throughout the twentieth and early twenty-first century, however benevolent and reasonable its intentions, has constantly found its will subverted and mocked by the very people it set out to help. Human intractability, in a very different context, has similarly frequently blighted the efforts of non-governmental organisations (NGOs). Even today, however, policy makers pay limited attention to the forces of tradition and the resourcefulness of the human material they seek to shape. This book will have served a deeper purpose if it reminds educationalists, social workers and childcare professionals that they are working with people with agency, however ignorant, abject and bereft, and that the state's intrusion into the lives of its citizens had to be negotiated when it first decided to take upon itself a significant part of child-rearing and still has to be negotiated today.

Notes

1. J. Bowen (1975–86) *A History of Western Education*, Paperback, 3 vols (London: Methuen), vols. 1 and 2; R. A. Houston (1988) *Literacy in Early Modern Europe. Culture and Education 1500–1800* (London: Longman), esp. chs 2 and 4; B. A. Elman and A. Woodside (eds) (1994) *Education and Society in Late Imperial China, 1600–1900* (Berkeley, CA: University of California Press), esp. conclusion; R. Dore (1992) *Education in Tokugawa Japan*, paperback (London: Athlone), esp. ch. 7.
2. Ki Che Leung, A. (1994) 'Elementary Education in the Lower Yangtse River in the Seventeenth and Eighteenth Centuries', in Elman and Woodside (eds), *Education and Society*, pp. 381–416 (for a detailed study set in a general framework).
3. Luther, M. (1955–86) 'To the Councilmen of All the Cities that They Establish and Maintain Christian Schools', and 'Sermon: On Keeping Children in School' in J. Pelikan and H. T. Lehmann (eds), *Luther's Works*, 56 vols (St Louis, MO: Concordia Publishing House), vol. xlv, pp. 341–77, and vol. xxvi, pp. 213–58.
4. In the case of France, see K. E. Carter (2011) *Creating Catholics. Catechism and Primary Education in Early Modern France* (Notre Dame, IN: University of Notre Dame Press).
5. J. Van Horn Melton (1988) *Absolutism and the Origins of Compulsory Schooling in Prussia and Austria* (Cambridge: Cambridge University Press), esp. chs 7 and 8.
6. Dates and statistics in P. Flora (1983–7) *State, Economy and Society in Western Europe 1815–1975. A Data Handbook in Two Volumes* (Frankfurt and London: Campus Verlag and Macmillan), i. ch. 10, and Y. N. Soysal and D. Strang (1989) 'Construction of the First Mass Education Systems in Nineteenth-Century Europe', *Sociology of Education*, 62/4, 277–88, at p. 278.
7. B. Eklof (1986) *Russian Peasant Schools. Officialdom, Village Culture and Popular Pedagogy, 1861–1914* (Berkeley, CA: University of California Press), pp. 285 and 293.
8. L. W. Cremin (1980) *American Education: The National Experience 1783-1876* (London: Harper & Row), *passim*; C. F. Kaestle (1983) *Politics of the Republic. Common Schools and American Society 1780-1860* (New York: Hill & Wang).

9. J. Murilo de Carvalho (2001) *Cidadania no Brasil: o longo caminho* (Rio de Janeiro: Civilização Brasileira), *passim*; G. A. Espinoza (2010) 'State, Primary Schools and Local Communities in the Region (*Departemento*) of Lima, 1821–1905', unpublished paper, pp. 27–9. Admittedly, neither had a significant proportion of children in school as late as the 1920s.
10. B. Curtis (1988) *Building the Educational State: Canada West 1836–71* (London: Falmer Press), esp. ch. 3; A. Barcan (1980) *A History of Australian Education* (Oxford: Oxford University Press), pp. 132–3.
11. H. Passin (1982) *Society and Education in Japan*, paperback (Tokyo: Kodansha International), esp. ch. 4.
12. S. Borthwick (1983) *Education and Social Change in China: The Beginnings of the Modern Era* (Stanford, CA: Hoover Institute Press), esp. chs 4–6; R. Hayhoe (ed.) (1992) *Education and Modernisation: The Chinese Experience* (Oxford: Pergamon); L. Bai (2008) 'Children as the Youthful Hope of an Old Empire: Race, Nationalism and Elementary Education in China, 1895–1915', *The Journal of the History of Childhood and Youth*, 1/2, 210–31.
13. UNESCO (1980), *Statistical Yearbook/Annuaire statistique* (Paris: UNESCO).
14. T. Parsons (1957) 'The School Class as a Social System', *Harvard Educational Review*, 29/4, 297–318.
15. J. Boli, F. O. Ramirez and J. W. Meyer (1985) 'Explaining the Origins and Expansion of Mass Education', *Comparative Education Review*, 29, 145–70; F. Ramirez and J. Boli (1987) 'Political Construction of Mass Schooling. European Origins and Worldwide Institutionalization', *Sociology of Education*, 60/1, 2–17; Soysal and Strang, 'Construction of the First Mass Education Systems in Nineteenth-Century Europe', pp. 277–88; J. W. Meyer, F. O. Ramirez and Y. N. Soysal (1992) 'World Expansion of Mass Education 1870–1980', *Sociology of Education*, 65/2, 128–49. John Boli also produced a full length study of the Swedish experience: Boli (1989) *New Citizens for a New Society. The Institutional Origins of Mass Schooling in Sweden* (Oxford: Pergamon).
16. A. Green (1990) *Education and State Formation: The Rise of Education Systems in England, France and the USA* (Basingstoke: Macmillan). The title does not reveal the book also studies Prussia.
17. M. S. Archer (1979) *Social Origins of Educational Systems* (London: Sage Publications).
18. Some allow the process of diffusion to be followed in minute detail; e.g. R. Grew and P. Harrigan (1991) *Schools, State and Society: The Growth of Elementary Schooling in Nineteenth-Century France. A Quantitative Study* (Ann Arbor, Mich.: University of Michigan Press).
19. For example, S. J. Heathorn (2000) *For Home, Country and Race: Constructing Gender, Class and Englishness in the Elementary School 1880–1914* (Toronto: University of Toronto Press).
20. J. A. Mangan (1988) *Benefits Bestowed? Education and British Imperialism* (Manchester: Manchester University Press). Mention should also be made of M. J. Maynes (1985) *Schooling in Western Europe* (Albany, NY: State University of New York Press). This, though, despite its title, does not go beyond 1880.
21. They range from a study of the Newfoundland School Society in the second quarter of the nineteenth century (W. P. McCann) to Britain's educational policy towards the indigenous inhabitants of Africa in the interwar and post-1945 eras (C. Whitehead).
22. The lack of access to non-English works was the principal weakness of Andy Green's otherwise sensitive study of England, France, Prussia and the United States: for his empirical knowledge of France and Germany, he relied on out-dated English language secondary sources.
23. A model of how the children's voice can be recovered for a later period is N. Stargardt (2005) *Witnesses in War. Children's Lives under the Nazis* (London: Jonathan Cape).
24. By the turn of the twentieth century, child development had become a science. For an introduction, see G. Jorland, A. Opinel and G. Weisz (eds) *Body Counts: Medical Quantification in Historical and Sociological Perspectives/La Quantification médicale,*

perspectives historiques et sociologiques (Montreal: McGill-Queen's University Press). For England in particular, see S. Shuttleworth (2010) *The Mind of the Child. Child Development in Literature, Science and Medicine, 1840–1900* (Oxford: Oxford University Press).

25. The key document is the 1847 report of the education committee of the Privy Council. Printed in H. S. Scott (1938) 'The Development of the Education of the African in Relation to Western Culture', *Yearbook of Education* (London: Evans Bros), pp. 693–739.

26. F. Smith (1931) *A History of English Elementary Education* (London: University of London Press), ch. ix.

27. L. Chang (2009) 'Learning to Read: Formation of the Young in Japanese Colonial Taiwan', unpublished paper given at the conference on mass education that was the starting point for this book. The author was unfortunately unable to complete the text for publication.

Part I

The British Isles

Introduction

Laurence Brockliss and Nicola Sheldon

In the eighteenth century, there was no uniform structure of elementary education in the three component kingdoms that would become the new union state of Great Britain and Ireland in 1801. Of the three, only Scotland had an embryonic national system of education, at least in the rural lowlands, where locally maintained parish schools had been universally established under the 1616 Act of Parliament. In England, there was no national system, but simply a mix of charity and fee-paying schools, particularly concentrated in towns and the south of the country; while in Ireland, besides the charity and fee-paying schools that largely served the Protestant minority, there was an amorphous network of itinerant 'hedge schools' patronised by the children of the better-off Catholics.[1] In the course of the nineteenth century, England and Scotland grew closer together. In both countries, for the first two-thirds of the century, the state relied on the established and dissenting churches to provide elementary education in the fast-expanding towns and was content to support their endeavours with an increasing level of subsidy. In both countries too, the eventual national systems of education set up in 1870 in England and in 1872 in Scotland built on rather than replaced existing provision: the state established locally funded and administered schools where none existed, and in Scotland brought the parish and burgh schools under the new locally elected boards; otherwise the voluntary system, as it was called, continued as before, subject to closer inspection.[2] In Ireland, on the other hand, the state took a much larger role from a much earlier date. The failure of private initiative to create mixed confessional schools in the early nineteenth century, as the British government had initially hoped, led to the establishment of a state-supported national system of education in 1831. Although the schools in the system were set up on local initiative and tended to be religiously homogeneous, they all provided the same state-approved secular education in the English language and used the same textbooks in return for central government funding.[3]

systems in the three countries did not significantly change
en the Irish Free State was founded in 1922, it brought
entral government the elementary schools run by the
d hitherto been independent but otherwise continued
ngland, greater coherence was brought to the system
.on Act, which brought all schools, state and voluntary,
.ı of the new Local Education Authorities (themselves subject
.ıed county and borough councils). LEAs, however, were not set up in
.ıand until 1918 (where they took the form of elected county committees), and
were never established in Ireland before Partition. Ideally in the late nineteenth
and early twentieth century, every child in the British Isles was supposed to be at
school from the age of five or six until the day they turned 14 but initially there
was a great deal of leeway. Attendance at school until the specified leaving age
was compulsory in Scotland from 1872 but did not become so in England until
1880 and in Ireland until 1927.[5] Even once attendance was obligatory, it was possible for older children to gain exemption, and it was only on the eve of the First
World War that the large majority of children would have spent eight years in the
classroom.[6] Initially, too, parents still had to pay fees but these were abolished for
pupils in all three kingdoms in the early 1890s.[7]

Throughout the three kingdoms, children in the early 1900s were subjected to a
relentless diet of the three R's and religion (denominational or broadly Christian),
enlivened by history, geography, and some nature study, with the emphasis on
memory learning. Although the curriculum became more child-centred after
1900 as the educational establishment came under the influence of the pedagogical ideas of Pestalozzi and Froebel, the changes were limited.[8] Only in Scottish
schools, where the tradition of going straight to university from the parish school
still lived on, were there advanced departments or supplementary courses laid on
for cleverer pupils for their last two years.[9] After the War, under the Fisher Act of
1918, the school-leaving age in England and Wales was finally raised to 14 without exception for all children, though some exemptions continued until 1921. At
the same time, the local authorities were ordered to introduce continuation day
schools where children between 14 and 18 could receive vocational training. But
the initiative was stymied by lack of funds and day release training only really
developed after 1945.[10] The 1920s did, however, see continued commitment to
reducing the amount of rote learning in the curriculum. The 1931 Hadow report
declared that primary education should be an active not a passive experience
concerned with acquiring facts.

The elementary schools largely formed a closed system. It was accepted that the
brightest pupils should be encouraged to move on to secondary education and
by the mid-1880s state/local government bursaries were available for those who
could not afford to do so.[11] But at this date most secondary schools were either
private institutions or charity foundations, or, as in Ireland, run by the Catholic
regular orders, and showed limited willingness to take on state scholars.[12] Access
was hard before the establishment of local government secondary schools, which
in England only became a commonplace after the passage of the 1902 Education
Act that demanded the establishment of such schools in every local authority

where there was no separate grammar school for boys and girls.[13] Even then, only a small proportion of elementary pupils moved on to secondary school and far fewer girls than boys. In Scotland where there was the greatest enthusiasm to maximise talent, one out of six to seven children embarked on a secondary course in 1914, although they only stayed a couple of years; in England, on the other hand, despite the fact that from 1907 a quarter of all places in state-supported secondary schools were free, the figure was only one in 22. The figure scarcely improved after the First World War. Only about 10 per cent of English 10- to 11-year-olds went on to secondary education in the 1920s and the figure was still under 15 per cent in the late 1930s. In rural Oxfordshire in 1924 only 40 elementary schools out of 212 in the county sent pupils to secondary school, and a mere eight of the 84 free-place children were the offspring of farm workers, though farming was the largest occupation.[14]

In the eyes of the educational establishment, the proportion of elementary pupils who would benefit from secondary education was always thought to be small, at the most 12 per cent.[15] The working class must know its place. In 1897, the secretary to the British Board of Education, Robert Morant, voiced the views of many, when he warned that 'working-class children must not be given an education which would give them too ambitious an outlook.'[16] Middle-class radical intellectuals, such as the Fabian socialist Sidney Webb, equally agreed that secondary education should be limited to the clever few. So too did the upper echelons of the National Union of Teachers, established in 1870, much to the disgust of a dissident member at the Union's 1911 conference, who thought an educational policy that barred the vast majority from advancing and lifted the clever few out of their class merely created 'a handful of prigs and an army of serfs'.[17]

The foundation of a national system of education in Ireland reflected a desire to ensure the loyalty of the Catholic and rural majority to the new Union state, an aim only heightened in the years following the system's formation by Daniel O'Connell's mass campaign for devolution in the 1840s. Irish children were to be turned into 'west Britons'. In Britain itself, the loyalty and patriotism of the population was scarcely an issue. The principal argument advanced for schooling the children of the poor was to raise their moral and intellectual character. While by the middle of the nineteenth century, there was general agreement that this was valuable, there remained considerable opposition for this being made a state concern. When the Newcastle Commission, established in 1858 to look at the provision and quality of elementary education in England, reported in 1861, it declared that the voluntary system, though deficient in certain respects, was sufficient.[18] What appears to have been the driving force behind the eventual establishment of a state educational system within a decade in both England and Scotland was the dawning realisation that the commission's optimism was unfounded and that the voluntary system was failing to cope with the growing number of urban children.[19] Too many were being raised in vice and ignorance at the very time Parliament had decided to give working men the vote (in 1867) and when there was a novel need for well-disciplined workers to meet the new industrial challenge from abroad. The pious and philanthropic feared for these children's souls. The worldly feared a breakdown in law and order if ill-disciplined and idle boys and girls were allowed to run wild on urban streets into their early teens, now they were excluded by labour legislation from gainful employment at a young age.[20] This fear was exacerbated in subsequent years by a new belief, promoted by the first social psychologists, that youth was a difficult time for all children, however perfect their upbringing. All children were potential juvenile delinquents.[21] According to one early twentieth-century school official in the capital, 'If it were not for her five hundred elementary schools London would be overrun by a horde of young savages'.[22]

Whatever its genesis, the elementary school system in all parts of the British Isles in the period under review was chiefly directed to turning out literate, numerate and civilised citizens of the future who would work hard, look after their families, obey the law, and accept parliamentary politics. From the turn of the twentieth century, the elementary school had also to ensure that the future citizens of the British Empire were physically in good shape. Across Europe, child-rearing was becoming scientised with the development of a new branch of medicine – paediatrics – which provided for the first time accurate information about children's nutrition, weight and height, and established healthy norms.[23] Schools were now expected to exercise their pupils' bodies as well as their minds and keep a close eye on their physical health. School medical officers were being appointed in some parts of England from the 1890s. The shock that the government received from the poor condition of army recruits during the Boer War only hastened the process. In 1906 Parliament passed a School Meals Bill, which empowered local authorities to provide a hot midday meal free for the neediest children, and in the following year a nationwide school medical service was created, financed from the rates.[24] The developing role of the school was made possible by the willingness of the state to subsidise local government costs. Across the period 1870–1910, annual public spending on education in Britain leapt dramatically from £1.27 million to £18 million.[25] As a result, by the outbreak of the First World War schools in the British Isles were comparatively well funded. According to a contemporary Spanish source, England and Scotland by this date headed a table of 17 European states in terms of per capita expenditure and Ireland came sixth (ahead of France).[26]

The first section of this book explores different aspects of citizenship education in the British Isles in the years 1870–1930. It begins with an account by Susannah Wright (Chapter 1) of the citizenship training given in the English classroom. She explores the fundamental characteristics of such training and the different views across time of its contents, and offers some thoughts on its effectiveness. *Pace* the belief of some writers that the British state made little attempt to use the school to promote support for the British Empire, Wright clearly shows there was a strong patriotic element in the curriculum which survived the First World War. There was also always a strong religious colouring to the system, despite complaints from secularisers. The voluntary schools obviously had a confessional identity, but the state schools also promoted a vigorous Protestant Christianity, albeit of a non-denominational kind.

The second essay (Chapter 2) by Heather Ellis helps to explain why elementary schools in England retained so many traditional features. The English system was heavily influenced in its development before the First World War by the ethos and structure of the traditional system of secondary and tertiary education, dominated by the privately financed 'public schools'. In that these public schools placed great emphasis on fostering pride in the Empire and creating Christian, mainly Anglican, gentlemen, it was inevitable that similar values would be inculcated in the new elementary schools, especially given the fact that the new national system was set up and run by men educated in those same public schools. The public schools were also an important force in ensuring a measure of social mobility was built into the state system from the beginning, although their general influence began to wane after 1900 as the elementary schools placed a new emphasis on teaching practical skills and understanding the local environment.[27]

The section concludes with an essay on Ireland by Deirdre Raftery and Martina Relihan (Chapter 3). The system of national education in Ireland in the decades before the First World War needed particularly careful handling by the British state. By the turn of the century, virtually all children passed through the national schools but the system was increasingly under attack from Irish nationalists for divorcing the young from their cultural birthright. To draw the nationalists' sting, the curriculum was liberalised: the promotion of Britishness was tempered and a growing place found for Irish history and the Irish language.[28] This gave the new Irish Free State a platform on which to build, but the national schools had left a permanent mark: the nationalists intended to use the elementary schools as a vehicle for promoting cultural nationalism but found it impossible to remove the English language and British culture from the new Irish classroom.

Notes

1. R. D. Anderson (1995) *Education and the Scottish People* (Oxford: Clarendon Press), ch. 1; F. Smith (1931) *A History of English Elementary Education, 1760–1902* (London: University of London Press), chs 1–2; J. Coolahan (1981) *Irish Education: Its History and Structure* (Dublin: Institute of Public Administration), pp. 8–12; M. G. Jones (1938) *The Charity School Movement* (Cambridge: Cambridge University Press); Antonia McManus (2004) *The Irish Hedge School and its Books, 1695–1831* (Dublin: Four Courts).
2. Smith, *English Elementary Education*, chs 5–9; Anderson, *Education and the Scottish People*, chs 4–8.
3. D. H. Akenson (1970) *The Irish Educational Experiment: The National System of Education in the Nineteenth Century* (London: Routledge, Kegan and Paul). The confessionalisation of the system was complete when the state agreed in the early 1880s to give financial support to denominational teacher training colleges.
4. Coolahan, *Irish Education*, p. 18.
5. Anderson, *Education*, p. 65; P. Flora (1983–7) *State, Economy and Society in Western Europe 1815–1975. A Data Handbook in Two Volumes* (Frankfurt and London: Campus Verlag and Macmillan), vol. 1, p. 597.
6. Various educational acts in the intervening years allowed for exemptions: in manufacturing towns older children were initially allowed by school boards to be part-timers so that they could begin earning a wage in the factories. Truancy was also a problem. See Sheldon, N. (2010) 'What Was the Effect of Compulsory Schooling on the Phenomenon of Working Children' in L. W. B. Brockliss and H. Montgomery (eds) *Children and Violence in the Western Tradition* (Oxford: Oxbow Books), pp. 199–205; and id. (2007) 'School Attendance 1880–1939: A Study of Policy and Practice in Response to

Truancy' (University of Oxford D. Phil. Thesis). 78.9 per cent of 5- to 14-year-olds were in school in Ireland in 1911; 78.7 per cent in England and Wales in 1920; and 82.6 per cent in Scotland in 1915: see Flora, *State*, vol. 1, pp. 594, 624 and 630.

7. Anderson, *Education*, pp. 189–90; Coolahan, *Irish Education*, p. 56.
8. R.J.W. Selleck (1968) *The New Education. The English Background 1870–1914* (Melbourne: Pitman).
9. Anderson, *Education*, pp. 251–61. They were not a success and few survived by 1914.
10. D.W. Thoms (1975) 'The Emergence and Failure of the Day Continuation School Experiment', *History of Education*, 4: 1, 36–50.
11. In England and Wales admission to secondary school was through an examination, usually oral, administered by the admitting school. Scotland had a national leaving examination, the 'qualy', from the turn of the twentieth century, but there was nothing similar south of the border until the interwar period. For the 'qualy', see Anderson, *Education*, pp. 259–60.
12. There were exceptions: Manchester Grammar School set aside 20 entrance scholarships for elementary schoolboys in 1877: see Smith, *English Elementary Education*, pp. 310–11. One way round the problem was for bursaries to be offered by outside bodies, such as the North Wales Scholarship Association set up in 1879: see *Oxford Dictionary of National Biography*, under 'Owen, Sir Hugh'.
13. In Wales government funds for establishing secondary schools were available under the 1889 Intermediate Act; in Scotland from 1892 county authorities used state funds to set up a network of secondary schools called 'higher grade' schools, which were the majority of secondary schools by 1914. In England some local councils established their own secondary schools long before the 1902 Act; the City of Oxford High School for Boys, for instance, was founded in 1881, as a counterpart to the privately run Magdalen College School. In Ireland, however, though some state funding was given to private denominational secondary schools from 1878, the secondary school system remained independent of government until the 1960s.
14. Anderson, *Education*, pp. 262–3; R. D. Anderson (1983) *Education and Opportunity in Victorian Scotland : Schools and Universities* (Edinburgh: Edinburgh University Press), p. 234; B. Harris (2004) *The Origins of the British Welfare State: Society, State and Social Welfare in England and Wales, 1800–1945* (Basingstoke: Palgrave Macmillan), ch. 17; G. Bernbaum (1967) *Social Change and the Schools, 1918–1944* (London: Routledge and Kegan Paul), pp. 92–3; P. Horn (1978) *Education in Rural England, 1800–1914* (Dublin: Gill and Macmillan), p. 270. In Ireland the chances of moving from a national to a secondary school were particularly poor: in 1924/5 the Free State only offered 471 secondary scholarships: Coolahan, *Irish Education*, p. 47.
15. Only 10 per cent according to Sir Henry Craik, in charge of the Scottish Education Department 1885-1904: see Anderson, *Education and Opportunity*, p. 211.
16. Horn, *Education*, p. 270. Morant was the author of the 1902 Education Act. He distinguished between 'education for leadership and education for followership'. For his influence on education, see P. Gordon, R. Aldrich and D. Dean (1991) *Education and Policy in England in the Twentieth Century* (London: The Woburn Press), ch. 2.
17. Horn, *Education*, p. 272; B. Simon (1974) *Education and the Labour Movement, 1870–1920* (London: Lawrence and Wishart), pp. 203–7.
18. Smith, *Elementary Education*, pp. 224–42.
19. The Newcastle Commission was only the first of three that reported on education in the British Isles in the 1860s. The Argyll Commission reported on Scotland in 1864; the Powis Commission on Ireland in 1868. All helped to shape the debate at the end of the decade.
20. Smith, *English Elementary Education*, pp. 220–3 and 281–2; A. Green (1990) *Education and State Formation. The Rise of Educational Systems in England, France and the USA* (Basingstoke: Macmillan Press), pp. 300–1. The Education Acts of 1870 and 1872 were

also part of a wider shift from a belief that social problems could be dealt with by voluntary effort to a belief that they needed state intervention: see G. Finlayson (1994)
Citizen, State and Social Welfare in Britain, 1830–1990 (Oxford: Clarendon Press).

21. H. Hendrick (1990) *Images of Youth: Age, Class and the Male Youth Problem 1880–1920*
(Oxford: Clarendon). The struggle against delinquency continued in the interwar
period: see V. Bailey (1987) *Delinquency and Citizenship: Reclaiming the Young Offender,
1914–1948* (Oxford: Clarendon Press).
22. G. A. N. Lowndes (1937) *The Silent Social Revolution: An Account of the Expansion of Public
Education in England and Wales, 1895–1935* (Oxford: Oxford University Press), pp. 15
and 19.
23. For the new interest in children's mental and physical development in Britain, see
S. Shuttleworth (2010) *The Mind of the Child. Child Development in Literature, Science and
Medicine, 1840–1900* (Oxford: Oxford University Press), esp. chs 11–14.
24. For the debate over whether to introduce school meals (Craik in Scotland was against),
see H. Hendrick (1997) *Children, Childhood and English Society, 1880-1990* (Cambridge:
Cambridge University Press), pp. 47–8 and 67.
25. B. R. Mitchell with P. Deane (1962) *Abstract of British Historical Statistics* (Cambridge:
Cambridge University Press), pp. 396–9. For the post-war expenditure on education,
apportioned between central and local government, see Harris, *British Welfare State*,
p. 264.
26. Cited in T. Garcia Regidor (1985) *La polemica sobre la secularización de la enseñanza
en España 1902–14* (Madrid:Instituto Universitario 'Domingo Lázaro', Universidad
Pontificia de Comillas), p. 43.
27. A similar development occurred in Ireland's national schools following the report of
the Commission on Practical and Manual Instruction set up in 1897.
28. Some concessions were also made to teaching in Gaelic in the Highlands from the
late 1870s and in Welsh in Wales at the beginning of the twentieth century after the
appointment of Owen Morgan Edwards as chief inspector of Welsh schools: see W. L.
Lloyd (1964) 'Owen M. Edwards (1858–1920)', in Glanmor Williams *et al., Pioneers of
Welsh Education: Four Essays* (Swansea: Faculty of Education, University College).

1
Citizenship, Moral Education and the English Elementary School

Susannah Wright

A range of concerns in the late nineteenth and early twentieth centuries, in England and beyond, led policy-makers, educational theorists, classroom teachers, churches, secularist organisations, scientists, and a range of social reformers to focus on the elementary school as an agent of moral reform. The effects of economic and social changes including urbanisation and industrialisation, new knowledge and ideas, the weakening of old traditions and beliefs all convinced contemporaries of the important role the school had to play.[1] Moral reform through the school, they believed, would mould the citizens of the future. Despite a common conviction of the socialising potential of the elementary school, however, there was no one idea about how this potential could be realised, or indeed a single clear notion of what citizenship was. Contemporaries disagreed on the basis of the values to be taught in elementary schools: was it to be a Christian morality, or a 'human' or social morality, without reference to God? They also differed on pedagogy – were moral values to be taught via direct moral instruction, or 'caught', imbibed indirectly through the social relationships of the school community, or absorbed from the content of other parts of the curriculum or activities such as organised games? Schools were, of course, not the only organisations involved in transmitting values to the young. Socialisation also occurred in the home, in the church, in organised youth movements, and – to the alarm of reformers – on the street.[2]

This chapter considers the role of the elementary school in England in socialising the rising generation, in teaching the values that would form responsible citizens, over the period 1870–1930. The first section offers background on the development of the elementary school system at that time. The central section examines the different ways in which elementary schools operated as agents of moral education. A concluding session considers what efforts to socialise elementary school pupils at this time achieved.

Citizenship and the elementary school system: 1870–1930

The state in England became involved in the provision of elementary education relatively late in comparison with other European countries, including Scotland.

Through much of the nineteenth century, the churches were the main providers of elementary education (elementary schools were also run by employers under the 1833 Factory Act and the owners of 'private venture' or 'dame' schools). The purpose of church schools was the basic elementary instruction and religious training of the poor. The role of church schools, as the Church of England's *National Society stated, was to 'communicate...such knowledge and habits as are sufficient to guide them through life, in their proper stations, especially to teach the doctrines of Religion'.[3] This was arguably closer to the churches' traditional pastoral duty of educating poor parishioners than an explicit agenda of state formation. Limited financial assistance was available from the central government from 1833. The stated intention of such funding was again the education of the poor, or, as it was put in 1860, the 'children belonging to the class who support themselves by manual labour'.[4]

From the 1860s, state involvement in financing and organising elementary education increased and for the first time a *Code of Regulations was issued by the government. The 1862 Revised Code established a common curriculum and a country-wide apparatus for inspection and funding – the 'payment-by-results' system whereby schools were awarded a grant on the basis of individual pupils' performance in reading, writing and arithmetic when examined by the inspector. With the 1870 Education Act, which provided school places for all children aged 5–12, the state was for the first time fully involved in establishing and running elementary schools. Where there were insufficient places for school-age children in existing voluntary schools, locally elected school boards were established and charged with building and running schools to 'fill in the gaps'. Under the 1902 Education Act, local education authorities (LEAs), which replaced school boards, were funded by the central government to establish secondary schools which would be made accessible to all through a competitive scholarship system, thus extending state involvement in education beyond the elementary school.

What motives lay behind this increased state involvement in elementary schooling for the mass of the population in the late nineteenth and early twentieth centuries? By the late 1860s, mounting evidence of a severe shortage of school places compared with the population of children put pressure on the government to act. Many young people were not attending school. This shortage was, apparently, particularly acute in large urban areas, as surveys in Manchester, Birmingham, Leeds and Liverpool attested.[5] This was, of course, a time when new techniques for counting, classifying, and measuring the population were developed, and linked to new forms of governance, in urban areas.[6] The pressure groups that emerged in the late 1860s – the National Education League and the National Education Union – gathered and publicised evidence of this sort in their campaigns for greater state involvement in elementary schooling.

Economic growth and the formation of citizens were cited throughout the period as reasons why all young people should receive an elementary education, and remain important as rationales for expanding compulsory education today. Looking first at economic growth, from the 1860s onwards, there were growing concerns that England would lose her industrial pre-eminence and fall behind her international competitors, notably the United States and Germany, and also other European countries. Contemporaries feared that limited educational opportunities might lead to industrial decline. As Mr. Anthony John Mundella, manufacturer of yarns and chairman of the Nottingham Chamber of Commerce put it in the 1880s: 'In Germany they are all well educated and it is to that fact that I attribute their greater progress.'[7] Government spokespersons also drew on such arguments when promoting the extension of state involvement in education. W.E. Forster introduced an education bill in 1870 with the assertion: 'Upon the speedy provision of elementary education depends our industrial prosperity...[if] we leave our work-folk any longer unskilled...they will become over-matched in the competition of the world.'[8] In a similar vein, in 1914 R.B. Haldane, then Lord Chancellor, urged the extension of educational opportunities for the simple reason that 'if our generation does not make an effort the nation will fall behind all others'.[9]

Citizenship, when it came up in educational debates in the nineteenth century, most often referred to membership of the social community of the nation, and the rights and duties which went with this membership. Citizenship was also, at times, related directly to the exercise of the franchise. To take the broad, general sense of citizenship first, the elementary school was seen as the place where the mass of young people could be collected together, and taught attitudes and behaviours that would remedy deficiencies of home and neighbourhood. From the early nineteenth century, if not earlier, a number of commentators had stressed the necessity of schooling for the masses for the comfortable and efficient functioning of society. During the 1830s and 1840s, there were calls for the expansion of elementary schooling in order to protect against the dangers of radicalism, and to prevent social unrest, particularly in poor, overcrowded urban areas.[10] A more immediate imperative, however, behind the 1870 Education Act was the expansion of the electorate in 1867 with the passage of the Second Reform Act. In an oft-misquoted statement, Robert Lowe claimed that 'it will be absolutely necessary that you should prevail upon our future masters to learn their letters'. Lowe was, in fact, arguing against an extension of the franchise, on the grounds that once this happened it would be necessary, in order to ensure 'the peace of the country', to develop a national system of education.[11] A direct connection between the Second Reform Act and the 1870 Education Act is hard to establish, but there was a strong perception of a link between a national system of education and the effective exercise of the vote. Arguments linking the extension of mass education and the extension of the franchise emerged again during the First World War, with H.A.L. Fisher, president of the Board of Education from 1916–22, stating in the House of Commons in 1917 that unless steps were taken to extend educational opportunities, to 'form and fashion the minds of the young', for example through continuation classes, they could not be expected to exercise the franchise in an intelligent way.[12] What sort of citizenship Lowe and Fisher wished to promote is not immediately apparent from such statements. They were, arguably, more concerned with developing controllable subjects who would accept their place, rather than autonomous individuals who could think for themselves.

Two key features of the system of elementary schooling shaped the ways in which schools were used for purposes of socialisation. The first of these was the balance between centralisation on the one hand and local initiative on the other. School boards from 1870 allowed for the representation of local minority interests: such opportunities existed to a lesser extent in local education authorities under the 1902 Act. The school board era is notorious for its highly centralised curriculum, inspection and funding system. Under the 1862 Revised Code, and the payment-by-results system, there was pressure on teachers to focus primarily on the three R's (reading, writing and arithmetic) that were the subjects examined by inspectors and where the level of attainment determined the school's funding by the state. Yet even under this common regime, some schools introduced a wide range of subjects. From the 1890s, changes to funding processes, along with greater flexibility in the centrally prescribed curriculum, offered schools more scope to define their curriculum.[13] This was possibly also encouraged by developments in educational thinking, which led to a focus less on a fixed teaching offer and more on the development of the individual child. However, even in the 1890s, government codes and curriculum suggestions still determined to a large extent what schools could teach, and a strong focus on reading, writing and arithmetic remained.

Second, there was what could be called a mixed economy of elementary educational provision, with voluntary church schools alongside board (after 1902 local authority) schools. Another source of variation was the socio-economic status of the neighbourhood of the school. Through this chapter, for the years up to 1918, individual examples of provision for citizenship and moral education will be taken from five schools in Birmingham and Leicester, which have been chosen to reflect these variations. In Birmingham, Edgbaston Church of England (CofE) School, opened in 1846, was located in a wealthy suburb, while Floodgate Street (Board) School, opened in 1891, was situated in one of the city's most notorious slum areas. A third Birmingham School, Severn Street School, was founded by the British and Foreign Schools Society in 1809. By the end of the nineteenth century the school was suffering financial problems and transferred to Birmingham School Board in 1901. In Leicester, St Saviour's was a CofE school opened in 1882 in the 'respectable' suburb of Spinney Hill, while Willow Street Board School opened in 1880 in a poor central area.[14]

The transmission of moral values in the elementary school: 1870–1900

It is useful for the purposes of this chapter to divide the years 1870–1930 into three shorter time periods. This division highlights the approaches to transmitting moral values in the elementary school that were emphasised at different times, reflecting developments in educational policy and thinking and broader political and social changes. However, it is important to note that different approaches did not start or finish in these periods. In the first of these time periods, 1870–1900, the most favoured means of transmitting moral values were school discipline (particularly systems of reward and punishment), drill, religious instruction, and the use of school texts to promote nationalism and citizenship.

The general discipline of elementary schooling was deemed an important tool for socialising working-class children. Mass elementary schooling in the late nineteenth century was, undoubtedly, seen as a way of dealing with unsupervised children, particularly in urban areas. However, the rhetoric of the time suggests a civilising mission alongside practical considerations. Attending elementary school in itself was perceived as a positive moral influence on the children of the poor, some of whom, after 1870, were brought into schools for the first time. At school, it was argued, such children would learn habits of cleanliness and discipline that they would not pick up at home or in their local communities. Nonetheless, the parents who resisted compulsory attendance were unconvinced about the importance of these habits, unsure about the effectiveness of schools in instilling them, or had other priorities such as increasing the family income.

How was school discipline used more specifically to breed good habits in elementary school pupils? Education Department guidance at this time focused on moral training through the 'ordinary management of the school'.[15] An important aspect of such general management would have been systems of reward and punishment, which promoted attendance and punctuality, and also hard work, orderly behaviour, and cleanliness. Attendance and punctuality received the most attention in such schemes. They were seen as virtuous qualities in their own right. Moreover non-attendance and lack of punctuality would have undermined attempts to teach these and any other qualities, while disrupting the school and potentially holding back the academic progress of individual pupils, which would in turn have affected the level of government grant. There were also the concerns about unsupervised children, particularly in towns, that have already been noted.

Elementary school log books offer examples of the systems of rewards and punishments which teachers developed. The first headmaster of Floodgate Street School, for instance, took children who had made a certain number of attendances to see the skeleton of a whale at Curzon Hall. He also 'promised to take all the regular children' to the Grand Pantomime in 1896. This strategy had an immediate impact: 'the improvement in attendance this week is most marked'.[16] Other approaches included extra break-time or an early end to the school day for punctual and regular attenders,[17] and timetabling popular lessons or activities when attendance could be low, such as Friday afternoons.[18] Regular attendance was also rewarded at formal prize-giving events, which offered opportunities for additional moral teaching, and promoting appropriate social deference, as in the following log book entry for Edgbaston School: 'Annual distribution of prizes this afternoon. Present: Vicar and Mrs Strange, Rev Edwards and E Handley Esq. The Vicar and Mr Handley addressed the boys, especially pointing out the importance of punctuality and regularity of attendance'.[19]

Rewards operated alongside a system of punishments. School Board attendance officers could visit the homes of absent pupils and compel pupils to attend, sometimes with the threat of a court case and fines. The headmaster of St Saviour's School, Leicester, was convinced that the threat of compulsion was more effective in improving attendance than any promise of reward.[20] Teachers themselves would also 'send after' absentees. The first headmaster of Floodgate Street School went himself to the truants' favourite haunts to round them up,[21] while the headmaster of Severn Street School wrote in 1882 that 'personal remonstrance with the parents' increased attendance.[22] Truants were frequently subjected to corporal punishment, which was also used, but to a lesser extent, for lateness.[23]

The period 1870–1900 also saw the emergence of drill as an approach to physical training and promoting discipline in schools. Drill was first included in the elementary school code as an 'alternative' activity in 1871, and by the late 1880s had become an established part of the curriculum in many voluntary and board schools. As John Hurt argues, it was valued for the training it offered to the children of the labouring poor in submission, order and obedience, and, more controversially, it was promoted by some as preparation for future military service.[24] Henry Major, in his first report as Inspector to Leicester School Board in 1877, elaborated on the potential benefits of drill, although how far these benefits were realised in practice is hard to tell: 'The habits of obedience, promptness, self-control, and silence of the drill [are] carried into the actual school work. ... This is very interesting work if attention be given to it, and well worth the labour it entails, from the comfort it brings into the school.'[25]

Religious instruction was similarly considered by many to be an essential feature of elementary schooling, in no small part because of the moral education it was thought to provide. Good was felt to result from teaching the subject irrespective of the different approaches typically used in voluntary and board schools. Voluntary schools offered religious instruction on a confessional basis, teaching the tenets of their particular denomination, using the catechism, the Book of Common Prayer, and carefully selected passages of scripture. Only such definite instruction, it was argued, would inspire pupils, and provide firm foundations for ethical behaviour.[26] Denominationally specific instruction, of course, also promoted allegiance to a particular church.[27] Such instruction was reinforced by the close links between the local church and school: often through physical proximity, and also through vicars' regular involvement in the life of the school, and teachers' involvement in the church.[28] Religious instruction in board schools, on the other hand, tended to take the form of Bible reading without comment, which, proponents urged, would provide the necessary religious sanction for moral behaviour and encourage good conduct.[29]

Log books provide only limited evidence about the content of religious instruction lessons. Most references are simply to 'scripture' or 'religious lessons', with no comment about what these entail and references to 'scripture reading', 'religious knowledge' and 'church history' are only a little more revealing.[30] Despite the perceived association between religious instruction and good conduct, it is difficult to find evidence of specifically ethical teaching. The log book for St Saviour's School contains several references to addresses on ethical matters; that they were exceptional is hinted at by the comment that they were given instead of the usual lessons.[31] The focus of such lessons, with themes such as temptation and the 'meaning of A Christian's name and its significance' is, arguably, more about personal conduct and attitudes rather than a broader social morality pertaining to nationalism or citizenship.

Despite this personal focus, advocates of both denominationally specific and non-denominational approaches pointed to the broader civic import of religious teaching. Christianity, they argued, was the basis for modern civilisation. Its ethical tenets underpinned the English legal code. Christian beliefs stimulated noble acts of patriotism and social service. Advocates of denominationally specific teaching in schools argued that such instruction would help retain the Christian roots of the nation. One argued that 'the sense of duty so characteristic of Englishmen and which had found expression in Nelson's famous signal at Trafalgar is largely the result of the impress that three hundred years teaching of the Church Catechism has left'.[32] On the other hand, Dr John Clifford, famous for leading the campaign of passive resistance against rate aid to church schools in the wake of the 1902 Education Act, was among the many Nonconformists who proposed that the Bible, with its wealth of biographical illustrations, and literary and poetical qualities, could be used to prepare children in the duties of citizenship.[33] Religious instruction in schools, therefore, was viewed as integral to national well-being.

Pupils were further exposed to values of nationalism and patriotism through the books that were used at school, chief among these being school readers. From 1880, the use of readers to improve the reading skills of elementary school pupils was mandatory, even if actual texts were not prescribed by the government. In consequence, cheap, mass-produced volumes of historical, geographical, literary, civics and home economics readers became widely used. At a time when many schools did not teach history and geography as timetabled subjects, readers became an important source for the transmission of patriotic and imperial ideals in elementary schools.

According to Stephen Heathorn, such readers promoted an imperialist project overseas and also what was deemed 'an appropriate domestic social identity for the lower rungs of society'.[34] Elementary school pupils were exposed to constructions of national identity based around the concept of an Anglo-Saxon race. Both cultural factors and biological traits were considered essential to English nationality – English rather than British tended to be used as the designation of nationality, and the focus in both historical and geographical readers was much more on England than Ireland, Scotland and Wales. There was slippage between the notion of national character and racial traits and origins. Thus 'English' characteristics including pluck, honesty, and fair play were seen as racial ones and the historic growth of English liberties through past constitutional struggles was attributed to a shared racial ancestry. With this stress on a common community of race, with a shared cultural heritage, Heathorn argues, pupils were encouraged to love king and country, and to accept their place in the social hierarchy, and class or gender roles.[35]

Among the most popular of the civics readers was H. Arnold-Forster's *The Citizen Reader*, first published in 1884, and by 1887 already in its eighth edition. Citizenship in this text was understood in a social rather than strictly political sense; it was about membership of a national and imperial community rather than just the franchise. W.E. Forster, architect of the 1870 Education Act, wrote in his preface to the eighth edition that 'there is a special fitness in the appearance of a book of this kind at a time when we have just added millions to the citizens who have the right of electing representatives'. He was presumably referring to the Third Reform Act of 1884, which greatly extended the franchise but still denied the vote to females and many unpropertied males.[36] Arnold-Forster's book described the country's legislative and administrative machinery, and also 'the duties owed by British Citizens to their country, their countrymen and themselves'.[37] Good citizenship was associated with qualities seen as essential to Englishness (rather than Britishness), such as love of liberty, fairness, patience and self-denial. Pupils read that it was their duty to uphold the honour of England. As Arnold-Forster wrote: '[those] who really love their country, and are truly proud of its great history, will be particularly careful not to do anything by which it may be dishonoured'.[38] This duty extended to the empire as a whole: citizenship in this book, as in other readers, had an imperial as well as a national remit. The English nation, Arnold-Forster wrote, 'extends everywhere where the English language is spoken by men who live under English law and under the English flag'.[39] Reference was made to historical figures whose actions saved the country from foreign oppressors and whose suffering and sacrifices produced the freedoms and liberties then enjoyed: military men such as Admiral Nelson, the Duke of Wellington and General Gordon, political leaders such as Edmund Burke, and 'martyrs' who died in the pursuit of freedom of thought such as Thomas More and Bishops Latimer and Ridley.

Similar depictions of Englishness and English citizenship can be found in textbooks of this period that were not officially prescribed readers.[40] There is also some overlap with the content of moral instruction texts addressing the theme of patriotism and discussed later in this chapter. Unfortunately little evidence exists to tell us what pupils took away from the texts they read in schools. Some ex-pupils, according to oral histories and autobiographies, remember the rote learning of battles and kings and place names and mention nothing of moral and civic values. Others remember inspiring lessons from enthusiastic and able teachers.[41] Although the values that authors intended to promote are clear, it cannot be assumed that moral messages were conveyed as the Education Department and authors of school books wanted, or that pupils reading texts absorbed what they read without question.

New approaches to moral education: 1900–1914

At the turn of the twentieth century, general systems of reward and punishment, drill, religious instruction, and readers remained important forms of moral teaching in elementary schools. However, new approaches to moral education, reflecting broader social and ideological changes, emerged. These included the introduction of secular moral instruction and organised games, and the promotion of the new emerging agendas of imperialism and national efficiency through, for example, extra-curricular activities such as Empire Day celebrations and teaching domestic economy.

Secular moral instruction was promoted by the secularist groups that emerged as an alternative to organised Christianity towards the end of the nineteenth century. Secularists, particularly those attached to the *ethical movement, argued that religious instruction in schools was not an effective form of moral education. The 'exigencies and complex responsibilities of the modern state', it was argued, required a different approach.[42] During the 1890s, the Sunday schools of the ethical movement had been used as a space to experiment with secular moral instruction lessons and advocates felt that such lessons could be promoted more widely. The *Moral Instruction League was established in 1897 to campaign for the introduction of timetabled secular moral instruction lessons in all elementary schools on the basis that such lessons were an essential aspect of a pupils' moral training.[43] It canvassed local education authorities, and the education department in London, developed curriculum materials (a syllabus and handbooks for teachers), and devised rudimentary mechanisms of professional development for teachers. While it never succeeded in its aim of gaining for moral instruction a compulsory position in the elementary school curriculum, the subject was part of an optional clause in the elementary school code from 1906 onwards. By 1908, 60 out of the 327 Local Education Authorities in England and Wales had made provision for some form of moral instruction lessons, while 20 had formally adopted the League's *Graduated Syllabus*.[44] Though never taken up in the majority of schools, this was more than a fringe interest.

Moral instruction lessons, where implemented, were most commonly 20 to 40 minutes in length, and took place once or twice a week. Schemes of moral instruction produced by the Moral Instruction League and others were based on social morality and duty to fellow humans, as distinct from Christian moral schemes centred on duty to God. The Moral Instruction League's *Graduated Syllabus*, to cover lessons for all elementary school students from infants up to Standard VII, provides a useful illustration. Values were expressed in the syllabus as abstract nouns. Lessons for younger children were to focus on personal duties and duties to the immediate family, such as cleanliness, kindness, good manners, courage, hard work, fairness, truthfulness, self-control, work, perseverance, temperance, prudence, and obedience. Broader social duties and themes, such as justice, patriotism, ownership and war and peace, were suggested for lessons with older pupils.[45]

The Moral Instruction League's method aimed to engage the pupil not through discussion of abstract moral principles but through concrete illustrations of moral subjects derived from a range of sources: literature, mythology, and history.[46] The approach varied with the age of the pupil: 'picture teaching' for the youngest children (simple fables and made up stories), concrete examples of lives of historical and contemporary individuals for 7-to 14-year-olds, and discursive methods for the oldest pupils. The books were, according to authors, intended merely for guidance and outline, and were to be supplemented or adapted as teachers saw fit. It is unclear, however, how teachers used these books in practice: there is a suggestion from local inspection reports from Birmingham and Leicester that some teachers showed less imagination, flexibility, or enthusiasm than authors had hoped.[47]

In some respects, the ideals imparted to pupils through moral instruction texts resemble those in other school books of the period. Lessons on patriotism, for example, aimed to inspire in pupils a love for their country and a desire to work for their country's benefit. Pupils were urged, as they were in historical readers, to preserve the country's position in the world, and her political freedoms. Exemplars of patriotism, nearly all men, included English (rather than British) historical and military heroes (Wellington, Nelson, Alfred the Great, General Gordon), international leaders (George Washington), and figures from Greek and Roman history (Marcus Curtius, King Codrus of Athens). This selection is similar to the exemplars found in other textbooks and readers, although the international element is perhaps stronger. However, a detailed reading of the content of individual lessons within moral instruction texts reveals that some offer a politically progressive reading that diverges somewhat from the norm of elementary school books of the period. F.J. Gould, for example, included in his idea of patriotism the motivation of political movements such as the Polish movement for freedom against Russia, the Irish claim for self-rule, and the Indian desire for a greater part in ruling their country, as well as the actions of the usual gallery of military and political leaders. Gould also questioned blind obedience, discussed the injustice of poverty and deprivation, and criticised the treatment of groups disadvantaged on the basis of creed, race, nationality, gender, and political views. He implied in one lesson that all religions are equal – this particular lesson generated extensive publicity and criticism and appears to have deterred some education authorities and schools from using his books.[48]

This period also witnessed increased emphasis on organised games, which, it was argued, had physical and moral benefits. Enthusiasm from the *Committee of Council on Education is evident in its report of 1897:

> Increasing attention is being paid in elementary schools to physical exercises. We have observed with much satisfaction the efforts which are being made by large numbers of teachers to help in the organisation of school games, and thus to secure for the scholars in elementary schools some of the advantages of that side of school discipline and comradeship which has become a characteristic feature of higher grades of English education.[49]

After the turn of the century, physical exercise was to be promoted more strongly, partly due to concerns that the poor physical condition of the urban poor would be detrimental to the efficiency of the nation as a whole. Thus in 1906 the elementary school code allowed, for the first time, games during school hours. The central government Board of Education outlined the expected benefits of this change, physical and moral:

> The children ought to win, not only something of the physique of the boys and girls in our Secondary Schools, but also the control over their personal

desires and impulses which goes far to form character. Victory or defeat, their individual success or failure, will be far less important than 'playing the game,' and from their pride in 'the school' and its good name will spring a stronger love of fair play, the power to give and take which counts for so much in the rough and tumble of life.[50]

These comments resonate with public school discourses of athleticism common in the late nineteenth century, although the explicit references to empire and leadership are missing here.[51]

The enthusiasm for games evident in this comment from the Board of Education is easy to account for, as most members of the board would have had a public school education themselves. There was also enthusiasm on the part of teachers, as entries in some school log books indicate. For example, teachers at Willow Street School in Leicester appear to have expended much effort to develop provision for games. The football club was started 'at the expense of the teachers' and equipment for cricket was purchased 'out of the school fund'.[52] Similarly, a football club was also started at Severn Street School before its transfer to Birmingham School Board in 1901.[53] (From the 1890s local school football associations were formed in large towns and cities, including London and Birmingham, and the English Schools Football Association was formed in 1904.)[54] The game of choice at Edgbaston School was cricket: the school team which won local tournaments during the 1890s and 1900s was also, presumably, funded and coached by volunteers.[55] The fullest discussion of the expected benefits of games, and also the lack of suitable space for them, a problem faced by many elementary schools, was in the log book for St Saviour's School, Leicester. The headmaster wrote as follows:

I took the boys in 'Organised Games' – rounders in the school yard; St[andard] I v II, III v IV, V, VI, VII in sides, explaining how the game should be played, with smartness, fairness, no wrangling, with vigour & with their 'heads' & not in any haphazard way. Such demonstrations do them an immense amount of good. I wish the yard was larger & better paved so that other games could be taken.[56]

There is no mention of games at Floodgate Street where the focus was very much on drill.

A further development was the emergence of a strong imperial agenda for the elementary school by the turn of the twentieth century. 'Its business is to turn out youthful citizens...preparing children for the battle of life (a battle which will...be fought in *all* parts of the British Empire', wrote Edmond Holmes of *Her Majesty's Inspectorate in 1899).[57] Interest in the imperial role of the school was evident in renewed enthusiasm for military drill at this time, in the adaptation of geography syllabuses to emphasise colonial expansion, and in the content of textbooks and the elementary school readers discussed earlier.[58] Its most obvious manifestation, arguably, was in the emergence of the Empire Day movement in elementary schools.[59] Empire Day was the brainchild of the 12th Earl of Meath, who got the idea from the celebrations which took place from the 1890s onwards in Canada each year on 24 May, Queen Victoria's birthday. The Earl of Meath outlined his ideas in an open letter to the press in 1905, which was reissued in subsequent years. He stressed that Empire Day aimed to inculcate ideals of good citizenship, by promoting qualities of imperial and national patriotism, loyalty to the monarch and obedience to authority – '[teaching the] rising generation...to subordinate the individual to the common interest'.[60] The programme he suggested included hoisting and saluting the flag, explanations of the meaning of Empire Day and singing of the national anthem with other suitable patriotic songs. There was initial interest, with 5,540 elementary schools in the country celebrating Empire Day in 1905, but also caution: many Local Education Authorities opted out of observance, and the House of Commons in 1908 voted against a proposal for official recognition. Radicals and socialists among parents and local education committee members objected to the militarist and imperialist message of the Empire Day movement.[61] Yet the popularity of the movement increased during and after the First World War.

School log books offer illustrations that illuminate this national picture. Leicester Education Committee sanctioned observance of Empire Day in 1913, but Willow Street and St Saviour's Schools introduced celebrations some years earlier, in 1906 and 1908, respectively. The observances in St Saviour's School very much followed the Earl of Meath's suggestions. In 1908 the headmaster 'spoke to the children about Empire Day soon after prayers this morning, explaining its meaning, the aims & objects of the society presided over by the Earl of Meath', and 'read to the children his letter & gave the children a few statistics concerning the British Empire & endeavoured to instil the lessons & spirit of Patriotism'. In later years, there were more elaborate ceremonies, such as the pageant in 1912 at which 'Britannia [received] visits from persons from different British dominions, all dressed in the proper dress of the country, each bearing some particular production of the country, an address of greeting by each chief representative'.[62] Observance at Willow Street School took on a more militaristic flavour. For example, on 24 May 1906, 'At play time children assembled in yard and sang "God bless our Native Land" and after a short address by Head Master, marched round the yards and for a short distance in the street headed by the flag'.[63] Despite the lack of official sanction by Birmingham Education Committee, Severn Street School observed Empire Day for the first time in 1914, not with a ceremony but through 'lessons...given...throughout the school, particular attention being paid to the personal qualities which are necessary if we are to maintain the conditions of our ancestors'. However, by 1916, celebrations in this school followed the more common pattern of the 'singing of patriotic songs, followed by an address by the [head teacher]'.[64] There is no mention of Empire Day in the log books of Edgbaston and Floodgate Street schools.

How far were pupils' beliefs and attitudes influenced by the celebration of imperialism in schools? Autobiographies suggest that celebrations like Empire Day were remembered well into adult life. Some accounts suggest patriotic pride. In other accounts, it was the ceremony, the break from the school routine, and (in some cases) the treat of a half-holiday that was remembered more than the message the celebration aimed to instil.[65] As with school texts, it cannot be assumed that all pupils simply absorbed the message of Empire Day. However, an enthusiasm for empire, reinforced as it was through a range of other media (theatre, cinema, radio, and juvenile literature), is likely to have permeated the thinking of at least some of the working-class children attending elementary schools.[66]

National efficiency was a further emerging agenda that came to influence elementary schooling in the early twentieth century. Advocates were convinced that the future well-being of the nation and empire could be enhanced through the improvement of the physical and moral fitness of the young in elementary schools, an argument that combined an emerging agenda of improving social hygiene and imperial interests. For girls, this was to be achieved through the inclusion of domestic training in the elementary school curriculum. The future wives and mothers of the working classes attending elementary schools, it was argued, could fulfil their civic and imperial duty through their efforts in the home, feeding and caring for their children, creating a clean, healthy, and comfortable environment for their family. Grants had already been available for the teaching of cookery from 1882, laundry work from 1890, and 'housewifery' from 1900. In 1905, following the recommendations of the government's *Interdepartmental Committee on Physical Deterioration which reported the previous year, domestic training was made compulsory for all girls attending elementary schools.[67] Advocates of domestic training argued that, as well as teaching the skills required for girls to undertake household duties, it instilled in individuals valuable moral qualities such as discipline, cleanliness, neatness, and service to others.[68] The Board of Education in its *Handbook of Suggestions* emphasised the value of such training to the nation: 'the training should lead the scholars to set a high value on the housewife's position, and to understand that the work of women in their homes may do much to make a nation strong and prosperous'.[69] Some parents, however, objected that the teaching of domestic subjects was inappropriate for their daughters who were not accustomed to such work at home and were not expected to find future employment that used these skills.[70]

Citizenship during the First World War and post-war period: 1914–1930

Approaches to the transmission of moral values in the elementary school were affected by the circumstances of the First World War, and again in the aftermath of war by emerging ideals of reconstruction and internationalism. During the First World War, new educational practices were introduced, or older practices were adapted for wartime purposes, with the intention of promoting patriotism and commitment to England's role in the conflict, and also of offering practical help to the war effort. There was explicit teaching about the war. Existing timetabled lessons, such as geography and history, were adapted to include teaching about the war and the part England was playing.[71] In this vein, the log book for Severn Street School contains the following entry at the start of the war: 'The present being a time of great national trial, lessons are being given on the share of our country in the war, and the simple reason for our engaging in it – duty...God grant our arms success.'[72] Educational periodicals contained hints for teachers on how to incorporate the war into lessons, including arithmetical questions about war savings and numbers of warships, and songs and verses for younger pupils about being a soldier.[73] Schools were involved in community service and fundraising. For example, in Birmingham, boys from Edgbaston CofE School helped on farms during the school holidays in 1915, while Severn Street collected for the 'Fund for Sick and Wounded Horses'.[74] In Leicester, older pupils and staff at St Saviour's School helped write out 'sugar cards' and 'meat cards' and assisted with voter registration, and pupils at Willow Street School knitted garments for soldiers at the front and held a 'rummage sale' in aid of the Mayor's Scheme for disabled soldiers and sailors.[75] Patriotism was also encouraged through the material culture of schooling.[76] Elementary school pupils in London, for instance, received certificates in lieu of prizes during the war illustrated with pictures of Britannia and soldiers and sailors, the Union Jack, and school classroom objects. These illustrations were selected carefully, obviously intended to instil patriotism and encourage support for British troops at war, while encouraging further hard work at school.[77]

The Empire Day movement received a significant boost during the War. By 1919, Empire Day was celebrated in 27,323 schools, training colleges and institutions in the UK, and the majority of LEAs had offered their official sanction. Central government support for Empire Day was forthcoming in 1916, a decade after it had become a statutory holiday in most of the Dominions.[78] The mode of observance also altered at this time, to include explicit references to the conflict. In St Saviour's School, celebrations in 1915 ended with 'three cheers for the king and his soldiers and sailors', and in 1916 the headmaster emphasised, as Leicester Education Committee had requested, 'the part played by our colonies and fleet in the great war now waging & the duty of all people to spend as little as possible & to save as much as possible'.[79]

The Moral Instruction League also adapted its propaganda to wartime conditions. A change of name in 1916 to the Civic and Moral Education League revealed a shift from a focus in its activities from individual morality to a broader agenda of civic education and the moral qualities required of the citizen. The League predicted that people would be more attuned to moral issues during the war and there would be openings that did not exist before for 'developing the civic spirit'.[80] Despite such optimism, however, pressure on finance and staffing limited opportunities for activism, and the League went into decline after the war, becoming absorbed into the Sociological Society in the early 1920s.

There were widespread demands during the War for a sweeping programme of reconstruction once the conflict was over. Frederick James Gould of the Moral Instruction League declared in 1917: 'The shock given to religion, politics, economics and the spirit of nationality by the…War…has been so severe…that reconstruction, wide and deep, is inevitable, and, indeed, generally expected.'[81] Educational reform was seen as an essential element of a programme of reconstruction. A range of wartime concerns relating to industrial supply, shortages of trained teachers, high levels of juvenile labour, and juvenile delinquency required, it was argued, the extension of educational opportunities for adolescents and improved teacher training and pay (these issues had been discussed before the war but the war, arguably, galvanised politicians and different interest groups into action). David Lloyd George in September 1918 put it this way: 'An educated man is a better worker, a more formidable warrior, and a better citizen. That was only half comprehended before the war.'[82] According to Lloyd George and others who argued in this vein, the state's commitment to educating the masses now had to extend beyond the elementary school.

Contemporaries had high hopes of an education bill which would deliver extended educational opportunity to the masses. In 1917, H.A.L. Fisher, then president of the Board of Education, argued his bill was 'an essential condition of a larger and more enlightened freedom, which will tend to stimulate civic spirit, to promote general culture and technical knowledge, and to diffuse a steadier judgement and a better-informed opinion through the whole body of the community'.[83] Continuation schools in particular were deemed essential in this respect, with the Labour Party's Advisory Committee of Education arguing that they could potentially become the 'greatest training ground of democracy which the world has seen'.[84] (The committee may have been looking back to A.H.D. Acland's syllabus on citizenship, introduced into the evening continuation schools curriculum in 1885.)[85]

The provisions of the 1918 Education Act included the removal of all exemptions from schooling up to the age of 14 and called for part-time continuation schooling for 14- to 16-year-olds (with the possibility of subsequent extension of continuation schooling for 16- to 18-year-olds). LEAs were also empowered to raise the school leaving age to 15 and allot maintenance grants to scholarship pupils in secondary schools.[86] Thus, the Act had the potential to extend formal educational provision, with all its possibilities for more deeply socialising the masses. However, few of the reconstruction plans for education were realised. The provision of part-time continuation schooling was lost under the cuts in the education budget in the early 1920s. Herbert Lewis, private secretary of the Board of Education, criticised this decision on the grounds that an opportunity to save adolescents from hooliganism and make them good citizens would be lost for the sake of short-term financial expediency.[87] At the systemic level, as Sherington has argued, the upheaval of the war did not lead to radical change. Lessons learned during the war did not seem so pressing once Britain emerged victorious from the conflict, and saving money became the most important consideration.[88]

Despite the limitations of reform, government remained convinced that schools could be used to develop desirable behaviours and ideals. The consensus among most teachers and educationalists appears to have been, as it was before the First World War, that the values of citizenship were best promoted not through direct teaching of moral instruction or 'civics' as a separate subject, but indirectly through the teaching of existing subjects in the school curriculum.[89] Throughout the inter-war period, history continued to be considered a key subject for developing national pride and civic virtues in pupils. New approaches to the teaching of history in schools were developed by historians such as M.V.L. Hughes and Helen Madeley, including a move to more interactive teaching methods, and a focus on local and social as well as political aspects of history, in order to engage pupils and help them understand better the development of their country and its institutions over time. At the same time, in the post-war atmosphere the rampant jingoism and uncritical imperialism of earlier texts was widely criticised. Nonetheless, for many educationalists the primary focus was still on national history and the aim to inculcate love and loyalty to the nation was retained as an important goal.[90] The historian, Graham Gooch, for instance, in a lecture – 'History as Training for Citizenship' – at the Conference of Educational Associations in January 1930, argued that learning about England's history would help pupils to understand the evolution of national institutions and social relations, and also encourage pupils to strive to serve their country.[91]

Empire Day continued to be observed in many schools in the inter-war years. Empire Day adapted to the changing ideological climate by incorporating remembrance of the dead from the War and internationalist versions of citizenship (for example through inclusion of the League of Nations in celebrations). In this way, older forms of imperialism were presented as compatible with an emerging emphasis on peace-making and international understanding. It could be argued, however, that ideological certainties that accompanied the celebration of Empire Day before the First World War were lost, and during the inter-war years it became the target of sustained campaigns of anti-imperialist protest.[92]

At the same time, international citizenship emerged in the inter-war period as an important agenda in elementary schools, public schools and universities.[93] The *League of Nations Union, founded in 1919, was one of a number of educational organisations in Britain determined to promote international understanding in order to prevent future conflicts. It campaigned for teaching about the work of the League of Nations in elementary and secondary schools, and to reform the teaching of history to emphasise internationalism and reduce jingoistic and militaristic elements. A degree of success was achieved. League of Nations junior branches were established in elementary and secondary schools: numbers rose from 293 in 1926 to 1400 by the end of 1934. Some schools held League of Nations events such as short talks by teachers, model League assembly meetings, and pageants at which different national costumes were worn. A number of educationalists promoted teaching about the League of Nations in history lessons, and the Board of Education's *Suggestions for the Consideration of Teachers* of 1927 contained a whole appendix of information for teachers about the League. Overall, however, the League had only a limited impact on the curriculum in elementary schools. Throughout the 1920s, it was criticised by members of the *Historical Association, the school Inspectorate and the Conservative Party for bringing bias and propaganda into state schools. Many schools appear to have ignored the League's call for international teaching. For example, research conducted by the League of Nations Union in the late 1920s found that many history texts used in schools, rather than promoting peace and the value of different nations, continued to emphasise militarism and Anglo-Saxon racial superiority. Some of this inevitably was due to financial constraints during the war and in its aftermath, which would have stopped schools from purchasing some of the new texts brought out during the 1920s. The deteriorating international situation in the 1930s damaged further the credibility of the Union's arguments for the promotion of international citizenship. After 1936, following their impotence during the Abyssinian crisis, the League of Nations, and its educational arm, the Union, rapidly lost support.[94] A nationally focused, Christian form of citizenship won out as the preferred strategy for protecting England from the advance of the extreme, secular political ideologies taking hold elsewhere.[95]

Conclusion

This chapter has examined attempts to socialise the young within a mass elementary education system from 1870 to 1930. This period witnessed the promotion of different and to an extent competing moral ideals: religious, secular, nationalist, imperialist, and internationalist. At the same time, there was continuity across different approaches with the aim of developing in young people the attitudes and behaviours that would enable them to love and serve their country. There was, arguably, also a general intention to socialise young people into becoming controllable subjects rather than autonomous, independent-thinking citizens. Moral education, by and large, reinforced rather than challenged existing class and gender roles: although some moral educators encouraged pupils to question what they deemed unjust aspects of the existing status quo they were in a minority. Overall, the 'masses' in elementary schools were expected to follow rather than lead, and to stay within appropriate limits. This was not, however, a simple and coherent project of social control. Young people were exposed to intensive attempts to instil desirable values and behaviours at an impressionable age. But moral education was promoted by various interest groups, many outside the formal remit of the state education system, with different agendas and priorities. Their efforts were uncoordinated. It seems unlikely therefore, given this lack of coordination, and also the heterogeneity of the 'masses' in elementary schools, that the socialising aims of educators were ever fully realised – the limited influence of some initiatives, and the varied response of pupils has been noted in this chapter.

Reaching a solid conclusion as to the level of success of this socialising project, on the other hand, is impossible, for it is difficult to find clear evidence about what 'worked'. Part of the problem is a lack of simple measurable outputs, for instance there are no examination results to analyse. Moreover, what would constitute success is difficult to determine: if the aim was the formation of citizens, one would not necessarily have expected immediate results, and long-term developments would be difficult to trace back to the school. There are some indications of moral improvement within the school: for example, systems of rewards and punishment for attendance and punctuality were perceived to have had some positive results, while local evidence from Leicester and Birmingham also suggests that moral instruction lessons could have a positive effect on pupil behaviour in schools.[96] Predictably, there is less evidence of impact outside the school. The repeated calls, in the national press and locally in Leicester and

Birmingham, for improved moral teaching in schools in order to combat the bad behaviour of young people on the streets might be interpreted as a sign of limited effectiveness.[97] The popularity of Sunday schools and organised youth movements through the period could also, arguably, point to a perception that the school itself was not enough to socialise the young into appropriate attitudes and behaviour and that alternatives were required. Conversely, a decline in juvenile convictions for non-indictable offences after 1910 might, as Gillis suggests, point to the long-term success of schools, along with other youth organisations, in influencing and improving the behaviour of the young.[98]

This chapter has, on occasion, referred to the views of pupils and parents. However, overall we know very little of what pupils themselves thought of the moral education they were exposed to.[99] What pupils felt they got out of religious instruction or moral instruction lessons, whether they were receptive to the patriotic and imperialist messages to which they were exposed, whether games and drill had the intended moral benefits or were purely physical activities, remains, to a large extent, a mystery. Evidence in autobiographies and oral histories suggests a range of attitudes to schooling on the part of pupils, some negative, some positive, some mixed, and it seems plausible that attempts to inculcate moral values evoked the same range of responses as other aspects of schooling. There is similarly little direct evidence of parental views. That which exists – for example on domestic training – suggests disagreement with the aims of educators. However, it is possible that while dissident voices were heard, a 'silent majority' accepted, or even approved, socialisation in schools.

What is striking is the strength of the conviction that the elementary school could and should be used as a key site of cultural formation and moral development, despite the limited *evidence* of effectiveness. Contemporaries were well aware of the importance of other agencies of socialisation, particularly home and family, but also churches and other bodies such as youth movements, and, more broadly, popular culture, leisure activities, the 'media'. Advocates of moral education in schools knew that schools were only one influence among many, and could only do so much (for instance, against 'antagonistic home influences' as one proponent put it). In some ways, then, it is surprising that they fought so hard to promote the benefits of their cause. Was this a matter of blind faith? The triumph of hope over experience? Or was it more a matter of convenience: once a mass elementary education system was established, young people of school age were a captive audience, and therefore different constituencies targeted elementary schools as the easiest way to reach the young population and promote whatever cause they felt was important for the rising generation.

Beyond 1930, there was both continuity and change in the use of the elementary school as a moral agent. Contests between Christian and secular conceptions of citizenship continued, though against a changing backdrop of international events and greater cooperation between different Christian denominations than previously. As a consequence, a Christian version of English citizenship was presented as a bulwark against the secular extremism found in Nazi Germany and Stalinist Russia: such arguments were used to justify the introduction of compulsory religious instruction in the 1944 Education Act (by this time the different denominations were able to cooperate to produce a combined syllabus). The *Association of Education for Citizenship argued, however, that religious approaches were ineffective and direct teaching on a secular basis was required.[100] There was also a continued emphasis on imperialism: observance of Empire Day in schools increased during the inter-war period, and incorporated new technologies such as films. Indeed, despite the efforts of the League of Nations Union and others to promote internationalist teaching, many texts used in schools retained a British, or English, focus, even after the Second World War.

The questions considered in this chapter have a contemporary resonance, although against a changed backdrop of multiculturalism, immigration and international terrorism. A range of concerns – about delinquent youth, political apathy, and a lack of clear cultural identity – have led to a revival of interest in the teaching of citizenship in British schools. In 2002 citizenship was made compulsory for all 11- to 16-year-olds, and more recently there have been attempts to use schools to develop a sense of 'Britishness'. The observations of *Ofsted and others have led to questions about the effectiveness of such teaching – whether introduced in the form of timetabled lessons or via a cross-curricular approach. With a new *GCSE in citizenship there are now possibilities to calculate 'success' through exam results, but this on its own is unlikely to be a useful measure of the effectiveness of efforts to socialise the young in the state's schools.

Timeline

1808: Royal Lancasterian Society (later British Society) founded by non-conformist Protestants to provide elementary education for poor children. Called after Joseph Lancaster (see below p. 85)

1811: National Society for the Education of the Poor in the Principles of the Established Church founded

1833: Factory Act: provided funding for some employers to establish schools

1861: Report of the Newcastle Commission: investigated state of popular education in England and Wales

1862: Revised Code: established a common curriculum and country-wide apparatus for inspection and funding. Under the system of payment-by-results a school's funding was affected by individual pupils' achievement in examinations

1867: Second Reform Act: extended the franchise to include propertied men in urban boroughs

1870: Education Act: ensured the provision of school places for all children in England and Wales age 5–12. Where there were insufficient places in existing voluntary schools, locally elected school boards were established and charged with building and running board schools to 'fill the gaps'

1876: Elementary Education (Sandon) Act enabled local authorities to take cases to magistrate's court to have truanting children sent to so-called industrial boarding schools. Local authorities were enabled to set up their own industrial schools and fund them from the local rates

1880: Elementary Education Act – made attendance at elementary school compulsory from the age of 5–10 years old. Industrial Schools Amendment Act allowed courts to remove girls from brothels or circumstances where they were considered to be at risk of sexual exploitation

1882: Revised Code of Education – allowed university graduates to become elementary school teachers for the first time

Third Reform Act: property provisions relating to urban boroughs of the Second Reform Act extended to men in the counties

1886–7: The Cross Commission – appointed to assess the working of the Elementary Education Acts of 1870 and 1880

1893: Education Act: minimum leaving age raised to 11

1895: Revised Code of Education: grants allocated according to the performance of the school as a whole rather than individual pupils

1897: Moral Instruction League founded

1899: Education Act: minimum leaving age raised to 12

1902: (Balfour) Education Act: school boards abolished and replaced by Local Education Authorities, which were charged with running what had been board schools and establishing secondary schools accessible to all pupils through a competitive scholarship system. Additional government funding was made available for voluntary schools

1918: (Fisher) Education Act: minimum school leaving age raised to 14. Proposals to restrict employment of children and for the part-time education of all young people to 18 through 'continuation classes' were not realised

1919: League of Nations Union established

Glossary

Association for Education in Citizenship: educational pressure group founded in 1935 to promote a greater emphasis on the teaching of citizenship in the country's schools.

Code of Regulations: annual publication from the Education Department first issued in 1862 setting out regulations re funding, administration, organisation and management of elementary schools, curriculum, inspection arrangements. From 1905 suggestions on the curriculum were issued in a different document, and the Code referred to administrative and organisational matters. Separate codes of regulations existed for secondary schools and teacher training colleges.

Committee of Council on Education: Central government educational body founded in 1870 with responsibility for elementary education (the successor to the Education Department). The Science and Arts Department had responsibility for technical and commercial education. The two merged in 1899 to become the Board of Education.

ethical movement: The ethical movement was a loose association of different ethical societies, which despite differing aims and programmes, all envisaged a universal and synoptic morality which was sufficient for a rule of life and would form the basis for union of individuals of different creeds. The first ethical societies in England emerged in London in the late 1880s, modelled on the Society for Ethical Culture founded in New York in 1886 by Felix Adler, a lapsed Jew from a rabbinic family.

GCSE: Terminal examination for secondary schooling in England, Wales and Northern Ireland taken at age 16.

Her (or His) Majesty's Inspectorate (HMI): Her Majesty's Inspectorate was established in 1839 by the Privy Council on Education. Responsible for the inspection of elementary schools in the nineteenth century and, after the passage of the Board of Education Act in 1899, secondary schools.

Historical Association: Founded in 1906 to promote and support history education in schools and in higher education in the UK.

Interdepartmental Committee on Physical Deterioration: The Interdepartmental Committee was established in 1903 after many would-be recruits to the army from working-class areas during the South African War (1899–1902) had been unable to fight owing to their poor health or physique. The committee reported in 1904, with recommendations about education, housing and health care.

League of Nations Union: organisation founded in 1919 to promote the League of Nations among the British public. This included promoting teaching about the League, and more generally ideals of international understanding and peace in existing lessons, in elementary and secondary schools.

Moral Instruction League: Educational pressure group, founded under the auspices of the ethical movement, to campaign for the introduction of moral instruction lessons in the country's elementary schools.

National Society for the Education of the Poor in the Principles of the Established Church: organisation set up in 1811 by the Anglican Church to establish elementary schools in England and overseas.

Ofsted: Schools inspection service covering England and Wales, set up in 1992.

Notes

1. For example see M. Sadler (1908) 'Introduction', in M.E. Sadler (ed.) *Moral Instruction and Training in Schools. Report of an International Inquiry. Volume I* (London: Longmans, Green & Co.), pp. xiii–xlix, at pp. xxi–xxii.
2. J. Springhall (1998) *Youth, Popular Culture and Moral Panics* (Basingstoke: Macmillan), pp.11–97; J. Springhall (1977) *Youth, Empire and Society. British Youth Movements, 1883–1940* (London: Croom Helm).

3. Cited in P. Silver and H. Silver (1974) *The Education of the Poor. The History of a National School 1824–1974* (London: Routledge & Kegan Paul), pp. 8–9.
4. 1860 elementary school code cited in J. Lawson and H. Silver (1973) *A Social History of Education in England* (London: Methuen), pp. 268–70.
5. J.S. Hurt (1979) *Elementary Schooling and the Working Classes, 1860–1918* (London: Routledge & Kegan Paul), p. 55.
6. See, for example, P. Joyce (2003) *The Rule of Freedom: Liberalism and the Modern City* (London: Verso) for a discussion of these issues.
7. Cited by A. Wolf (1998) 'Politicians and Economic Panic', *History of Education*, 27/3, 219–34, at p. 232.
8. Cited in P. Horn (1989) *The Victorian and Edwardian Schoolchild* (Gloucester: Alan Sutton), p. 16. Forster is widely cited as the architect of the 1870 Act.
9. Cited in G. Sherington (1981) *English Education, Social Change and War* (Manchester: Manchester University Press), p. 38.
10. Lawson and Silver, *A Social History of Education*, p. 271.
11. Cited in Hurt, *Elementary Schooling and the Working Classes*, pp. 21–2.
12. Cited in Sherington, *English Education, Social Change and War*, p. 180.
13. See P. Gordon and D. Lawton (1978) *Curriculum Change in the Nineteenth and Twentieth Centuries* (London: Hodder and Stoughton) for an overview.
14. These schools were selected from a sample of 14 (seven in Birmingham, seven in Leicester) examined as part of my doctoral research. S. Wright (2006) 'The Struggle for Moral Education 1879–1918' (unpublished PhD thesis, Oxford Brookes University), ch. 6 and appendix 1.
15. Education Department (1875) *New Code of Regulations for Elementary Schools 1875* (London: HMSO), p. 6 (Article 19A).
16. Floodgate Street School Log Book 1891–1920, 11 Dec. 1892, 21 Feb. 1896, S68/2/1, Birmingham Archives and Heritage Services, Central Library, Birmingham, B3 3HQ (BAHS).
17. For example, Floodgate Street School Log Book 1891–1920, 14 Jul. 1902; Severn Street School Log Book (Boys) 1886–1921, 10 Nov. 1899, S178/1/2, BAHS.
18. For example, Severn Street School Log Book (Boys) 1886–1921, 10 Nov. 1899; St Saviour's School Log Book 1882–1919, 6 Oct. 1890, 18D68/1, Record Office for Leicester, Leicestershire and Rutland, Wigston Magna, Leics. LE18 2AH (RLLR).
19. Edgbaston CofE School Log Book 1881–1906, Week Ending (WE) 19 Dec. 1890, S62/1/1, BAHS.
20. St Saviour's School Log Book 1882–1919, 16 Dec. 1887, 11 Jan. 1889, 9 Sept. 1891, 5 June 1893.
21. Floodgate Street School Log Book 1891–1920, 29 Mar. 1895, 26 Mar. 1897, 1 Oct. 1897, 15 Oct. 1897, 4 Mar. 1898, 23 Sept. 1898, 21 Oct. 1898.
22. Severn Street School Log Book (Boys) 1864–86, 8 Sept. 1882, S178/1/1, BAHS.
23. Floodgate Street School Log Book 1891–1920, 9 Sept. 1892, 11 Nov. 1892, 25 Nov. 1892, 15 Mar. 1895, 22 Mar. 1895, 21 Oct. 1898; St Mark's School Log Book 1874–1901, 15 May 1899, DE3893/23, RLLR.
24. J.S. Hurt (1979) 'Drill, Discipline and the Elementary School Ethos' in P. McCann (ed.) *Popular Education and Socialization in the Nineteenth Century* (London: Methuen & Co. Ltd.), pp. 167–90. An emphasis on military drill in the 1870s was replaced by the turn of the twentieth century by a programme of physical training, but the qualities it was thought to promote were much the same.
25. H. Major, *Report on the Leicester Board Schools May 1 to July 31 1877*, p. 7, Pamphlets Vol. 50, RLLR.
26. B. Sacks (1961) *The Religious Issue in the State Schools of England and Wales, 1902–1914* (Albuquerque, New Mexico: University of New Mexico Press), pp. 114–16.
27. Hurt, *Elementary Education*, p. 176.

28. J.T. Smith (2002) 'The Real Milch Cow? The Work of Anglican, Catholic and Wesleyan Clergymen in Elementary Schools in the Second Half of the Nineteenth Century', *History of Education*, 31:2, 117–37; J.T. Smith (2008) *A Victorian Class Conflict?' Schoolteaching and the Parson, Priest and Minister, 1837–1902* (Brighton: Sussex Academic Press, 2008); Silver and Silver, *Education of the Poor*, pp. 103, 142; Wright, 'Struggle for Moral Education', pp. 224–5.
29. Sacks, *Religious Issue*, pp. 123–4.
30. Severn Street School Log Book (Boys) 1886–1921, 7 Jan. 1901; St Saviour's School Log Book 1882–1919, 19 Mar. 1883, 12 Jul. 1910.
31. St Saviour's School Log Book 1882–1919, 4 Mar. 1908, 30 Nov. 1916. See also 9 May 1907, 3 Sept. 1912.
32. Reverend Dymott cited in Sacks, *Religious Issue*, pp. 114, 173.
33. Sacks, *Religious Issue*, pp. 124–5.
34. S. Heathorn (1995) ' "Let us Remember that we, too, are English": Constructions of Citizenship and National Identity in English Elementary School Reading Books, 1880–1914', *Victorian Studies*, 38:3, 395–427, at p. 396.
35. Heathorn, '"Let us Remember"', pp. 399–401.
36. H.O. Arnold-Forster (1887) *The Citizen Reader*, 8th edn (London: Cassell & Company Ltd.), p. iv. For a wider survey of citizenship in elementary school readers see Heathorn, '"Let us Remember"', pp. 413–21.
37. Arnold-Forster, *Citizen Reader*, p. 11.
38. Ibid., pp. 18, 25.
39. Ibid., p. 14.
40. P. Horn (1988) 'English Elementary Education and the Growth of the Imperial Ideal: 1880–1914' in J.A. Mangan (ed.) *Benefits Bestowed? Education and British Imperialism* (Manchester: Manchester University Press), pp. 39–55; W.E. Marsden (2000) '"Poisoned History": A Comparative Study of Nationalism, Propaganda, and the Treatment of War and Peace in the Late Nineteenth- and Early Twentieth-Century School Curriculum', *History of Education*, 29:1, 29–47.
41. J. Rose (2001) *The Intellectual Life of the British Working Classes* (New Haven: Yale Nota Bene), pp. 146–86.
42. H. Johnson, *Moral Instruction and the Education Bill. An Address Delivered before a Meeting of the Nonconformist Committee of Members of the House of Commons, Wednesday October 28 1908*, Social Pamphlets R188675, Deansgate Library, Manchester, M3 3EH.
43. F.J. Gould (c.1897) *A Plan of Moral Instruction Adopted by the Moral Instruction League* (London: Moral Instruction League), p. 3.
44. H. Johnson (1908) *Moral Instruction in Elementary Schools in England and Wales. A Return Compiled from Official Documents* (London: David Nutt), pp. xi–xii.
45. Moral Instruction League (1902) *A Graduated Syllabus of Moral Instruction and Training in Citizenship for Elementary Schools* (London; Moral Instruction League). Elementary schools were organised into Standards. Pupils were designated by achievement rather than age, so the ages noted above are approximate.
46. Gould, *A Plan of Moral Instruction*, pp. 3, 14–15; Moral Instruction League, *Graduated Syllabus*; Moral Instruction League (1900) *Our Future Citizens* (London: Moral Instruction League), pp. 6–7.
47. S. Wright (2007) 'Into Unfamiliar Territory? The Moral Instruction Curriculum in English Elementary Schools 1880–1914', *History of Education Researcher*, 79, 31–41. Moral instruction lessons were introduced by Birmingham School Board in 1879 and Leicester School Board in 1901. Unfortunately moral instruction lessons are not mentioned in the school log books examined for this chapter.
48. F.J. Gould (1907) *Children's Book of Moral Lessons. Fourth Series* (London: Watts & Co.), p.56. For extended discussion of moral instruction texts see S. Wright (2009) '"Our Future Citizens": Values in Late Nineteenth and Early Twentieth Century Moral Instruction Books', *History of Education and Children's Literature*, 4/1, 157–77.

49. Committee of Council on Education (1897) *Report of the Committee of Council on Education, England and Wales with appendix 1896–97* (London: HMSO), p. xx.
50. Board of Education (1906) *Report of the Board of Education for the year 1905–1906* (London: HMSO), pp. 24–5.
51. J.A. Mangan (1981) *Athleticism in the Victorian and Edwardian Public School: The Emergence and Consolidation of an Educational Ideology* (Cambridge: Cambridge University Press).
52. Willow Street School Log Book 1880–1905, 6 Oct. 1898, 17 May 1899, 19D59/VII/437, RLLR.
53. Severn Street School Log Book (Boys) 1886–1921, 21 Dec. 1900 (see also 11 Apr. 1902).
54. Details on school football in London can be found in the archives of the Institute of Education, University of London.
55. Edgbaston School Log Books 1881–1906, WE 15 Sept. 1893, 14 Sept. 1894, 6 Sept. 1895, 28 Aug. 1903, 30 Aug. 1907.
56. St Saviour's School Log Book 1882–1919, 23 Apr. 1907.
57. Board of Education (1900) *Report of the Board of Education for 1899–1900* (London: HMSO), pp. 254–6.
58. Horn, 'English Elementary Education', pp.41–6; Heathorn, '"Let us Remember that we, too, are English"'; J.S. Mackenzie (1984) *Propaganda and Empire. The Manipulation of British Public Opinion, 1880–1960* (Manchester: Manchester University Press), pp. 173–97.
59. See Horn, 'English Elementary Education', 48–51, and J. Springhall (1970) 'Lord Meath, Youth, and Empire', *Journal of Contemporary History*, 5/4, 97–111, at pp. 105–10.
60. Meath's open letters on Empire Day were reproduced in the educational press. See *School Guardian*, 19 May 1906, pp. 476–7.
61. Horn, 'English Elementary Education', pp. 48–50.
62. St Saviour's School Log Book 1882–1919, 22 May 1908, 24 May 1912.
63. Willow Street School Log Book 1905–28, 24 May 1906 (see also 27 May 1908, 24 May 1909, 24 May 1910, 24 May 1911), 19D59/VII/438, RLLR.
64. Severn Street School Log Book (Boys) 1886–1921, 25 May 1914, 24 May 1916.
65. M. Keen, *Childhood Memories 1903 to 1921*, n.d, p. 9: 2–449, Working Class Autobiographical Archive (WCAA), Brunel University Library, Uxbridge, UB8 3PH; M. Rainer, *Emma's Daughter*, n.d., p. 31: 2–644, WCAA. See also Horn, 'English Elementary Education', p. 50 and J. English (2006) 'Empire Day in Britain, 1904–1958', *The Historical Journal*, 49/1, 247–76, at pp. 249–53.
66. Mackenzie, *Propaganda and Empire*, passim.
67. Horn, *Victorian and Edwardian Schoolchild*, pp. 49-50; Gordon and Lawton, *Curriculum Change*, p. 113; A. Turnbull (1987) 'Learning her Womanly Work: the Elementary School Curriculum, 1870–1914' in F. Hunt (ed.) *Lessons for Life. The Schooling of Girls and Women 1850–1950* (Oxford, Basil Blackwell), pp. 83–100, at pp. 92–96.
68. Turnbull, 'Womanly Work', pp. 88–9, 95.
69. Board of Education (1905) *Suggestions for the Consideration of Teachers and others Concerned in the Work of Public Elementary Schools* (London: HMSO), pp. 78–9.
70. Turnbull, 'Womanly Work', p. 97. No reference to such objections was recorded in the school log books investigated.
71. Marsden, '"Poisoned History"', pp. 33–4.
72. Severn Street School Log Book (Boys) 1886–1921, 27 Aug. 1914.
73. See, for example, issues of *Teachers World* from 1914 and 1915. See also Marsden, '"Poisoned History"', pp. 33–4, 38–40.
74. Edgbaston CofE School Log Book (Boys) 1906–31, 16 Jul. 1915, S62/1/2, BAHS; Severn Street School Log Book (Boys) 1886–1921, 23 Apr. 1918.
75. St Saviour's School Log Book 1882–1919, 28 Sept. 1917, 22 Mar. 1918, 25 Apr. 1918; Willow Street School Log Book 1905–28, 27 Oct. 1914, 1 Feb. 1915, 23 Sept. 1916, 1 Jul. 1918.

76. I. Grosvenor (1999) '"There's no Place like Home": Education and the Making of National Identity', *History of Education*, 28:3, 235–50.
77. Certificates awarded to Stanley Wright (my grandfather), held by family.
78. Horn, 'English Elementary Education', p. 48; Springhall, 'Lord Meath, Youth, and Empire', p. 105.
79. St Saviour's School Log Book 1882–1919, 21 May 1915, 24 May 1916.
80. *Moral Education League Quarterly*, 38, 1 Oct. 1914, pp. 2–3; Moral Education League (c.1914–15) *Notes to Members and Friends, Circular M6*, p. 1.
81. F.J. Gould (1917) *British Education after the War* (London: Watts & Co.), p. 1.
82. Cited by Sherington, *English Education, Social Change and War*, p. 128.
83. Ibid., p. 108.
84. Ibid., p. 145.
85. J.T. Smith (2002) 'The Beginnings of Citizenship Education in England', *History of Education Society Bulletin*, 69, 6–16, at pp. 10–11,
86. P. Gordon, R. Aldrich and D. Dean (1991) *Education and Policy in England in the Twentieth Century* (London: Woburn Press), pp. 49–50.
87. Sherington, *English Education, Social Change and War*, p. 161.
88. Ibid., p. 181.
89. See J. Keating (2010) 'Civics, citizenship and patriotism – the experience of the London County Council, 1918-1939', Paper presented at the History of Education Society Annual Conference, 26–28 Nov. 2010, for detail on London County Council.
90. On history teaching in the 1920s and its relation to the aims of citizenship education, see G. Batho (1990) 'The History of the Teaching of Civics and Citizenship in English Schools', *The Curriculum Journal*, 1:1, 91–100, at pp. 92–95; J. Wong (1997) 'Rhetoric and Educational Policies on the Use of History for Citizenship Education in England from 1880–1990', *Education Policy Analysis Archives*, 5:14 (Electronic journal. At: http://epaa.asu.edu/epaa/v5n14.html [accessed 30/06/2008]).
91. Published as G. P. Gooch (1930) 'History as a Training for Citizenship', *The New Era*, 11/42, 67–70.
92. English, 'Empire Day', pp. 260–67; H. McCarthy (2010) 'The League of Nations, Public Ritual and National Identity in Britain, c. 1919–56', *History Workshop Journal*, 70, 108–32, at p. 118.
93. On public schools and internationalism see, for example, C. Watkins (2007) 'Inventing International Citizenship: Badminton School and the Progressive Tradition between the Wars', *History of Education*, 36/3, 315–38.
94. B.J. Elliott (1977) 'The League of Nations Union and History Teaching in England: a Study in Benevolent Bias', *History of Education*, 6, 131–41; Marsden, '"Poisoned History"', pp. 34–5, 43–4.
95. R. Freathy (2008) 'The Triumph of Religious Education for Citizenship in English Schools, 1935–1949', *History of Education*, 37/2, 295–316.
96. Wright, 'Into Unfamiliar Territory'.
97. Wright, 'The Struggle for Moral Education', ch. 5.
98. J. Gillis (1975) 'The Evolution of Juvenile Delinquency in England 1890–1914', *Past and Present*, 67, 96–126.
99. An extensive search through existing oral histories and autobiographies from the period examined, might, potentially, turn up further evidence.
100. Freathy, 'Triumph of Religious Education'.

2
Elite Education and the Development of Mass Elementary Schooling in England, 1870–1930

Heather Ellis

> The object of all schools is not to ram Latin and Greek into boys, but to make them good English boys, good future citizens.[1]

The above quotation is taken from *Tom Brown's School Days*, the famous public school novel by Thomas Hughes, which first appeared in 1857. Published more than a decade before mass elementary schooling was introduced throughout England and Wales and a training in citizenship came to play a central role in the education offered to millions of working-class children, Hughes suggested that the primary aim of all schooling was not instruction in particular subjects but the formation of good citizens. In the historiography of English elementary education the *public schools have attracted relatively little attention; indeed, they have usually been treated as a separate, unconnected system of education restricted in significance to the middle and upper classes.[2] This tendency reflects the important role that class distinctions have played in the analysis of the history of English education. When the public schools and universities are mentioned within the context of the development of elementary schooling, they tend to be seen as part of a somewhat cynical effort by the English middle and upper classes to use mass education as an agent of social control.[3] Here, by contrast, it will be suggested that despite catering to very different sections of the population, the public schools nonetheless acted as an important model for the development of elementary schooling in England between 1870 and 1900. It was only after the turn of the century, in particular after the end of the First World War, that the maintenance of class distinctions came to play a significant role in education policy and the influence of the public school model declined.

As the first section will show, the Newcastle Commission, which reported in 1861 on the 'state of popular education in England', and which was the starting point for the 1870 Elementary Education Act, drew significantly on the experience of the public schools and the recent reform of the elite universities in a number of ways. The second section goes on to consider the growing importance of the public schools and universities as a model in the reform of elementary schooling after 1870. In particular, it will suggest that a certain ideal of national and imperial citizenship, promoted at the public schools from the late 1860s onwards, was drawn upon when designing both the academic curriculum and the provision of physical exercise in the elementary schools after 1870. The assumption that those directing reform of the elementary system in this period deliberately separated the curricula of the elementary and public schools in order to control working-class access to higher education is also challenged. Rather, it is suggested that moves were increasingly initiated in both types of school to adopt a modern syllabus with a view to improving the overall quality of education provided; likewise the distinction between military-style drill and team games, which is often insisted upon by scholars when comparing the curricula of the public and elementary schools, is shown to have been nowhere near as rigid as is often assumed. The third section examines the various personal connections between elite and popular education, which developed in the last decades of the nineteenth century. Instead of seeing such connections in terms of a rigid power dynamic between the middle and working classes, it is suggested that middle-class educators and government officials sought, particularly in the Cross Commission of 1886–7, to establish a variety of new connections between the two levels of schooling in an effort to raise both the quality of teaching and the educational achievement of elementary pupils. Of particular interest was the possibility of involving the *ancient universities more directly in the training of elementary school teachers and pupil teachers. Ways to render the existing scholarship and exhibition system more accessible and effective were also discussed in more detail than ever before.

In the years after 1900, however, the public schools were increasingly criticised as failing to serve the needs of the British nation and empire. Against a background of growing rivalry with European and extra-European powers and mounting anxiety about racial degeneration at home, they were often charged with failing to provide a sufficiently scientific or military education. Elementary education began to assume a more vocational character in an effort to remedy this apparent lack. After the end of the First World War, the influence of the public schools and ancient universities upon the reform of the elementary system continued to decline. The elementary curriculum continued to become more practical in nature, while the expanding secondary sector, confined largely to the provision of free places in the traditional *grammar schools, was characterised by a middle-class classical curriculum modelled on that of the public schools. Although it was argued at the time that this type of education was simply the best available, it also ensured that those working-class children who received free grammar school places would be socialised in a middle-class environment. In the very different post-war climate, with growing fears about the spread of socialist ideas among the urban poor in particular, this was considered far from undesirable by Conservative government ministers and civil servants at the Board of Education.

Elite education and the Newcastle Report 1861

It will be argued here that the introduction of mass elementary education in England and Wales in 1870 deserves to be seen as part of a national reorganisation of schooling at different levels of society. Beginning with the parliamentary commissions examining the education provided at the ancient universities of Oxford and Cambridge in 1850, there followed the Newcastle Commission, which investigated the state of 'popular' education in 1861, the Clarendon Commission in 1864, which examined the nine leading public schools and the Taunton Commission in 1868, which focused on all those schools that fell in between the scopes of the other two commissions.

It is certainly not new to note the strong influence which public school and university-educated men exercised on the development of English elementary education after 1870. However, in the majority of studies, such influence has been seen in terms of the middle classes trying to maintain their socio-economic position. As Barry H. Bergen has claimed, 'it would be difficult to overemphasize the degree to which elementary education in England in the nineteenth century constituted an imposition of the middle class on the working class.'[4] R.H. Tawney argued similarly that 'the elementary schools of 1870 were intended in the main to produce an orderly, civil population with sufficient education to understand a command'.[5] While such motivations may well have had a role to play in the nineteenth century and did indeed assume a greater importance in post-1918 education policy, without the strong influence of the public schools, there might never have been an Elementary Education Act in 1870. Reformers keen to extend the benefits of education to the working classes, in particular the urban poor, knew only too well that they had to work within the confines of what their own society considered acceptable. It is all too easy from our modern perspective to underestimate what a radical and important step the introduction of mass elementary education was in the late nineteenth century. Indeed, to be understood properly, it needs to be seen as part of a much broader effort to transform the whole educational landscape of Victorian Britain, to create for the first time a truly national system of education.

The first step towards the creation of a national elementary school system was the appointment in 1858 of the Newcastle Commission to 'inquire into the present state of popular education in England, and to consider and report what measures, if any, are required for the extension of sound and cheap elementary instruction to all classes of the people.'[6] It is true that the entire commission (with the exception of Edward Miall)[7] had been educated at the leading public schools and universities.[8] Indeed, all except Henry Pelham, Duke of Newcastle, Edward Miall and William Rogers had been elected fellows, tutors or professors at Oxford or Cambridge.[9] However, that the commission represented nothing more than a self-interested attempt on the part of the establishment to direct the introduction of mass education so as best to secure their own position is not the only interpretation one can draw from these facts. The commission included many men who had shown considerable commitment to educational reform at various levels.

John Taylor Coleridge, for example, had been appointed a commissioner under the Oxford University Act of 1854[10] and helped to bring about the appointment of the Clarendon Commission in 1861 with his 1860 lecture *On Public School Education*. W.C. Lake was likewise prominent in the cause of university reform,[11] while Goldwin Smith was one of the two secretaries of the Oxford University Commission of 1850.[12] Nassau Senior wrote in support of liberal reform at Oxford in the mid-to-late 1840s[13] and William Rogers worked hard as a curate in inner-city London to increase the provision of elementary schooling in the capital.[14] As the report itself makes clear, the public schools and universities frequently furnished the intellectual context within which the commission's thinking about elementary education was worked out. To some extent, the influence of the public-school and university system was inevitable as it constituted the vast majority of the educational experience of the commissioners charged with the task of designing a new system of elementary schooling.[15] In many cases, more-over, the public schools and universities did offer a useful model for the commissioners to work with. It was thought, for example, that if elementary schools were organised along the lines of the *great public schools, they might exercise a comparable moral influence over pupils. Of particular importance here was the idea that pupils of different social ranks learned important moral lessons from being educated together. 'In the great public schools, such as Eton and Harrow, and at the Universities', wrote one assistant commissioner, Patric Cumin, 'it is an obvious advantage both to noble-men and to commoners that their children should be brought up together. It is an equal advantage to the farmer and the shopkeeper that their children should be brought up with the farm servant and the day labourer. This is the only cure for foolish pride on the one hand, and a cringing spirit on the other.'[16]

However, more than simply using their experience of the public school system as a context for thinking about improvements in elementary schooling, the commission endeavoured to create much stronger links between elite and popular education. In addition to suggesting that more connections between individual schools should be established, it recommended that endowed elementary schools, together with the public schools and universities, be placed under the supervision of the Education Committee of the Privy Council. 'It already possesses considerable powers in relation to the highest of our endowed places of education, the Universities, their Colleges, the Colleges of Eton and Winchester', the report declared. Considerable improvements in organisation and cost-effectiveness, it was hoped, would result from 'placing our whole system of public education, so far as it is connected with the government, in the same official hands'.[17] In the commission's investigations into popular education abroad, particularly in France and Germany, similar attention was paid to schemes designed to improve connections between elite and elementary education. The *Foreign Assistant Commissioners, including leading English university reformers like Mark Pattison, were specifically asked to find out whether 'Universities, academies, and other learned bodies, more or less connected with and recognized by the State, discharge any functions in regard to popular education'.[18]

The method most often recommended by the commissioners for establishing firmer ties between elite educational institutions and the elementary schools was an extension of the existing (albeit extremely limited) scholarship and exhibition system. When the universities and older public schools were founded, the report argued, there had been more than adequate provision for the talented poor to be raised 'above their class and carried forward to the high places of the Church and the liberal professions'.[19] In the intervening centuries, however, such scholarships and exhibitions as there were had become increasingly restricted to the middle and upper classes and no longer fulfilled their original function.[20] Despite stressing the need for scholarships to the public schools to be given only to those 'boys whose talents would enable them to maintain themselves at the level of their education',[21] the Newcastle Commission put forward quite a radical vision of an integrated national system of education. Building on the recent progress made in widening access to the ancient universities, they saw 'the open scholarships at...Oxford and Cambridge, the number and value of which have been greatly increased by recent legislation' as forming 'the highest part of a graduated system of educational charity, through which remarkable merit might ascend from the lowest to the highest grade'. 'The more you can expand every institution', they argued, citing the assistant commissioner, John Hare, 'and every restriction you can take away, there is so much to gain...If every school in the country was open to every child it would be beneficial'.[22] At times, the tone becomes almost visionary. Such a system, Patric Cumin declared, 'meets the wants of every class...It will draw forth from obscurity many a brilliant intellect which must otherwise waste its power in neglect and indigence...It will go some way to put an end to that separation between the upper and lower classes, the rich and the poor, which does more, perhaps, to prevent an efficient and economical system of education than any other circumstance'.[23]

Another common suggestion for building links between the elementary schools and elite education was that the ancient universities should become more closely involved in the administration and organisation of elementary education. Thus, it was suggested that the universities might assume a variety of responsibilities with regard to elementary schools including carrying out regular inspections[24] and examinations of the pupils themselves.[25] Particularly prominent was the notion that Oxford and Cambridge might take a central role in the training of elementary teachers, for example, by assuming responsibility for the certification of teachers, both male and female.[26] Once again, the moral advantages of the public school and university environment were stressed when proposing these institutions as a model for the development of elementary teacher training colleges. Many important features of public school life including regular chapel attendance, high table and communal dining as well as the presence of resident masters were recommended to the principals of training colleges and were indeed taken up by them.[27] The report likewise recommended that more elementary teachers should be recruited from among university graduates.[28]

Public school citizenship and the elementary curriculum, 1870–1902

It is evidence of the degree to which elementary school reform was tied up with changes to other parts of the educational system that it took some nine years for many of the recommendations of the Newcastle Report to be given the force of law in the Elementary Education Act of 1870. This delay allowed the accumulated findings of several other education commissions (most importantly the Clarendon and Taunton Commissions) to be taken on board. Both these commissions resulted in major Acts of Parliament – the Public Schools Act of 1868 and the *Endowed Schools Act of 1869 – which had a significant impact upon the kind of elementary education system envisaged in the Act of 1870. While we have seen that the public schools formed an important reference point, and in many cases a working model, for elementary education in the 1861 Newcastle Report, by the time the new elementary system came up for its first full-scale review with the Cross Commission in 1886–7, their role had become even more important with particular emphasis placed upon the moral benefits of a public school education, especially the inculcation of a certain ideal of imperial citizenship.

This connection has been recognised before but has usually been interpreted in the same way as the general influence of the public schools on the elementary system – as a means of social control. Such an interpretation has been put forward by historians like John MacKenzie who have referred to the presence of pro-imperial textbooks, rituals and festivals in the elementary system as nothing less than 'imperial propaganda', imposed upon the working class by the elite in an effort to keep them in their place.[29] Even historians of elementary education like Stephen Heathorn, who have recently argued against the 'myth of a conspiratorial ruling elite' in the late nineteenth century and have sought to show that middle-class educators 'were similarly immersed in the nationalist hegemony of their day', maintain that official encouragement of imperialism in elementary schools was to a degree 'socially manipulative', the product of 'middle-class anxieties' about working-class social mobility.[30] Although retaining the somewhat limiting notion of 'propaganda', J.A. Mangan has called for a closer investigation of the role of public schools in the transmission of an ideal of imperial citizenship. 'Intensive, comprehensive and comparative studies of general attitudes to imperialism within the schools are required', he wrote, 'to trace the nature of the association between public school and state school in the promulgation of imperial enthusiasm'.[31] An important first point to note is that the ideal of imperial citizenship represented by the public schools, which Pamela Horn has described as a combination of 'diligence, obedience, thrift, self-denial, endurance, and "indomitable pluck"',[32] was a fairly recent development within the public schools themselves. A particular emphasis on the empire and imperial citizenship only appeared in the wake of the 1861 Clarendon Commission and came into its own in the early 1870s following the Public Schools Act of 1868. After this date, historians speak of the 'reformed public schools' and of the 'public-school system', which increasingly incorporated boys' preparatory schools as well.[33] In the Clarendon Report itself, it is possible to detect a shift in tone from what Heathorn has described as an emphasis on individual 'character reformation, moral worthiness, personal salvation and a view of society as the aggregate of responsible, morally upstanding individuals' towards 'a more secular and collectivist or communitarian conception' of citizenship.[34] Thus, in the Clarendon Report of 1864 we read that 'the great object of education, next to the training of the mind to overcome difficulties... is to train the man for discharging certain definite functions and relations towards his fellow-citizens, his own countrymen'.[35] In line with this, over the course of the 1870s we see a significant shift in many public schools towards an emphasis on organised games and the cultivation of team spirit and collective responsibility, virtues which came to define the public-school ideal of citizenship by the final quarter of the nineteenth century.[36]

Historians seeking to emphasise the importance of class distinctions between elementary and public school education in the late nineteenth century have often stressed the fact that although an increased interest in physical exercise is noticeable at both levels, organised team sports were almost entirely restricted to the public schools with a preference for military-style drill prevailing in the elementary schools.[37] Although one of the assistant masters at Eton, Edmond Warre, mentioned in the course of his evidence to the Clarendon Commission that military-style drill was less popular at Eton than the other main activity of the voluntary rifle corps, namely shooting, he spoke in positive terms about the moral and physical effects of drill and of its continuing popularity among Eton pupils. 'It has brought out a class who would neither row nor play cricket', he said.[38] The boys took considerable pride in being 'able to show themselves off on a grand day like the 4th of June,[39] or if anybody comes down to inspect them'.[40] The commissioners themselves expressed the view that 'as a gymnastic exercise' drill was particularly valuable, praising 'the effects... on [pupils'] bodies, in developing their frames and giving them heartier appetites'.[41] 'We can only express our opinion', they wrote, 'that the school authorities would do well to give it all practicable and suitable encouragement'.[42] There is no sense in the Clarendon Report that military-style drill was seen as a pursuit more suitable for the working classes. Indeed, the commissioners regarded it as entirely compatible with the traditions of the public schools, linking it in the case of Harrow to the long-standing instruction of pupils in archery, a practice going back to the foundation of the school in the sixteenth century.[43] This being the case, it is entirely possible that the increasing use of drill in elementary schools was, in some degree, related to its growing popularity in the public school system and was not, as many have argued, designed as a special means of keeping working-class children in line. By the same token, organised games such as cricket and football were far from unknown in working-class elementary schools.[44] Social reformers advocating the benefits of team games over military drill acquired significant support among those involved in elementary schooling in the late nineteenth and early twentieth centuries, particularly when they stressed the moral benefits of such sports with reference to the successful formation of imperial citizens.[45]

The public schools may have played a similar role in promoting a particular notion of imperial citizenship when it came to the development of the academic curriculum in elementary schools. Once again scholars have tended to view middle-class control over the textbooks and readers used in elementary school classrooms within the context of an over-arching strategy of social control.[46] Much has been made in this context of the supposed division between the classical curriculum pursued in middle-class schools which opened the doors to higher education and socio-political influence and the modern curriculum followed in elementary schools based on English literature, history, geography and a limited amount of physical science. In fact, both middle-class and elementary education were marked in the final decades of the nineteenth century by a modernisation of the syllabus. Thus, one of the most notable features of the post-Clarendon public schools is a much greater enthusiasm for the teaching of modern subjects. Such a move was explicitly called for in the Clarendon Report itself. In their 'General Recommendations', the commissioners declared that:

> In addition to the study of the classics and to religious teaching, every boy who passes through the school should receive instruction in arithmetic and mathematics, in one modern language at least, which should be either French or German, in some one branch at least of natural science, and in either drawing or music. Care should be taken to ensure that the boys acquire a good general knowledge of geography and ... modern history, and a command of pure grammatical English.[47]

One of the greatest incentives for the public schools to devote more time to modern subjects was the parallel development of new honours schools in these subjects at the ancient universities. In the appendix to the Clarendon Report, Charles Waldegrave Sandford, the Senior Censor of Christ Church, Oxford, spoke of the importance for the universities of a broader curriculum at the public schools:

> The University course is, doubtless, affected by the unsatisfactory manner in which the great public schools prepare their boys for matriculation ... If ... boys come from school with their intellectual tastes cultivated with a greater knowledge of modern history, or some branch of physical science, a larger number might be expected to pursue these studies on entering the University, the lecturers would be able to penetrate more deeply into their subjects, and the examiners in awarding honours would be able to fix a higher standard.[48]

In particular, the commissioners recommended that the universities offer more prizes 'for newer and more special branches of knowledge', in particular, mathematics, modern history and physical science to encourage public schools to pay more attention to these subjects prior to matriculation at the universities.[49]

Just as the encouragement of modern subjects at the public schools was linked to the foundation of new honours schools in these subjects at the universities, so was the decision to introduce a modern academic curriculum at the elementary schools after 1870. This connection is particularly visible in the way in which university-trained men, including many who actually worked at Oxford and Cambridge as academics, came to dominate as authors of history, literature and civics readers for use in the elementary school classroom. Indeed, Heathorn can speak of the development of a 'symbiotic relationship' between academics and publishers. On the one hand, publishers became increasingly keen to have university men as authors as it raised the reputation of their series with the public and helped them get their books onto the carefully controlled selection lists drawn up by school boards, themselves dominated by public school and university-educated men; on the other hand, academics working in the emerging fields of modern history, English literature and geography wanted to write these books as it helped justify their aspirations for professional status and aided the establishment of new academic disciplines at the universities.[50] Some of the most popular history readers were written by men of the stature of Samuel Rawlinson Gardiner, Professor of Modern History at both Oxford and Cambridge, T.F. Tout, Professor of Medieval and Modern History at the University of Manchester, Frederick York Powell, Regius Professor of Modern History at Oxford and Oscar Browning, who, as a fellow and lecturer at King's College, Cambridge, did much to establish modern history as an independent degree subject in that university.[51] This burgeoning relationship between higher and elementary education was also reflected in the increasing involvement of the university presses in the production of readers for elementary schools. As Peter Sutcliffe tells us in his history of Oxford University Press, from the 1860s onwards, 'the Clarendon Press series became the most heterogeneous series imaginable, ranging from...reading books...at 4d through the editions of the classics to Mr Veitch's *Irregular Greek Verbs* at 10s'.[52] The outcome of this was, in the words of Heathorn, that 'the same or similar authors were responsible for writing books for university, secondary, and elementary schools systems', doing much to integrate the different levels of English education.[53] This meant, somewhat inevitably, that there was also a coalescing of messages about citizenship, nationality and the empire included in the books read by pupils at both elementary and public schools. Although elementary school pupils may not have been reading expensive textbooks produced mainly for use in middle-class schools like Rudyard Kipling and C.R.L. Fletcher's jingoistic *History of England*,[54] they were using readers written by a small cadre of writers of the same educational background, many of whom included similarly patriotic messages in their elementary school readers. From the 1880s onwards, we see a similar concentration on national origins, character and mission in these books – whether history, geography, literature or civics readers.[55] Imperial heroes like General Gordon were presented as role models for public school and elementary pupils alike.[56] Similarly, passages from popular history books such as J.R. Green's *Short History of the English People*[57] and J.A. Froude's *History of England*,[58] which glorified the narrative of Anglo-Saxon history and the importance of English racial identity, were used in both elementary and public schools. This suggests once more that the distinction often insisted on by scholars between the classical curriculum of the public schools and the modern syllabus of the elementary schools was not as clear as it is often presented.[59] Increasingly, 'the model societies of the Greeks and Romans' were no longer 'the main examples' for pupils in the public schools and students in the elite universities. Lessons drawn from the history of the English people and comparisons with 'the now subordinated peoples of the empire' found their way as much into middle-class education as they did into the instruction provided in elementary schools.[60]

Personal connections between public and elementary schools, 1870–1902

Insofar as scholars have examined the personal connections between the elementary and public schools, they have tended to concentrate on the extent to which former public school pupils were able to dictate the form of schooling received by working-class children. Thus, it is often pointed out that almost all members of the Board of Education and those appointed to sit on the various education commissions as well as many members of school boards and H.M. Inspectors were educated at the public schools and universities.[61] This is undoubtedly true; indeed, as we saw, middle-class influence over the elementary curriculum actually grew after 1870 with the professionalisation of school-reader authorship, which saw the market increasingly dominated by public school and university-educated men.

Despite these facts, however, the connections established between the elementary and public school systems in the late nineteenth century were much more varied than such a picture suggests. Moreover, in many cases, the motivations driving such connections had little to do with crude notions of social control. There was frequently a genuine desire to improve access to elite education for the children of working-class families and to enhance the quality of elementary instruction. Thus many of those chosen to take part in education commissions, who had attended the public schools and universities, had also extensive experience of educational reform. This was particularly true of the 1886 Cross Commission, which included among others Cardinal Henry Manning, a tireless advocate for greater Catholic elementary school provision; Sir John Lubbock, a dedicated promoter of scientific and technical education for the masses; Robert Gregory, the long-serving treasurer of the *National Society for Promoting the Education of the Poor; and Sydney Charles Buxton, a reformist member of the London School Board.

In addition, the Cross Commission showed itself more flexible towards the idea of promoting elementary teachers to higher posts within the education system, in particular, into the ranks of the inspectorate, a move specifically rejected by the Newcastle Commission of 1861.[62] 'Very distinguished' elementary school teachers might be allowed to become H.M. Inspectors, the report declared. They must, however, remain 'able men of liberal education'.[63] The commissioners also mentioned a variety of ways in which the average education of the elementary teacher might be improved. In particular, they recommended much greater involvement on the part of the public schools and universities in the training of elementary school teachers and pupil teachers. There was, for example, considerable enthusiasm for modelling elementary teacher training colleges on public schools and the colleges at Oxford and Cambridge. According to Canon Cromwell's evidence before the Cross Commission, teachers boarding at a training college ought to 'derive something of the same kind of advantage that a boy derives from going to one of our great public schools, and they would lose all those advantages if they were trained in day colleges'.[64] It was precisely the opportunity which residential training colleges provided for living closely with 'men of superior education', by which were meant the lecturers and principals, many of whom had been educated at the public schools and universities, which constituted the principal advantage of these institutions for the commission.[65] It was likewise suggested that 'we should bring some of [the universities'] social amusements, and society arrangements, or athletic organisations to the training colleges' to help recreate the intimate atmosphere of an Oxford or Cambridge college.[66] The commissioners were also fond of using analogies taken from the universities to suggest improvements at an elementary school level. Comparisons were often made, for example, between the role of the elementary school teacher and that of the university professor and between that of the pupil teacher and that of the university 'coach'.[67] Also fairly common was the comparison between elementary school headmasters and university tutors.[68]

As well as seeking to make the atmosphere at teacher training colleges more closely resemble that experienced at the public schools and universities, the Cross Commission suggested ways in which elementary school teachers might gain first-hand experience of life at the universities. The Revised Code of 1882 allowed university graduates to become elementary teachers for the first time, a move which also made it easier for elementary teachers to undertake the duties of an H.M. Inspector of Schools. Indeed, Patric Cumin was asked explicitly whether 'the idea of raising the elementary schools to the standard of Eton and Harrow' lay behind this change in policy. Although Cumin denied that the goal was as straightforward as this, he did stress the point that the aim was to improve the overall quality of education provided. 'There are a great many persons', he answered,

> who have...a disposition towards being schoolmasters, and the better the class they come from, the better the teaching is likely to be...In Scotland, where you have that connexion between the elementary schools and the Universities, you get a better class of teachers; and the intention was to elevate the condition of the teachers, and to improve education generally.[69]

Following this change of attitude, the question also arose as to whether elementary teachers might actually be able to complete some of their training at the universities themselves. Suggestions ranged from an additional third year's training at one of the universities,[70] to asking Oxford and Cambridge to make it easier for trainee teachers to receive honours degrees by, for example, allowing two years at a training college to count for one year of an honours course.[71] Such an argument gained strength from the fact that growing numbers of qualified elementary teachers, trained at training colleges, were going on to win university honours at London, Cambridge, Dublin and the Royal University of Ireland.[72] It was even suggested that Oxford, Cambridge and the newer provincial universities might receive government grants to allow them to provide the entire course of training for elementary school teachers. This idea was advocated, in particular, by the *Education Reform League*, which sent a deputation to the vice-president of the Privy Council asking for just such a reform.[73] The principal motivation, it seemed, remained the improvement of the quality and rigour of teaching provided. As Canon Warburton explained in his evidence before the commission: 'I hope to live to see a closer approximation of our training college system with the liberal culture of our universities, so that all that is best and highest in modern education may be brought within the reach of those to whom the teaching of the great mass of the children of this and coming generations will be entrusted'.[74] Nor does it seem that such enthusiasm for greater contact between elite and working-class education came simply from those in charge of reforming the elementary system. Canon Warburton reported his belief 'that there would be no unwillingness to cooperate on the part of the authorities of Oxford and Cambridge'.[75] Indeed, discussions were already underway to strengthen formal ties between the ancient universities and the training of elementary teachers. Canon Cromwell had spoken to the authorities at Cambridge about directly affiliating a number of training colleges to the university[76]; Canon Warburton had likewise made enquiries with Oxford's vice-chancellor about the possibility of setting up facilities at the university to allow a certain proportion of female elementary teachers to complete a year's training there. 'I should like them to be resident on the spot', he wrote, 'and to imbibe the spirit of the place'. 'The Oxford authorities', he continued, 'feel strongly what a great advantage it would be to our teachers if they could come up to Oxford and hear high class lectures'.[77]

The report also contains information about experiments already taking place, which aimed to draw directly on the experience of the public schools and ancient universities to improve the quality of elementary teaching. We are told, for example, about a recent initiative called the Teachers University Association, which gave trainee elementary teachers the opportunity to reside for three weeks at Oxford during the long vacation and, alongside a demanding academic curriculum which included instruction in Greek and Latin grammar, to take an active part in university cricket and rowing. The commissioners commented, in particular, upon the degree to which such a practice was 'valuable as cultivating feelings and taste' as well as a sense of 'social brotherhood'.[78] Similar initiatives were developed for the benefit of pupil teachers. The former principal of a pupil teacher centre at *Toynbee Hall, Edmund Beale Sargent, spoke of various 'social training' schemes recently established including organised visits to Oxford and Cambridge, where pupil teachers were chaperoned by university students, toured the colleges and observed traditional student recreations like boating.[79] The principal aim, we are told, was to provide them with 'opportunities of mixing with persons of higher culture, and thus acquiring respect for themselves and for others, good and pleasing manners, liberality of thought, and above all the spirit of chivalry'.[80] For the training of pupil teachers, the practice of organized team sports which had developed in the public schools from the late 1860s was considered particularly valuable. As Edmund Beale Sargent complained,

> There has been no organised physical training [for pupil teachers]. I mean no such sports and recreation in common as enter so prominently into the life at a public school. In rural districts there is opportunity for individual recreation, but there being no community of interest with others nor adequate supervision, the disciplinary effect of games is lost.[81]

We also hear of the promotion of cricket and football by the *London Pupil Teachers' Association, an organisation, which, it was claimed, 'was shaped to resemble the athletic unions of the houses of a public school' and to 'afford a like education' to its members.[82]

Finally, in a spirit which built on the recommendations of the Newcastle Commission, we see a much greater determination to widen access to public schools and higher education for elementary pupils. When asked 'whether it was a real advantage to a boy belonging to the working classes to give him a literary exhibition and help him forward ultimately to the University', Matthew Arnold, a Chief Inspector of Schools, replied firmly that 'if he can hold his own with those he finds at the University, it is a decided advantage to him to enter into a higher battle of life'.[83] The ideal of a 'ladder of learning' allowing poor but talented pupils to progress through the various levels of education, from the elementary school to the universities, received unprecedented support. Another Chief Inspector of Schools, T.W. Sharpe, was able to provide specific examples of 'boys being thoroughly nursed through by one system in the same school, from the lowest round of elementary school up to being scholars of Balliol'.[84] J. Nunn, Chairman of the Manchester School Board, spoke similarly in his evidence of the 'ladder by which a poor boy may rise from a public elementary school to the Manchester Grammar School and, as we have seen lately, to Oxford and Cambridge.'[85]

The second report of the Cross Commission contained an appendix listing all the scholarships and exhibitions available within elementary schools belonging to the London School Board along with details of pupils who had been awarded scholarships in recent years. These tables provide evidence that it was indeed possible for a minority of elementary school pupils to rise by means of the scholarship system all the way to the ancient universities. In the year 1875, for example, two boys, both from St. Michael's elementary school in Bromley had won Drapers' Company scholarships to continue their education at Merchant Taylors' School and afterwards at St. John's College, Oxford and St. John's College, Cambridge, respectively. The first boy, the son of a shipwright, went on to be placed in the first class for Classical Moderations in 1883 and to achieve a top place in the Civil Service Entrance Examinations. The second, the son of a joiner, went on to attain a first class in the Theological Tripos Part I and a second class in Part II. He also won a number of university prizes and at the time of the commission was about to enter holy orders.[86]

Perhaps the best evidence of the growing interest in promoting easier move-ment between the different levels of education is the mention made in the final report of the Cross Commission of a new initiative on the part of the Charity Commissioners designed to make each H.M. Inspector familiar with all the schol-arship opportunities available in his district and to encourage promising children to apply. All inspectors received an 'exhaustive list of about 1,000 schemes, made under the Charitable Trust and Endowed Schools Acts, now in operation, under which exhibitions are granted to scholars from elementary schools so as to enable them to enter higher schools'. The initiative behind this development seems, however, to have come from the inspectors themselves. 'At present', declared J.G. Fitch, Chief Inspector of Training Colleges for Schoolmistresses, 'we have no such knowledge. As we move about among schools, and come in contact with clever and promising children, it would be a great advantage to us, if we were officially cognisant of the means of secondary instruction which exist in the district, and which we might advise the managers and parents to avail themselves of'.[87]

The declining influence of elite education upon elementary schooling, 1902–1930

Until the last years of the nineteenth century, the public schools remained a valu-able source of inspiration for those interested in reforming the elementary system introduced in 1870, both inside and outside the government. Although there was no doubt always an aspect of social control present, there was also a genuine desire to improve the quality of education provided and to integrate both elite and elementary education into an efficient and meritocratic national system. The position began to change, however, as the century drew to its close, in large part in response to increasing anxieties, particularly in government circles, about the security of Britain's international position and the viability of the empire. A chief cause of this anxiety was the growing rivalry between the European powers, par-ticularly following the unification of Germany in 1870. Britain's lack of success in the Boer War (1899–1902) did not help to stabilise fears about the country's inter-national position; indeed, the discovery of the poor state of health of many army recruits during the conflict only compounded existing fears about the 'degenera-tion' of the English race.[88] The public schools were not unaffected by these grow-ing anxieties nor was the system of elite education in England excluded from the increasingly widespread criticism of the establishment which sought to find the cause of Britain's apparent malaise. Against the background of growing worries about the country's ability to compete with its European and extra-European rivals, it was the perceived failure of the public schools to provide a proper sci-entific training which caused many to criticise them so strongly. Even the then prime minister, Arthur Balfour, declared in a speech in 1903 that most public school boys 'do not care a farthing about the world they live in except so far as it is concerned with the cricket-ground, or the football-field, or the river'.[89] Writing in *Macmillan's Magazine* in 1907, Charles Bruce, himself an army officer educated at Harrow and Repton, wrote despairingly of public school boys out of touch with the modern world and the demands which it placed upon Britain. 'Their educa-tion', he wrote, 'has never taught them to look the realities of life in the face, to think out what they are going to do, to feel the necessity of fitting themselves for the work of the world. In almost every part of our Empire public-school boys and university men find themselves in the same perilous condition'.[90] Without a thorough reform of public school education, how was Britain to keep up with 'the rapid advance of the United States of America, of Germany, and perhaps above all, of Japan, in the spheres of administration, industry, and social progress?'[91] On the eve of the First World War, the apparent failings of the public school system had merited a monograph-length study by Herbert Branston Gray, public school head-master and former scholar of Winchester and Queen's College, Oxford. Explaining his reasons for writing *The Public Schools and the Empire*, which appeared in 1913, he remarked: 'I regard the existing condition of English Education with anxiety, as being chaotic, inefficient and ill-suited to the temper of the times and the country in which we live'.[92]

Even before the outbreak of war, these kinds of anxieties had caused those responsible for developing elementary education in England to move away from the late nineteenth century enthusiasm for drawing elite and elementary school-ing closer together. Writing in 1914, Charles Birchenough remarked upon the fact that government policy, particularly in the years since 1900, had been 'giv-ing to elementary education a character of its own'. 'There has been', he wrote, 'an increasing tendency to…make schoolwork more practical and less bookish, to develop, in short, handiness and practical capacity'.[93] New subjects including physical geography, mechanics, physiology, botany (and domestic economy for girls) were encouraged by the Board of Education. To a large extent, this change was due to a growing dissatisfaction with the lack of practicality in English ele-mentary education. In 1904, the Board declared that 'The purpose of the public elementary school is…to fit [pupils] practically as well as intellectually, for the work of life.'[94] This view translated itself not only into a curriculum which was more strongly focused on subjects not in the main taught at the public schools, but also into a type of education much more closely adapted to the particular geographical regions in which elementary schools were situated. The most obvi-ous example of this was the new emphasis placed on nature study from 1902 with schools in rural areas taking up appropriate agricultural tasks such as bee-keeping and poultry-raising and with schools in towns adopting mechanics and chemistry.[95]

Such changes were also encouraged by the growing influence of progressive foreign educational theorists in Britain such as *Dewey, Herbart and Froebel. The American John Dewey, in particular, recommended making schoolwork more meaningful to children 'by bringing it into closer relationship with the home and the life of the neighbourhood'.[96] Indeed, Birchenough was to describe this tendency towards an increasingly localised form of elementary schooling as 'the new spirit in education'.[97] This was the very opposite of the public school approach which emphasised the value of removing children from their home environments and instilling a national-imperial loyalty to king and country. Another factor which arguably contributed to the move of elementary schools away from the public school model after 1900 was the growing ratio of female to male teachers in elementary education. While there were still slightly more male than female elementary teachers in 1870, by 1914, nearly three quarters were women.[98] As a consequence, some scholars have spoken of a 'maternalisation' or 'feminisation' of the elementary teaching profession in this period and an associated retreat from a primarily bookish or academic curriculum in favour of more practical, homely subjects such as domestic economy and nature study.[99]

However, a move towards a more vocational curriculum in elementary schools after 1900 may also have been driven, in part, by the fear that the provision of an overly intellectual education for a majority of working-class children tended, in the words of Birchenough, 'to manufacture economic misfits' and give such children undue 'pretensions'.[100] Such views gained particular prominence amid growing fears about the spread of socialist ideas among England's urban poor and the threat of working-class insurrection in the early years of the twentieth century. That said, before the outbreak of war in 1914, most efforts to reform the elementary system were concerned not so much with maintaining class distinctions as with implanting the idea of Britain's imperial greatness more firmly into the minds of working-class children. Most important here was the Empire Day Movement which was promoted enthusiastically by the Earl of Meath from the early 1900s, when he adopted the idea from the practice of schools in Canada. Emphasising the importance of citizenship, national and imperial patriotism and obedience to authority, celebrations included raising and saluting the Union Jack, singing the national anthem and pointing out to the children the scale of the British Empire on large wall maps.[101]

It was the experience of the First World War that brought the issue of social class to the forefront of the political agenda. As Brad Beaven and John Griffiths have written, 'For social commentators and academics charged with constructing a viable notion of citizenship from the debris of war, it became clear that some acknowledgement to social class had to be reworked into any new notion of citizenry'.[102] Played down in the wave of jingoistic nationalism which had preceded the war, class tensions became increasingly visible in the context of the widespread civil unrest in 1919, industrial strikes in the 1920s and the growth of socialism as a political force in the post-war years.[103] At the same time, class distinctions became more apparent in Britain's school system. The most significant change in these years was the expansion of a state-aided secondary sector, which built on the 1902 Balfour Education Act and the increased provision after 1907 of grammar school places under the direct-grants scheme. However, despite the fact that greater numbers of working-class children had access to free secondary education in the interwar years,[104] the system was heavily marked by class distinctions. This is perhaps most apparent when we compare the subjects most commonly studied at elementary schools with the curricula of the state-aided grammar schools.[105] While the elementary curriculum became increasingly vocational in nature, with special emphasis on 'handy' subjects such as carpentry, mechanics, agriculture and domestic economy, grammar schools, which offered free places, continued to provide a traditional classical curriculum, 'patterned', in the words of Gail Savage, 'after the education offered by the public schools'.[106] Indeed, she has maintained that this division was deliberately encouraged by civil servants at the Board of Education in the interwar years. Officially, the policy was justified by the argument that as secondary schools educated 'the country's future leaders', the quality of education received should be of a demonstrably higher standard. For Board officials, this meant 'an academic, non-vocational course of study that would mould the character as well as train the mind'.[107] Moreover, they were careful to stress that all children capable of benefiting from secondary education, whatever their social background, should be allowed the opportunity. The point remains, however, that they did not think the numbers of such children would ever be particularly high.[108] Likewise, although the expanded system of free places provided an important means of social mobility for a limited number of working-class children, the education they received and the socialisation process to which they were exposed were distinctly middle-class in nature, thus helping to maintain class distinctions. That a degree of anxiety about the potential spread of socialist ideas in schools lay behind the Board's enthusiasm for strongly differentiated curricula in elementary and state-aided grammar schools in this period is suggested by their reactions to Labour's proposal in 1929 for a unified system of post-primary education. S.H. Wood, private secretary to the president of the Board, criticised the plans, designed to minimise the significance of class difference in schools, as 'dangerous…and not in the best interests of education or the children'.[109]

Commentators like Cyril Norwood, the future headmaster of Harrow, who continued to argue, as the late Victorians had done, that the public schools and ancient universities could provide useful models for elementary as well as secondary education found themselves distinctly out of step with the new emphasis on a class-based system. As late as September 1928, when he gave the presidential address to the Educational Science section of the British Association for the Advancement of Science, Norwood could still speak of the need for the public school spirit to infuse 'every part and parcel of our educational system.' All schools, he declared, would benefit from taking up the founding idea of the public school system, 'that education is more than instruction, that character counts for more than brains and lives more than learning'.[110]

With the renewed emphasis upon practical and vocational subjects in the elementary schools, the influence of the public schools and universities upon elementary education continued to decline in the 1920s. Moreover, and somewhat ironically, with the expansion of state-aided grammar schools offering a non-vocational, academic course of study, the overall cultural significance of the public school system as a distinct style of education was also reduced. Enrolments at all the major public schools as well as the numerous smaller institutions fell sharply in the years after 1918 and many encountered severe financial problems.[111] Interestingly, this was also the period which saw the popularity of public school fiction decline significantly, suggesting, as Jenny Holt has argued in her recent study, that the image of the public school boy, famous since the publication of *Tom Brown's Schooldays* in 1857, had lost much of its broader cultural appeal by the interwar years.[112] By the end of our period, protests against the perceived division between working- and middle-class schooling were increasingly heard. At the centre of this opposition were figures connected with the Labour Party. In 1929, during the second Labour government, plans for bringing together all forms of post-primary education in a new system of comprehensive schools came before the Board of Education, proposed by a research group connected with Labour. However, as Gail Savage has shown, C.P. Trevelyan, then president of the Board, showed no interest in the plans and Board officials voiced their strong opposition. 'With no sponsor inside the Board', she concluded, 'the idea that the state should organize such schools made no headway until comprehensive schools became a part of Labour education policy after the second world war'.[113]

Conclusion

Insofar as the public schools and ancient universities have been considered by historians of English elementary education they have usually been treated as a distinct system of education having little directly to do with the working classes. If any relationship has been observed, it has been seen in terms of a clear power dynamic with middle-class, public school-educated men making use of their control over the structure and content of elementary education in order to reinforce their own social and political position. The promotion of a particular ideal of national and imperial citizenship in the late nineteenth century has often been treated as part of this strategy – an attempt to appeal to an overarching British identity superseding class interests.

What has been argued here, by contrast, is that the relationship between elite and popular education in this period was considerably more complicated than such a picture assumes. Firstly, it was suggested that, to some extent, the influence of the public schools and ancient universities in the early days of elementary school reform was inevitable as such institutions constituted, in many cases, the sum total of the educational experience of those responsible for developing the new system. Moreover, reform of the elementary sector should not be separated from changes introduced at all levels of education (including the elite schools and universities) from the 1850s onwards. This being the case, it is more accurate to see attempts to develop mass elementary education in the context of a national project of educational reform. Although there must always have been an element of social control present, in a number of cases, particularly with the growing dominance of the elementary school readers' market by university-trained academics, this had far more to do with the growing connections between the different levels of education. Thus academics undertook to produce such readers as a way of justifying the existence of new disciplines such as modern history and English literature at the universities. The motivation most frequently cited in the various educational commissions as driving not only the proposed general reform of the elementary system but specifically the desire for a closer relationship between elite and popular education, was the wish to raise the quality of teaching provided in elementary schools and to improve prospects for working-class children. This is perhaps most clearly seen in the myriad attempts to involve the ancient universities more closely in the training and certification of elementary school teachers and to improve the effectiveness of the existing scholarship system. Far from attempting to close off elite education to working-class children and elementary teachers we see increasing moves, particularly with the Cross Commission of 1886–7, to bring the curricula pursued in elite and elementary schools closer together as well as to raise the level of education achieved by elementary school teachers, particularly by providing opportunities for them to access university instruction.

The influence of the public schools and universities as models in the reform of the elementary system was however limited to a particular period of time. It reached its peak before the turn of the century and then diminished. Growing international rivalries and anxiety about the viability of Britain's empire over the course of the 1890s and first years of the twentieth century encouraged a loss of confidence in the public school system as a pattern for the education of the mass of children. It was increasingly seen as unable to equip pupils for the modern world, particularly in its perceived failure to provide a sufficiently practical or scientific education. As a result, the elementary curriculum, influenced too by new pedagogical ideas from abroad, assumed an increasingly workaday character in the years leading up to the First World War. In the period after 1918, the influence of the public schools and universities upon elementary education continued to decline. While the latter continued to become more vocational in nature, the newly expanded secondary sector, confined largely to the state-aided grammar schools, was characterised by a curriculum closely modelled on that of the public schools. This difference was justified by the argument that secondary (as opposed to elementary) schools required the 'best' syllabus available as they were responsible for training the country's future leaders. However, at a time when fears were growing about the spread of socialism among Britain's urban population, it was felt to be no bad thing that those working-class children who received a secondary education would attend grammar schools alongside their middle-class peers and hopefully imbibe similar values and attitudes.

Timeline

1850: Appointment of the Oxford University Commission

1850: Appointment of the Cambridge University Commission

1854: The Oxford University Act

1856: The Cambridge University Act

1861: Report of the Newcastle Commission – investigated state of popular education in England and Wales.

1861: Appointment of the Clarendon Commission – investigated the nine leading public schools in England.

1864: Publication of the Clarendon Report

1868: Public Schools Act

1868: Appointment of the Taunton Commission – investigated endowed grammar schools in England and Wales not covered by the Newcastle and Clarendon Commissions.

1869: Endowed Schools Act

1870: Elementary Education Act – introduced mass elementary schooling into England and Wales for the first time

1880: Elementary Education Act – made attendance at elementary school compulsory from the age of 5 to 10 years old

1882: Revised Code of Education – allowed university graduates to become elementary school teachers for the first time

1886–7: The Cross Commission – appointed to assess the working of the Elementary Education Acts of 1870 and 1880

1902: Balfour Education Act – replaced school boards with LEAs (Local Education Authorities)

1918: Fisher Education Act – increased the minimum school leaving age from 12 to 14 and made provision for 'continuation' classes up to the age of 18

Glossary

ancient universities: the universities of Oxford and Cambridge.

Dewey, Herbart and Froebel: John Dewey (1859–1952) was a functional psychologist who wrote a number of pioneering works on education at the turn of the twentieth century, including *The School and Society* (1900) and *The Child and the Curriculum* (1902). Dewey believed that the school should be an institution to develop the potential of the individual child while making him a model democratic citizen. This could only be done by interactive learning. For the German educationalists, Herbart and Froebel, see below, p. 113.

Education Reform League: a movement founded in 1884 by the London vicar and social reformer, Samuel Barnett, to campaign for the reform of state elementary education, in particular, to make it compulsory and free until the age of 15 or 16.

endowed schools: usually used to refer to those schools in receipt of some form of government funding. They included both elementary and secondary schools.

foreign assistant commissioners: those who were appointed as part of a Royal Commission to investigate and report on the situation in foreign countries.

grammar schools: secondary schools which tended to teach a classical curriculum (including Greek and Latin grammar) and most often prepared middle-class boys for the professions or for entry into the universities. In the early years of the twentieth century, many such schools accepted government funding for so-called free places which were restricted to pupils who had attended state-run elementary schools.

great public schools: usually used to refer to the nine public schools investigated by the Clarendon Commission of 1861 (Eton, Harrow, Winchester, Westminster, St. Paul's, Merchant Taylors', Rugby, Charterhouse and Shrewsbury).

The London Pupil Teachers' Association: Based at Toynbee Hall, this organisation enrolled over 2,000 male and female pupil teachers from the twelve pupil-teacher centres across London and sought to provide entertainment as well as a training in citizenship for its members.

National Society for Promoting the Education of the Poor: a movement campaigning for greater elementary school provision established by the Church of England in 1811.

public schools: private, fee-paying schools, mostly attended by the British middle and upper classes. Many were boarding schools although there were 'day schools' too such as Merchant Taylors.

Toynbee Hall: set up in 1884 by Samuel Barnett as a place where students from the ancient universities of Oxford and Cambridge, together with their teachers, could live and work alongside the urban poor in London's East End. Toynbee Hall is perhaps the best known example of the Settlement Movement.

Notes

1. T. Hughes (1857) *Tom Brown's School Days* (London), p. 69.
2. In a recent study, Jenny Holt has considered the wider appeal of public school fiction in the late nineteenth and early twentieth centuries. See J. Holt (2008) *Public-School Literature, Civic Training and the Politics of Male Adolescence* (Farnham: Ashgate).
3. See, for example, Bergen, B.H. (1988) 'Only a Schoolmaster: Gender, Class and the Effort to Professionalize Elementary Teaching in England 1870–1910' in J. Ozga (ed.) *Schoolwork: Approaches to the Labour Process of Teaching* (Milton Keynes: Open University Press), pp. 46–68; J.M. MacKenzie (1984) *Propaganda and Empire: The Manipulation of British Public Opinion* (Manchester: Manchester University Press).
4. Bergen, 'Only a Schoolmaster', p. 48.
5. R. H. Tawney (1924) *Education, The Socialist Policy* (London: Independent Labour Party), p. 22.
6. Education Commission (1861) *Report of the Commissioners Appointed to Inquire into the State of Popular Education in England. Vol. I.* (afterwards *Newcastle Commission* Vol. I) (London: George E. Eyre and William Spottiswoode), p. 1.
7. Edward Miall attended St. Saviour's Grammar School in London before entering the Congregationalist ministry.
8. Henry Pelham, Duke of Newcastle, Sir John Taylor Coleridge, William Rogers, Goldwin Smith and Nassau Senior all attended Eton and Oxford. William Charles Lake attended Rugby and Oxford. Rugby School and Thomas Arnold were also important links for these members of the commission. John Taylor Coleridge was a contemporary and close friend of Arnold at Corpus Christi College, Oxford; Lake was one of his pupils at Rugby.
9. Coleridge was a fellow of Exeter College, Oxford. Senior was appointed Drummond Professor of Political Economy at Oxford, Goldwin Smith was made Regius Professor of Modern History at Oxford and Lake was appointed a tutor at Balliol College, Oxford.

10. Harvie, C. (1997) 'Reform and Expansion' in M.G. Brock and M.C. Curthoys (eds) *The History of the University of Oxford Volume VI. Nineteenth-Century Oxford Part 1* (Oxford: Oxford University Press), p. 699.
11. Ward, W.R. (1997) 'From the Tractarians to the Executive Commission' in Brock and Curthoys (eds) *History of the University of Oxford*, Vol. VI, p. 316.
12. Ibid.
13. See, for example, N.W. Senior (April 1845) 'Oxford and Mr. Ward', *Edinburgh Review*, 81:164, 385–98.
14. Thomas Seccombe, 'Rogers, William (1819–1896)', revised M. C. Curthoys, *Oxford Dictionary of National Biography*, Oxford University Press, 2004; online edn, May 2006 [http://www.oxforddnb.com/view/article/24004, accessed 4 Sept. 2010].
15. G.L. Savage (April 1983) 'Social Class and Social Policy: The Civil Service and Secondary Education during the Interwar Period', *Journal of Contemporary History*, 18:2, 261–80, at p. 263.
16. Education Commission (1861) *Reports of the Assistant Commissioners Appointed to Inquire into the State of Popular Education in England. Vol. III.* (afterwards *Newcastle Commission III*) (London: George E. Eyre and William Spottiswoode), p. 74.
17. *Newcastle Commission I*, p. 475.
18. Education Commission (1861) *Reports of the Assistant Commissioners Appointed to Inquire into the State of Popular Education in England. Vol. IV* (afterwards *Newcastle Commission IV*) (London: George E. Eyre and William Spottiswoode, 1861), pp. 11–12.
19. *Newcastle Commission I*, p. 459.
20. Ibid., pp. 459–60.
21. Ibid., p. 502. The report made clear that 'To give a high education to boys whose talents will not enable them afterwards to maintain themselves at that level, is merely to send them into life with expectations doomed to be disappointed, and with sensibilities which will make disappointment bitter' (pp. 502–3).
22. Ibid., p. 503.
23. *Newcastle Commission IV*, p. 351.
24. Education Commission (1861) *Appendix. Minutes of Evidence Taken Before the Commissioners. Vol. VI* (afterwards *Newcastle Commission VI*) (London: George E. Eyre and William Spottiswoode), p. 194.
25. *Newcastle Commission IV*, p. 305.
26. Education Commission (1861) *Answers to the Circular of Questions. Vol. V.* (London: George E. Eyre and William Spottiswoode), p. 78; *Newcastle Commission I*, p. 482. This would have given Oxford and Cambridge a role in the training of teachers similar to that played by the single *université* in France before the 1880s.
27. *Newcastle Commission I*, p. 141.
28. *Newcastle Commission VI*, p. 116.
29. MacKenzie, *Propaganda and Empire*, p. 4.
30. S. Heathorn (2000) *For Home, Country, and Race: Constructing Gender, Class, and Englishness in the Elementary School, 1880–1914* (London: University of Toronto Press), pp. 18, 4.
31. Mangan, J.A. (1986) ' "The Grit of our Forefathers": Invented Traditions, Propaganda and Imperialism' in J.M. MacKenzie (ed.) *Imperialism and Popular Culture* (Manchester: Manchester University Press), p. 136.
32. Horn, P. (1988) 'English Elementary Education and the Growth of the Imperial Ideal: 1880–1914' in J.A. Mangan (ed.) *'Benefits Bestowed'? Education and British Imperialism* (Manchester: Manchester University Press), p. 40.
33. On the incorporation of boys' preparatory schools in the public-school system, see Leinster-Mackay, D. (1988) 'The Nineteenth-Century English Preparatory School: Cradle and Crèche of Empire?' in Mangan (ed.) *'Benefits Bestowed'?*, pp. 56–75.
34. Heathorn, *For Home, Country, Race*, p. 203.

35. (1864) *Report of her Majesty's Commissioners Appointed to Inquire into the Revenues and Management of Certain Colleges and Schools, and the Studies Pursued and Instruction Given Therein* (afterwards *Clarendon Commission Report*) (London: George Edward Eyre and William Spottiswoode), p. 300.
36. On this, see the comments of Dr. John Percival of Clifton College in L.W.B. Brockliss (ed.) (2008) *Magdalen College, A History* (Magdalen College: Oxford) p. 405.
37. See, for example, Heathorn, *For Home, Country, and Race*, p. 193.
38. *Clarendon Commission Report*, p. 185.
39. The '4th of June' is an annual holiday at Eton which commemorates the birthday of George III, the school's most important patron.
40. *Clarendon Commission Report*, p. 185.
41. Ibid., p. 186.
42. Ibid., p. 42.
43. Ibid., p. 42.
44. C. Birchenough (1914) *History of Elementary Education in England and Wales from 1800 to the Present Day* (Oxford: University Tutorial Press), p. 297.
45. See, for example, T. Chesterton (1909) *The Theory of Physical Education in Elementary Schools* (London), p. 118; Heathorn, *For Home, Country and Race*, p. 194.
46. See, for example, B. Simon (1965) *Education and the Labour Movement, 1870–1920* (London: Lawrence & Wishart).
47. *Clarendon Commission Report*, p. 52.
48. *Clarendon Commission Report: Appendix to Report*, p. 10.
49. Ibid., p. 21.
50. Heathorn, *For Home, Country and Race*, pp. 16–17.
51. Ibid., p. 44.
52. P.H. Sutcliffe (2002) *The Oxford University Press: An Informal History* (Oxford University Press: Oxford), p. 23.
53. Heathorn, *For Home, Country, and Race*, p. 17.
54. C.R.L. Fletcher and R. Kipling (1911) *A History of England* (Oxford: Clarendon Press).
55. Heathorn, *For Home, Country, and Race*, p. 11.
56. See, for example, H.O. Arnold-Forster (1904 edn) *The Citizen Reader*, p. 27. Cited in Heathorn, *For Home, Country, and Race*, p. 51.
57. J.R. Green (1874) *A Short History of the English People* (London: Macmillan).
58. J.A Froude (1860) *History of England from the Fall of Wolsey (to the Defeat of the Spanish Armada)* (London).
59. Heathorn, *For Home, Country, and Race*, p. 133.
60. For the popularity of notions of race at the ancient universities, see P.R. Deslandes (January 1998) '"The Foreign Element": Newcomers and the Rhetoric of Race, Nation and Empire in "Oxbridge" Undergraduate Culture, 1850-1920', *Journal of British Studies*, 37:1, 54–90.
61. See, for example, R.H. Tawney (1938) *Equality* (London: Allen and Unwin), p. 157; Savage, 'Social Class and Social Policy', pp. 261–3.
62. Elementary Education Acts (1886) *First Report of the Royal Commission Appointed to Inquire into the Working of the Elementary Education Acts. England and Wales* (afterwards *Cross Commission, First Report*) (London: Eyre and Spottiswoode), p. 107.
63. Elementary Education Acts (1887) *Third Report of the Royal Commission Appointed to Inquire into the Working of the Elementary Education Acts. England and Wales* (afterwards *Cross Commission, Third Report*) (London: Eyre and Spottiswoode), p. 564.
64. *Cross Commission, First Report*, p. 468.
65. Ibid., p. 468.
66. *Cross Commission, Third Report*, p. 617.
67. *Cross Commission, First Report*, p. 444.
68. See, for example, *Cross Commission, Third Report*, pp. 269, 273.

69. *Cross Commission, First Report*, p. 64. For more information on the relationship between universities and elementary schools in Scotland, see R.D. Anderson (1983) *Education and Opportunity in Victorian Scotland: Schools and Universities* (Edinburgh: Edinburgh University Press).

70. *Cross Commission, First Report*, 289; *Elementary Education Acts. Appendix to the Final Report of the Royal Commission Appointed to Inquire into the Working of the Elementary Education Acts. England and Wales* (London: Eyre and Spottiswoode, 1888), p. 467.

71. See, for example, a specific request to this effect made by H. Martin, the Principal of the Winchester Training College. Training College Returns (1888) *The Royal Commission Appointed to Inquire into the Working of the Elementary Education Acts (England and Wales). Information Obtained in Answer to Inquiries Made by Circular Addressed to the Principals of Training Colleges in Receipt of a Government Grant* (London: Eyre and Spottiswoode, 1888), p. 85.

72. *Cross Commission, First Report*, p. 444.

73. *Cross Commission, Third Report*, pp. 468–9.

74. Elementary Education Acts (1888) *Final Report of the Commissioners Appointed to Inquire into the Elementary Education Acts. England and Wales* (afterwards *Cross Commission, Final Report*) (London: Eyre and Spottiswoode, 1888), p. 289.

75. Ibid.

76. *Cross Commission, First Report*, p. 476.

77. Ibid., p. 289.

78. *Cross Commission, Third Report*, p. 479.

79. Ibid., pp. 463–4.

80. Ibid., p. 463.

81. Ibid.

82. Ibid., pp. 463–4.

83. *Cross Commission, First Report*, p. 230.

84. Ibid., p. 239.

85. Elementary Education Acts (1887) *Second Report of the Royal Commission Appointed to Inquire into the Working of the Elementary Education Acts. England and Wales* (afterwards *Cross Commission, Second Report*) (London: Eyre and Spottiswoode), p. 796.

86. *Cross Commission, Second Report*, p. 1058.

87. *Cross Commission, Final Report*, p. 170.

88. See, for example, J.M. Smith (1998) 'Degeneration and Eugenics: Late-Victorian Discourses of the Ending of the Race', *Australasian Victorian Studies Journal*, 4, 55–66.

89. Cited in Sir N. Lockyer (1903) *On the Influence of Brain Power on History; An Address Delivered, before the British Association for the Advancement of Science, at Southport on September 9th, 1903* (New York: The Macmillan Co.), p. 26.

90. C. Bruce (November 1905) 'Our Public Schools and the Empire', *Macmillan's Magazine*, 1:1, p. 74.

91. Ibid., p. 76.

92. H.B. Gray (1913) *The Public Schools and the Empire* (London: Williams and Norgate), p. viii.

93. Birchenough, *Elementary Education*, p. 286.

94. Cited in P. Gordon and D. Lawton (1978) *Curriculum Change in the Nineteenth and Twentieth Centuries* (London: Hodder and Stoughton), p. 22.

95. Birchenough, *Elementary Education*, p. 294,

96. Ibid., p. 312.

97. Ibid., p. 313.

98. C. Steedman (1985) '"The Mother Made Conscious": The Historical Development of a Primary School Pedagogy', *History Workshop Journal*, 20:1, p. 158.

99. See, for example, ibid.

100. Birchenough, *Elementary Education*, p. 297.

101. Horn, 'Growth of the Imperial Ideal', pp. 48–9.

102. B. Beaven and J. Griffiths (June 2008) 'Creating the Exemplary Citizen: The Changing Notion of Citizenship in Britain 1870–1939', *Contemporary British History*, 22:2, 203–25, at p. 212.
103. Ibid., p. 211.
104. For specific figures, see B. Harris (2004) *The Origins of the British Welfare State: Society, State and Social Welfare in England and Wales, 1800–1945* (Basingstoke: Palgrave Macmillan), pp. 274–5.
105. It should be noted that selective 'central' schools, founded in London, Manchester and elsewhere in the early years of the twentieth century, offered a form of secondary education with a more vocational curriculum. However, the numbers of pupils attending such schools constituted only a small proportion of the total number receiving free secondary education. The vast majority were accommodated within the free-place scheme at state-aided grammar schools.
106. Savage, 'Social Class and Social Policy', p. 276.
107. Ibid., p. 276.
108. Ibid., p. 271.
109. Ibid., p. 274.
110. C. Norwood (September 1928) 'Education: the Next Steps' (presidential address to the Educational Science section, *British Association for the Advancement of Science, Glasgow*) in *British Association for the Advancement of Science, Report of the Ninety-Sixth Meeting, Glasgow, 1928* (London: Office of the British Association, 1929), p. 212.
111. Savage, 'Social Class and Social Policy', 271.
112. Holt, *Public-School Literature*, p. 209.
113. Savage, 'Social Class and Social Policy', p. 269.

3

Faith and Nationhood: Church, State and the Provision of Schooling in Ireland, 1870–1930

Deirdre Raftery and Martina Relihan

Introduction

Education in Ireland in the nineteenth and early twentieth centuries was characterised by involvement of, and tensions between, church and the state. For most of the nineteenth century, Protestantism enjoyed a position of strength, Ireland was part of the United Kingdom, and education was harnessed in support of these two forces. After 1870, following the disestablishment of the Church of Ireland and the eventual repeal of the Act of Union in 1920, there commenced an increase in the power of the Roman Catholic Church and a move towards Ireland's separation from the United Kingdom, which was completed in 1922 when the Irish Free State was formed. During that period, the Catholic Church greatly strengthened its hand in education, while the fledgling state mobilised schools and teachers in support of its aim to rebuild the Irish nation. The radical shift in the relative power of Protestantism/Catholicism and of the British/ Irish states across the period covered by this chapter involved a recalibrating of the education machinery. This chapter examines that recalibration, while commenting on the role that schooling played in changing ideas of citizenship, modernisation and nationhood.

Throughout the period under review, laity and parents remained benign forces in education, leaving matters of education policy and administration in the hands of churchmen and politicians. In this chapter, the formation of education policy, and the governance and management of schools in Ireland will be scrutinised in an attempt to assess how these issues reflected the dramatic change that the country underwent in the closing decades of the nineteenth century and the early decades of the twentieth century. The chapter, then, is a study of educational change, and it will repay the reader to have an overview of education provision in Ireland during the period in which formal schooling in Ireland was developed: the eighteenth and early nineteenth centuries.

Schooling in Ireland in the eighteenth and early nineteenth centuries

The explicitly political function of schooling in Ireland dates from the sixteenth century. To spread the influences of the Reformation in Ireland, Tudor policy included the passing of a series of laws to proscribe Catholic education and to harness schooling in the support of Protestantism and loyalty to the crown. It was from this point that the Catholic Church lost its public role in Irish education, and the Church of Ireland claimed that role: the significance of this was to be considerable in the two centuries that followed.[1]

The laws prohibited Catholics from having their children educated by Catholic priests and nuns, either at home or abroad, and banned Catholic teachers from running schools or teaching children. Education from this time forward became entwined in issues of religious and national identity. As Atkinson has noted, '...the Anglican Church, immersed in its role as an instrument of government policy, continued to look on proselytism as its immediate objective'.[2] Irish Catholics responded to the British policy for schooling in several ways; some – particularly the poor – availed of the education provided by evangelical Protestants. Others flouted the law and secretly sent their sons abroad to be educated in seminaries in France and Spain.[3] But the most popular Catholic response was to avail themselves of a subversive system of *'hedge schools', which spread throughout the country.[4] Hedge school masters conducted lessons in astronomy, land measurement, Greek, Latin, the English language, science, and mathematics, using barns and ditches as their 'school room', and appointing a pupil to keep watch for informers. The masters moved regularly from town to town to reduce the risk of being detected by the authorities. About 9,000 of these schools were in existence by the end of the eighteenth century, catering for the majority of the Irish school-going population – the Catholic poor.

Unsurprisingly, the success of the hedge schools was of concern to the hierarchy of the Established Church, and to the British government. There were repeated 'official' efforts to provide schools for the poor that would be an alternative to the hedge schools, and these included *charter schools, *royal schools, and parish and diocesan schools run by the Church of Ireland, but no legislation was passed to organise a system of mass education. By the early nineteenth century, government funding for schools was channelled through Protestant voluntary societies, such as the Kildare Place Society (KPS) founded in 1811, with the aim of affording 'the same facilities for education to all classes of professing Christians without any attempt to interfere with the peculiar religious opinions of any'. With a teacher training college in Dublin, and carefully designed classroom equipment, the KPS represented the first sustained attempt to develop a system of mass education in Ireland, utilising the theories of British educationists *Lancaster and Bell. Successive scholars who have chronicled the work of this society, and its legacy to education, have also noted that it fell into disrepute having been accused of discriminating against Catholics.[5] The KPS allowed the Bible to be read in classrooms 'without note or comment', a practice not accepted within the contemporaneous

Roman Catholic Church. The image of the KPS was further tarnished when it emerged that this non-denominational society was paying grants to schools supported by Protestant evangelical societies. Daniel O'Connell was at the forefront of public opposition to the KPS, arguing that this situation was unacceptable to Catholic parents. The increasing confidence of the Catholic Church meant that its rejection of the KPS as a possible national system of education was heeded, and Catholic children were withdrawn from schools funded by the KPS.[6] O'Connell, in his campaign for Catholic emancipation, agitated for a share in the parliamentary education grant for Catholic schools. He regarded as unacceptable the lack of state support for Catholic education, at a time when the majority of grants from the lord lieutenants' fund was going to Protestant schools, even though this fund had been created to support poor Catholic schools.[7] Archbishop John McHale of Tuam, and Bishop James Warren of Kildare and Leighlin, led a campaign for reform and a petition was presented to parliament in 1824, requesting a public inquiry into the state of education in Ireland.

The resulting Commission of Irish Education Inquiry (1825)[8] furnishes researchers with important evidence on the denominational tensions that surrounded education debate, and marks a tipping point in Irish education: once the commission returned its reports it became evident that Catholics had cause for grievance and education reform was unavoidable. The commission recommended that public funding should be withdrawn from Protestant education societies, and directed instead towards supporting a government board of education, which would be responsible for building and maintaining national schools. The solution to the problem of denominational tensions could be found by educating Catholic and Protestant children together for secular instruction, and separately for religious instruction. There were, however, objections from the churches to these proposals; the Catholic Church did not approve of mixed secular instruction, and wanted explicitly Catholic education for Catholic children, while the Established Church and the Presbyterian Church required scriptural reading to have a central position in education. Once again, control of schooling was a flashpoint for the churches and six years elapsed before the Chief Secretary of Ireland, Lord E.G. Stanley, formulated a system of non-denominational national education, to be managed by a National Board. By then, Catholic emancipation had been granted in 1829, allowing Catholics to be elected to parliament and it had become a matter of urgency 'to provide education for the lower classes and thus create a literate and loyal electorate'.[9]

At the time of the inception of the national system of education in 1831, out of a population of some 8 million people, 6.5 million were Catholic, and there was pressure on the National Board to succeed with non-denominational schooling rather than reverting once again to supporting schooling via Protestant agencies. Over decades in which the system faced criticism and many challenges, it nonetheless increased in popularity; in 1831 the national schools enrolled over 100,000 children, and this number increased to almost one million within 40 years. The new system was to provide 'if possible a combined literary and a separate religious education ... a system of National Education for the lower classes of the community'.[10]

However, while the newly formed National Board articulated the aim of non-denominationalism, it became flexible in its approach and the system became de facto denominational. This flexibility was, no doubt, facilitated by the fact that when the national system was put in place in 1831, there was no Act of Parliament to legislate for this major experiment in state-funded mass education.[11]

The National Board was given a fund of £30,000, which had previously been allocated to the KPS, and it commenced an important scheme which would include building schools, producing textbooks, and supplying teacher training and school inspection. Local schools could apply to the National Board for support, and while the Board looked with favour on joint applications from Catholic and Protestant groups, it became pragmatic in accepting that in a country which was overwhelmingly Catholic there were few opportunities for such co-operation. The Board supported applicants by providing two-thirds of the cost of building new schools, funding for schoolroom equipment, and gratuities for teachers. It was expected that applicants, typically parish clergy, would raise the remaining costs, including the teacher's salary, locally as well as supplying the site on which the new school would be built. In addition to providing for new schools, existing schools, such as those managed by Catholic orders such as the Presentation Sisters and the Christian Brothers, could also affiliate to the system. The Board supplied *gratis* to schools the five 'graded reading books' that teachers were obliged to use. These books were designed to provide a solid education in general knowledge, English literature and moral education, while excluding any instruction in the Irish language, history and culture. By the end of the first decade of its existence, the National Board had 1,978 schools operating under its control. In principle, national schools were to be co-educational, but in practice many of those with religious affiliations, such as convents, were single-sex schools.

Three model schools were set up at Marlborough Street, Dublin, together with a male training college. In 1838, a model farm was established on the edge of Dublin city, and in 1842 a training college for women was established. A set of instructions for National School inspectors was drawn up in 1836, and inspectors visited the schools to ensure grants were being spent correctly and to report on the general state of education. At the start of the system, inspectors were paid an annual salary of £250. Teachers had modest salaries that were determined by their position on a scale which classified them into three categories. As noted by Coolahan and O'Donovan, '1st class male teachers were allocated £20 salary; 2nd class £15 and 3rd class £12. The corresponding scales for females were £15, £12, and £10.'[12] This classification system was revised in 1848, to include small variations of award within grades, and between 1848 and 1849 some 2284 teachers were 'classified following detailed oral and written examination'.

In the decades that followed, despite objections to elements of the system from the churches, national schooling continued to grow. A proliferation of small denominational schools spread across the country, numbering over 8000 by the end of the century. The development of the national system was central to the provision of mass education in Ireland, and more than any other initiative, it determined the future of education in the country. The management and curriculum of the nineteenth-century national school reflected wider social and political changes with startling clarity. The school as an agent in social mobility became evident by the late nineteenth century, while the political function of schooling was articulated via successive editions of the school readers, and gradual changes in the curriculum. Central to both the social and political function of the national schools was the creation of the citizen, and the curriculum reflected a changing conception of citizenship as Catholics became increasingly articulate and the rhetoric of nationalism filtered through education institutions. It is to these changes that this chapter will now turn.

The politics of schooling: assent and dissent in the late nineteenth century

The complex administrative layers of the national system generated copious records that form an important legacy to the historian of education. The system had, as already noted, a National Board of Commissioners, who produced detailed annual reports including data on schools, enrolments and attendance, books and materials, and the training and payment of teachers. Each school had a patron, usually the local bishop or ecclesiastical authority, who in turn appointed a school manager who was also often a clergyman. The manager employed the teachers and managed the school, keeping records such as registers, roll books, discipline books and inspectors' reports.

Perhaps most useful are the graded reading books, which continued to be modified and used in schools into the early twentieth century and which were considered so well-produced and robust in quality that they were exported to the colonies for use in British schools. The first and second reader contained simple reading lessons, while the advanced readers included lessons on the British monarchy, the geography and history of England, and natural science. The books included extracts from evangelical writers such as Hannah More and Sarah Trimmer. Scholars generally concur with the view that the reading books strongly reflected Britain's cultural assimilation policy for Ireland. The Board also produced special 'female' readers, for use with girls. These books included instruction in domestic economy, and 'appropriate' female behaviour. The *Reading Book for Use in Female Schools* appeared in 1854, to be followed in 1864 by the *Girls' Reading Book for Use of Schools*. Three years later, the *Manual for Needlework* was published, and in 1885 *Short Lessons in Domestic Science* was produced. The appearance of these books marked the first formal gendering of the curriculum in Irish schools; while girls and boys had been instructed differently in charter schools and in some hedge schools, the emergence of a specific 'female curriculum' within the national system of mass education is noteworthy.[13]

The development of the national system of mass education was not without problems. In the early decades of its existence, the churches expressed dissatisfaction with elements of the system. The Presbyterian objection was to the denominationally mixed Board, and to the power the Board had over both the teachers and schoolbooks used in class. Additional difficulties were presented by the fact that the Bible had been removed from its central position in education, and by the regulation that religious instruction was to take place separately from literary instruction. The latter point was also contentious for the Established Church, which believed that its special role in education had been greatly compromised by the development of non-denominational schooling. The Catholic Church also had reservations about the system which, while improving provision for Catholic children, obliged them to partake in denominationally mixed schooling. Those who voiced dissent typically withdrew from contact with the national system. For example, the Church of Ireland established the Church Education Society (CES) in 1839, to support separate Protestant schooling in which there was scriptural education.[14] In a somewhat similar move, the Christian Brothers withdrew their schools by 1836, as a mark of objection to the pervasive influences of Protestantism and British culture that were implicated in the curriculum. Other religious orders carefully negotiated the requirements made by the Board, in order to continue to avail themselves of its support.[15] But one particularly contentious issue for the Catholic Church was teacher training. In 1863, Paul Cullen, Catholic Archbishop of Dublin, banned Catholics from participating in the non-denominational state system of teacher training, and Catholic teacher training colleges were established. In Dublin in the 1870s, a training college for male teachers was established by the Vincentian Fathers, and one for women was founded by the Mercy Sisters. In 1883, the government agreed to give state support to denominational training colleges, and by 1903 there was a total of seven colleges, five of which were Catholic.

Church interference in both political and educational affairs was not only commonplace but unavoidable at this time. Clergymen were involved in electioneering, and while they did not run for office they 'played a crucial role in deciding who would do so…clerical approval was a prerequisite for success' in Irish politics.[16] In an attempt to appease Catholic opinion, Gladstone's government appointed a royal commission on primary education under Lord Powis. In addition to mollifying Catholic unrest, this commission was to ascertain whether or not the Irish system of mass education represented a good economic investment. Its findings, published in 1870, cemented Irish education in a performance of education practices that fell out of step with modernising Western Europe, and arguably created an education culture which the country has not yet jettisoned.

The Powis Commission on Education 1870

The Powis Commission examined all aspects of the national school system and generated some recommendations that had an immediate effect on education. The commission demonstrated that enrolments did not reflect daily attendance at school, and in addition to high levels of absenteeism, many pupils were withdrawn from school at an early age.[17] As a consequence, the majority of pupils did not progress past the second graded reading book, and literacy levels were low.[18] In 1872, in response to these findings, a system of 'payment by results' was introduced. It provided a supplementary payment to teachers, in addition to their salaries, dependent on the performance of their pupils in annual assessments that were conducted by inspectors visiting the schools. A core curriculum was set, and pupils could be entered for the annual examinations only if they had attended school for not less than 90 days per annum. The payment by results system was successful insofar as retention rates improved, pupils progressed further at school, and the reading and writing proficiency of pupils increased dramatically. Negative consequences of the system were that schooling became narrow and focused on assessments, while teachers strove to motivate the able pupils who could succeed in examinations. With a strong emphasis on the English language, the vernacular was seriously compromised and scholars have identified national schooling as having contributed strongly to the demise of the Irish language.

There were, however, two important and interconnected outcomes from payment by results that reached into the twentieth century. Firstly, a need was created for a system of intermediate (or second level) education to which successful primary school children could progress. Intermediate education allowed those who could afford school fees to continue their schooling until about 16 years of age. The Intermediate Education (Ireland) Act 1878 established an examination system and funded scholarships and exhibitions for successful pupils. Modelled on the British grammar schools, *intermediate schools typically taught the classics, languages, mathematics, English language and literature, history and geography. The 'Intermediate Certificate' became the passport into civil service jobs and the universities, opening up well-paid careers and the 'learned' professions to Irish Catholics. The intermediate schools enhanced a network of Catholic secondary schools that already existed. Catholic secondary schooling was given robust support by the Catholic Church from the turn of the nineteenth century, and large diocesan boarding schools were founded by the bishops, for the education of Catholics and also to facilitate recruitment of future members of the clergy. St Patrick's College, Carlow (1793), St Jarlath's, Tuam (1800), St Finian's, Navan (1802), St John's, Waterford (1807) and St Peter's, Wexford (1819) all offered a classical education for Catholic boys, while also preparing some of them to become secular priests. Religious orders also expanded; the prestigious Jesuit college, Clongowes Wood, was established in 1814, and by 1867 there were 47 Catholic colleges for young men in Ireland, under the direction of religious such as the Dominican, Holy Ghost and Vincentian Fathers. For girls and young women, education was supplied at day and boarding schools run by many French orders, such as the Loreto, Ursuline and Dominican Sisters, while two Irish congregations, the Presentation Sisters and the Sisters of Mercy, established a network of girls' schools throughout the country.

A changing education landscape: Ireland at the turn of the century

By the end of the nineteenth century, much had changed in Ireland since the inception of the national system in 1831. The Irish masses had achieved a greater involvement in the democratic process, following reforms in the 1830s, and in 1840 Daniel O'Connell had created the first independent Irish political party, with some 30 MPs in the British Parliament. Irish political consciousness had been raised, and behind the politicisation of Irish society lay what McCartney has described as 'a national network which included political clubs, municipal councillors, poor law guardians and others.'[19] The spirit of emerging democracy was energised by the fact that people were receiving an education through the growing national school system, and through the spread of information via newspapers, ballad literature and through the Catholic Church. 'Schools, literacy, politics and religion were all interconnected' as increasingly the Catholic Church was involved in managing education.[20] The language of nationalism was honed and used not only at massive political meetings, but also by teachers, and much of the rhetoric centred on land agitation. Ireland in the 1840s had a population of about 8 million, about two-thirds of whom were living off the land. McCartney notes that 'four millions were to a large extent dependent on the potato, and about half of these depended absolutely on it for their existence.'[21] When the crop failed in the years between 1845 and 1849, the country suffered widespread and devastating famine, gross poverty and disease. By the time the census of 1851 was taken, approximately one million had died of starvation, and one million had emigrated. In the decade that followed, the population continued to fall and the Irish practice of early marriage and large families changed, with the result that the mid-nineteenth-century marriage rate in Ireland was one of the lowest in the world. Depopulation, emigration and gradual consolidation of small farms, together with the impact of changing worldwide economic and social factors, all contributed to new demands on education. English was the language of commerce, and indeed of the 'new world' which attracted emigrants, and education was viewed as providing a passport to a better future. It is perhaps not surprising, then, to find Irish schools maintaining a conservative yet ambitious outlook at the turn of the century.

Despite the falling population in the closing decade of the nineteenth century, investment in intermediate (or 'superior') education continued. McElligott has commented on the fact that by 1900 Ireland, with its over-emphasis on 'academic' education, showed 'many of the signs characteristic of a country emerging from a period of cultural deprivation',[22] favouring the kind of intellectual training suited 'to lawyers, doctors, clergymen, teachers, civil servants, and clerks of all grades'.[23] The census figures of 1881, 1891 and 1901 indicate how expenditure on intermediate education increased, and participation by Catholics in 'superior' schooling also increased (see Table 1).

In January 1898, following the report of the Belmore Commission on Manual and Practical Instruction, some changes were introduced, bringing Irish elementary education a little more in line with Europe. The payment by results system was abolished in national schools, and a revised programme of instruction was introduced in 1900. While this programme reflected the methodologies of Friedrich Froebel (1782–1852), including subjects such as drawing, elementary

Table 1 Number of pupils in superior schools in each of the years 1881, 1891 and 1901, together with their religious profession attending superior establishments

	1881	1891	1901
Catholics	12,064	15,430	25,647
Protestant Episcopalians	7854	7280	7335
Presbyterians	3063	3342	3638
Methodists	775	787	1011
Other Denominations	937	930	934
TOTAL	24,693	27,769	38,565

science, and cookery for girls, lack of resources meant that teachers were unable to make radical changes in their work. In 1904, and again in 1919, following further scrutiny, official reports recommended reforms such as the introduction of local education authorities to improve funding and co-ordinate schooling. Old tensions between church and state re-emerged, with the Catholic hierarchy firmly opposed to any interference in its control of Catholic schools. The Catholic Church had 'built for itself an imposing educational edifice at primary and secondary levels' and, as Titley has argued, 'any reform which undermined clerical power in the schools would be opposed'.[24] Education was one of the chief concerns of the Church; indeed, 'next to his liturgical duties it was the parish priest's most pressing responsibility'.[25] It was necessary for the Church to manage the schools on religious lines, both to show children 'the way to eternal life' and also to ensure that there would be a continuing supply of young persons for religious life.[26] According to Irish bishops, 'the purpose of education was chiefly to prepare man for the world to come'.[27] They stated that education implied 'the training and development of the whole man ... for the purpose not merely of fitting him for a career of usefulness and honour in this life, but also and still more for the purpose of guiding him to attain ... the life to come'.[28]

Akenson has made a compelling argument that the success of the Catholic Church in the field of Irish education lay not in the fact that it gained such extensive control of schooling, but that 'its hegemony was won not by the repression of popular sentiment but by articulating ideas and attitudes compatible with the popular will'. The Catholic bishops' distrust of state activities was not dissimilar to that of many civilians. When, in 1922, Ireland gained its political independence from Britain, the Catholic Church retained its monopoly in the education field. The Free State government was content to leave this area in the hands of priests, brothers and sisters; these religious continued to run their own day schools, boarding schools and colleges, while even the state national system retained a Catholic expression via church involvement in the management of national schools. While modernisation may have been the educational concern of liberal twentieth-century democracies, in Ireland education remained firmly linked to faith formation.

The dawn of a new century: Catholic supremacy
in education

In 1900 the Catholic hierarchy declared in a pastoral letter that the national school system was 'as denominational almost as we could desire'.[29] The combination of de facto control of a large proportion of individual schools, with state funding for them emanating from one central government body, provided a model of educational provision ideally suited to the Catholic Church. For the succeeding two decades prior to the establishment of the Irish Free State in 1922, it was to guard this model jealously by actively and successfully resisting attempts by the British government to introduce devolved structures and local funding as elements of Irish educational provision both in 1904 and 1907.[30] This approach of the Church was to have a deleterious effect on education in Ireland during the first two decades of the twentieth century as the government insisted that increased funding for the system was contingent on the acceptance of its administrative reform.[31] The introduction in 1919 of the MacPherson Education Bill proposed 'the idea of levying a local education rate for education and the establishment of local education committees which would have responsibility for the upkeep of schools, the organisation of medical and dental services for schools, the provision of school meals and a school-books scheme'.[32] The measure provoked the fury of the Catholic hierarchy with the Primate, Cardinal Logue calling for a 'national solemn novena in honour of St. Patrick to avert us from the threatened calamity'.[33]

The Irish National Teachers' Organisation (INTO) having been founded in 1866 was an established stakeholder in Irish education by this time. The Irish Protestant Teachers' Union (IPTU), which was affiliated to the INTO, was, together with Protestant educational interests generally, very supportive of the Bill. It was not however sanguine in relation to the prospects for its success, regarding the power of the Catholic Church as all-consuming on education issues. It summarised the latter body's stance on the Bill during its AGM of 1920 '...as denationalising and anti-Christian and as a Saxon device to rivet additional fetters on Irish youth ...'.[34] The IPTU passed a resolution 'as loyal subjects of the British Empire' lamenting the sorry state of Irish education and requesting that the position of Irish teachers be placed on an equal footing with that of their British counterparts.[35]

The debate in relation to the Bill became mired in the political tumult of the era. Irish nationalists were wont to cast a jaundiced eye on it. Emanating as it did from a British parliament, the Irish supporters of the measure were frequently derided as 'anti-national'. The Irish National Teachers' Organisation (INTO) while basically supportive of a bill which promised improved conditions for its members found it had to proceed with caution in order to avoid the dreaded 'anti-national' tag. At its Annual Congress of 1920, it passed a diffident resolution proposing a 're-adjustment' of the Education Bill 'so as to bring it more into harmony with the aspirations of the Irish people...'.[36] A teacher from County Galway in a letter published in the organisation's journal *The Irish School Weekly* resented the 'false position' in which the union had been placed as 'isolated individuals' propounded the view that '...the public were on one side and the teachers on the other – the public for faith and fatherland and the teachers for Mammon and denationalisation...'.[37] The rapidly unfolding political situation was shortly to render the issue superfluous. The native administration which assumed office in 1922 quietly shelved the question of an Education Bill, being presumably loath to enter into controversy with the Catholic Church on a matter of such contention.[38] The Catholic Church had assumed de facto control over elementary education in Ireland by the end of the nineteenth century. Its position in this regard was unassailable by the time political independence was conceded in 1922 and was accepted as such by the new political order.

The Free State era

The Irish Free State which developed after the concession by the British government of political independence for Ireland in 1922 effectively preserved the administrative structures of the national school system 'as if in amber'.[39] While the Irish educational system was operating in a radically altered political and cultural climate, the rationale underpinning the pre-1922 system was not re-evaluated. Coolahan notes the new administration's unwillingness to either establish a commission on education or to introduce legislation in the area.[40] While the Department of Education, which was to co-ordinate the functions of primary, secondary and technical education, was established in 1924, the new structure served merely to provide '...an umbrella for the maintenance unchanged of structures, policies and powers which had been defined in the imperial era...'.[41] Accordingly, officials of the department lacked a contextual framework within which to determine policy. There was a tacit assumption that the concept of 'combined secular and separate religious instruction', which had been the lodestar of the nineteenth-century school system, had in the absence of any alternative become the guiding principle of the new state's educational system. The administrative structures of the system which the native government inherited were regarded as unproblematic and were adopted more or less without question.

The educational deliberations of the new state were almost entirely dominated by the official obsession with 'strengthening the national fibre by giving the language, history, music and tradition of Ireland their natural place in Irish schools'.[42] The revival of the Irish language as the spoken language of the people was chosen as the talisman of the new state and its schools were the means through which this aim was to be effected. The teaching of the Irish language was made compulsory for all schools from March 1922. The stipulation that infant classes were to be taught more or less exclusively through the medium of the language was especially contentious but nonetheless pertained, at least officially, into the second half of the century. The senior classes of primary schools were actively encouraged to use Irish as a medium of instruction in other school subjects as far as practicable. The language was made compulsory for both state examinations, the Intermediate Certificate and the Leaving Certificate,[43] in 1928 and 1934, respectively.

Department of Education officials also lacked a coherent framework within which to determine policy on school textbooks and were operating in a vacuum in relation to deciding on the suitability or otherwise of content of an overt religious nature which some of the textbooks contained. In 1925, the Department of Education issued a memorandum for publishers of books for use in national schools.[44] Publishers were advised that textbooks should be:

> ...Christian in spirit, national in outlook and truthful as regards facts...They should include matter in prose and poetry drawn from the hero stories of Ireland and of the World; deal extensively with the important facts of life in Ireland and have an Irish outlook and a definite rural bias. They should be free from matter objectionable to any religious denomination.[45]

The implementation of these guidelines was especially problematic for the Department of Education when school authorities requested sanction for textbooks which reflected a specifically Catholic outlook. It was, for example, leery of a request to sanction a series of textbooks entitled *New Ideal Catholic Readers* despite coming under concerted pressure from a number of schools who wished to use them. The manager of a County Wexford school requested permission to use them for the practical reasons that the books had already been purchased and '...the boys attending our school are very poor...'.[46] The Department of Education's Chief Inspector was aware that the issue begged some fundamental questions vis-à-vis the philosophy underlying the education system. He wondered, both in relation to this issue and other matters such as 'the growing practice of introducing denominational pictures and statues into the National Schools' to what degree the rules of the National Board in relation to overt religious content in school textbooks could be applied.[47] He acknowledged that in an overwhelmingly Catholic jurisdiction, it 'was a source of annoyance to Catholic managers and teachers that these restrictions should apply to schools attended only by Catholic pupils on the ground that Protestant pupils may attend them.'[48] He favoured some flexibility in relation to the implementation of the rules especially in larger urban areas where Protestant pupils had easy access to schools of their own denomination.

Following a detailed examination of the textbooks conducted by a senior inspector in 1928, the secretary of the Department of Education concluded that the textbooks were unsuitable for use in the schools because of their denominational title and because they '...contain[ed] pictures and matter to which Protestants may object...'.[49] He did however concede that the issue impinged directly on the broader question of '...how far the restrictions which bound Catholic national schools should be relaxed or removed'.[50] By 1932, the vexed question had been resolved with a departmental ruling that three separate lists of sanctioned textbooks were to be compiled. The first of these contained books suitable for use in all schools while the second approved texts in exclusively Catholic schools with the third applying to pupils in Protestant establishments.[51]

In the following year, the department published its *Notes for Teachers*, which was intended as a guide for teachers in relation to the teaching of the various subjects on the curriculum. This guide stated that the teaching of the Irish language was not only an aim in itself but was part of a broader process which was the restoration of '…the characteristically Gaelic turn of mind and way of looking at life…'.[52] In the absence of the cultivation of this 'Gaelic attitude', the Irish people were destined to become 'amorphous' and 'a hybrid people.' The fostering of this outlook was to provide the antidote to 'foreign penetration by newspaper, book and cinema.'[53] The departmental guidelines were unsurprisingly reflected in the various series of Irish language school textbooks which were published by the leading educational book publishers in the 1930s. The 'Gaelic' and 'Catholic' elements of the material were frequently intertwined. A junior text in one such series opens with a verse the title of which translates as, 'Our Little Native Country, Ireland.' The verse translates: 'We are learning diligently/The language which God gave us – Irish/ And we will practise it willingly/In our little native country, Ireland'.[54] The text also makes references to specifically Catholic religious practices. It contains a short piece on the recitation of the family rosary with each family member reciting an individual 'decade' of the prayer. Another story in the textbook tells of the children going to Mass in their parents' horse and cart on Sunday.[55] The various series of Irish language textbooks did not uniformly treat these subjects with such an intensity of evangelical fervour. None the less the textbooks of the period frequently and unselfconsciously conflated the promotion of the 'Gaelic ideal' and Catholicism.

The teaching of history in the new state was also formulated exclusively along Catholic/Nationalist lines. *Notes for Teachers* advised that teachers should regard the 'important movements' of the nineteenth century as 'the struggles for Catholic rights, for possession of the land, and for national independence…'.[56] Teachers were exhorted to stress the continuity of the separatist ideal from Wolfe Tone to Patrick Pearse. Treatment of the 1916 Rising should provide little difficulty for teachers as 'the struggle that followed it will be so fresh in (their) minds' with the 'great language movement' providing 'the inspiration of the leaders'.[57] The teacher was thus afforded the convenient opportunity 'of dealing as a whole with the cultural and language struggle'.[58] This approach to the teaching of history was, in the view of Farrell Moran, unsurprising as it enabled the Irish Free State 'to reinforce itself with a curriculum based upon the nationalist model of Irish history, tying itself to a teleological history wherein the ancient past led to and legitimated the new state'.[59]

Protestant-run schools in the post-independence era

The issue of obtaining 'suitable' school textbooks for Protestant schools was one of the most pressing issues which engaged the Church of Ireland authorities as they attempted to adapt its network of schools to the requirements of the new regime. The Church of Ireland's Board of Education report of 1923 noted the difficulties which it was experiencing in obtaining 'suitable' Irish language textbooks for its schools. It noted that '...nearly all the books in the market contain phrases and teaching not in accordance with Protestant beliefs...'.[60] Similar difficulties were experienced by the authorities in relation to the exclusively Catholic/Nationalist narrative reflected in the history textbooks of the new state. In order to rectify the situation, the authorities sought either entirely different textbooks, or textbooks which had been purged of references that they regarded as either inappropriate or offensive for use in their schools. The issue was never fully resolved during the succeeding decades. The Church of Ireland authorities submitted a list of textbooks which it deemed to be acceptable to the department, and this was duly sanctioned. However, the church authorities were obliged to repeat this process annually. The Church of Ireland's unease with this situation was reflected in its decision in the 1940s to publish a history textbook which it commissioned for use in its schools.[61]

The Protestant authorities were also distinctly uneasy with the new state's policy of 'compulsory Irish' in schools. The state was sensitive to the Church of Ireland's position on the matter and took an incremental approach to the implementation of the policy especially in Protestant schools in the northern counties of Cavan, Monaghan and Donegal, which straddled the border with Northern Ireland. However, in spite of repeated requests from the Church of Ireland's Board of Education during the 1930s and 1940s, the state refused either to dilute the policy or to offer the authorities any formal derogation from its operation.[62] Of more practical import for the church authorities was the maintenance of its scattered network of several hundred national schools, many of which catered for small numbers of pupils in remote locations. The government's scheme to subsidise the transport of pupils to their nearest Protestant school was introduced in 1934. The scheme ensured the survival of many such schools and was much appreciated by the Church's Board of Education. Akenson has contended that the Protestants in the new Irish Free State were variously 'treated with great generosity' and 'hectored, bullied or ignored' in their position as a religious and cultural minority following the political settlement of 1922.[63] In the state's dealings with the difficulties which the Church of Ireland experienced in relation to the changes in the educational system, it is possible to discern elements of all these characteristics.

Concluding comments

By the 1930s, the fundamental tenets of the educational system of the Irish Free State had been established. This system involved elements of both continuity and change from that which had pertained under the British administration of the pre-1922 era. Dramatic changes in the national school curricula were instigated. The range of subjects taught was significantly reduced with the peremptory elimination from it of drawing, elementary science, cookery, laundry and needlework. Hygiene and nature study were both dropped as obligatory subjects. This narrowing of curricular scope was undertaken in order to maximise the time to be afforded the teaching of the Irish language, which was the all-consuming policy preoccupation of the government in relation to the education system. However, although the native administration in the 1930s derided the national school system which had evolved under the British government from 1831, it ironically maintained the distinguishing features of that system: the education system remained highly centralised and state-subvented, while none the less under rigid denominational control. As over 90 per cent of national schools within the Irish Free State jurisdiction were under Catholic management, the position of that Church was virtually hegemonic in relation to elementary schooling in the Ireland of the 1920s and 1930s. It equally controlled the provision of almost all second-level education. Its dominance of the educational system had been achieved by the start of the twentieth century, and was merely consolidated under the native administration.

Timeline

1811: Kildare Place Society founded to provide non-denominational education to all Christians in Ireland.

1831: National system of education established Ireland under a National Board

1870: Powis Commission on primary education in Ireland

1878: The Intermediate Education (Ireland) Act for the establishment of a second-level examination system, and the funding of awards, scholarships and exhibitions

1900: revised programme of studies for Ireland's national schools

1922: Teaching of Irish language compulsory in all Irish schools

1933: *Notes for Teachers* issued in Ireland for the cultivation of a 'Gaelic attitude' in schools

Glossary

charter schools: schools of the Incorporated Society for Promoting English Protestant Schools in Ireland. Founded in the late eighteenth century, they had royal and parliamentary support. The aim of the schools was to convert the Irish Catholic poor to Protestantism.

hedge schools: informal and illegal elementary schools for Catholic children, which developed in the eighteenth century.

Intermediate schools: part of a system of ancient endowed schools providing second level education. There were no 'state' intermediate schools. Second level education in Ireland remained the preserve of a small minority, as the schools were mostly private/fee-paying ventures.

Lancaster and Bell: Joseph Lancaster (1778–1838) and Andrew Bell (1753–1832) were known for introducing the monitorial, or 'mutual instruction' system of tuition, by which abler pupils instructed those at an earlier stage of learning, thus enabling the teacher to cope with many more pupils.

royal schools: founded in the early Stuart period (1603–49) to provide a classical grammar school education to the sons of Protestant settlers in Ireland. Seven royal schools were established with generous endowments. By the end of the eighteenth century, they had gone into decline.

Notes

1. Raftery, D. (2009) 'The Legacy of Legislation and the Pragmatics of Policy' in S. Drudy (ed.) *Irish Education: Challenge and Change* (Dublin: Gill and Macmillan). The author acknowledges Gill and Macmillan for permission to reproduce parts of that chapter here.
2. N. Atkinson (1969) *Irish Education: a History of Educational Institutions* (Dublin: Allen Figgis), p. 65.
3. Ibid., pp. 51–58.
4. For a comprehensive study of hedge schools see A. McManus (2002) *The Irish Hedge School and its Books, 1695–1831* (Dublin: Four Courts Press).
5. See for example D. Akenson (1970) *The Irish Education Experiment: The National System of Education in the Nineteenth Century* (London: Routledge & Kegan Paul), p. 90; S.M. Parkes (2010) *A Guide to Sources for the History of Irish Education, 1790–1922* (Dublin: Four Courts Press), p. 33. Studies of the KPS include H. Kingsmill Moore (1904) *An Unwritten Chapter in the History of Education, Being the History of the Society for Promoting the Education of the Poor in Ireland, 1811–1831, Generally Known as the Kildare Place Society* (London); S.M. Parkes (1984) *Kildare Place: the History of the Church of Ireland Training College, 1811–1969* (Dublin: C.I.C.E.); H. Hislop (1990) 'The Kildare Place Society: an Irish Experiment in Popular Education' (unpublished PhD thesis, Trinity College Dublin).
6. Kingsmill Moore, *An Unwritten Chapter*, pp. 52–70; Parkes, *A Guide to Sources*, p. 33.
7. Akenson, *The Irish Education Experiment*, pp. 83–4.
8. Parliamentary Papers (P.P.) 1825 *First Report of the Commissioners of Irish Education Inquiry*, XII [400]; P.P. 1826–7 *Second report of the Commissioners of Irish Education Inquiry*, XII [12].
9. Ibid., p. 39.
10. Letter from the Secretary for Ireland to His Grace the Duke of Leinster on the formation of a Board of Education. 1837. [485] ix 585, in Á. Hyland and K. Milne (1987) *Irish Educational Documents*, Vol. I (Dublin: C.I.C.E.).
11. Raftery, 'The Legacy of Legislation', p. 17. The experimental nature of the national system has been noted by Akenson, *The Irish Education Experiment*, and J. Coolahan (1981) *Irish Education: its History and Structure* (Dublin: Institute of Public Administration).
12. J. Coolahan and P. F. O'Donovan (2009) *A History of Ireland's School Inspectorate, 1831–2008* (Dublin: Four Courts Press), p. 23.
13. See D. Raftery and S. M. Parkes (2007) *Female Education in Ireland, 1700–1900: Minerva or Madonna?* (Dublin and Ontario: Irish Academic Press).
14. The CES attracted children away from the national schools in the 1840s and 1850s, but by the 1860s it was unable to finance its separate system of schooling. Its schools gradually entered the national school system. For a discussion of this see Parkes, *A Guide to Sources*.
15. For a discussion of this see D. Raftery and C. Nowlan-Roebuck (2007) 'Convent Schools and National Education in Nineteenth-Century Ireland: Negotiating a Place within a Non-denominational System', *History of Education*, 36/3, 353–65.
16. E.B. Titley (1983) *Church, State and the Control of Schooling in Ireland, 1900–1944* (Kingston and Montreal: McGill-Queen's University Press and Macmillan), p. 11.

17. PP 1870 *Royal Commission of Inquiry into Primary Education* (Ireland) [Powis Commission], vol. VI, *Educational census: returns showing number of children actually present in each primary school, 25 June 1868, with introductory observations and analytical index* XXVIII [C 6-V], pt v. 1.
18. See J. M. Goldstrom (1972) *The Social Context of Education 1808–1870: a Study of the Working Class School Reader in England and Ireland.* (Shannon: Irish University Press); Coolahan, *Irish Education,* and Raftery and Parkes, *Female Education in Ireland.*
19. D. McCartney (1987) *The Dawning of Democracy: Ireland 1800–1870* (Dublin: Helicon Ltd.), p. 149.
20. Ibid., p. 150.
21. Ibid., p. 167.
22. T.J. McElligott (1981) *Secondary Education in Ireland, 1870–1921* (Dublin: Irish Academic Press), p. 60.
23. Ibid.
24. Titley, *Church, State and the Control of Schooling,* pp. 11,12.
25. D.H. Akenson (1975) *A Mirror to Kathleen's Face: Education in Independent Ireland, 1922–1960* (Montreal and London: McGill-Queen's University Press), p. 107.
26. Ibid.
27. Ibid., p. 96.
28. Roman Catholic Church in Ireland (1929) *Acta et Decreta Concillii Plenarii Episcoporum Hiberniae... 1927* (Dublin: Browne and Nolan), pp. 155–6, cited in Akeson, *A Mirror to Kathleen's Face,* p. 97.
29. Quoted in Coolahan, *Irish Education,* p. 37.
30. The Irish Free State was established following the signing of the Anglo-Irish Treaty in December 1921. Its jurisdiction comprised 26 of Ireland's 32 counties. The remaining six predominantly Protestant counties located in the north-east of the country retained links with Britain while maintaining a devolved administration in Belfast.
31. Coolahan, *Irish Education,* p. 37.
32. Ibid., pp. 37–8. The bill was introduced in the wake of the publication of the *Report of the Vice-regal Committee of Inquiry into Primary Education 1918.*
33. Quoted in S. O'Buachalla (1988) *Education Policy in Twentieth Century Ireland* (Dublin: Wolfhound Press), pp. 53–4.
34. Report from the AGM of the Irish Protestant Teachers' Union (IPTU) as published in *The Irish School Weekly,* 10 Jul. 1920. *The Irish School Weekly* was the official publication of the Irish National Teachers' Organisation.
35. Ibid.
36. *The Irish School Weekly* 3 Apr. 1920.
37. Ibid., 3 Jul. 1920.
38. The question was shelved for a further eighty years. The Irish parliament did not pass an Education Act until 1998.
39. Akenson, *The Irish Education Experiment,* p. 390.
40. Coolahan, *Irish Education,* p. 39.
41. Akenson, *A Mirror to Kathleen's Face,* p. 33.
42. Extract from speech made by newly appointed chief executive of education, Bradley addressing the members of the old 'National Board' on the occasion of the dissolution of that body. Reported in the *Irish Times* 1 Feb. 1922.
43. The Department of Education established two examinations for second-level students in 1924: the Intermediate Certificate and the Leaving Certificate. From 1928, it became obligatory to obtain a pass in the examination in Irish in order to be awarded the Intermediate Certificate. This condition was extended to the Leaving Certificate in 1934.
44. National Archive, Dublin. Ed/File No. 22299 Box 495.
45. Ibid.

46. Ibid.
47. Ibid.
48. Ibid.
49. Ibid.
50. Ibid.
51. *Rules and Regulations for National Schools under the Department of Education, 1932* (Dublin: Stationery Office), p. 32.
52. (1933) *Notes for Teachers* (Dublin: Department of Education), p. 55.
53. Ibid.
54. (early 1930s) *An Bhrideog* (Dublin: Fallons), p. 6 (translation: M. Relihan). Textbook part of the *Leitheoiri Bhride* series.
55. *An Bhrideog*, p. 24.
56. *Notes for Teachers*, p. 26.
57. Ibid.
58. Ibid., p. 27.
59. Moran, S.F. (2003) 'History, Memory and Education: Teaching the Irish story' in L. McBride (ed.) *Reading Irish Histories – Texts, Contexts and Memory in Modern Ireland* (Dublin: Four Courts Press), p. 214.
60. Report of the Board of Education of the General Synod of the Church of Ireland 1923, p. 215.
61. D. Casserley (1941) *History of Ireland* (Dublin: Church of Ireland).
62. M. Relihan (2008) 'The Church of Ireland and its Relationship with the Irish Education System 1922-1950 with Particular Reference to the Irish Language and Gaelic Culture', (Unpublished PhD thesis, University College Dublin), pp. 128–93.
63. Akenson, *A Mirror to Kathleen's Face*, p. 134.

Part II

Continental Europe

Introduction

Laurence Brockliss and Nicola Sheldon

The first two-thirds of the nineteenth century saw the establishment of national systems of elementary education in virtually all parts of continental Europe except Russia. It is quite clear, however, that in most states it proved extremely difficult to make these systems a working reality. At best, as in France, school buildings were ill-suited to their function, classroom materials were in short supply, and children reluctant to attend school; at worst, as in Spain, it proved impossible to establish a network of rural schools in the first place. The one part of Europe where contemporaries felt that the elementary-school system was functioning satisfactorily in 1870 was the congeries of states headed by Prussia that would form the new German Empire (though even here conditions were not always perfect).[1]

Over the next 60 years, the majority of states struggled valiantly to bring their systems up to the German level. Large numbers of new schools were founded and equipped; teacher training was extended so that virtually all teachers were certificated; *mutual methods of teaching (where earlier adopted) were laid aside and more interactive 'scientific' forms of classroom learning promoted; corporal punishment was largely abolished; children in the larger schools were divided into separate forms according to age and attainment; and attendance for both boys and girls was made compulsory (where it was not already). Everywhere too there was an attempt, particularly after 1900, to develop the curriculum beyond the three R's and enliven the classroom experience of older children with lessons in national history and geography, nature study, singing, needlework (for girls) and gymnastics and/or games. In a number of states, this was coupled with a new interest in the physical well-being of pupils. The Danes were particularly precocious. The Danish town of Fredericksberg was serving midday meals from 1877, and in 1889 the Danish state made hygiene one of the subjects included in examinations taken by schoolteachers.[2] There were still laggards. In Spain, the percentage of school-age children attending school was only 51.8 per cent in 1931.[3] But in most parts of western and central Europe by 1930 effective systems of mass elementary education had been erected and illiteracy all but wiped out.

The systems were never exactly the same. Northern Europe was far richer than the Mediterranean south. This inevitably affected the amount of money that could be spent on elementary education, and this in turn affected teachers' pay and conditions, and the standard of classroom facilities. It also limited the number of years that a child had to spend at school, especially as it was recognised everywhere that one of the best ways of ensuring that parents sent their offspring to school was to abolish tuition fees. Even as late as 1911, Portuguese children, for instance, were only expected to spend three years at school rather than the standard seven or eight.[4] The size of the financial budget equally determined the speed with which graded schooling could be established and the new methods of teaching absorbed. Most states established institutes of education or pedagogy attached to universities where the ideas of child-centred learning espoused by *Froebel and his followers, the findings of late nineteenth-century psychology, and the new research into child development and child-rearing produced by the so-called *Genevan school in the early twentieth century (Claparède, Ferrière, Piaget et al.) was discussed and tested. However, despite the innumerable educational journals that sprang up to popularise the new ideas and the support, in general, they received from the teachers' associations and unions in the different states, it proved difficult to effect a pedagogical revolution in the classroom without the resources. Spain had a Museum of Primary Instruction, devoted to the dissemination of the ideas of Froebel from 1882, and the same year saw the meeting of the country's first pedagogical congress. But the fact that it was another 40 years before Spain's leading progressive educationalist, Lorenzo Luzuriaga, began the *Revista de Pedagógiá* is evidence of how limited an interest there was in the museum's activities in a country with very limited resources.[5]

There was also a distinctive difference between historically Protestant and Catholic countries. The former were normally quite happy for elementary schools to be co-educational, even if girls and boys as they grew older did not follow exactly the same curriculum, while Catholic states preferred girls and boys to be educated separately wherever possible. The Catholic states themselves were not homogeneous, as different political regimes had very different views over the degree to which the church should have any influence over the system. Republican, secular France eventually banned priests from the classroom, as it did religious education *tout court*, while the Portuguese republicans who took over the state in 1910 attempted to use the elementary school to promote anticlericalism and new civic rituals.[6] Monarchical Spain, on the other hand, saw the church as an ally: it retained the right to inspect the orthodoxy of classroom religious teaching, and helped out the state by running a complementary network of private elementary schools staffed by the regular orders.[7] There were differences of opinion too across Europe over how centralised and bureaucratic the system should be that reflected historic differences between states. France was notoriously centralised, while Scandinavian states left management of the schools to local committees, which from the mid-1920s included parental representatives.[8] Yet, however decentralised the system, all states had come to realise by the eve of the First World War that elementary education could not be funded from local sources alone and had to be subsidised by national government. The Danish government began to contribute to elementary education in 1856 when it agreed to fund teachers' pensions. By 1923 three-quarters of the expenditure came from national funds. In Greece from 1895 the whole cost was borne by the state.[9]

As in the case of Britain, the primary purpose of these mass educational systems was to serve the needs of society as much if not more than the individual's. Children were to be disciplined for the general good. In the words of the Portuguese Commission of Public Instruction in 1864: 'To build a school leads to the demolition of a prison'.[10] Much more than in Britain, however, mass education was an instrument of nation-building in most continental countries. In the opinion of some enthusiasts, it would be the starting point for economic greatness. For others, it was the only bulwark against national collapse in a predatory world and had to be shaped accordingly. Greece only became independent from the Ottoman Empire in 1830. National unity was still weak towards the end of the century, and fears of impending implosion were only compounded when the country was defeated in war in 1897. Critics increasingly called for the elementary educational system to be used to strengthen the national spirit. As early as 1885, one commentator was worried that 'we have no schools like those of the German Emperor that create national grandeur'. In 1910, in a moment of particular national soul-searching, the newly founded Association for Education claimed to be 'convinced that both the deep cause and the result of our psychic, social and political decadence is the Greek school which has taken a wrong turn.'[11]

Establishment educationalists therefore seldom had much interest in the value of elementary education for the individual. What was important was the contribution the individual could make to forging national unity. This is not to say that there was no support on the continent for the role education might play as an agent of social mobility. As early as 1848, an assembly of German professors had voiced support for the creation of a hierarchical educational system whereby the talented could move on from primary to secondary schooling and eventually to university. And similar sentiments were frequently articulated in the years before and after the First World War. In 1916 a group called the *Compagnons de l'université nouvelle* was founded in France who argued not simply that individuals had the right to maximise their talents, but that it was only thereby that the country would be rebuilt after the war: 'All French children have the right to acquire the fullest instruction that the Fatherland can dispense. And the Fatherland has the right to exploit all the intellectual riches that it possesses.'[12] But even the richest liberal democracies of the era usually only paid lip service to the idea before 1930. Some national systems, notably the Italian, where only 3 per cent of 11- to 19-year-olds were in high schools (academic or technical) in 1910, provided no mechanism at all for the talented poor to move up the educational ladder.[13] It was normally only where socialists and social democrats came to power after the Great War that access to secondary education was significantly eased. Denmark was committed from 1899 to allowing the able to transfer from communal schools to the *gymnasium at the age of 11. In 1903 this was made easier with the creation of middle schools, usually on the same site as the *Folkschule*, which taught the first four years of the high school course. However, though a sixth of the places were free, entrance was through a competitive examination. It was only in 1928, with a left coalition in power, and after ten years of discussion, that transfer became automatic. Thereafter about a third of elementary school pupils in Copenhagen entered the middle school, although only 70 per cent of these completed the course.[14]

This second part of the book explores the development of mass education in the three largest European states. The first chapter by Gunilla Budde looks at Germany (Chapter 4), the state with the most developed and settled system of mass education on the creation in 1871 of the new German Empire. Though dominated by the Protestant Prussian elite, the unified federal state was confessionally divided and this was reflected in its school system during the period. Although the elementary schools were public institutions, administered by the *Länder*, the churches still had an important role in education, and children went to either Protestant or Catholic schools. There they learnt to be good Germans, know their place, and distrust the radical social and political ideas of Europe's largest socialist party, the SDP. Although Germany was the continent's industrial behemoth, there appears to have been little interest in expanding the pool of well-educated workers. Germany's system of mass education provided next to no access to the elite-dominated secondary schools (either the *Realschule or the gymnasium). The disintegration of the Empire at the end of the First World War brought hardly any change to the existing educational system. The Weimar Republic that succeeded the Empire claimed to be progressive, but though it discussed and flirted with creating a more meritocratic and secular system of education it altered little.

Continuity was also the hallmark of French elementary education during the period, as Jean-François Chanet reveals in the following chapter (Chapter 5). France throughout the period was a republican and democratic state but one where a high proportion of the population still worked on the land, heavy industry was limited, and many did not use French as their first language. Born out of defeat in war against Germany in 1871, the Republic was also beset by internal enemies in the early decades of its existence. Since France was already a country with a high level of school attendance and a well-established national system of education, so the republicans were determined to use the state's schools to create a strong, culturally homogeneous and patriotic nation to weaken the influence of the Catholic Church and residual regionalism. Like the German imperialists, the republican establishment showed little interest in using schooling to promote social mobility: the primary aim was turn 'peasants into Frenchmen', in a phrase made famous by Eugene Weber.[15] And, as Chanet reveals, the First World War proved no more of an educational turning point than in Germany. Despite France's huge losses, the demand of groups such as Les Compagnons de l'université nouvelle that the system be overhauled largely fell on deaf ears.

The final chapter in the section (Chapter 6) in contrast, written by Ben Eklof, examines the history of elementary education in the one state where the First World War did lead to dramatic change to the system. Russia was the most populous but one of least developed countries in Europe in 1870. The decades before the war not only brought rapid economic growth, but were accompanied by an impressive state-led expansion in the provision of elementary education that aimed to pull the peasantry into the towns. The purpose was not to liberate the individual but furnish the state with industrial workers. The collapse of the Russian Empire brought to power a Bolshevik clique interested in reshaping all the country's institutions along completely new ideological lines. The chapter shows, however, how difficult this was to achieve in the field of education. The Bolsheviks wanted to create an integrated system of education that would be a vehicle for real social mobility. But they were also influenced by radical ideas about pedagogy and lacked the resources to build the new educational Jerusalem with the result that the new system descended into chaos. It would be left to Stalin in the 1930s to establish an effective meritocratic system but one that was pedagogically conservative.[16]

Glossary

Folkschule: name for the elementary school in Denmark

Froebel, Friedrich Wilhelm August: German educationalist and father of the kindergarten (1782–1852). Froebel believed that children were individuals with unique capacities and that the best way to learn was through play.

Genevan School: collective name for the founding fathers of experimental child psychology who worked at the Rousseau Institute, a private Genevan academy set up by Edouard Claparède in 1912. Their aim was turn educational theory into a science.

Mutual methods of teaching: refers to systems of classroom teaching inspired by the practice of Joseph Lancaster and Andrew Bell in early nineteenth-century England that allowed large numbers of children to be taught in a disciplined fashion by a single teacher. Essentially each of the three R's would be broken down into levels of difficulty: a boy or girl who had mastered a particular skill, such as the ability to read two-letter words would be given the task of imparting this knowledge by rote to others.

gymnasium: Danish and German academic secondary school.

Realschule: German secondary school which concentrated on modern and practical subjects. The name was adopted in other countries for schools providing a similar education.

Notes

1. Yasemin Nuhoglu Soysal and David Strang (1989) 'Construction of the First Mass Educational Systems in Nineteenth-Century Europe', *Sociology of* Education, 62: 4, 277–88, at p. 278; Colin Heywood (1988) *Childhood in Nineteenth-Century France: Work, Health and Education among the 'Classes Populaires'* (Cambridge: Cambridge University Press), ch. 3; C. Strumingher (1983) *What Were Little Boys and Girls Made of? Primary Education in Rural France, 1830–1880* (Albany: SUNY Press), ch. 1; Lorenzo Luzuriaga (1919) *El Analfabetismo en España* (Madrid: J. Cosano), p. 44;

Karl A. Schleunes (1979) 'Enlightenment, Reform, Reaction: The Schooling Revolution in Prussia', *Central European History*, 12: 4, 315–42; Hans-Ulrich Wehler (1987) *Deutsche Gesellschaftsgeschichte, 1818–1845/49* (Munich: Beck), pp. 478–90.

2. W. Dixon (1958) *Education in Denmark* (London: G. G. Harrap), p. 92.
3. A. Escolana Benito (2002) *La Educación en la España contemporánea. Politicas educativas, escolarización y culturas pedagógicás* (Madrid: Biblioteca nueva), pp. 72–3. At this date Spanish children were expected to spend eight years in school; initially, under the 1857 law, it had been only three: ibid., p. 27.
4. Candida Proença, M. 'A República e a democratizaçao do ensino', in *id.* (ed.) *Sistema de ensino em Portugal. Séculos XIX–XX* (Lisbon: Colibri), pp. 61–2. This was increased to five in 1919. Even then the requirement was optimistic: apparently only 25.6 per cent of eligible children were in school in that year. For some idea of the relative per capita spending on children in 17 European countries during the Great War, see the figures in pesetas given in T. García Regidor (1985) *La polémica sobre la secularicatión de la enseñanza en España 1902–14* (Madrid: Instituto Universitario 'Domingo Lázaro', Universidad Pontificia de Comillas), p. 43.
5. Benito, *Educación*, pp. 90–9. Spain also boasted the independent Free Institute of Education founded in 1877 that published an annual bulletin promoting progressive education until 1936. Lorenzo Luzuriaga was one of its leading lights.
6. Proença, 'A Républica', p. 56; for France, see below, p. 122ff.
7. A fifth of Spanish primary schools were private in 1915: Benito, *Educacion*, p. 79. Under the 1857 education law, the parish priest could also be the schoolmaster in small villages. The power of the Church over the system was contested: see Regidor, *Polémica*, *passim*.
8. In Scandinavia local control became gradually more democratic across the period, thereby ending the automatic right of local landowners and the parson to oversee appointments etc.
9. Dixon, *Denmark*, pp. 78–9 and 129; J. Gennadius (1925) *A Sketch of the History of Education in Greece* (Edinburgh: Lindsay and Co.), p. 23.
10. Cited in Portuguese in Fernandes, R. 'Génese e consolidaçao do sistema educativa nacional (1820–97)', in Proença (ed.), *Sistema*, p. 39.
11. Cited in French in C. Koulouri (1991) *Dimensions idéologiques de l'historicité en Grèce (1834–1914)* (Frankfurt-am-Main: Peter Lang), pp. 85–6.
12. Cited in French in Amado, C. 'A escola única em Portugal: Do debate doctrinal nos anos 20 e 30 às realizaçôes democráticas', in Proença (ed.), *Sistema*, p. 89.
13. Tannenbaum, E. R. (1974) 'Education', in *id.* and E. P. Noether (eds) *Modern Italy. A Topical History since 1861* (New York: New York University Press), p. 237.
14. Dixon, *Education*, pp. 100, 104, 122 and 147. Under the 1928 law communal schools could also have a *Realschule* attached to them, so that those unfitted for the gymnasium course could continue their studies. From 1937, two sorts of middle school were created – for the able and the less able – with the intention of ensuring most children had nine years of education rather than seven. Attempts to offer extended, noncompulsory education for the less able were made in several countries which followed France in creating upper primary schools: see below, pp. 120, 134–5.
15. E.Weber (1976) *Peasants into Frenchmen: The Modernization of Rural France* (London: Chatto & Windus).
16. The 1930s also saw the first genuine moves to a meritocratic educational system in several other European countries where left-wing regimes were in power. Besides Denmark, mentioned above, the most notable case was Spain where a commitment to radical reform was enshrined in the Republican constitution of 1931: see A. Molero Pintado (1977) *La reforma educativa de la Segunda Republica española. Prime biennio* (Madrid: Santillana). The Spanish socialists had adopted a programme of free education at all levels at its 1911 congress: Benito, *Educación*, pp. 112–3.

4

From the *'Zwergschule'* (One-Room Schoolhouse) to the Comprehensive School: German Elementary Schools in Imperial Germany and the Weimar Republic, 1870–1930

Gunilla Budde

The teacher Albert Sixtus (1892–1960) with his picture book 'Rabbit School' fixed the cliché of a cheerful und well-ordered daily life in German elementary schools.[1] Yet it was not only German children's book authors and illustrators who eagerly helped to spread this cliché.[2] Around the middle of the nineteenth century, the Englishman Joseph Kay contributed to this image by planting his travel impressions in the minds of many of his fellow countrymen: 'There were no rags, and no unseemly patched and darned clothes. The little girls were neat, their hair was dressed with a great deal of taste, and their frocks were clean and tastefully made. Their appearance would have led a stranger to imagine that they were the children of parents belonging to the middle classes of society.'[3] If one believes the proud reports in the German press, Kay must have been continually stumbling upon other Englishmen with an interest in education.[4] Those among them whose pedagogical gaze was less fixated upon aesthetic notions of order also saw, despite the relative progressiveness, the darker side of German elementary education.

I shall attempt, in five steps, to outline the basic features of the development of elementary school education from the Wilhelmine period to the Weimar Republic. First I will sketch the quantitative and qualitative expansion of elementary schools between 1870 and 1930. Second, I will turn to the question of when and how state-mandated compulsory education was pushed through. Third, I will discuss the extent to which this development was able to contribute to making the entrenched borders between the social classes more porous. Fourth, I will examine the influence of the church on elementary school education in Germany's multi-confessional society. Fifth and finally, I shall turn to the internal life of schools, to the teachers and pedagogical concepts, teaching materials and teaching methods.

The expansion of the elementary school system

The expansion of the German elementary school system in the nineteenth century did not by any means follow a straight path towards modernisation. If in the context of the *Humboldtian educational reforms, the basic outlines of a liberalisation and differentiation were already recognisable at the beginning of the century, the restorationist tendencies after the failed Revolution of 1848 thwarted these ambitions. Elementary school teachers, in Prussia and across the German states, were regarded by those at the highest levels of authority as bearing a considerable measure of co-responsibility for encouraging the revolutionary movement. Three regulations 'on the establishment of Protestant *seminary, *preparatory and elementary school instruction' were enacted on 1, 2 and 3 October 1854, which were supposed to put them in their place. According to these 'Stiehlsche Regulations' the level of training for elementary school teachers, as opposed to secondary school teachers, was determined by the scope of instruction in a single-class, one-room schoolhouse in which all the children of a village from 6 to 14 years were taught together. The essential task of the elementary school was, according to a principle in the regulations, to educate 'youth in a Christian, patriotic spirit and in domestic virtue'. The provision of instruction above all in religion and the German language with a bit of basic mathematics and singing was regarded as sufficient to achieve this goal.

Regardless of such directives, processes of differentiation began to make themselves apparent as early as the 1860s. Above all in state elementary schools, the division of the primary school into four age-based classes or grades increasingly became the norm. When, after the foundation of the German Empire in 1871, Adalbert Falk, a Liberal, was put in charge of the Imperial Ministry for Spiritual, Educational and Medicinal Affairs, the 1854 regulations were replaced by the so-called General Directives (*Allgemeine Bestimmungen*). Herein five different types of 'normal elementary school institutions' were named[5]: (1) the single-class elementary school, which long continued to predominate above all in the rural areas; (2) half-day schools, which had been established in order to reduce the size of classes, so that the teacher could instruct one half in the mornings and the other half in the afternoons; (3) the two-class school with two teachers; (4) the three-class school with two teachers; and (5) the increasingly popular fully elaborated school with three or more classes, which, above all in the larger cities, soon became the rule. The normal lesson plan was considerably expanded. To the subjects which in the earlier regulations were named as primary subjects were added 'Geometry' and at the intermediate level 'History' and 'Natural Science'. Beyond this there was 'Gymnastics' for the boys and 'Handicrafts' for the girls. On the other hand, the number of hours reserved for instruction in Religion was reduced to a total of four per week.

Seen as a whole, however, the forces of change and resistance long balanced each other out. Above all the urban–rural divide remained. According to the figures recorded by Ernst Engel, Head of the Royal Office of Statistics, the number of pupils at state elementary schools in 1869 amounted to 806,922 in the cities and 2,131,757 in the countryside.[6] This also meant that 8.5 per cent of urban and 0.6 per cent of rural pupils attended private rather than state elementary schools and/or preparatory schools.[7] Even ten years after the foundation of the Empire, the single-class, one-room schoolhouse still dominated in the countryside until, from the 1890s onward, even here the multiple-class elementary school gradually began to establish itself. In 1906, 11 per cent of all schoolchildren still attended schools with only one class, while no fewer than 30 per cent went to an elementary school with seven classes.[8] The situation in the individual classes also improved. In the last decade of the nineteenth century, the average classroom contained 'only' 51 pupils, down from 72. Yet in 1911, a teacher at a rural school still had to teach between 120 and 200 children. The improvement in the teacher–student ratio, which primarily took place in urban areas, was largely a consequence of the hiring of more and more teachers. Across Germany between 1871 and 1914 the number of teachers had doubled, reaching the figure of 187,500. Of these 40,000 were, thanks to the women's movement, now women.[9] Yet the pupil population was also steadily increasing. By the outbreak of the First World War, their number had risen to 10.6 million, marking an increase of 68 per cent.

In order to properly 'school' them, the construction of elementary schools boomed in the first three decades of the twentieth century. In 1911, there were still only 32,451, whereas by 1931 52,961 elementary schools were listed. The pronounced urban–rural divide was also diminishing. In 1914, 85 per cent of German schools were in rural areas; in 1931 this figure still stood at 76 per cent but by then they catered for only a minority of Germany's children. In an effort to reduce class sizes, which were still large, the number of elementary school teachers continued to rise, reaching 195,946 by 1921. Among them, the percentage of women also grew from 22 to 25 per cent by 1933, when there were 48,300 female elementary school teachers in Germany.[10]

The structural developments of the Wilhelmine period functioned as a 'conservative modernisation from above',[11] which, while gradually advancing an improvement in primary education, nevertheless – through the coexistence of numerous and various private institutions, especially in elementary education – helped to entrench a two-class society. In contrast, education policymakers after the November Revolution of 1918 attempted to institute a *Grundschule* (or primary school) that was mandatory for everyone, a demand that had previously been made repeatedly by the Social Democrats. Thus was it stated in Article 145, the article on schools of the 1919 Constitution of the Weimar Republic: 'School attendance is compulsory. The implementation of such is served fundamentally by the elementary school comprising at least grades one to eight and of the subsequent secondary school up to the age of eighteen. The instruction and teaching materials in the elementary and secondary schools are free of charge.'[12]

The long road to the enforcement of compulsory education

By the time of the establishment of the Weimar Republic, compulsory education had already broadly established itself in Germany. Yet the road to this point had been long and rocky. Up to the turn of the century, a precarious alliance of agricultural landowners, industrialists, parents, clergy and certainly also a few teachers succeeded periodically in circumventing or at least weakening compulsory education. The question, 'How is one to prevent deliberate truancies, to render them – unavoidable as they are – as harmless as possible?'[13] was one that occupied contemporaries throughout the 'long' nineteenth century.

At the beginning of the nineteenth century, when there would have been approximately 2.2 million children of school age in Germany, only 60 per cent of them actually attended school.[14] This was the case despite the fact that there were already legal provisions such as the Prussian Legal Code (*Allgemeine Landrecht*) of 1794 that mandated school attendance for children between the ages of 5 and 14. Yet the series of exemption clauses simultaneously showed how half-heartedly the mandate on compulsory schooling was enforced. In Article 45 of the Prussian Legal Code a dispensation was granted to those children 'who due to domestic tasks' or to 'certain necessary labours' could not regularly attend school at certain times of year.[15] Schooling not only suffered from long interruptions but also the length of a child's school career was by no means uniform. This is evident from the wording of the provision, which states that school instruction should continue 'until a child has, in the judgement of a clergyman, achieved the requisite level of knowledge of a reasonable person of his social standing'.[16] Such a formulation allowed for immeasurable leeway, opening the door to arbitrariness.

Critical contemporaries such as the statistician Ernst Engel were well aware of this difficulty. He noted worriedly that pupils were classified as 'attending school' who missed lessons for weeks or months at a time because they had been hired out as shepherd boys or, as with the Swabian children, who were offered to farmers for a harvest season.[17] Even though over the course of the nineteenth century, the local authority figures, such as the clergyman or the squire, were increasingly divested of the power to decide on the compulsory education of members of the community, it is safe to assume that, particularly in rural areas, the schooling of many children was interrupted by frequent gaps or many a school career was broken off long before the mandatory eight years.

In industrial regions, as well, the need for cheap labour competed with compulsory education. Once again, industrialisation and literacy – two phenomena of modernisation – stood in each other's way. Especially in regions with manufacturing trades like the textile industry, in which children were traditionally employed, it remained difficult into the 1860s to consistently enforce schooling. Even drastic punishments proved an ineffective deterrent. In Krefeld, a centre of soap manufacturing in the Ruhr, the school department reported in 1885 that for a total of 7,922 elementary school pupils, 3,409 parents – or more than 40 per cent – were summoned to discuss their children's absence from school, and no fewer than 2,662 received jail sentences.[18]

Measures taken by the state to counteract this problem, such as the Child Protection Provisions (*Kinderschutzbestimmungen*) of 1839 and 1853, which initially applied only to those children who were employed in larger factories, could be circumvented by parents and employers by deploying the children primarily as cheap labour in the still-widespread cottage industries or as 'beer boys' in inns. It was only with the passage of the Worker Protection Law (*Arbeiterschutzgesetz*) on 1 June 1891 that the ban on child labour was extended to 'children under 13 years' and to 'enterprises that cannot be characterised as factories with ten and more workers'. For many teachers, who were the foremost campaigners for regular school attendance, this was not broad enough. They were aware of the many loopholes that such a provision left open. Yet not only pedagogical responsibility but also material interests drove the elementary school teachers to the barricades. After all, their salaries depended on the number of their pupils. Under pressure from the German Teachers' Association, child protection was extended in 1903 to cover even smaller enterprises. The ban on child labour still did not apply to agricultural work; this end was achieved only in the 1970s.

In any event, many school departments made only half-hearted use of the legal possibility to mandate school attendance. A network of dependencies often had an obstructive influence. Theodor von der Goltz, an agronomist at the University of Königsberg, brought this precarious constellation of forces to a point in his famous 1874 disquisition 'The question of rural workers and its solution' when he wrote: 'The large as well as the small agricultural enterprises employ to a great extent school-aged children and youths during the mandated school period as wageworkers'. This led to the situation 'that a large number of school-aged children receive virtually no schooling in summer' while in the winter long and difficult journeys to school as well as adverse weather conditions prevented them from going to school. Frequently 'dependent on the local landowner for their already meagre material existence', teachers only seldom dared to draw his attention to his illegal exploitation of child labour. 'Many a teacher', Goltz continued, 'has been forced to pay a high price for his professional zeal when he was so bold as to criticise the squire or his inspector for keeping children from their lessons'. The situation was complicated still further by the fact that the mothers of the schoolchildren often had to work for the local landowner as well, with the consequence that older siblings had to stay home and look after their younger brothers and sisters during the school day.[19]

The few childhood memories that have been survived support his view. Wenzel Holek, who was born the son of an agricultural worker in 1864, looked back on a very patchy school career:

> Once again autumn passed without my having gone to school. [...] Again I had to stay home and look after my siblings. Later, when my brother was able to perform my job, I had to join my parents in the field and take part in the work.

Once again, there was no talk of my going to school. Only in winter were there a few days when Mother did not have to go and thresh grain and I did not have to fetch firewood or charcoal. Then I could get to see the inside of the school again. It continued on like this until my twelfth year. After that there was no mention of school anymore.[20]

Child labour in the countryside remained into the twentieth century the decisive structural problem, and one which in many areas stood in the way of the enforcement of regular school attendance for the children of the lower classes but also in part those of wealthier farmers. A census carried out in 1904 found that 1,769,803 children were employed in agricultural work, of whom more than 1 million were under the age of 12.

There was little protest against this, as Wenzel Holek recalled. Initially, his still young and clearly idealistic teacher did not want to tolerate the boy's absence from school and 'complained and threatened to report [the boy's parents] to the authorities'. However, he 'gradually adapted to the conditions in the areas and quietened down'.[21] In part, this change of heart was influenced by the regular payments in kind, which financially strapped elementary teachers gladly accepted. Not infrequently they turned a blind eye when a child, instead of learning arithmetic, spent a summer on a farmer's land, herding goats. Even if Holek's teacher had not succumbed to fatalism and had reported the parents to the authorities, his efforts would probably have come to nothing. At most, one level up the chain of command his complaint would have fallen on deaf ears, for, as Holek reports, the local school council 'which was all too aware of the material destitution of the local poor... never passed complaints on to the school authorities, with the result that the *real state of affairs* never became known.'[22]

As this surely not uncommon example makes clear, the hierarchically organised chain of administration could no longer function if one link slipped out of place, thereby driving the already high number of unreported cases of school absenteeism even higher. At the top-most level, which complaints rarely reached, stood the Department of Religious and Educational Affairs of the respective communal government. The leading positions were usually filled by jurists with no relevant experience in the field of education. Under them stood the school councils, on which sat pedagogically well-versed experts, who frequently had a number of years of teaching experience under their belts. At the bottom of the administrative ladder stood the county and local school inspectors, both of which positions in the nineteenth century were largely held by clergymen. This differentiated bureaucracy, which the Imperial German civil service looked upon with such pride often functioned paradoxically as a modernising instrument with an anti-modernising effect.

Frequently it was also the same people who on the one hand advocated unbridled progress and on the other signed petitions that were directed against the 'too extensive schooling' of the children of the lower classes. The arguments that were appealed to were manifold. Some moralised by referring to the pedagogically beneficial effect of habituation to regular work; above all factory owners pressed the case for pragmatically weighing the question of whether the necessary closure of their enterprises, should they be compelled to forego their small and cheap labour force, would not be more detrimental to the solution of the pressing 'social question' than a few missed lessons on the part of proletarian children. Although in industrial areas or on landed estates they confronted one another as 'class enemies', on this question business owners, landowners and parents frequently sang from the same hymn sheet. Adult members of the lower classes had themselves not experienced school attendance as a vehicle for potential social mobility but rather as an impediment to earning money. In contrast to the preparatory schools that the children of the middle class attended, elementary schools and the knowledge they dispensed were not perceived as a springboard to higher education but rather as a one-way street to the usual misery. For: 'The elementary school leaving-certificate entitled one to nothing'.[23] Parents' attitudes towards mandatory schooling were correspondingly indifferent, sceptical and sometimes even hostile. Thus the mother of Adelheid Popp, a weaver's daughter born in 1869, who herself had been sent 'into service' at the age of 6 without ever having attended school, was an 'enemy of the 'new-fangled laws', as she called compulsory education.[24] In the mid-1860s she managed, by means of numerous 'petitions', to get her sons excused from school at age 10 and set them to work on the looms. Yet when her daughter, also called Adelheid, reached school age in the 1870s, this was no longer so easy. 'Now', the daughter recalled, 'the school administration reported the case to the authorities and mother was sentenced to twelve hours in jail'. However, afraid of risking her new job, she did not appear to serve her sentence: 'At six in the morning on Easter Sunday, two gendarmes came and took her away. Afterwards she was humbled before the head teacher, who admonished her to send me to school, as I was very gifted'.[25] Precisely on this point the mother had her doubts, and she moved with her daughter to next-largest city, where, at city hall, she did not register her 10-year-old daughter as a 'child' and thereby managed to slip out of the crosshairs of the local school authorities.[26]

Even if according to the statistics kept in Imperial Germany compulsory schooling was in force and was largely complied with, there continued to exist a multitude of possibilities for evading it. As long as parents did not see their child's attendance at elementary school as an opportunity to improve their position in society, they contributed greatly to spoiling the education of their sons and daughters, even those who were eager to learn. In their eyes, the elementary school was not only an inconvenient tool designed by the authorities to further their own interests and enforce social discipline; it also infringed on their rights as parents and failed to open up options for the future. Deliberate limits placed on education stood in the way of educational aspirations. This mutually reinforcing constellation of factors prevented the elementary school from being seen as a place not merely of compulsory but also of voluntary learning until the beginning of the twentieth century.[27]

The elementary school as a 'social one-way street'?

When travelling through Germany, Joseph Kay was well aware that the 'orderly, clean, and respectable-looking children' that he saw on their way to school only appeared to belong to the 'middle classes of society'. In reality – and this struck him above all, because he contrasted them in his mind with the bedraggled look-ing working-class children in England – they were 'sons and daughters of the poorest artisans and labourers'.[28] Yet this superficial resemblance of the classes was misleading. For one thing, Kay was looking at a Swabian village and not an industrialised metropolis such as Berlin or the Rhineland, in which the differ-ences would have been more conspicuous. Carl Zuckmaier, who was born the son of a factory owner in 1896 and grew up in the city of Mainz, could well recall the different clothing of the schoolchildren there. With a kind of envy he looked at the sons of workers and tradesmen, who 'ran around in worn out garments, some with patches on the sleeves and trouser legs. [...] I would have felt much more comfortable and been able to move much more freely in them than in the pressed sailor-suit that I wore'.[29]

The worker's and tradesmen's children must have viewed things differently. In contrast to the factory-owner's son, they were not free to choose to continue their education after completing elementary school. In Imperial Germany, the elemen-tary school remained a dead end, thwarting any possibility of social mobility. As long as the strict division between the proletarian *Volksschule* and the bourgeois *Vorschule* existed, the borders between the social classes were strictly drawn. Only the preparatory school, which frequently was already linked to a *Gymnasium*, set the course for secondary school. 'In the harsh reality of today's school system', remarked the Social Democrat Heinrich Schulz pointedly in 1911, 'it is not the desire or aptitude of the individual child that determines what school he will attend but rather a factor that it is indifferent to both his physical and mental abilities: his father's money!'[30] And his fellow Social Democrat Otto Rühle stated tersely: 'We don't have a *Volksschule*; what goes by that name is nothing other than a school for the poor and the poorest of our people'.[31]

For bourgeois parents, who in any event only hesitantly placed their trust in public education because the 'levelling principle of school', as one Berlin mer-chant's wife put it in her diary in 1886, denied their children individual encour-agement, this division was very convenient.[32] Only in rare cases – often when the father was a pastor and had supervisory authority over the local elementary school – were the sons and daughters of the middle class sent to one. Gertrud Bäumer, who was born in 1873, was among this group, and as a child was sur-prised by the furore that her father's decision sparked among the local digni-taries.[33] Her little proletarian friend, the daughter of a cobbler, was well aware that this inter-class friendship would be brief: 'Soon Gertrud will go to the girls' school and she won't look at me anymore'.[34]

In fact, we know from a multitude of ego documents that children – whether consciously or unconsciously – developed a feeling for different class positions very early in life. This is attested to not least by the small-scale class warfare that regularly broke out between elementary school and Gymnasium students. According to Eduard von Hippel, a professor's son born in 1895, such street battles had to 'take place from time to time according to an unwritten code of honour'.[35] 'Since time immemorial', confirmed Franz Rehbein, the son of an agricultural labourer, 'a terrible feud had been going on between elementary school and Gymnasium pupils which not infrequently degenerated into open warfare. On the street veritable battles took place between the two sides, in which rulers and snowballs but also dangerous objects were used as weapons of battle'.[36]

What further divided working-class and middle-class children was the fundamentally different attitude that their respective parents held towards school attendance. For bourgeois parents, the primary-school years were but the first step in a long educational career, and expectations in terms of achievement were high already. Working-class parents, on the other hand, while they generally had been raised to respect the teacher as an embodiment of the state, had less regard for the knowledge that the school was supposed to dispense. The 'school system with its internal barriers, demands and selection mechanisms' only represented 'a practicable channel for mobility for those who, through their socialisation and experience prior to school, i.e. above all in their families, had been properly prepared'.[37]

While during the Imperial period the system of secondary education continued to expand and become more differentiated, primary education tended to stagnate. The task of the elementary school was to convey to the lower classes in the cities and the countryside a modicum of basic knowledge as well as qualities such as punctuality, hard work and submissiveness, which were regarded as conducive to their smooth integration into Wilhelmine society. Even if the percentage of pupils being taught in one-room schoolhouses decreased from the 1880s, this did not mean that the channels for social advancement through education were now open. Of high-school graduates in Berlin between 1907 and 1911, 62.2 per cent still hailed from the educational or economic bourgeoisie, 31.8 per cent from the families of self-employed tradesmen and merchants, and 5.3 per cent from the aristocracy. Only 0.7 per cent were the sons of employed tradesmen and workers[38] – there were no daughters among them.

In the Imperial period, the elementary school did not succeed in uniting a highly heterogeneous population. On the contrary, the lines between the classes would appear to have deepened. It was only after the end of the First World War and of the monarchy that there was for the first time a real opportunity to create a primary school that would truly be for everyone.[39] The responsibility for realising this fell to the educational policy experts of the 'Weimar Coalition', which had formed after the elections of 1919 and was composed of representatives of the Social Democratic Party (SPD), the left-liberal German Democratic Party (DDP) and the Catholic Zentrum. Above all the former saw the integration of the various segments of the population as a task whose urgency had only been made more acute as a result of the war and the Revolution. As people whose connection to education was not just political but also for the most part professional, they declared education to be the key to the solution of the 'social question'.[40]

The desire to weaken if not to break down the walls between the social classes was the driving force behind the 'school' article of the Weimar Constitution. Alongside Article 145, which established a free and 'fundamental' universal compulsory eight-year education at an elementary school, above all Article 146 was supposed to put an end to its dead-end character: 'The public school system should be organised organically. Intermediate and secondary education are built upon the foundation of an elementary school designed for everyone'. Now the elementary school, too, was supposed to become a door that could lead to higher educational institutions, as was expressly emphasised: 'For this structure, the diversity of life-long vocations is decisive, just as the talents and proclivities of a child – not the economic and social position or religion of his parents – are decisive for his acceptance into a particular school.'[41]

At least on paper, the private schools previously frequented by the bourgeoisie were simultaneously supposed to become a thing of the past, as the text of Article 147 tersely states: 'Private preparatory schools are to be abolished'.[42] This statement amounts to a declaration of war by the educational policy makers of the Weimar Republic on the type of school reform that the socialist, Wilhelm Liebknecht, had denounced in his famous 1888 speech 'Knowledge is Power – Power is Knowledge'; a type of reform that deprived 'the people of the possibility of education'.[43] Hereby the course was set for a loosening up of the dual-track school system and a relaxation of class barriers. Yet the preparatory schools together with their proponents would prove more intractable than had been hoped. Far from being closed down overnight, they continued to exist for years and in no small numbers due to a generous period of grace that lasted until 1930. Nevertheless, despite protests staged by middle-class parents and Gymnasium teachers, the 'Law relating to primary schools and the phasing-out of preparatory schools' was passed on 28 April 1930. In the meantime, the chorus of democratically minded educational experts had grown loud enough to make themselves heard at the enormous Imperial School Conference in Berlin in 1920, which, with 722 participants attending, was a conference of superlatives. Here incredibly modern-seeming and controversial subjects were discussed. For at least a few participants, the aim was to achieve a more just distribution of educational opportunities as well as the democratisation of schools and individualisation of teaching. Yet even if in Berlin a few proponents of progressive teaching methods got to have their say, the mood was clearly infused with tensions. The unmistakable impression that emerges from the sometimes heated discussions (they are documented in a transcript volume extending to nearly a thousand pages) is that elementary and Gymnasium teachers collided with one another as if they inhabited different worlds. Taken aback, the Liberal Interior Minister Erich Koch-Weser remarked upon the 'dreadful intellectual arrogance of the secondary school teachers'.[44]

Across the board, the liberalising tendencies in elementary school education had by no means prevailed, and certainly not in people's heads. Shortly after the revolutionary euphoria had begun to wane in the early 1920s, the brakes began to be applied to the noble idea of the comprehensive school. After the parliamentary elections of late 1924, the Interior Ministry, which was responsible for schooling, fell to a member of the conservative German National People's Party, and he seized the opportunity to revise the law. With the 'Small Primary School Law', which was enacted in April 1925, 'especially quick-witted school-children' could henceforth be excused from elementary school after three years. Furthermore, many pupils continued to attend private preparatory schools. When, in February 1927 the abolition of private schools was finally tied by the Weimar Republic to the legal settlement of the question of compensation (and the requirement for the state to build new schools to replace them), this effectively guaranteed their continued existence.[45] How strongly the preparatory school continued to be used is also reflected in the statistics: in 1921, 47 per cent of Prussian *Sextaner* (or first-year Gymnasium students) might now have come from an elementary school, but 42 per cent had previously attended a private preparatory school.[46] Among the female students who attended one of the mushrooming number of *lycées*, the percentage of former preparatory school students was much higher, namely 67 per cent, while only 25 per cent had come from a state elementary school.[47]

State–church–school: a precarious co-existence

If it was difficult to attempt to dissolve class barriers by means of a primary school that was mandatory for everyone, the effort to break down religious barriers in multi-confessional Germany would prove an even greater challenge. When the German Empire was founded in 1871, some 30 million Germans were members of the Protestant Church, around 16 million were Catholics, 560,000 were Jews and another 30,000 were followers of others religions. The *Kulturkampf* spearheaded by Chancellor Otto von Bismarck, the aim of which was to reduce the influence of the Catholic Church in all areas of culture, ultimately had the opposite effect, actually leading to a re-confessionalisation. For all of the emphasis that was placed on secularisation in Imperial Germany, it remained surprisingly important what confession one belonged to. Parents therefore placed correspondingly great value on sending their children to a school of their confession.

Precisely in the area of elementary school education the church was, alongside the commune, the second social force with which the state had to engage when it came to setting school policy. Already during the Revolution of 1848, the abolition of clerical supervision of schools was among the core demands. During the Kulturkampf in the 1870s, the issue was once again on the agenda, if the tenor of the debate had changed. This time the discussion was guided not by the liberal notion of a clear separation between church and state but rather by the desire, now that a German state had been outwardly founded, to achieve its 'inner foundation', a 'cultural homogenisation',[48] under which all the forces of division were supposed to be rounded up and domesticated. Above all the Catholic Church, its claims to universality having just been reinvigorated by the Zentrum Party, appeared to thwart this process. If the school was seen as a key instrument of national integration, then the Catholic Church's overarching claims in the field of education harboured a great potential for conflict.[49]

With respect to the school system, the Kulturkampf in Prussia began by closing down the Catholic Department at the Ministry of Culture and replacing the church-friendly minister of education and cultural affairs, von Müller, with Adalbert Falk on 22 January 1872. Among the latter's first orders of business was to enact the 'Law on the Supervision of Schools', which stated that the supervision of all public educational institutions fell exclusively on the state. Previously clergymen had occupied a special position, particularly vis-à-vis elementary school teachers, whose direct superiors they more or less were, wielding a great deal of influence not only on what was taught but also over the daily lives of teachers. At the same time, the Prussian Ministry of Education and Cultural Affairs demanded the foundation of *Simultanschulen*, or confessionally mixed schools, in which the pupils would be divided into separate confessional groups only during Religion class.

The clergy thereby lost a considerable amount of power, and they reacted with a corresponding degree of indignation, issuing notes of protest and circulating mass petitions. At least initially they enjoyed some successes. They were aided in their endeavour by the fact that the speed and rigour with which the law was enforced evidently depended on local conditions. In ultra-Catholic Münster (capital of the Prussian province of Westphalia), for example, where the majority of the population welcomed the close symbiosis between schools and the church, the signs all pointed to de-escalation. The supervision of individual schools remained largely unaffected; only in particular cases were clergymen stripped of their supervisory function.[50] Only around three years later did a wave of firings take place. In the entire administrative district of Münster, 142 priests were discharged from the various school boards in 1875.[51] And Westphalia was not the only place where things began to heat up: on orders from the state, the locks on many schools were changed so that clergymen could no longer enter them with their old keys in order to dispense unscheduled religious instruction. Policemen stood guard at the entrances to elementary schools, and in some cases charges were brought against individual clergymen.[52]

Yet when, from the 1890s onwards, the state and the church found themselves confronted by a common enemy in the form of parties of the left espousing social democracy, the two drew closer together again. In the countryside, the powerful influence of the church had not waned and had remained relatively unscathed by the Kulturkampf. Together with farmers, many clergymen continued to assist parents in circumventing federal laws on compulsory school attendance and to influence both lesson plans and the hiring and firing of teachers. In the School Compromise of 1904, it was once again emphasised that the supervision of schools was a secular task. At the same time, however, religious schools were recognised as mainstream schools, whereas the previously supported Simultanschulen were once again marginalised. Before the First World War, 95 per cent of all Catholic and 90 per cent of Protestant children in Imperial Germany attended religious schools.

Even when the political cards were reshuffled after the First World War, the question of the interrelationships between the state, schools and the church remained central in debates about educational policy in the early years of the

Weimar Republic. As the Social Democrats had never made any bones about the fact that in their eyes the church had no business in the running of schools, after the socialist parties took power in November 1918, far-reaching changes in educational policy were only to be expected. Here Prussia once again played a pioneering role. On 12 November 1918, the majority socialist Konrad Haenisch and the independent socialist Adolph Hoffmann together took over the Ministry of Education and Cultural Affairs. The second decree they issued was entitled 'Suspension of compulsory religious instruction in schools' and it included a series of corresponding provisions. According to these, no teacher could be obliged to give instruction in Religion nor to perform any other church-related activity; no pupil could be compelled to attend Religion classes; the prayer previously recited at the beginning of the school day was to be omitted; religious holidays need not be observed; Religion was no longer to be an examination subject; and it was forbidden to assign homework for Religion class.[53] The vehemence of the criticism that this edict provoked showed how deeply entrenched the church still was among many segments of the German population. The preservation of the 'Christian school' was now subject to negotiation, and the task at hand was to defend it.

And indeed there was some backpedalling on the issue. What remained in the 1919 Constitution was the 'Weimar Compromise'. This stipulated that: (1) the Simultanschule would be recognised as a mainstream school and parents would decide over the question of religious instruction; (2) 'At the desire of parents', religious schools would continue to exist, and the details pertaining to their organisation would be clarified in a federal law. However, as this constitutional obligation was disregarded by the Catholic Centre Party, which until 1933 resolutely torpedoed any legislation on the subject, this article 'effectively functioned as a restrictive clause against the Simultanschule'.[54] Consequently, the confessional bifurcation of education remained largely unchanged in the Weimar Republic; merely the supervision of schools was placed in secular hands. As in previous decades, Protestant children largely continued to attend Protestant schools and Catholic children the Catholic schools. Each confessional community therefore retained its own schools.

The inner life of the elementary schools: teachers, curricula, methods and pedagogical concepts in flux

'On the headmaster's birthday, the desk and the blackboard were festooned with garlands. Diederich even decorated the cane'.[55] It was not only in novels like Heinrich Mann's *Der Untertan* (The Loyal Subject) that Wilhelmine school life was painted in the darkest of colours. 'Those who know Germany only from literature', wrote the pedagogue Friedrich Paulsen in 1912, must 'conclude that in no period in history have youths ever been treated so mercilessly'.[56] Cane-wielding teachers also dominated contemporary autobiographies – across class lines. The teachers in working-class memoirs in particular, most of them elementary school teachers, were seldom depicted as positive figures.

The professional training of elementary school teachers had neverthe-less improved markedly in Imperial Germany. Only a few decades previously, 'schoolmasters' had frequently been artisans or former soldiers without educa-tional training who 'held school' on the side. Elementary-school teaching as a separate profession began to emerge in the period preceding the Revolution of 1848, and some members of the lower middle classes sought to use it as a social springboard. With the abolition of the old Prussian Stiehlsche Regulations, teacher training in the new German state became both more regimented and more nuanced. Future elementary school teachers usually studied for three years at a preparatory institute, followed by three years at a teacher training college. While there were 64 in 1871, by 1914 their number had risen to 204, 16 of them special training colleges for female teachers. The latter were, as Otto Rühle complained, 'located with preference in small, remote towns... The idea is to retard the intellectual development of future educators of youth as much as possible by making them spend years in backwaters far from culture and touched little or not at all by the current of life'.[57] This form of teacher training, surely described here in somewhat exaggerated terms, ended only in 1926 with the establishment of pedagogical academies. Elementary school teachers' desire for a university education, driven by the hope of equal status with secondary school teachers, was not yet fulfilled, at least on the level of training.

It did occur on another plane, however. Three decades previously the teachers had succeeded in winning a major victory in their constant struggle for better training and social recognition. In 1896, the secondary school teachers' right to 'one-year voluntary service' was also conceded to graduates of the teacher train-ing colleges. This meant that the usual two- or three-year term of military service demanded of German males was reduced to a single year. Afterwards, the men gained the right to bear the title of 'officer in the reserve'. The fact that up to 1913 nearly half of all male elementary school teachers availed themselves of this quite costly option shows how prestigious it was. This may well be the origin of the infamous drill-sergeant style of the Wilhelmine school. Thus according to a ped-agogical lexicon, 'When the teacher enters the pupils are to stand up sharply all at once, like a battalion riding in a military parade. [...] At the break pupils must exit the classroom like soldiers in an orderly goose step. [...] The boys' heads and shoulders are to be held erect in class in a military stance, so that the eye of the school commander sees no deviation wherever he looks'.[58]

Even the increasing presence of female teachers in the schools does not appear to have alleviated the harsh barracks tone. Beginning in the 1860s, more and more unmarried daughters, particularly from the lower middle classes, opted for the teaching profession. Unlike most other professions, it was deemed socially acceptable because in keeping with women's allegedly 'natural' talent for chil-drearing. By the outbreak of the First World War, one-fifth of all elementary school teachers were women.[59] This was the case despite the fact that women teachers generally earned 20–25 per cent less than their male colleagues and were subject to the degrading ban on marriage, which was still largely in place even in the 1920s.[60]

In the eyes of many women, the constant improvements in employment conditions may have outweighed such inequities. In 1897, the Public Employees' Salary Act introduced a uniform yearly base salary of 900 marks for the first time, which was supplemented by housing allowances and age-dependent payments of 130–240 marks. This brought elementary school teachers a good deal closer to their long-held aspiration to the status of lower and middle civil servants. Despite these improvements, however, even at the turn of the century, there was still a huge gap between urban and rural teachers. Thus around 1,900 elementary school teachers still had to perform the lowly duties of a church sexton and accept some of their payment in kind. Social control by the local clergy also remained strict, and they were denied the right to stand for election to public office.

Convinced of their important role in society and inspired by a strong desire for social mobility, elementary school teachers were nevertheless soon self-confident enough to organise politically to assert their interests. Even before the Revolution of 1848, elementary school teachers began to organise, but after 1850, political repression and bureaucratic coercive action brought much of this organising to a standstill. Nevertheless, the teachers' associations had revived by around 1860. The General German Teachers' Conferences, which for fear of repressive measures were poorly attended in the period of reaction, attracting only about 270 teachers, became major events again after 1862 with thousands of participants. The German Teachers' Association (DLV) was founded in 1870.

This said, the improvement of teachers' status proceeded at a snail's pace. In Imperial Germany and into the Weimar Republic, being an elementary school teacher was certainly not a dream profession. In light of the class sizes mentioned before, young teachers, many of them inadequately trained, frequently found themselves in overcrowded classrooms full of hungry children exhausted by labour and long walks to school. Unjust punishments and mindless rote learning are topics that recur in memoirs of school life.[61] There were exceptions, of course: teachers who recognised and sought to encourage their pupils' talents, who knew how to make lessons interesting and absorbing or, since they often came from the lower classes themselves, embodied the possibilities of social mobility: 'I would have liked to become a teacher', recalled Adelheid Popp, 'my model was my teacher, a beautiful, refined young lady whose tasteful clothing I always admired'.[62]

There were at least two reasons for the state's growing interest in teachers and the elementary schools during the Wilhelmine period: on the one hand, a recognition of the formative role of the elementary school, and on the other, a desire to gain greater control over it for that very reason. The aspiration to guide every last aspect of school life particularly dominated the 'School Oversight Act' of 15 October 1872. This law prescribed the classroom furnishings as well as the 'indispensable means of instruction' in precise detail. The classroom should be large enough to ensure 'that there was at least 0.6 square metres of space for each pupil'. The room should also be 'bright and airy' with good ventilation, provide 'protection against the elements' and be 'equipped with adequate window curtains'. All children should be able to sit and work 'without detriment to their health'.[63] In addition to sufficient benches, the classrooms should be equipped with a blackboard and stand, a chalkboard on the wall, a lectern or 'teacher's desk with a lock' and a cupboard for storing books, notebooks, chalk and sponges. The fact that by the 1870s the geographical radius of instruction extended beyond the pupils' immediate surroundings, and was intended to awaken a 'global' awareness made further accessories necessary. Thus, apart from a copy of the mandated textbook, a globe, a wall map 'of the home province', a wall map of Germany, a wall map of Palestine and several pictures for teaching Political Geography were included among the classroom necessities. Joseph Kay had already noted with approval the 'remarkable taste for music' in German elementary schools, in which every musical child received especial encouragement from an early age.[64] Minister Falk was convinced that every elementary school classroom should have a violin.

The sources do not reveal how often it was used and what pieces were played. The stipulations regarding the contents of instruction were left vague, giving teachers substantial scope. Apart from teaching basic skills such as reading, writing and arithmetic, the elementary schools were primarily concerned with training pupils in obedience, humility, self-sacrifice and modesty. The fact, for instance, that teaching materials for the fairy tale 'Mother Hulda' following the five-step *Herbartian model – preparation, presentation, association, summary, application – end with the question, 'If one of the girls becomes a housemaid, why is the story so appropriate?'[65] demonstrates that pupils were to be trained to be satisfied with their own social position. This applied to girls and boys equally. Apart from the separation for girls' handicraft lessons and boys' gymnastics, gender-specific differences in the curriculum were rather minor. German elementary schools were generally coeducational, more out of necessity than principle. Beginning at the turn of the century a few separate boys' and girls' schools arose, but only in the larger cities. Boys and girls alike, it was repeatedly emphasised, should also be taught to love 'the traditional ruling dynasty'.[66] School memoirs confirm that many teachers did their best in this regard. This was only to be expected in that at the end of the nineteenth century many of them profited from a gradual nationalisation of the school system, which was intended to improve elementary education both qualitatively and quantitatively in the long term. The fact that state intervention led to a more uniform and significantly improved system of pay would have been a positive experience for many teachers, and perhaps also one that commanded loyalty.[67]

Emperor William II's cabinet order of 1 May 1889 stipulating that the schools 'in their various gradations' were to be used 'to counteract the spread of socialist and communist ideas' accordingly met with little criticism.[68] According to the recollections of the worker's son Moritz Bromme, the implementation of this notion in a German elementary school might have looked as follows: as the teacher informed a class of 11-year-olds, 'There is now a sort of person, they call themselves Social Democrats, who aim to destroy marriage and family life, abolish the state and the kings and all private property'.[69] As a 12-year-old, August Winnig had a teacher who 'spoke ill of the Social Democrats'. 'He portrayed them as rebellious, disrespectful people who wanted to destroy all authorities and level high and low. This was quite wrong, for just as there are roses and nettles in Nature, so among people there are lazy and hardworking and rich and poor.' Clearly, though, these 'lessons' had little effect on the pupils. Some of them were plainly pleased at the Social Democrats' electoral victory and waved a newspaper special edition announcing it around in the classroom. Angered, the teacher now threatened to change his tune and began the next day's lesson with canings.[70] That this style of pedagogy was not effective in stamping out social democracy is demonstrated by studies of the electoral behaviour of former elementary school students. According to this research, a politically and religiously conservative education aimed at raising loyal subjects tended to produce oppositional voting patterns.[71] The fact that the Social Democrats and left-wing Liberals nearly attained a majority in 1912 after 40 years of Wilhelmine elementary education illustrates the limits of the schools' influence.[72]

Whether this stance gave way to universal patriotism during the war and the imperially mandated social truce has not been studied thus far. At any rate, most schools participated in the organisation of lavish victory celebrations and the re-enactment of battles in the classroom. Soon after the war ended, however, people changed their tune. In the Preamble to the so-called November Decree of 27 November 1918, Konrad Haenisch demanded that in future, instruction and the 'authority of the teacher' should no longer be misused to exert political influence. 'We steadfastly insist...that the schools never again become sites for inciting national hatred and glorifying war'.[73] These were lofty ideals, which were doubtless contradicted by quite a few teachers returned from the war who now spread the so-called stab-in-the-back legend. And doubtless many teachers will have dictated the letters of protest from pupils against the decree promulgated in September 1919. This decree stipulated that 'pictures of the former emperor and his families' were to be left out of the new textbooks, 'since their sole purpose was to glorify the dynasty and cultivate the previous notion of the state'.[74]

The forces supporting the status quo, as we have seen with regard to the influence of the church, may frequently have stood in the way of reform attempts in everyday school life. Nevertheless, the enthusiasm for pedagogical change will have begun to penetrate everyday instruction, if only gradually. Thus in the 1920s, influenced by the ideas of reform pedagogy, the new subjects of civics and *Arbeitsunterricht*, practical studies in crafts and home economics, were introduced. In quite a few classrooms the rigid rows gave way to group tables or benches arranged in a semi-circle. After 1900 and increasingly in the 1920s this reform pedagogy, which was strongly influenced by the youth movement, began to disseminate a new idea of childhood and childrearing. The name of one contemporary best-seller, 'I must walk through the country of the child's psyche' became the motto of a pedagogy 'proceeding from the child'. In the multiplicity of pedagogical writings that flooded the market youth was glorified as the epitome of all things original, natural and pure, as yet untouched by the 'corruption' of civilisation.

Great emphasis was now placed on the pupils' self-motivation, and 'holistic' and 'child-centred' completed the trio of concepts that runs through the pedagogical literature. Children should learn to understand the world by observing natural and life processes on educational walks. The schools should nourish an emotional attachment to their native land in close connection with children's own 'life circles'. Tellingly, in Albert Sixtus' *Rabbit School*, 'gardening' is the young rabbits' favourite subject. Apart from nature study, the children's creative impulses were also to be encouraged, and high hopes were placed in art education in particular. People now spoke of the 'art of education', which as such could not be regulated.[75] Many of the educationalists who now voiced their opinions were inspired by a boundless pedagogical optimism, and they believed that the solution to society's problems lay above all in the right kind of educational system. The elementary school should no longer train the 'narrow minds of loyal subjects', but instead aid in the formation of children's personalities.

But other voices could be heard among the liberal vocabulary. The firm rejection of 'education for religious and middle-class respectability', of the rigid inculcation of conformist virtues, was not juxtaposed with the notion of self-assured, democratic-minded citizens. The ideal was not the republic, but rather the 'German cultural nation' invoked in the countless culturally pessimistic pamphlets that peddled their visions of doom in those days. It was the 'creative forces of youth as a blessing for the national community' that required room to develop, and the teacher as a charismatic leader was to lead the way.[76] Just as the general *zeitgeist* of the Weimar Republic was marked by a struggle between disparate concepts, the pedagogy of the period was dominated by the coexistence of liberal and nationalist ideas, a euphoric devotion to individualism and a longing for a national community.

Conclusion

'He who has the schools has dominion over the future and over the world'.[77] In Imperial Germany, this dictum by Heinrich von Sybel on the power of schools became anchored in the minds of educational policy makers. In the Weimar Republic, school and education became deeply felt issues that were loaded with great expectations by the whole of society and invested with powerful emotions. The many participants in the struggle over the schools pluralised the interests involved and brought conflicts to the fore. In all this, little consideration was given to the pupils, although after the war some thought was given to allowing them a degree of co-determination. The products of the Wilhelmine and Weimar elementary schools, however, were neither solely subservient subjects nor self-motivated citizens. Furthermore, despite attempts at increased state, church and pedagogical control, the schools consistently retained substantial latitude to regulate their own affairs, resisting outside influence, whatever the prevailing socio-political power structure.

Timeline

1854: Prussian regulations of elementary teachers' training

1870: Formation of the German Empire under Prussian leadership

1870: German Teachers' Association founded

1871: Adalbert Falk regulations

1896: Reduction in military service for male teachers extended to those in elementary schools

1904: School Compromise recognising religious schools in the state system

1918: November Revolution

1919: Weimar Republic established – new Constitution agreed. Articles 145–147 – free elementary schools and compulsory attendance established

1920: Imperial School Conference

Glossary

Froebel, Friedrich Wilhelm August: German educationalist and father of the kindergarten (1782–1852). Froebel believed that children were individuals with unique capacities and that the best way to learn was through play.

Genevan School: collective name for the founding fathers of experimental child psychology who worked at the Rousseau Institute, a private Genevan academy set up by Edouard Claparède in 1912. Their aim was turn educational theory into a science.

gymnasium: German academic secondary school.

Herbartian: after Johann Friedrich Herbart (1776–1841), German educationalist. Herbart believed that the role of education was to develop an individual's potential. He was particularly interested in the way that knowledge should be taught so that it was successfully inculcated.

Humboldtian: after Wilhelm Humboldt (1767–1835), educational reformer and founder of the University of Berlin, From 1808 to 1810, Humboldt was in charge of the section of the Prussian Interior Ministry dealing with Ecclesiastical Affairs and Education. Humboldt believed strongly in universal education and that education's primary role was to develop character and moral sense.

Kulturkampf: campaign launched by the German chancellor, Bismarck to reduce the influence of the Catholic Church in the new German Empire.

lycées: French academic secondary schools usually for older teenagers, first established by Napoleon in 1802; a number of secondary schools were founded in other countries along the same lines and using the same name.

seminaries: the name for teacher training colleges in Germany.

Volksschule: name for the elementary school in Germany.

Vorschule: in Germany, a private school used by the middle-classes to prepare their children for the gymnasium.

Notes

1. A. Sixtus (1924) *Die Häschenschule. Mit Bildern von Fritz Koch-Gotha* (Leipzig: Alfred Hahn's Verlag).
2. H. Schiffler and R. Winkeler (eds) (1991) *Bilderwelten der Erziehung. Die Schule im Bild des 19. Jahrhunderts* (Weinheim/München: Juventa).
3. J. Kay (1850) *The Social Condition and Education of the People in England and Europe. Vol. II: The Education of the People* (London: Longman, Brown, Green and Longmans), p. 296.
4. *Allgemeine Zeitung* Augsburg, No. 227, 4.10.1867.
5. Falk, A.(1961) 'Allgemeine Bestimmungen', in G. Giese (ed.), *Quellen zur deutschen Schulgeschichte seit 1800* (Göttingen: Musterschmidt), pp. 168–74.
6. Drewek, P. and Tenorth, H.-E. (2001) 'Das deutsche Bildungswesen im 19. Und 20. Jahrhundert. Systemdynamik und Systemreflexion' in H.J. Apel et al. (eds) *Das öffentliche deutsche Bildungswesen. Historische Entwicklung, gesellschaftliche Funktionen, pädagogischer Streit* (Bad Heilbrunn: Verlag Julius Klinkhardt), pp. 49–83, at p. 53.
7. P. Lundgreen (1980) *Sozialgeschichte der deutschen Schule im Überblick. Teil I: 1770–1918* (Göttingen: Vandenhoeck & Ruprecht), p. 97.
8. H.-U. Wehler (1995) *Deutsche Gesellschaftsgeschichte, Vol. 3* (Munich: C.H. Beck), p. 1195.
9. Ibid., p. 1194.
10. H.-U. Wehler (1995) *Deutsche Gesellschaftsgeschichte, Vol. 4* (Munich: C.H.Beck), p. 454.
11. P. Lundgreen (1981) *Sozialgeschichte der deutschen Schule im Überblick Vol. 2* (Göttigen: Vandenhoeck & Ruprecht), p. 11.
12. Giese, *Quellen*, p. 240.
13. F.K. Schnell (1850) *Wie sind mutwillige Schulversäumnisse zu verhüten, unvermeidliche aber möglichst unschädlich zu machen?* (Berlin).
14. Drewek and Tenorth, 'Das deutsche Bildungswesen im 19. Und 20. Jahrhundert, p. 53; F.-M. Kuhlemann (1992) *Modernisierung und Disziplinierung. Sozialgeschichte des preußischen Volksschulwesens 1794–1872* (Göttingen: Vandenhoeck & Ruprecht), p. 108.
15. Cited in Kuhlemann, *Modernisierung*, p. 109.
16. Ibid.
17. The 'Schwabenkinder', so-called, were the children of farmers from Vorarlberg, Tirol, Südtirol and Switzerland, who hiked every year in spring to the 'childrens-markets' at Oberschwaben to offer their labour to the farmers there each season.
18. Kuhlemann, *Modernisierung*, p. 115.
19. Ibid., p. 117.
20. Wenzel Holek (1909) *Lebensgang eines deutsch-tschechischen Handarbeiters* (Jena: Diederichs Verlag), p. 43.
21. Ibid., p. 47.
22. Ibid., p. 72.
23. Berg, C. (1977) 'Volksschule im Abseits von "Industrialisierung" und "Fortschritt"' in K. Herrmann (ed.), *Schule und Gesellschaft im 19. Jahrhundert* (Weinheim: Beltz), pp. 243–64, at p. 251.
24. A. Popp (1991) *Jugend einer Arbeiterin* (Bonn: Verlag J.H.W. Dietz) [following the edition of 1921], p. 29.
25. Ibid., p. 33.
26. Ibid., p. 35.
27. M. Klewitz (1981) 'Preußische Volksschule vor 1914. Zur regionalen Aufwertung der Schulstatistik', *Zeitschrift für Pädagogik* , 27, 551–73, p. 552.
28. Kay, *Social Condition*, Vol. II, p. 297.
29. C. Zuckmayer (1966) *Als wär's ein Stück von mir. Horen der Freundschaft* (Hamburg: Fischer), p. 167.

30. H. Schulz (1911) *Die Schulreform der Sozialdemokratie* (Berlin: Kaden Compagnie), p. 14.
31. O. Rühle (1903) *Die Volksschule wie sie ist* (Berlin), p. 5.
32. Budde, G. (2003) 'Familienvertrauen-Selbstvertrauen-Gesellschaftsvertrauen. Pädagogische Ideale und Praxis im 19. Jahrhundert' in Ute Frevert (ed.) *Vertrauen. Historische Annäherungen* (Göttingen: Vandenhoeck & Ruprecht), pp. 152–84, at p. 164.
33. G. Bäumer (1933) *Lebensweg durch eine Zeitenwende*, 6th edn (Tübingen: Reiner Wunderlich Verlag), p. 27.
34. Ibid., p. 28.
35. E. von Hippel (1975) *Meine Kindheit im kaiserlichen Deutschland* (Meisenheim am Glan: Verlay Anton Hahn), p. 19.
36. F. Rehbein (1911) *Das Leben eines Landarbeiter* (Jena: Eugen Diederichs Verlag), p. 27.
37. Kocka, J. (1979) 'Stand-Klasse-Organisation. Strukturen sozialer Ungleichheit in Deutschland vom späten 18. bis zum frühen 20. Jahrhundert im Aufriß' in H.-U. Wehler (ed.) *Klassen in der europäischen Sozialgeschichte* (Göttingen: Vandenhoeck & Ruprecht), p. 137–65, at p. 153.
38. H. Becker and G. Kluchert (1993) *Die Bildung der Nation. Schule, Gesellschaft und Politik vom Kaiserreich zur Weimarer Republik* (Stuttgart: Klett-Cotta), p.13.
39. G. Kluchert (2007) 'Schule der Einheit? Die Einführung der für alle gemeinsamen Grundschule in der Weimarer Republik' in *Recht der Jugend und des Bildungswesens. Zeitschrift für Schule, Berufsbildung und Jugenderziehung*, 55/3, 306–16.
40. Ibid., p. 307.
41. Cited ibid.
42. Cited ibid., p. 311.
43. Liebknecht, W. (1979) 'Wissen ist Macht – Macht ist Wissen. Festrede gehalten zum Stiftungsfest des Dresdner Arbeiter-Bildungs-Vereins am 5. Februar 1872' in L. Fertig (ed.) *Die Volksschule des Obrigkeitsstaates und ihre Kritiker* (Darmstadt: Wissenschaftliche Buchgesellschaft), pp. 123–59, at p. 158.
44. Wehler, *Deutsche Gesellschaftsgeschichte*, Vol. 4, p. 454.
45. Kluchert, 'Schule der Einheit', p. 315.
46. Lundgreen, *Sozialgeschichte*, Vol. II, p. 105.
47. Kluchert, 'Schule der Einheit', p. 310.
48. Christoph Sturm (2006) '"Wer die Schule besitzt, der besitzt die Herrschaft über die Zukunft und über die Welt" – Die Auseinandersetzung um die katholischen Elementarschulen in Münster während des Kulturkampfes (1872–1888)', *Westfälische Forschungen*, 56, 187–212, at p. 188.
49. Becker and Kluchert, *Bildung der Nation*, pp. 32–3.
50. Cf. Sturm, 'Wer die Schule besitzt', p. 195.
51. Ibid., p. 199.
52. Ibid., p. 201.
53. Becker and Kluchert, *Bildung der Nation*, p. 164.
54. Wehler, *Deutsche Gesellschaftsgeschichte*, Vol. 4, p. 452.
55. H. Mann (2008) *Der Untertan* (Frankfurt on Main: S. Fischer), p. 8.
56. Paulsen, F. (1912) 'Schuljammer und Jugend von heute' in F. Paulsen, *Gesammelte Pädagogische Abhandlungen*, ed. E. Spranger (Stuttgart and Berlin: J. G. Cotta), p. 471.
57. Rühle, *Volksschule*, p. 30.
58. Cited in H. John (1981) *Das Reserveoffizierskorps im Deutschen Kaiserreich 1890–1914. Ein sozialgeschichtlicher Beitrag zur Untersuchung der gesellschaftlichen Militarisierung im Wilhelminischen Deutschland* (Frankfurt on Main: Campus), p. 331.
59. Wehler, *Deutsche Gesellschaftsgeschichte*, Vol. 3, p. 1198.
60. I. Hansen-Schaber (1999) 'Vom Kaiserreich zur Weimarer Republik. Alltag von Lehrerinnen und Lehrern der Volksschule im historischen Wandel' *Pädagogik*, 51/6, 25–9.

61. J. Loreck (1977) *Wie man früher Sozialdemokrat wurde. Das Kommunikationsverhalten in der deutschen Arbeiterbewegung und die Konzeption der sozialistischen Parteipublizistik durch August Bebel* (Bonn and Bad-Godesberg: Verlag Neue Gesellschaft), p. 133.
62. Popp, *Jugend*, p. 34.
63. Ibid., p. 169.
64. J. Kay (1846) *The Education of the Poor in England and Europe. Vol. I* (London: J. Hatchard & sons), p. 236.
65. Cited in Hansen-Schaberg (1999) 'Alltag von Lehrerinnen und Lehren', p. 28.
66. Though this happened less in the schools than has long been assumed, as demonstrated in the recent dissertation by Carolyn Grone, 'Schulen der Nation? 1914' accessible at http://ebookbrowse.com/02-carolyn-grone-doktorarbeit-pdf-d46637857
67. Bölling, R. (1989) 'Elementarschullehrer zwischen Diziplinierung und Emanzipation. Aspekte eines internationalen Vergleichs (1870–1940)' in K.-E. Jeismann (ed.) *Bildung, Staat, Gesellschaft im 19. Jahrhundert. Mobilisierung und Disziplinierung* (Stuttgart: Franz Steiner Verlag), pp. 326–42, at p. 340.
68. Cited in B. Michael and H.-H. Schepp (eds.) (1993) *Die Schule in Staat und Gesellschaft. Dokumente zur deutschen Schulgeschichte im 19. und 20. Jahrhundert* (Göttingen and Zurich: Muster-Schmidt), pp. 184–6, at p. 184.
69. M. Th. W. Bromme (1905) *Lebensgeschichte eines modernen Fabrikarbeiters* (Jena: Diederichs Verlag), p. 60.
70. Cited by Loreck, *Wie man früher Sozialdemokrat wurde*, p. 134–5.
71. M. Wölk (1980) *Der preußische Volksschulabsolvent als Reichstagswähler 1871–1912. Ein Beitrag zur Historischen v in Deutschland* (Berlin: Colloquium Verlag), pp. 448–9.
72. Wehler, *Deutsche Gesellschaftsgeschichte*, Vol. 3, p. 1197.
73. Cited in Giese, *Quellen*, p. 232.
74. Cited in Becker and Kluchert, *Bildung der Nation*, p. 235.
75. Ibid., p. 141.
76. Ibid., pp. 397–8.
77. Cited in J. B. Kissling (1911) *Geschichte des Kulturkampfes im Deutschen Reich*, vol. 1 (Freiburg: Herder), p. 326.

5

'Schools Are Society's Salvation': The State and Mass Education in France, 1870–1930

Jean-François Chanet

At the beginning of the 1870s, there was undoubtedly no country in which politicians and scholars had a greater tendency to overestimate the influence of education on the evolution of society than France. There were three main reasons for this. The first was that France regarded itself as the birthplace of the Enlightenment and the 1789 Revolution. As Condorcet declared to the Legislative Assembly in 1792, the liberal and legally egalitarian nature of that revolution imposed on the state a duty to constitute the education of the people as a public service. The fact that the industrial revolution began at the same time as demands for democracy were making themselves felt only made this duty all the more pressing. Victor Hugo paid particular attention to it in the chapter of *Les Misérables* in which the author acts as the physiologist of the 'Paris urchin': for him, a childhood of deprivation and destitution was 'a disease that must be cured by light'.[1] This idea was widely shared in nineteenth-century Europe. Charles Dickens expressed it with as much force as humour in 1852, when he was campaigning for the *ragged schools despite their inadequacies:

> The compulsory industrial education of neglected children, and the severe punishment of neglectful and unnatural parents, are reforms to which must come, doubt it who may. We can no more hope to make any great impression upon crime, without these changes, than we could hope to extinguish Mount Vesuvius, in eruption, with a watering-pot, or stop its flow of lava with a knitting-needle.[2]

However, the logical connection between this question and the more general role of political institutions explains why the rapid succession of regimes and their instability ensured that only partial progress was achieved; in France more than elsewhere this was likely only to fuel debate rather than put an end to it.

Soon after the second Restoration (1815), Louis XVIII had recognised that both urban and rural areas of his kingdom were lacking 'a very large number of schools'.[3] However, his edict of 29 February 1816 merely gave the appearance of breaking with the Napoleonic state's habit of offloading responsibility for primary education on to local government. Under the July Monarchy (Louis-Philippe, 1830–1848), the notion – still a bourgeois one – that individual merit had become 'the main driving force and the primary condition for success in life'[4] was given political expression by *Guizot, Minister for Education. Merit, a personal quality that could be positioned initially on a moral scale of values and was inseparable from 'ability', now emerged as a principle of social hierarchy. The protestant Guizot was convinced that, in order to put an end to the cycle of revolutions, Catholicism had to be reconciled with the new France. However, he faced a double difficulty. The first was to distinguish between the Church and Christian faith more broadly in order to base a shared morality on religion. The second was to reconcile the respective rights of fathers and of the state in a country in which individuals were declared to be equal before the law and in which, in accordance with the Concordat of 1801, the new constitutional Charter recognised Catholicism as the majority religion. The success of the law of 28 June 1833, which placed an obligation on each commune to maintain a school and to ensure that education was free for poor children, cannot be denied: by 1847, there were 3,213 communes without a school, compared with 10,400 in 1832.[5] Nevertheless, the left-wing opposition could not declare itself satisfied because of the inadequate resources the state made available and the space it left for the Church.

The rapid fall of the Second Republic (1848–1852) convinced its supporters that universal suffrage, a necessary but not sufficient condition for democratic stability, had to be supplemented by state education. Such thinking was also not alien to the leaders of the Second Empire (1852–1870), since Louis-Napoléon Bonaparte claimed the legitimacy of the return to a dynastic regime would be ultimately secured by the reintroduction of universal suffrage. The policy adopted by his Minister for Education Victor Duruy arose out of a rational analysis of the institutional liberalisation that got underway in 1860, after the Italian war of 1859. In addition to the law of 29 March 1867, which compelled communes with more than 500 inhabitants to set up a state school for girls,[6] mention must also be made of the extension of free schooling and the establishment of adult classes and of school libraries. Thanks to these initiatives, by the time free and mandatory elementary education was finally established during the Third Republic (1870–1940) under the Lois Ferry of 1881 and 1882, the proportion of French people able to read had increased by 20 per cent. This was as great an increase as that achieved in the 20 years during which the *Jules Ferry Acts were in force.[7] As François Furet and Jacques Ozouf have already shown, on the eve of the adoption of these laws, the battle for schooling could be 'regarded as won'.[8]

If the work of *Jules Ferry, his collaborators and his successors in the field of education was regarded by the French as one of the main achievements of the Third Republic, it was because it was intended not only to extend existing provision but also to endow the country with an education system able to contribute to its reconstruction after defeat in the Franco-Prussian war and the civil war into which Napoleon III had dragged it, and to re-establish national unity by separating state education from religion. This ambition illustrates the third reason for the overestimation of the education system's influence that we mentioned at the beginning: in addition to the ideological and social motives that had guided the previous regimes, there was now a third motive, a patriotic and spiritual one this time, which made the obligation on the state to become the people's educator ever more pressing.

'Schools are society's salvation' (Edouard Laboulaye)[9]

In 1871, in the immediate aftermath of what the French call 'our disasters' (the defeat by Prussia and the resulting civil war), two institutions took on a particular significance in the debates and thinking about the country's future; they were the education system and the army. The connection between the two was all the more widely accepted at the time because the French were accustomed to seeing the latter filling the gaps in the former. Two million men are said to have attended the army's regimental schools between 1839 and 1863.[10] The author of an *Etude sur l'instruction scientifique et littéraire dans l'armée française*, published in 1870, went so far as to declare that 'the Ministry of War in France has done more for the education of men, particularly those in rural areas, than the Ministry of Public Education'.[11] Following the Battle of Sadowa in 1866 where Austria was defeated by Prussia, it had often been said that the victory was attributable primarily to Prussian primary school teachers.[12] This argument was accepted by citizens who in other respects held divergent opinions. Some, such as the republican Jean Macé, founder of the *Ligue de l'Enseignement (a pressure group for free and compulsory education) in this same year, 1866, were worried about the backwardness of mass education in France; others, including most of the members of the legislative body, became advocates for the cause because they balked at the imperial plan to reintroduce compulsory military service.

The defeat and the Commune of 1871 led to the reintroduction of conscription, which in turn gave new weight to the army as an instrument of education. As early as 1872, there was broad unanimity on the notion that the conscript army should henceforth be a citizenship training school.[13] There were three complementary reasons for this. Firstly, the principle of conscription had been re-established with so many exceptions that the burden of military service still fell disproportionately on the poor, and the poor were most in need of citizenship training. Secondly, the fact that soldiers on active service were banned from standing for office or even voting seemed to be a safeguard against their meddling in politics. Thirdly, the army could be used in this role relatively easily. Moving the structure of France's existing educational system in a 'republican' direction required time: it could only be done once the republicans had the parliamentary majorities required for the reforms they had planned to be adopted. Educational reform was the republicans' greatest concern, but they had to be patient because their approach to the education question was far from being generally accepted.

The republicans' aims were well-known: to rebuild the defeated and divided country, to fight the cause of universal suffrage, to provide primary education for all, and to extend primary education beyond the elementary school. That meant both taking responsibility for young children's schooling and developing a form of higher primary education originally sponsored by Guizot, the *école primaire supérieure, in which the best pupils could obtain the education required for intermediate-level jobs.[14] The republicans were also interested in making part of the national system the privately run *salles d'asile* (*dame schools or embryonic *écoles maternelles* that catered for the very young), which were set up from the 1830s as a place of refuge for the children of working-class women. These were now to become real schools, in which learning took place, even though it might be concealed in play, and in which children were led by the hand on the road to knowledge.[15] This set of objectives was a reflection of both principles and circumstances. Their openly declared patriotism could not be dissociated from more universal justifications. Schools were to teach the upcoming generations that 'for courageous men, the homeland is everywhere' and that France in aspiring to educate its colonial peoples was fulfilling a duty towards the indigenous populations that was comparable to that of the state towards children in metropolitan France, disfigured as the 'hexagon' was by the loss of Alsace-Lorraine.

The lack of consensus on this policy was due less to its stated ambitions than to its ideological presuppositions and the resources devoted to it. On 14 July 1872, the republican leader Gambetta had demanded 'a truly national education, that is an education that is compulsory for all'.[16] However, education that was free and compulsory and, above all, secular, was not acceptable to conservatives. For republicans, the aim was to dispense with a triple sophism. They proclaimed children's right to education, thereby restricting fathers' freedom. In response to those who thought, like the Minister for Education Falloux in 1849, that there could be no education without religion, they affirmed the right to freedom of thought and the need to separate morality from religion in order to strengthen both families and the national community. Finally, rather than continuing to restrict the benefit of free education to the poor and making those who could do so pay the appropriate price for education, they declared it was the state's duty to ensure equality of access to the public service of education.

While they treated the Catholic Church as an enemy, the republicans did not challenge freedom of education. It is important to understand that, in France, the distinction between public and private schools did not coincide with that between secular schools and church schools: in principle, lay teachers could teach in private schools and, conversely, nuns in public girls' schools. This was tantamount to agreeing to a contest in which the state was a latecomer. The Falloux Act of 1850 encouraged the rapid expansion of female religious orders, which, by the end of the Second Empire, were running the majority of both state and private schools. When the republicans came to power, the state made available the financial resources required to build schools in those communes too poor to find the necessary funds and in those municipalities where there was a lack of will, as well as teacher training colleges in the *départements* where the elite primary school teachers, both men and women, were to be trained. The 1886 *Goblet Act stipulated that all teaching staff in state schools should be secular, while that of 19 July 1889 made primary school teachers employees of the central state. Vigorously contested at every stage, this legislation was notable for its progressiveness. Historians have refuted the accusations of Masonic or 'Judeo-Protestant' plotting that came from the right. While the male congregational teachers were to be replaced by lay teachers within five years, the women were to be replaced as posts fell vacant. Jules Ferry, who was of the view that rural France had to be conquered if the Republic was to be consolidated, placed his faith in patience and the passage of time.[17] Similarly, neither he nor his successors challenged the separation of the education system into two orders, primary and secondary, however much it may have appeared to contradict the principles they espoused. What Stendhal called *'mérite pauvre'* ('weak merit')[18] was respected, sometimes even honoured, because the egalitarian legal foundation of French society demanded it rather than because it was recognised as an agent in the construction of the republican order. On the one hand, there were the people's schools and, on the other, the classical humanities; the former offering the symbolic endorsement of the *certificat d'études (school certificate) awarded to those who successfully completed their primary school education, the latter dedicated to preparing pupils for the *baccalaureate*, which alone provided access to higher education, the senior civil service and the liberal professions. The establishment of a 'higher' segment of primary education, crowned by the two écoles normales supérieures, Saint-Cloud for boys and Fontenay-aux-Roses for girls, did not remove the 'barrier' that the sociologist Edmond Goblot was to criticise in 1925,[19] but was accompanied rather by a rigorous 'inculcation of boundaries'.

The education system established during the Republic embodied and extended the revolution in teaching that had been taking place from the mid-nineteenth century onwards. Schoolmasters and mistresses were now expected to interact with pupils so that they had a chance to speak French. The silence rule that had formerly borne sway had been dictated by the need to maintain discipline in overcrowded classes. As André Chervel suggested, it 'is undoubtedly one of the reasons for the delay in the use of the French language in the provinces',[20] a delay that the Republic sought to make up for by stipulating in Article 14 of the standard set of rules for primary schools that: 'Only French will be used in schools'. From Mona Ozouf to Philippe Martel, all the historians who have been concerned with the fate of the regional languages have noted the absence of any reference to the language question in Jules Ferry's speeches and in those of his opponents.[21] This absence from a debate that was focused on the question of secularism confirmed the very real consensus that existed within the country on the importance of extending the use of French.[22] In such regions as Brittany, where rural children were both numerous and dispersed, the slow progress of French language can be explained less by the resilience of Breton than by the difficulty in getting children into school at all, whether secular or church schools.

When it came to drawing up the syllabuses, the subject that posed the greatest difficulty was not French but moral philosophy which took first place in the curriculum. For the republicans, 'moral and civic education' was to replace 'moral and religious education'.[23] Their moral education, which was unconnected with any religious dogma but not anti-religion, emphasised that life was necessarily hard but forbade physical violence, at least in theory. The message to be imparted was one of austerity but also of humility: pupils were to be taught that the secret of happiness was to be satisfied with one's lot, particularly since fortune was fickle, and that they should accept the risk of insecurity, provided it was not a consequence of sloth, 'the mother of all vices'. Arithmetical problems delineated the social topography of a country of landowners, shopkeepers, craftsmen and manual workers concerned with the sale of their wheat, their pieces of work or their profits. Geometry was introduced in Article 1 of the law of 28 March 1882, because schools were to impart practical knowledge to their pupils. All workers would need to be able to calculate an area or a volume. History and geography were also elevated to the rank of important subjects. History, above all national history, as hierarchised by *Ernest Lavisse, with an emphasis on promotion of the Gauls, rehabilitation of the good kings and gratitude for the Revolution, constituted the real 'schooling in patriotism' according to *Gabriel Compayré, who also added this piece of advice: 'In order to love one's country, begin by loving your native region. Observe the soil on which you live, its products and its riches. Ask yourself which great men were born in your village, your town or your province'.[24] The teaching of geography, which was inseparable from history, was expanded in imitation of the German conquerors. Incidentally, Ernest Lavisse left it up to his brother Emile to publish a handbook that made clear to schoolboys the objective of their studies: 'You will be a soldier'.[25] And what of the girls? On leaving school, they were to devote their lives above all to the proper upkeep of their homes and to ensuring that they were governed by the virtues of cleanliness, thrift and temperance inculcated in school with the support of or, if necessary, in opposition to their families. They were the guardians of order and incarnations of the most important of the patriotic virtues, namely finding personal fulfilment in sacrificing themselves for others; once they became mothers, they also emerged as agents of mobility, since it was the woman of the household, whether she was a mere manual worker or domestic help, who often turned out to harbour the greatest ambitions for her children.[26]

Social change and the separation of church and state in education

To look through the homework book of a schoolgirl from the Haute-Loire, a senior class pupil in the year 1896, is to understand how deep-rooted and culturally influential the republican education system was. Twenty-five years earlier, if she had gone to school at all, this same child would undoubtedly have been entrusted to the care of a *béate*, a sort of lay nun found in many of the villages of the Velay at that time, whose piety and skill as a lace maker made it easier to accept her low level of education. The exercise book, well looked after and kept within the family (the girl was the author's great-grandmother), was filled between 19 October 1896 and 16 January 1897 and then replaced by a second one, which lasted until the end of the year and the examination, the *certificat d'études*, that marked the end of Marie Lafont's schooling. 'Lexicological exercises' alternated in an ordered sequence with arithmetical problems, dictations alternated with essays and calligraphy alternated with drawing. This is the first sentence written with Marie's nib pen: 'A conscience without God is a court without a judge'. In these regions, which remained devout and where books in general took up little room, it was regarded as normal to have prayer books, school text books and books awarded as prizes all side by side on the same shelf at home.

Seen from Paris, however, the general situation in the primary schools was giving rise to renewed criticisms from their detractors and even some concerns on the part of their defenders. Although supporters of Dreyfus followed Zola in seeing school teachers as the 'shepherds of the lowly',[27] they were aware of how weak their influence was, given the short time that children spent in school. Furthermore, teacher recruitment was suffering from reforms that had made the training more demanding and abolished the exemption from military service, which young men had seen as a compensation for the low pay they received at the start of their careers. The toughness of the profession and, in some cases, that of the men employed in it, is confirmed by the persistence of corporal punishment, despite the fact it was outlawed by the state. In the *département* of Seine, for instance, when there was a complaint and an enquiry by an inspector, the pupils who had been beaten often acknowledged that they had behaved badly and accepted that 'the right to punish was shared by their fathers and their teachers', a sign of respect for the institution of the school. Thus there was a degree of tolerance, due to the circumstances in which these acts of brutality occurred. Teachers in the urbanising areas worked alone in overcrowded classes with poor discipline among pupils from humble backgrounds whose parents scarcely had time to look after them at home. Thus it was deemed acceptable that teachers demonstrated greater firmness towards those who committed infractions. Displacement of the culprit to another school was the commonest penalty. At the same time, inspectors and primary school principals often tried to dissuade parents from complaining to the authorities, because it would have suggested that the school administration was unable to enforce its own principles and regulations.[28]

The social profile of the Lyon schools was similar to that of the Parisian ones in terms of the share of working-class children, supplemented by the children of craft workers, clerical workers and shopkeepers. The attitudes of the working classes in these cities to the provision of schooling are more varied and complex than might be imagined, and were not simply determined by material constraints, religious loyalties or ideological convictions. At the beginning of the century in Lyon, whether in the old working-class districts such as la Croix Rousse or in more recent ones such as la Guillotière, more than a third of pupils spent less than a year and almost two-thirds less than three years in the same school. Thus it was the exception rather than the rule for children to complete their education from the age of 6 to 13 in the same school. The first explanation for this instability, the damaging effect of which on lessons and pupils' progress is not difficult to imagine, is certainly family mobility. However, it is not the only explanation. Account also has to be taken of those whom headmasters, who had little time for them, called 'school swappers', and who were usually regarded within the education system as an inevitable cohort of 'dunces' rather than a population whose failure at school had to be analysed and dealt with as a problem caused by the city's rapid economic and social change. Even families with modest means did not hesitate to change schools, even moving between the public and private sectors, in order to take advantage of social assistance or the existence of a canteen, or so that their children could benefit from allegedly better preparation for the *certificat d'études*. By their own standards and with the resources at their disposal, they were clearly turning compulsory schooling into a means of social advancement.[29]

Having been entrusted with the task of providing the nation's children with the means to become honest citizens, primary school teachers themselves had to restrict their own personal ambitions and give their all to securing the Republic. Even the great republican and wartime leader, Clemenceau, lamented the fact that they sometimes behaved as 'prophets dazzled by the new Word'.[30] However, we should be wary of generalisations. In rural areas, deference to the authorities was the norm. It was unwise to attract the prefect's attention, to displease the school inspectors or not to side with the mayor.[31] The village schoolmaster, Jean Coste, the eponymous hero of Antonin Lavergne's novel of 1903, lost the post of secretary to the town council, a valuable supplement to his salary, because he had campaigned against the outgoing mayor in the municipal elections.[32] However, the risks of commitment did not prevent the emergence of a militant avant-garde who managed to establish a 'trade union culture'[33] that the government was at pains to channel. The need for solidarity among individuals who often experienced strong feelings of isolation, particularly at the beginning of their careers, was a factor in the establishment of the National Federation of Primary Schoolteachers' Associations of France and the Colonies, whose founding conference was held in Bordeaux in 1901 and whose permanent statutes were adopted in 1906 and then revised in 1911.

This need for support was due in no small part to the intensity of the 'education war' from the early 1880s that had been revived by the anticlerical policy of the Coalition of the Left and the Church's reaction to it. The prime minister, Émile Combes, did not confine himself to using the Act of 29 July 1901, on the right of association, as a weapon against the religious orders, whose request for the authorisation they were obliged to seek he refused. In 1902, he ordered any crucifixes remaining in state schools to be removed and suspended the salaries of any priests who taught the catechism in Breton.[34] The Act of 7 July 1904 excluded the religious orders from involvement in the education system altogether and paved the way for the legislation on the separation of church and state, which was passed on 5 December 1905. The dissolution of the teaching religious orders had given rise to very different opinions within the Church and revealed that it had a remarkable capacity for adaptation.[35] Although the legislation was not to be implemented in full for 10 years, the Church did not wait so long to acknowledge the need to sacrifice the religious orders: in 1902, almost all teachers in Catholic schools were members of religious orders; by 1905, they were all lay people, or nearly so. For the Church, the key was to defend Christian schools that had been secularised and were now described as 'free' (i.e. free from state control and privately funded by the church and parental fees). The supervision and management of the schools were transferred to the lay clergy, under the authority of the bishops, whose position was strengthened by Rome's intransigence in the period immediately after the separation. Two years after the publication of the *Pascendi* encyclical condemning modernism, the cardinals, archbishops and bishops of France published a collective letter on 14 September 1909, in which they expressed their disapproval of 14 moral and civic education textbooks then being used in state schools. This letter triggered the second 'textbook war', following the one initiated by the Sacred Congregation of the Index when it had published, in January 1883, a decree condemning the moral textbooks written by Gabriel Compayré, the zoologist Paul Bert, the Inspector General and protestant Jules Steeg and a Mrs. Gréville. As in 1883, the resources mobilised in the ensuing struggle reflected the influence of the community-based organisations that still flourished in rural areas; this time, however, they were further strengthened by the contribution of 'powerful formal organisations'. As a result, the movement turned out to be more strongly polarised. Yves Déloye has identified three categories of *départements*. The first group consisted of those in which the clergy's determination inspired the population to vigorous resistance. They were about 20 in number and can be divided into four regional subgroups: Brittany, Normandy and the Vendée in the West, Nord-Pas-de-Calais, part of Eastern France (Jura, Haute-Marne, Haute-Saône and Vosges) and, finally, the Northern Alps, extending into the Ardèche (the only other *département* of this type in the Massif Central was the Corrèze). On the other hand, from Picardy to the Charente and the Auvergne and throughout the whole of the Mediterranean region, with the exception of Gard and the Eastern Pyrenees, some 30 *départements* in all, people remained largely unmoved by the whole affair. In all the other *départements*, there were only isolated incidents. However, the scarcity of these incidents did not prevent the state schools losing pupils to the 'free' schools. This was the case in the Lower Loire, although to a lesser extent than in the Morbihan or the Côtes-du-Nord, where the reduction in pupil numbers between 1909 and 1913 was between 5 and 9 per cent depending on the precise time and locality, while enrolment in the 'free' schools increased by between 15 and 29 per cent.[36]

While it was capable of stirring people into action and inspiring portrayals as evocative as *La guerre des boutons* (1912) by the secular primary school teacher Louis Pergaud,[37] the notion of the 'two Frances' was a theme whose meaning was mythical rather than historical. The pope's intransigence was far from being shared by the vast majority of Catholics. The rivalry between schoolmasters and priests, which Marcel Pagnol was able to invest with a certain folksy charm in the 1950s,[38] should not conceal the fact that, for the majority of French people, the two types of schooling were, with the exception of a few moments of crisis, complementary rather than incompatible. On rereading the autobiographies of schoolmasters of the Belle Époque collected by Jacques Ozouf, Philippe Boutry discerns in them the characteristics of a 'spiritual power'.[39] 'Just as the priest embodies something of the divine', suggests François Dubet, 'so the schoolmaster embodies something of the Republic, of Reason and of high culture'.[40] It was this sharing of roles that enabled the spiritual division within families to be rendered more harmonious and peaceful. In *Les beaux quartiers* (1936) by Louis Aragon, Armand Barbentane, who is enrolled in a secular school because of the radical opinions espoused by his father, a doctor, says the rosary under the table, using 'a small rosary of amethysts that his mother had brought back from Fourvières'.[41]

In fact, families' expectations of their children's schools were very similar, regardless of whether they attended secular or denominational schools. In both cases, the school culture attached great importance to the learning of French. It was based on exercises that had become, so to speak, canonical; these included practical criticism, dictation and recitation. And indeed, children learned to recite but not really to speak, just as they learnt to read in order to learn rather than to acquire a taste for reading.[42] Thus the academic authorities observed that school and public libraries were little used. This failure to encourage the reading of 'good books' gave rise to much criticism of the newspapers and songs that chimed more with popular tastes; this was another thing the church and the schools had in common. The 'good books' par excellence were those awarded to the most deserving pupils at the prize-giving ceremonies that brought the school year to a solemn close. But did they have the same value for parents as the savings bank passbooks promised to those who performed most brilliantly in the *certificat d'études*? In his last essay, in the summer of 1914, the poet and essayist and socialist turned Catholic, Charles Péguy, who perceived more clearly than anyone the awkwardness of the school teachers' position, described these passbooks as 'a veritable bible for the modern world, a guarantee of the tranquillity of the modern world'.[43]

It was clearly the wish of its founders that the republican school system should educate parents through the agency of their children. As Alain Choppin has noted, the dividing line between schoolbooks and popularising books was not clearly defined, because 'the overlap between domestic use and school use was only belatedly – and perhaps never fully - eliminated for certain categories of books', such as reading books and collections of selected extracts.[44] This phenomenon was not restricted to France. In the United Kingdom, Ian Michael has also observed this difficulty in separating books written for specifically didactic purposes from those that seek to entertain while educating.[45] Similarly, *Il Viaggio per l'Italia di Giannettino* (1876) by Carlo Collodi, a book written for children, attained the status of a schoolbook, while *Le tour de la France par deux enfants* (1877) by G. Bruno, which was explicitly intended for use in school, was read at family gatherings as much as in classrooms.[46]

In France, however, the Dreyfus affair and the turn-of-the-century debates on the army gave the question of adult education particular importance. 'There is not a single French republican today who does not regard the education of adults as our democracy's most pressing need.' Thus began the book by the chief education officer Raphaël Périé entitled *L'école du citoyen. Histoire et morale à l'usage des cours d'adultes*, published in 1899 and which by 1913 was in its fourth edition. There were two reasons in particular why this new mission was added to the one that primary school teachers already had in respect of children: 'firstly, the needs of a Republican state, whose very existence is at risk if the people do not receive a strong civic education and, secondly, the excessively short duration of basic primary education, which ends at an age at which children are incapable of absorbing such education'.[47] In both urban and rural areas, primary education did indeed finish at an early age. The Act of 11 January 1910 set the minimum age for taking the *certificat d'études* as 12. In many families, once a child had reached this age and taken the examination, he or she left school. On the basis of a study of small industrial towns in the Doubs, Jacques Gavoille identified a type of early but abbreviated schooling that was similarly found in the largest cities.[48] Work on the land also continued to require a great deal of labour, which itself was becoming scarcer as a result of the rural exodus and this was the cause of high levels of absenteeism between spring and autumn.

The need to find a way of continuing the moral and civic instruction of boys between their leaving school and entering the army justified the commitment that the then Chief Inspector Edouard Petit gave to this cause. Here too, the rivalry and emulation between secular and Catholic militancy played a full part, and action was expected from the municipalities, since they could no longer confine themselves to merely providing premises and staff. However, the budgetary resources remained limited. The volume of resources determined in part the degree of enthusiasm displayed by school teachers accustomed to repeated calls on their goodwill and to the 'symbolic' bonuses they were awarded in recompense for their efforts. The solution favoured by the Ligue de l'Enseignement at its conference in Amiens in 1904 was to recommend the establishment of 'secular educational clubs'. For its part, the Libre Pensée (a republican association of freethinkers) sought to keep young adults on the right track by recruiting mainly in working-class areas, where school teachers were regarded as part of the intellectual elite. The Catholics followed similar strategies. The example of the people's universities espoused by the intellectuals who supported Dreyfus was taken up by Marc Sangnier, a tireless propagandist for popular Catholic education modelled on the church clubs for young people. He was one of those who had understood that, although it had been disrupted by the exodus of religious orders and the decline in the number of priestly vocations, the catechetical mission had to be extended to adolescents and adults, particularly in urban working-class milieux. And indeed, his campaign found a particular echo in the textile manufacturing centres of northern France.[49] For Jacqueline Lalouette, this was indicative of a 'paradox that was certainly one of the underlying reasons for the failure of this movement': although its philosophical aspirations made exhaustive learning desirable, its campaign tended rather to reflect 'the noisy bustle of the public place and the extreme simplifications of militancy'.[50]

The ultimate paradox of the pre-war period was that, faced with repeated attacks from right-wing nationalists, republican leaders, who theoretically eschewed violence, expected school teachers to encourage their pupils and former pupils

to take part in gymnastics and shooting practice, the sort of military preparation that was made all the more necessary by the shortening of the period of
military service to two years in 1905. There was even a provision that, from 1908
onwards, the Ministry for War could give its authorisation to associations of this
type whose usefulness and republican sincerity had been recognised; conversely,
the ministry could refuse to give such authorisation to Catholic associations.
At the same time, however, the authorities were concerned about the effects of
socialist propaganda and believed they could detect, in the early manifestations
of a trade union movement that was not yet authorised to speak its name, signs
of an increase in anti-militarism, or at the very least of a crisis of patriotism. In
reality, in the France of the 1910s, school teachers who organised gymnastics
clubs would have been on friendly terms with those who enthusiastically read the
pacifist articles of the socialist leader, Jean Jaurès, in the *Revue de l'enseignement
primaire*. On the other hand, those who helped to preserve in their localities the
memory of the 'lost provinces' of Alsace and Lorraine were no less representative
than those who considered it necessary to affirm universal fraternity.[51] None of
them, assuredly would have declared themselves anti-patriotic. In August 1914,
the conditions under which France had to mobilise were to show how similar
the contributions of the two types of schooling had in fact been to the reconstruction of French patriotism. Both had contributed to what we will call, to use
Mona Ozouf's expression, a 'transfer of sacredness'[52] to the benefit of the mother
country, without which the 'Sacred Union',[53] the united front presented by the
French against the enemy, and the war effort would undoubtedly have been much
weaker.

The 'Sacred Union' and the wounds of war

'No other sentiment is any longer a match for it':[54] such was the opinion expressed
in 1901 on the subject of 'love of the mother country' by the sociologist Célestin
Bouglé, who was to exert great influence in the world of education after the war.
In view of the role that it had played in strengthening this sentiment from the
1870s onwards, the education system was to be called on to mobilise on two
fronts at the start of the new school year in 1914. The military mobilisation
affected a quarter of male school teachers. The vast majority of them were to
serve as non-commissioned officers, and it is well known that the new face of
war was to make these subaltern ranks very important. The symbol of the soldier
becoming a teacher responsible for giving the 'first class' in French in a village
in reconquered Alsace was disseminated very rapidly, in memory of the success
of Alphonse Daudet's story, *La dernière class*, after the annexation of 1871.[55] Thus
the military mobilisation could not be dissociated from the other one taking
place on the home front. This one concerned women teachers, some of whom,
unable to vote but often better educated than elected municipal councillors,
were to take over the post of secretary to their town councils, as well as retired
teachers and the pupil-teachers in the teacher training colleges, who were called
on to replace those who had enlisted. The request made by the minister, Albert

Sarraut, that school teachers should act as the chroniclers of war in their communes demonstrated the trust the state had in them.[56] They took part en masse in many different tasks made necessary by the war, whether it was collecting money and linen, helping with work in the fields, helping families with allowances or pensions or sending parcels to soldiers or to prisoners. They also gave up 2 per cent of their monthly salaries to help fund national assistance and welfare organisations. Those who claimed to shape opinion, and even those of them who had been the harshest critics of the secular school system before the war, did not hesitate to acknowledge, with Ferdinand Buisson, former national director of primary education, 'what reserves of absolute patriotism had been accumulating within these schools, which have sometimes been suspected of having rather sacrificed love of the mother country for love of humanity in general'.[57] In truth, French patriotism claimed to reconcile these two loves. School children had repeatedly been told in the pre-war period that 'all men have two homelands, their own and France'. For primary school teachers, to make sense of the war was, firstly, to justify the defence of French soil and the struggle against an invader. Teachers promptly denounced the atrocities committed when Belgian neutrality was violated and constantly reminded their pupils that the French were fighting for the rule of law and democracy.

Olivier Loubes has carried out a balanced analysis of this 'ambivalence of wartime patriotism' in French schools. He cites the exercise book of a schoolboy in the Eure, a war orphan, whose teacher had made him copy out in his best handwriting on 25 March 1918 the sentence: 'Always have a hatred for the Germans', but who had previously written in a civic education essay on the army on the 31 January: 'war is a great misfortune, so we should not wage war'.[58] We should be mindful here of the time and place of the war. The longer the war went on, the more important mourning became; it inspired hatred of the enemy, undoubtedly, but even more of the war itself. It also encouraged a reversion to old habits, including absenteeism. 'Everything is an excuse for missing class', complained the schools inspector in the Allier in his report for the year 1917–18; in this case, attendance had been about 20 per cent better before the war.[59] Many of his colleagues echoed this complaint, and not just with regard to rural schools. It is significant that in the departments they occupied the Germans ensured that compulsory schooling was enforced.

All the subjects taught reflected and helped to sustain the war culture: in moral education, pupils celebrated over and over again the beauty of individual effacement for the sake of the collective good; in history, greater efforts than ever before were made to explain the present in terms of the past; in geography, teaching focused above all on the regions that were the theatre of military operations and on the countries fighting the war; in French, pupils recited patriotic poems, particularly Victor Hugo's 'Hymne' of 1831, whose opening line, *'Ceux qui pieusement sont morts pour la patrie'*, was to inspire the parodic opening line of Jacques Prévert's *'Tentative de description d'un dîner de têtes à Paris-France'*, written a hundred years later.[60] And many of the texts used for dictation and the subjects for essays were also connected in some way with war. In arithmetic, pupils could learn, as the chief education officer for the Doubs recommended in 1916, to 'assess the value of all the savings that could be made in the most modest homes'.[61] Conversely, the war helped soldiers to become much more aware of the true value of education. The social mixing that took place in the trenches meant there were many more opportunities for them to feel ashamed of their ignorance, and in particular to regret that they were unable to express their thoughts 'in good French' when they were writing to their loved ones. On these occasions, they envied those who had mastered the style of primary school essays, that exercise which, in the same way as Latin unseen translation for grammar school pupils, helped to familiarise 'the whole of the French population with certain ways of writing and certain stylish turns of phrase that might be regarded as the expression of educated speech'.[62]

Thus the victory of 1918 was also a victory for the education system. It enabled it to find a new equilibrium. From 1919 onwards, women, who had since 1906 accounted for the majority of teachers in state primary schools if the staff of the *écoles maternelles* are included (60,700 compared with 56,109 men), were paid the same salaries as their male colleagues and the pay for both sexes was raised above the level paid before the war. The Roustan Act of 30 December 1921 facilitated access for married couples to 'dual posts' as primary school teachers, which enabled them to establish their influence in towns and villages. In 1924, the government supported by the *Cartel des gauches* (Coalition of the Left) gave state employees the right to join a trade union. From then on, female primary school teachers, who were still excluded from universal suffrage, as indeed were all women, gained the right to vote and were eligible to stand for election to the board of public education in each *département*. The needs of the reconstruction process also attracted attention to a sector, that of vocational training, in which the Ministry of Public Education had long struggled to gain acceptance for its point of view. The Astier Act of 25 July 1919 laid the groundwork for a unified vocational education for apprentices and instituted continuing education courses for workers. After the lengthy debates of the pre-war period and the experiences of wartime, the state took responsibility for a part of education that had previously been left to private initiative, in many cases to employers and in others to municipalities. Greater attention too was paid to practical education in the elementary school. The 1923 syllabuses for elementary primary education made official the combination of three disciplines, mathematics, art and manual work, that had been current since 1909 in higher primary education.[63]

And yet, the dominant impression in the 1920s was that the 'republican model' of education was running out of steam. This change first became apparent in the early 1920s. The price of victory had been so high that primary school teachers, very much aware of the praise heaped on them by those who gave them some of the credit for having made it possible, were also aware of the criticism that they bore part of the blame for the 'brainwashing' that had taken place. Thus there was deep ambivalence within the profession: not only were teachers having to deal with the impossibility of returning to the patriotic ways of before the war but they had also been given a new role as 'guardians of the memory'. Each year on 11 November, they had to take their pupils to the war memorial in their commune.

But what meaning could they give to the commemoration? A ministerial circular issued in 1920 required particular homage to be paid to primary school teachers who had been killed in action (almost a quarter of those who had enlisted, approximately 8,000 out of 35,000)[64] and recommended that, for each of them, a marble plaque and portrait should be affixed to the memorial as an appropriate means of cultivating 'the truly intimate and familial aspects of the cult of memory'. For the survivors, widows and successors, however, the memory of war inspired above all a feeling of the futility of so many sacrifices.

This in turn led to the development of pacifism among school teachers, who were inclined to declare 'war on war' and, as André Delmas, general secretary of their national trade union from 1932 to 1940, related, 'to mandate their leaders to work without flinching and on all levels to prevent its recurrence'.[65] As a result, they were to be found in prominent positions in ex-servicemen's associations.[66] In 1922, the question of 'warmongering textbooks' appeared on the agenda at the third international conference on moral education in Geneva and the following year saw the publication of the first volume of the survey conducted by the *Carnegie endowment on the same subject. It was also debated in France at the annual conferences of the national teachers trade union, particularly in Lyon in 1924, until campaigns to delist certain books were launched in the *départements*, where it was the job of teachers to draw up, at the cantonal pedagogic conferences and under the authority of the chief education officers, the list of textbooks to be used in schools in their districts. It is significant that the spread of pacifism was the driving force behind Georges Lapierre and Louis Dumas's 1927 plan to use their contacts with English and German colleagues to set up an international federation of schoolteachers' associations (FIAI). In the course of a meeting held at the Kroll Opera in Berlin during the Easter holidays of 1928, in front of an audience of 6,000, 'teachers from countries that were until recently enemies proclaimed that schools in all countries should take it upon themselves to develop the spirit of peace and to ensure the triumph of fraternity among all men'.[67]

The year of the Carnegie survey, 1923, also saw the reform of the organic laws governing primary education, as well of primary school syllabuses. In 1981, the authors of a book entitled *Cent ans d'école* – the anniversary being that of the Ferry Act of 16 June 1881 on free education – suggested that after the 'period of certainties' (1881–1923), this reform marked the beginning of 'the period of searching'.[68] And indeed, the continuity of curriculum content and teaching methods could not conceal the fact that questions were being asked at the institutional, pedagogical and moral levels. The first is summarised, as it were, in the commitment to the ambiguous notion of the *'école unique'* or 'single school', which could be taken to mean either the establishment of a monopoly for state education or the unification of elementary education through the merger of the 'people's schools' with the junior classes of the *lycées*, where the children of the middle classes received their primary education. The idea had been launched in the middle of the war by a group of teachers of all categories then serving in the armed forces that went under the name of the *Compagnons de l'Université nouvelle*. In 1920, they set out a clear objective, which seemed to be justified by the levelling effects of conditions at the front; it was 'to give all young children the same education under the direction of primary school teachers'.[69] But an institutional separation and social hierarchy between primary and secondary schools had developed, among teachers, a strong feeling of belonging to two distinct bodies: in the junior classes of the *lycées*, teachers were proud of belonging, so to speak, to the Latin empire – while the elementary school teachers remained attached to the primary world, without Latin. Thus, the opposition of secondary school teachers and the existence of two irreducible professional and trade union cultures prevented this reform from being achieved, although a 1925 decree authorised the appointment of primary school teachers to the junior classes of the *lycées* and a 1926 order brought these classes' syllabuses and timetables into line with those of the primary school.

The need to replace an education system based on orders or ranks with one based on stages was eventually to give rise to the idea that an intermediate level should be established between primary schools and *lycées*; this was the *collège*, and its introduction made it possible gradually to extend free secondary education from the sixth class (11- to 12-year-olds) to the third class (14- to 15-year-olds) from 1930 onwards.[70] However, although it was then free, the entry into the sixth class did not become automatic at the end of primary education. Every pupil had to pass an entrance exam, which was maintained until 1959. In 1945, still only 20 per cent of pupils gained access to secondary education by this route.

Pedagogic reform also remained limited. The question of whether or not to adapt syllabuses that were considered excessively heavy and academic to the realities of life and work, which was raised repeatedly, did not receive a comprehensive answer. The dread of rural depopulation caused the plan to introduce separate curricula for schools in urban areas to be abandoned, in the name of defending rural schools. And the most daring innovators, such as *Célestin Freinet, were eventually to be forced to stop pursuing their experiments and their careers within the state education system.[71] While teachers made greater use of pictures in their lessons, including cinematography, particularly in the 'people's lectures' that replaced the adult classes of former times, and while more of them took their pupils on class outings, the education system in general was hardly receptive to the childhood culture and sociability acquired outside of school, unless it was to make space during break time for games such as marbles or hopscotch, with their rules mysteriously handed down from generation to generation.

With regard to secularism, finally, the public school system was forced onto the defensive. The re-establishment of diplomatic relations between the French Republic and the Vatican in 1921 encouraged the cardinals and archbishops of France to renew their declaration of 'war on secularism and its principles until the iniquitous laws emanating from it have been abolished'.[72] In this they were aided by the *Davidée* movement, which had come into being in 1916 and whose name was taken from a novel by René Bazin, *Davidée Birot*, published in 1912.[73] Like the novel's heroine, a secular primary school teacher who had converted to Catholicism, its followers, who numbered 3,500 in 1925, sought to exert a Christian influence over their pupils and their colleagues. In 1924, on forming his government, Edouard Herriot declared his intention of implementing the law on the separation of church and state in the 'recovered territories of Alsace and Lorraine'. However, this plan met with such resistance in the territories that Herriot had to abandon it before the end of the year, which explains why even today the three departments in question remain subject to the Concordat that was in force in France before 1905. Times had certainly changed compared with the pre-war period, so much so that in 1929 the ceremony planned in honour of Ferdinand Buisson, who had been director of primary education in the Ministry of Public Education without a break from 1879 to 1896, was finally cancelled. The fiftieth anniversary of the Ferry Acts was celebrated two years later. The historian Georges Duveau, who witnessed the celebration organised for the occasion in Cahors, Gambetta's birthplace, remembered it as a sad event: schoolmasters who, in his eyes, had become 'saints without hope' listened to the 'emphatic yet scepti-cal' chief education officer 'as he reeled off a string of clichés'.[74]

In its imagination and its culture as much as in its politics, the France of 1930 remained a rural country governed from Paris. It was not until the 1931 census that the share of the population living in towns with more than 2,000 inhabit-ants just crept past the 50 per cent mark. Between innumerable villages and the 'City of Light', the seedbed of the small towns was characterised by a slow pace of life and a propensity to look backwards that was described by the historian Marc Bloch in *Strange Defeat*.[75] Primary schools naturally reflected the traditions and anxieties about its identity of a country that had paid too high a price for victory in 1918. The France of 1930 was also celebrating the centenary of its conquest of Algeria, where the republic had established in Bouzareah a teacher training col-lege on the metropolitan model offering three-year courses for the colonists and a training college offering one-year courses for the Algerians, thereby instituting a division laden with ambiguities. On the other hand, in France and in Indochina, the Colonial Exhibition of 1931 undoubtedly marked the beginning of the pro-cess of adapting schools to some extent to local realities.

The French secondary education system of this period is often described in terms of the contrast between two social types, the heir and the bursary holder, as analysed by Albert Thibaudet in a famous chapter of his 1924 essay, *La République des professeurs*,[76] and taken up by Pierre Bourdieu and Jean-Claude Passeron.[77] The plan to establish the *école unique* had its origins in a desire to dismantle the barrier between primary and secondary education, which only the best primary school pupils could cross, those who succeeded in the competition for grants to attend the *lycées* and *collèges* and who consequently risked being treated with contempt by the children of the bourgeoisie and being wrenched, like the young Albert Camus, 'from the warm and innocent world of the poor'.[78] However, this institu-tional and cultural duality could not simply be decreed away. The 'primaries' were proud of being what they were: they had with dignity appropriated an adjective that had been turned into a noun only in order to caricature them. The very num-ber of primary school teachers and the high level of trade union membership were to ensure that, after the Second World War, they wielded lasting influence in the National Education Federation. When all is said and done, society had itself agreed that its schools should be the instrument for a slow and gradual transformation of society. While they produced only a fictitious equality, the fiction at least was widely accepted in France and gave rise to a trust that the disenchantments of the inter-war period scarcely weakened.

Timeline

1833: Loi Guizot: every French commune has to maintain a school, which is free for the poor

1867: Communes with more than 500 inhabitants had to set up a school for girls

1881: Loi Ferry: free state elementary education for all established

1882: Loi Ferry: elementary education made compulsory and secular

1883: beginning of the first 'textbook war' after the Sacred Congregation of the Index condemned a number of classroom texts prepared for the Republic's schools

1886: Goblet Act: all teaching staff in state schools had to be members of the laity. The French regular orders were removed from the state classroom.

1901: founding conference of the National Federation of Primary Schoolteachers' Associations of France and the Colonies

1904: the Catholic religious orders were banned from teaching in all schools, public or private

1909: beginning of the second 'textbook war' after the French Catholic Church objected to a 14 moral and civic textbooks

1910: minimum age for taking the *certificat d'études* set at 12

1919: Astier Act: sets up a national system of vocational courses for apprentices and provides for continuing education courses for workers

1923: first steps taken towards ending the separation of elementary and secondary education

1926: syllabuses of the elementary schools and the junior classes of the *lycées* (which served the middle-classes) brought into line

Glossary

Certificat d'études: French elementary school leaving diploma in the Republican era.

Compayré, Jules Gabriel: French educationalist and politician (1843–1913); author of *Elements d'éducation civique* (1881) which was attacked by the Catholic Church.

dame schools: private schools run by old women from their homes in Victorian England where the poor could leave 2- to 5-year-olds while they went to work.

école primaire supérieure: French schools which offered a more developed curriculum than the ordinary elementary school but were not part of the secondary-school system. They chiefly gave courses in practical geometry, natural science, history and geography. Established by Guizot (q.v.) in 1833, they were finally abolished in 1941.

écoles maternelles: name gradually adopted for France's state sponsored nursery schools in the Republican era which replaced the earlier network of private *salles d'asile* or children's refuges.

Ferry, Jules: French republican politician (1832–1893). Responsible for the legislation that established compulsory, free and secular education in France in 1881 and 1882.

Freinet, Célestin: French pedagogue and educational reformer (1866–96); became an elementary teacher in Le Bar-sur-Loup in 1920 in where he developed his ideas about collaborative and hands-on learning. Author in 1946 of *L'Ecole moderne française.*

Guizot, François: French protestant politician and historian (1787–1874): in 1833 he oversaw legislation establishing a national system of elementary schools at the level of the commune (the lowest tier of local government).

Lavisse, Ernest: French historian (1842–1922); professor of history at the Sorbonne; director of the Paris Ecole Normale; author of classroom history textbooks and editor of the multi-volume *Histoire de France depuis les origines jusqu'à la Révolution* (1900–11).

Ligue de l'enseignement: French educational pressure group. Established in 1866 by Jean Macé it campaigned for free, compulsory and secular elementary education. At the turn of the twentieth century, it was particularly interested in strengthening civic republicanism through the development of youth organisations and the provision of continuing education.

lycées: French academic secondary schools usually for older teenagers, first established by Napoleon in 1802; a number of secondary schools were founded in other countries along the same lines and using the same name.

ragged schools: charitable schools in Victorian Britain set up to provide free education and other support for poor children in London and the big industrial cities. Their resources were pooled to form the Ragged Schools Union in 1844.

Revue de l'enseignement primaire et primaire supérieur: privately published weekly journal that ran from 1890 to 1929 and was read by a fifth of teachers in 1912. It played an important part in the campaign for teachers' unionisation and one of its frequent contributors was the socialist leader, Jean Jaurès.

Notes

1. V. Hugo (1863) *Les Miserables*, trans. C. E. Wilbour (New York: Carleton), III/i/10, 'Ecce Paris, ecce homo', p. 14.
2. C. Dickens (1963) 'Households Words: A Weekly Journal' in P. Collins *Dickens and Education* (London: Macmillan), p. 72.
3. Edict of 29 Feb. 1816.

4. F. Guizot (1860) *Mémoires pour servir à l'histoire de mon temps*, III (Paris: Michel Lévy frères), p. 12. See also P. Rosanvallon (1985) *Le moment Guizot* (Paris: Gallimard).
5. A. Prost (1979) *Histoire de l'enseignement en France, 1800–1967* (Paris: Armand Colin), p. 97.
6. The limit for this legal requirement was 800 inhabitants in the Falloux Act of 1850.
7. Plessis, A. (1997) 'Pouvait-on penser librement sous le Second Empire?' in J. Tulard (ed.) *Pourquoi réhabiliter le Second Empire ?* (Paris: Bernard Giovanangeli), p. 102.
8. F. Furet and J. Ozouf (1977) *Lire et écrire. L'alphabétisation des Français de Calvin à Jules Ferry*, vol. 1 (Paris: Les Éditions de Minuit), p. 172.
9. E. Laboulaye (1869) *Discours populaires* (Paris: Charpentier), p. 280. Laboulaye (1811–83) was a jurist, poet and author.
10. C. E. Bourdin (1868) *Recherches statistiques sur l'instruction primaire dans l'armée française* (Strasbourg).
11. D. Louis (1870) *Etude sur l'instruction scientifique et littéraire dans l'armée française* (Péronne), p. 19.
12. A. Claveau (1913) *Souvenirs politiques et parlementaires d'un témoin, I, 1865–1870* (Paris: Plon), p. 146.
13. A. Crépin (2009) *Histoire de la conscription* (Paris: Gallimard), p. 283. See also A. Forrest (2009) *The Legacy of the French Revolutionary Wars: the Nation-in-Arms in French Republican Memory* (Cambridge; New York: Cambridge University Press).
14. There were only 12 écoles primaires supérieures in 1870; their number then expanded radically and the number of students doubled in 20 years, from 24,200 to 55,900 between 1881 and 1901. F. Mayeur (1981) *De la Révolution à l'école républicaine*, vol. 3 of Louis-Henri Parias (ed.), *Histoire générale de l'enseignement et de l'éducation en France* (Paris: Nouvelle Librairie de France), p. 550.
15. J.-N. Luc (1997) *L'invention du jeune enfant au XIXe siècle. De la salle d'asile à l'école maternelle* (Paris: Belin), pp. 261–4. Between the late 1860s and the mid-1880s, the numbers of children enrolled in these schools increased from slightly fewer than 450,000 to almost 700,000. For an idea of how the republicans rebranded these schools, see (1885) *Journal de l'instruction primaire. Revue des examens. Devoirs d'élèves. Bulletin hebdomadaire des instituteurs et des institutrices...*, 15 Aug., pp. 7–8.
16. Gambetta, L. (1881) 'Discours', La Ferté-sous-Jouarre, 14 Jul. 1872 in J. Reinach (ed.) *Discours et plaidoyers politiques*, vol. II (Paris: G. Charpentier), p. 387.
17. M. Crubellier (1993) *L'école républicaine, 1870–1940* (Paris: Editions Christian), pp. 40–3.
18. Stendhal (1977) *Lucien Leuwen* [1834–1835] in H. Martineau (ed.) *Romans et nouvelles*, (Paris: Gallimard, Bibliothèque de la Pléiade), p. 1368.
19. E. Goblot (1925) *La barrière et le niveau. Étude sociologique sur la bourgeoisie française moderne* (Paris: F. Alcan).
20. A. Chervel (2008) *Histoire de l'enseignement du français du XVIIe au XXe siècle* (Paris: Retz), p. 399.
21. Ozouf, M.(1984) 'Jules Ferry et l'unité nationale' [1982] in id. (ed.), *L'École de la France. Essais sur la Révolution, l'utopie et l'enseignement* (Paris: Gallimard), pp. 407–8; P. Martel (2007) *L'école française et l'occitan. Le sourd et le bègue* (preface by R. Lafont, Montpellier: Presses universitaires de la Méditerranée).
22. J.-F. Chanet (1996) *L'École républicaine et les petites patries*, preface by M. Ozouf (Paris: Aubier).
23. J.-M. Mayeur (1997) *La question laïque, XIXe–XXe siècle* (Paris: Fayard), pp. 63–9.
24. G. Compayré (1880) *Eléments d'éducation civique et morale* (Paris: P. Garcet, Nisius & Co.), pp. 55–7, and id. (1890) *Organisation pédagogique et législation des écoles primaires (Pédagogie pratique & administration scolaire)* (Paris: Librairie classique Paul Delaplane), p. 109. See A.-M. Thiesse (1997) *Ils apprenaient la France. L'exaltation des régions dans le discours patriotique* (Paris: Ed. de la Maison des sciences de l'homme), pp. 15–34.

25. E. Lavisse (1887) *'Tu seras soldat', histoire d'un soldat français, récits et leçons patriotiques d'instruction et d'éducation militaires* (Paris: Armand Colin).
26. See A.-M. Sohn (1996) *Chrysalides : femmes dans la vie privée (XIXe–XXe siècles)* (2 vols., Paris: Publications de la Sorbonne).
27. E. Zola (1996) *Vérité* ed. C. Becker and V. Lavielle (Paris: Le Livre de Poche classique), p. 16.
28. See J. Krop (2008) 'Punitions corporelles et actes de brutalité dans les écoles primaires publiques du département de la Seine (1880-1914)', *Histoire de l'éducation*, 118, 109–32.
29. M. Thivend (2006) *L'école républicaine en ville: Lyon, 1870–1914* (Paris: Belin), pp. 133–44.
30. G. Clemenceau (1995) *Le grand Pan* [1896], ed. J.-N. Jeanneney (Paris: Imprimerie nationale), p. 212.
31. See Agulhon, M. (1984) 'La mairie' in P. Nora (ed.) *Les lieux de mémoire, I, La République* (Paris: Gallimard), p. 173.
32. A. Lavergne (1903) *Jean Coste ou l'Instituteur de village* (Paris: Paul Ollendorff), pp. 236–45.
33. J. Girault (1996) *Instituteurs, professeurs: une culture syndicale dans la société française, fin XIXe–XXe siècle* (Paris: Publications de la Sorbonne).
34. See F. Broudic (1997) *L'interdiction du breton en 1902. La IIIe République contre les langues régionales* (Spezet: Coop Breizh) and Chanet, *L'École républicaine*, pp. 209–10.
35. A. Lanfrey (2003) *Sécularisation, séparation et guerre scolaire. Les catholiques français et l'école (1901–1914)* (preface by Cardinal Jean Honoré, Paris: Cerf).
36. Y. Déloye (1994) *École et citoyenneté. L'individualisme républicaine de Jules Ferry à Vichy: controverses* (Paris: Presses de la FNSP), pp. 230–51.
37. L. Pergaud (1968) *The War of the Buttons*, trans. S. and E. Hochman (New York: Walker). The title of the novel refers to the fights between the pupils of two rival schools of the same village, the secular school and the Catholic one. The winners ripped out the losers' trouser buttons.
38. See M. Pagnol (1986) *My Father's Glory*, trans. R. Barisse (San Francisco: North Point Press). Originally 1957.
39. Boutry, P. (2009) 'L'instituteur comme pouvoir spirituel au village', in *Hommage à Jacques Ozouf*, Cahiers du Centre de recherches historiques, no. 43 (Paris: EHESS), pp. 77–92.
40. Dubet, F. (2003) 'Paradoxes et enjeux de l'école de masse', in O. Donnat and P. Tolila (eds) *Le(s) public(s) de la culture. Politiques publiques et équipements culturels* (Paris: Presses de Sciences Po), p. 36.
41. L. Aragon (2000) *Les beaux quartiers*, ed. under the direction of D. Bougnoux (Paris: Gallimard, Bibliothèque de la Pléiade), p. 85.
42. Chervel, *Histoire de l'enseignement*, pp. 499–504.
43. C. Péguy (1992) 'Note conjointe sur M. Descartes et la philosophie cartésienne', posthumous text (Jul. 1914), in id., *Œuvres en prose complètes*, ed. R. Burac, vol. III (Paris: Gallimard, Bibliothèque de la Pléiade), p. 1442.
44. A. Choppin (2008) 'Le manuel scolaire, une fausse évidence historique', *Histoire de l'éducation*, no. 117, p. 27.
45. I. Michael (1979) 'The Historical Study of English as a Subject: a Preliminary Inquiry into some Questions of Methods', *History of Education*, 8/3, 193–206, at p. 202.
46. C. Collodi (2006) *Il Viaggio per l'Italia di Giannettino*, 3 vols (*Italia superiore*, 1880; *Italia centrale*, 1883; *Italia meridionale*, 1886) (Bergamo: Leading edn); Fouillée, A. (pseudonym G. Bruno) (2006) *Le tour de la France par deux enfants. Devoir et patrie* [1877], in J.-P. Rioux (ed.) *Tableaux de la France* (Paris: Omnibus). See also D. Maingueneau (1979) *Les livres d'école de la République 1870–1914* (Paris: Le Sycomore); Ozouf, M. and J. (1984) 'Le tour de la France par deux enfants: le petit livre rouge de la République', in Nora, *Les lieux de mémoire*, pp. 291–321; J. Strachan (2004) 'Romance, Religion and the Republic: Bruno's *Le tour de la France par deux enfants*', *French History*, 18/1, 96–118;

Pazzaglia, L. (2007) 'I libri di testo: il caso del *Giannetto* di Parravicini' in P. L. Ballini and G. Pécout (eds), *Scuola e nazione in Italia e Francia nell'Ottocento. Modelli, pratiche, eredità. Nuovi percorsi di ricerca comparata* (Venezia: Istituto Veneto di Scienze, Lettere ed Arti), pp. 141–88; P. Cabanel (2007) *Le tour de la nation par des enfants: romans scolaires et espaces nationaux, XIXe–XXe siècles* (Paris: Belin).

47. R. Périé (1913) *L'école du citoyen. Histoire et morale à l'usage des cours d'adultes* (Paris: Gedalge), p. viii.
48. J. Gavoille (1981) *L'école publique dans le département du Doubs, 1870–1914* (Paris: Les Belles Lettres), p. 54.
49. See for example (1904) 'Un banquet populaire présidé par Marc Sangnier, M. l'abbé Lemire, M. Eug. Duthoit' in *L'Effort* (bulletin mensuel de la Fédération de la Jeunesse catholique de Roubaix), 15 Mar., p. 191.
50. J. Lalouette (1997) *La libre pensée en France 1848–1940* (Paris: Albin Michel), p. 102.
51. J.-F. Chanet (2001) 'Pour la Patrie, par l'École ou par l'Épée? L'école face au tournant nationaliste', *Mil neuf cent. Revue d'histoire intellectuelle*, 19, 127–44.
52. M. Ozouf (1976) *La fête révolutionnaire 1789–1799* (Paris: Gallimard), pp. 317–40.
53. In his message to the French Parliament of 4 Aug. 1914, President Raymond Poincaré said France would be 'heroically defended by all her sons whose Sacred Union, facing the enemy, shall never be broken'.
54. Bouglé, C. (1901) 'Patrie' in M. Berthelot et al. (eds) *La Grande Encyclopédie*, vol. 26 (Tours: E. Arrault & Co.), p. 99.
55. As early as August 1914, a small part of Southern Alsace was conquered and placed under military administration. 89 French schools were open. Teaching staff consisted of 113 women including 90 congregational teachers and 99 men including 65 soldiers. J. Senger and P. Barret (1948) *Le problème scolaire en Alsace et en Lorraine* (Paris: Temps Futur), p. 65. For the 'first class', see A. Balz (1914) 'La Restauration du Français en Alsace' and 'Revue de la Presse. La Première Classe en français', *Manuel général de l'instruction primaire*, 5 Dec., pp. 88 and 94. For the Daudet story, see A. Daudet (1930) 'La dernière classe. Récit d'un petit Alsacien' [*Contes du lundi*, 1873], in *Œuvres complètes illustrées*, vol. 1 (Paris: Librairie de France), pp. 1–7.
56. Circular of the Minister of Education Albert Sarraut, 18 Sept. 1914. See J.-J. Becker (1977) *1914. Comment les Français sont entrés dans la guerre* (Paris: Presses de la FNSP), p. 262.
57. Buisson, F. (1915) preface to A. Moulet *L'École primaire et l'Éducation morale patriotique* (Paris: Hachette), p. viii.
58. O. Loubes (2001) *L'école et la patrie. Histoire d'un désenchantement, 1914–1940* (Paris: Belin), p. 38.
59. Report of the chief education officer (*inspecteur d'académie*) of the Allier on the situation of primary education in the *département* during the year 1917, Moulins, 10 Aug. 1918, p. 145.
60. V. Hugo (1835) 'Hymne' 1831, *Chants du crépuscule*, no. III; J. Prévert (1972) 'Tentative de description d'un dîner de têtes à Paris-France' [1931], in *Paroles* (Paris: Gallimard). Hugo wrote his poem for the first anniversary of the revolution of July 1830. See Stéphane Audoin-Rouzeau (1993), *La Guerre des enfants, 1914–1918: essai d'histoire culturelle* (Paris: Armand Colin).
61. Report of the chief education officer of the Doubs on the situation of primary education in the *département* during the year 1915–16, pp. 28–33.
62. Chervel, *Histoire de l'enseignement*, pp. 710–12.
63. R. D'Enfert (2007) 'L'introduction du travail manuel dans les écoles primaires de garçons, 1880-1900', *Histoire de l'éducation*, 113, 31–67, at p. 65.
64. Loubes, *L'école et la patrie*, p. 45.
65. A. Delmas (1979) *Mémoires d'un instituteur syndicaliste* (Paris: Albatros), p. 342.

66. A. Prost (1977) *Les Anciens combattants et la société française, 1914–1939*, vol. 2, *Sociologie* (Paris: Presses de la FNSP), pp. 159–60.

67. Delmas, *Mémoires*, p. 218.

68. Groupe de travail de la maison d'école à Montceau-les-Mines (1981) *Cent ans d'école* (Seyssel: Champ vallon), p. 131.

69. 'Les "Compagnons" et l'école unique', *Journal des instituteurs*, 10 Jan. 1920. See B. Garnier (ed.) (2008) *L'Université nouvelle. Les Compagnons* (Lyon: INRP) and John E. Talbott (1969) *The Politics of Educational Reform in France, 1918–1940* (Princeton, NJ: Princeton University Press).

70. Prost, *Histoire de l'enseignement*, p. 409.

71. See C. Freinet (1993) *Education through Work: A Model for Child-Centered Learning*, trans. J. Sivell (Lewison: E. Mellen). The main concepts in Freinet's pedagogy are: pedagogy of work, meaning that pupils learn by making useful products or providing useful services; co-operative learning, based on co-operation in the productive process; enquiry-based learning, involving group work; the natural method, based on an inductive, global approach; centres of interest, based on children's learning interests and curiosity.

72. Minutes of the third meeting of the Assembly of cardinals and archbishops of France, 1 Mar.1921, Collection of J.-A. Chollet, archevêque de Cambrai, 1 B. 3.

73. R. Bazin (1912) *Davidée Birot* (Paris: Calmann-Lévy).

74. G. Duveau (1957) *Les instituteurs* (Paris: Le Seuil), p. 171.

75. See 'A Frenchman Examines His Conscience', third part of M. Bloch (1949) *Strange Defeat: A Statement of Evidence Written in 1940*, trans. G. C. Hopkins (New York: Oxford University Press), pp. 126–76.

76. A. Thibaudet (1927) *La République des professeurs* (Paris: Grasset), ch. x, 'Héritiers et boursiers', pp. 120–49.

77. P. Bourdieu and J.-C. Passeron (1964) *Les héritiers. Les étudiants et la culture* (Paris: Les Éditions de Minuit).

78. A. Camus (1994) *Le premier homme* (Paris: Gallimard), p. 163.

6
Russia and the Soviet Union: Schooling, Citizenship and the Reach of the State, 1870–1945

Ben Eklof

> Of course, ethnic and cultural incoherence were not new problems for Russian nationhood; they had been a defining feature of it from the earliest times.
>
> – Stephen Lovell

The period examined in this chapter witnessed extraordinary upheaval in Russia. The emancipation of the serfs (1861) was followed by Sergei Witte's industrialisation campaign of the 1890s, generating rapid economic and social change. A massive, ultimately failed revolution (1905–1907) preceded Prime Minister Stolypin's land reforms, which sought to transform in a single generation the way of life of Russia's peasantry, which made up 80 per cent of the population. The eastern front of the First World War was fought largely on Russian territory, and a horrific civil war (1918–1921) reduced industrial output by 90 per cent and left the country, in Isaac Deutscher's words, 'bled white, starving, shivering with cold, consumed with disease, and overcome with gloom'.[1] A brief period of recovery and reconstruction – the NEP era (1921–1929), which however also witnessed enormous experiments in culture, politics and society – concluded when Stalin launched a ruthless collectivisation campaign. This murderous assault on Russia's peasantry, along with industrialisation, urbanisation, and the establishment of a vast Gulag system, utterly transformed the country's social, cultural and institutional landscape. The result was both a rigidly structured, monolithic and hierarchical state and economy, and what Moshe Lewin has called a 'quicksand society'. Finally came the unprecedented catastrophe of the Second World War, resulting in the loss of 27 million Soviet lives, unimaginable hardship and devastation, but ultimately also a victory which rebuilt the ideological foundations of the Soviet state.[2]

Seen from this perspective, the launching of mass education as a state project seems but a footnote to the larger dramas of turmoil, collapse, and rebuilding in a great nation and empire. It would be tempting to ignore schools as peripheral to these developments, and reasonable to assume, given the scale of upheaval, that little progress was achieved. But this would be wrong; it was precisely in this interval that Russia 'learned to read', that universal literacy and schooling were achieved and that, in my view, a distinctive Russian classroom culture emerged, one that has persisted despite radical and frequent shifts in the political order.[3] Sadly, the pursuit of universal literacy, initially seen by society and many statesmen as an emancipatory project fundamental to the well-being of the country, concluded with the installation of one of the most vicious dictatorships of the twentieth century. Yet the enormous social mobility resulting from educational expansion was also a major source of the legitimacy of the Soviet system, especially as, in the post-Stalin era, Marxism-Leninism lost all relevance to reality for most people in the USSR.

Rewriting Russian history: some recent themes

Education must not be treated in isolation from 'big history'. In recent decades, both in Russia and the West, our textbook understanding of much of modern Russian history has been challenged and often rewritten. Briefly put, a sustained effort has taken place to normalise Russia's development, to establish continuities between pre- and post-revolutionary periods, to describe the limitations of state power (particularly at the local level), to highlight the 'push-back' of society to state initiatives and even to find a flourishing civil society by the early twentieth century. Historians have sought to ascribe agency to a peasantry earlier treated largely as mute beasts of burden, and to depict daily life as something other than 'nasty, brutish and short', despite the undeniable conflict and tragedy which punctuated this story. After all, not so long ago, the title of one of this generation's best monographs, *Russia at Play*,[4] would have been greeted as oxymoronic. Finally, it is now axiomatic that few aspects of Russian history can be considered without addressing issues of empire.

All of these strands bear upon the tale of how popular education emerged in Russia and the Soviet Union, and must first be addressed in brief. We begin with a few comments upon modernisation, civil society, the 'peasant state', citizenship and national identity, the 'failure of local government' and continuities between Tsarist and Soviet history in terms of 'slow history'.[5] Then we turn to mass education itself, considering who built schools and why, how control was exerted or contested, the role of teachers, curriculum, textbooks and schedules, and outcomes.

The term 'modernisation' is of course problematic,[6] but is still widely used to describe both the policies of Russian statesmen and the processes underway in the late Imperial and Soviet period. Russia was undeniably a 'latecomer' to modernisation, and most educated Russians, while proud of their country's status as a great power and empire, viewed Russia as backward. As recent studies have confirmed, the Russian economy grew steadily after 1881 (measured in per capita terms, even during a population explosion). And by 1914, Russia was the world's fifth largest industrial power. Yet the trope of backwardness persisted, and was felt especially strongly in the sphere of education; so much so that educators tended to understate progress at home, and in so doing grossly exaggerated achievements abroad.[7] This was only magnified by a Soviet historiography determined to malign the old order and highlight progress since 1917. But modernisation theory also describes a society progressively transformed, enlightened and emancipated, with education playing a major role in this process.

The vaunted powers of the autocratic and Soviet state have also been subject to scrutiny. While earlier, historians debated the existence of a 'hypertrophic' state in Muscovite Rus', recently historians such as Mark Raeff have highlighted the commonalities between European and Russian enlightened absolutism in the eighteenth and nineteenth centuries. Another historian of the eighteenth century, Roger Bartlett, makes a global comparison by labelling the *post-Petrine state a 'peasant state'.[8] By this definition, a peasant state is one in which the central government limits itself to the collection of taxes, conscription of recruits and suppression of popular disorders. Local (communal) peasant life subsists largely without state intervention. Indeed, several historians have pointed out that nineteenth-century Russia was 'undergoverned,' with far fewer officials in relation to population than the states of Western Europe, including Britain. C. Gaudin has argued that it was precisely when the state began actively to intervene in peasant communal affairs in the late nineteenth century that social tensions rapidly mounted in the Russian countryside.[9] Others have noted that the weakness of local government was the 'Achilles heel' of Tsarist (and Soviet) power, that it brought down the Provisional Government in 1917, and that it persisted well into the Soviet period. The argument also exists that it was the failure of Prime Minister Stolypin's local government reforms in 1908 (rather than the vaunted land reforms which sought to eliminate the peasant commune)[10] not the First World War, that determined the fate of the autocracy. This shift in historiography makes more readily understandable the depiction below of the state as only one actor in the momentous turn-of-the-century mobilisation campaign to achieve universal literacy. It also underscores the radical departure involved in Stalin's wedding of statism and mass education and the Soviet state's efforts to monopolise teacher training. Finally, this shift brings into focus the recent trend to study developments across the traditional divide of the 1917 revolution; some see the origins of the Soviet 'surveillance' state in the First World War, while others focus upon the persistence of institutional practices and sets of mind in the family, schools, civil service and elsewhere.[11]

Notions of citizenship are central to understanding the relationship between the state and mass education. Although much recent scholarship[12] has investigated voluntary organisations and horizontal ties outside the state in Russia, the vast majority of the Empire's 'subjects' were peasants still rooted in communal ways (which included as Robert Redfield long ago pointed out, sustained interaction with the city), and the huge and diverse minority populations of the borderlands, while often possessing multiple 'identities' and affiliations, in most cases, would have put 'nation' and 'citizenship' far down the list.[13] Even in Russia's 'heartland' (itself a problematic concept), national identity, it has been argued, was very weak indeed among workers and peasants, who made up more than

80 per cent of the population of European Russia, and certainly was secondary to class affiliation. The entire issue of the popular response in Europe to the outbreak of war in 1914 has recently come under renewed scrutiny, and I am inclined to agree with Hamilton and Herwig[14] that it is not a topic the sources allow us to answer with any real confidence. In Russian studies too, patriotism and the First World War have recently been a cottage industry, but it is fair to say that earlier observations, namely that Russian peasants tended to identify themselves first by the village and region they came from, then as 'Orthodox' but with little allegiance to the modern 'imagined community', have not been profoundly altered; all the more so for the Finnic, Turkic, and German Mennonite populations of the Volga region, and the Tatar and other Muslim ethnic groupings south and east of Kazan and Orenburg.

One unaddressed question is the allegiances of the country's multinational elite. Russian nationalism played a prominent role in the country's new parliament after 1906, and was deployed instrumentally by Stolypin to promote an agenda of conservative reform. Romantic nationalism and *Pan-Slavism also had deep roots among the Russian educated public. Yet the focus on this 'ideology of compensation' and its links with parallel trends in Germany[15] is connected with a *Sonderweg historiography seeking to explain Russian exceptionalism. Today, as with the Austro-Hungarian Empire but with even more justification, historians are generally concerned with explaining the longevity of the Russian Empire, describing how it 'worked' on a daily level, and no longer accept the teleological focus upon social conflict and political stalemate leading inexorably to revolution.[16]

Along with this has come the argument, succinctly put by Geoffrey Hosking, that Russia was 'a state before it was a nation'. Policies of co-option made Russia's ruling elite distinctly multinational; 15 per cent of the bureaucracy in St. Petersburg was of German origin; half of the 'Russian' nobility was Polish, but there were also Georgians, Tatars, Armenians and many others at the top. And even if, at the turn of the century, many universities and secondary schools were hotbeds of political protest, the vast majority of graduates of these institutions entered their adult life and the working world with an ethos of profound loyalty to state and empire rather than nation. Yet there is no research on the connection between secondary schooling and this ethos, which extended even to Russia's liberal opposition when it briefly came to power in the Provisional Government in 1917. Recent historiography, however, has tended to downplay the conflict between educated society and the state, finding, instead, a relationship of mutual dependency, compromise and negotiation, as much as conflict and coercion. To what degree Russia's longstanding 'dual culture' of traditionalist peasantries and Europeanised elites (both state and societal) had been altered is still an open question for historians.[17]

How, then, did Russia's school system emerge, and do the themes described above also inform the history of Russian education? Some of the dynamics sketched below will surely find parallels on the global level, in terms of the strains of latecomer status, the tensions of state building, the landscape of 'dual economies' and 'dual cultures' and both the revolutionary and the neo-colonial responses to empire.

Building a school system

The 'system' of 'Russian' education was built from the top down. In the eighteenth century, rulers first created an academy of sciences as well as so-called *cypher schools aimed at imparting the nobility skills required to serve in the military or civil service. Then Moscow University was founded, and under Catherine the Great orders went out to establish secondary schools in provincial and district centres, though little funding accompanied these decrees. Alexander I created a Ministry of Enlightenment and as part of the Great Reforms emancipating the serfs, in 1864 a School Statute sketched out a model for tuition-free three-year terminal schools[18] to be built and funded by local self-governing, all-class *zemstvos and municipal dumas, but supervised by state inspectors. This legislation (modified in 1874), the 1875 regulations bestowing privileges upon military recruits with a school leaving certificate, a Model Curriculum Programme of 1897, and the School Bill of 1908 set the parameters for popular schooling in the Russian Empire. In 1915, during the First World War, a reformist Minister of Education, Ignat'iev, sought to open up this system by providing 'rungs' on a ladder integrating primary and secondary education and promoting decentralisation by making school inspectors subject to local control and changing their role from supervisors to 'facilitators.' But fierce internal opposition from conservatives as well as the chaos of war swept away this initiative.[19]

When the Bolsheviks came to power, a 1918 decree established the *unified school lasting three to four years, eliminating all class distinctions, removing the church from any role in education and, over time, instituting a progressive curriculum with no regard to the traditional disciplines, placing labour and 'learning by doing' at the core, and sidelining the authority of the teacher and textbook in the classroom. However, the catastrophic effects of civil war, famine and rampant disease, the ensuing collapse of industrial output and the 1921 decision to decentralise funding for the schools, as well as fierce resistance from a teaching profession, which initially resisted Bolshevik rule in favour largely of a multiparty socialist state,[20] and from parents appalled by the lack of discipline and seeming chaos in such schools, halted progress at best.[21] In addition, a policy decision in the 1920s to emphasise adult literacy programs reduced the resources available for basic schooling for children and may have actually led to a decline in enrolments. Beginning in 1931, however, Stalin, now firmly in control, reversed the *NEP policies of the 1920s, re-established with modifications the traditional disciplines and authority of the teacher, and installed monolithic state control of every aspect of schooling including, for the first time, teacher training.

This was, in fact, a profound reversal of the direction schooling had taken in the more than half-century following the Great Reforms of the 1860s. In that interval, state and society had been engaged in a lively tug of war over control of the schools and the nature of the curriculum.[22] In fact, the 'state' itself was, as we now know, far from a monolithic actor in schooling as elsewhere, and historians now see its policies as divided, driven by ad hoc decisions more than cogent policy, and not only in education.[23] Within the state itself, a struggle between the Orthodox Church (Holy Synod) and the Ministry of Education led to parallel elementary school systems and the failure of the Duma in 1908 to pass a School Bill enacting profound changes in elementary education. Several other ministries (war, interior, finance, etc.) even had their own schools, although mostly secondary, and private education had begun to flourish, also at the secondary level. At the same time, in European Russia, the state was engaged in another tug of war with the semi-autonomous zemstvo institutions set up to manage local affairs. Zemstvos were entrusted with founding schools and managing the economic affairs of local schools, while the state was to supervise the curriculum. In reality, these zemstvos, which hired teachers (and later sometimes funded additional state inspectorate positions), provided textbooks, built schools and libraries and were intimately engaged in all aspects of popular schooling, even if often harassed by state regulations.[24] Outside European Russia, in the empire's vast, multinational and multi-confessional borderlands (Russians were a bare majority in the country's population by 1900), a bewildering variety of arrangements promoted or limited popular schooling. In the Western borderlands, the Polish church, Jewish organisations, and Lutheran schools, all were engaged in negotiations with an uneasy state about who could fund and control elementary schooling, how teachers were selected, what languages of instruction were allowed, and what role religion played.[25] In the Caucasus and Central Asia, as well as along the Volga River, from the time of Catherine the Great the state had established an official Muslim hierarchy entrusted with the promotion and control of religious schools. But increasingly in the second half of the nineteenth century, Tsarist authorities had become uncomfortable with this arrangement, partly because of growing pressure for Russification of the empire, and partly because of the rapid spread of Islam in the southeastern reaches of the country.[26]

These brief comments offer only a hint of the complexity of educational politics among national minorities: even outside the 'core' Russian areas around Moscow, along the Volga, more than 20 percent of the population was 'non-Russian' (largely Turkic and Finnic); in Viatka province for example, many districts had to make arrangements for instruction of groups of children who spoke two or three different languages at home, and whose entry into the school marked their first exposure to Russian. Indeed, a major issue in teacher training at the time was finding qualified applicants who could converse in the several languages needed in the Volga region to interact with the children from the Finnic and Turkic populations, making most schools 'mixed' institutions. Accommodating minority languages where Russian was the medium of instruction was a growth industry in pedagogy; the language of instruction and place for minority languages, and the content of 'Bible' lessons were recurring topics both at local teachers' congresses and in the national press (the one concerned largely with pragmatics, the other with politics). In Kazan, Russia's 'third capital' on the Volga, I recently came across a file about a hapless Russian school inspector accused in 1906 of anti-government activities in the schools. His response to the charge could be summed up as follows: 'How could I be responsible for popular disorders in the village if, after all, I am inspecting the schools of German colonists? I can't even understand their spoken German, and they know almost no Russian!' (This of course raises a question about the quality of his inspection work, since he could understand nothing of what was being said in class.) In neighbouring Viatka, I found an inspector's annual report on the eve of the First World War in which he sheepishly acknowledged that in his district of roughly 200,000 people and 100 official schools, he had recently 'discovered' 15 unofficial Muslim schools operating openly but not on the ministry files. Moreover these schools had been founded almost two decades previously! So much for central control over minority education, even close to the heartland of Russia.[27]

Who built the schools and why?

But this story is incomplete, even distorted, for well before the state began to play a sustained role, beyond enabling legislation, in schooling, the population had established a widespread network of *'vol'nye' or 'free' schools across European Russia. Recognising the utility of literacy and numeracy, from the late eighteenth century many peasant communities had hired itinerant teachers, retired soldiers, unemployed clergy, to teach their children, largely but not only boys, how to read and count. Indeed, while the usual narrative of Russian popular schooling has 'society' (i.e. the educated elite running the zemstvos) stepping in during the 1860s to take advantage of the new legislation permitting the establishment of schools and providing the initiative for educational expansion, many of the 'new' schools set up during this period were built upon foundations already established by such vol'nye schools. It was only in the 1890s, with the rise of popular discontent (labour strife and peasant disorders) as well both noble and intelligentsia frustration with a recalcitrant state, that elite efforts to promote popular education became a genuine 'campaign' and mass education became the elixir that would solve Russia's problems. Thus began a campaign to achieve universal enrolment, and thereby to overcome Russian backwardness, narrow the frightening cultural gap between the educated elite and a 'dark' and violent peasantry and working class, improve the quality of the military in a time of increasing international tensions, enhance labour discipline and productivity, provide a means to disseminate and improve agricultural practices, and better unify the empire.

In this mix of familiar considerations, which by the turn of the century were increasingly shared by officialdom, it is impossible to separate out the emancipatory from the darker, Foucauldian impulses.[28] Up until the huge wave of violence marking the revolution of 1905, the emancipatory impulse most likely held sway among the educated public, locked in a struggle with the autocracy for basic political rights, while the state, when promoting education, was overwhelmingly concerned with utilitarian issues of productivity and control. After the violence of 1905–1907, the views of state and public actors merged; while differences remained over curriculum, language of instruction, and control of the schools,[29] there was general agreement on the need for a unified empire, a strong state as well as public order and both fundamental skills and social discipline.[30] By 1914 the state and local elites were in agreement, and working hard, to achieve universal primary education in Russia, with a target date of 1922 for reaching that goal.[31] Given a long tradition of compulsory state modernisation projects in Russia, many public figures were suspicious of that approach, and after some hesitation, decided that the goal should be universally accessible, not state-mandated, elementary education. Because of this, even while the length of primary schooling was set at three to four years, the school age cohort included children from age 8 to 14 (with no compulsory entry age, parents could enroll their children when convenient, or when spaces opened up in the schools). As will be clear below, this was to cause some confusion in measuring results.

To be sure, despite the consensus that schools needed to be built, Russian pedagogy was, in the dual capital cities of St. Petersburg and Moscow, polarised between conservative and progressive proponents. The country's recently established national parliament (the Duma, first convened in 1906) was locked in a struggle between proponents of a religious and of a secular education, over the priority to be given to the Russian language or to Orthodoxy in the schools, and over the degree of centralisation proper for the schools. But outside the capital cities, at summer teacher training courses, among school inspectors and directors as well as zemstvo employees; that is, at the level of practice, by the turn of the century a consensus had emerged about how schools should be run, what teachers should teach and how, what kind of disciplinary measures were appropriate, and what results could be expected from the three- to four-year school. This mainstream pedagogy was distinct in that it emphasised a tightly structured schedule, textbook learning, much rote learning combined with memorisation, classroom recitations, oral calculations, as well as 'explanatory readings' and a focus upon the use of visual aids (*nagliadnye posobiia*),[32] and, everywhere, the unchallenged authority of the teacher. At the same time, it banished corporal punishment from the schools and promoted a benevolent view of the intrinsic goodness of the child. The emphasis upon a structured environment stemmed from the rigours of one teacher being responsible simultaneously for two to three groups of students, while the benevolent view of childhood, especially peasant childhood, had deep roots in nineteenth-century Russian culture.[33] The result was that at the local level, co-operation rather than conflict between teachers, zemstvo educators, and local inspectors was the rule,[34] and a distinct culture of Russian schooling emerged, quite at odds with the conflict over education which raged at the national level. The success of this approach was evident in the results achieved, which I discuss below.[35]

As for peasants, their contribution to the early expansion of schooling has been mentioned above. But once the state and educated society began to intervene on a large scale, peasant strategy involved both expanding access to education and limiting its scope. In fact, popular attitudes changed little in the half century after emancipation. The impulse to literacy and numeracy was there from the start, but was, and remained, largely a defensive impulse. This was a complex and dangerous world and children needed to learn how to read and write in order to navigate their way around the city, where many of them would work. They also needed these skills to protect themselves from rapacious local officials, the nobility as well as merchants and others with whom a growing money economy brought them into contact. Increasingly too, peasants saw the value of literacy for girls, and when openings appeared in local schools for girls, they rapidly filled up.[36] But peasants were simultaneously engaged in an effort to limit the impact of schooling on their children's world views. The authority of (women) teachers challenged patriarchal authority at home; the types of vistas presented in some school readers opened up a new world of discourse, geographic realms, modes of living, promoting what developmental economists across the globe have described as the 'backwash' effect: that is, inputs into schooling in rural communities ultimately leading to the draining of human capital from the countryside in search of new opportunities elsewhere. For peasant families, this was seen as a net loss, so they struggled to provide their children with enough schooling to function, but not enough to leave the village. As can be imagined, this often led to tensions and misunderstandings between the school and the community.[37]

As a result of these conflicting impulses in the peasant community, the dynamics of enrolment in popular schools were complex, and need to be deciphered. While most children in European Russia were in school by 1914 (see below), they commonly left school at the point at which, after two years or so, the parents felt the child had learned how to read, write and cope with the modern world. Using both massive statistical studies carried out by local zemstvos, as well as equally large surveys of peasant opinion collected by local correspondents, it can be demonstrated that this was not an 'educational failure' but rather a marker of peasant agency. While opportunity costs played some role, more important was the attempt to reduce the impact of the 'hidden curriculum' and protect the boundaries and hierarchy of peasant culture. Traces of this strategy can be discerned both in enrolment patterns and in measurements of the outcomes of schooling, discussed below.

Returning to the narration of school expansion, I argue that for a brief period following the 1917 revolution and ensuing civil war, the emancipatory, even utopian, impulse prevailed over centralising 'statist' leanings. During the experimental NEP period from 1921 to 1927, marked by a mixed economy, progressive social legislation and marked creativity in the arts (albeit within the framework of a single-party state), a debate raged within education circles about the value of textbooks, the authority of the teacher in the classroom, the organisation and presentation of knowledge, and the relationship between school and society, as traditional disciplines were abandoned in favour of the 'labour school', and the 'democratic classroom'.

But many teachers, as well as parents preferred the traditional content and ambience: 'lessons, bells, and books'. The extreme material needs and acute shortages of the time generated hardships hardly conducive to reform and experimentation. These stringencies were exacerbated by the deplorable conditions endured by most children. It was at this time that the mass phenomenon of *bezprizorniki*, or homeless children, became an inescapable concern of educators and policy makers, and only worsened as time passed. Issues of survival, shelter, and nourishment became all important in the following two decades as the party and state struggled to address the desperate needs of children orphaned by revolution, civil war, or famine, left destitute by the imprisonment or execution of their parents during collectivisation and Stalin's purges, or cast aside during the horrors of the Second World War. As a result, for many educators, the social welfare functions of schools often took precedence over discovery and learning. Teachers became surrogate parents; extended day and boarding schools proliferated, and schools were often shelters for traumatised children. Conditions in such schools were often spartan and harsh, sometimes abusive, but a magisterial recent study argues that given the enormity of the upheavals which the Soviet Union experienced at the time, the effort made was heroic, and compares favourably with the treatment of abandoned children globally in the twentieth century.[38]

In these circumstances, the struggle between progressive educators and state-builders[39] determined to modernise Russia and restore Great Power status [they would have cringed at this vocabulary] was resolved in favour of the latter, and shortly after the rise of Stalin in 1929, the emancipatory impulse was crushed by the monolithic centralising, industrialising, and hierarchical ethos that was to prevail for the next half century.[40] Not only did the arrival of universal schooling mark the end of the emancipatory project of Russian intellectuals in favour of a darker impulse of control and hierarchy, perhaps wedded inevitably to the earlier stages of industrialisation, but collectivisation of agriculture marked the shattering of an autonomous peasant culture as well as a 'peasant pedagogy'. It is notable that Stalin's push for the 'elimination of illiteracy' was contemporaneous with the 'elimination of the kulak,' and that the acronym in Russian for the literacy campaign resembled that for the secret police (or Cheka). From that point on, to find agency in popular schooling in Russia, one must look at individual social mobility (to be sure, enormous) or at 'backstage' behaviour, the weapons of the weak and muted forms of resistance to Soviet culture, in the school, on the playground and streets, as elsewhere. As for independent youth culture, which flourished in the 1920s, both as militant *Komsomol* (Communist youth) organisations fervidly supporting radical agendas and as working class sub- and counter-cultures, these topics must remain outside the purview of this chapter.[41] Likewise, the extraordinary network of extra-mural institutions providing all manner of after-school cultural enrichment, sporting activities, and summer camps, which played a huge role in the lived experience of Soviet children and adolescents, but virtually disappeared along with free pre-school institutions after the collapse of the Soviet Union, must be bypassed here.[42]

Who were the teachers?

Across Europe, the initial governmental involvement in primary education came through teacher training, and by the end of the nineteenth century, the majority of teachers had passed through *normal schools imparting a specific curriculum and professional socialisation. From the 1860s, the Russian government also began to establish normal schools along the Prussian model, but efforts lagged and the state never achieved a true monopoly over teacher training until well into the Stalinist era. During the two first major school expansions (1895–1914 and the 1930s), a large proportion of new teachers had received their education in a variety of advanced primary and general secondary schools, often not having completed their studies. For this reason, in late Imperial Russia, summer refresher courses and teachers' congresses, organised and run by local institutions and educated society, played a major role in enhancing pedagogical training, promoting a distinctive classroom culture (see below) and reinforcing professional identity. As a rule, too, elementary school teachers, unlike secondary school teachers, were not state employees and their (low) salaries were set by local zemstvos and municipal Dumas. Although the state began to provide salary supplements in the 1890s, it was only after 1908 that a guaranteed minimum was established as a condition for local institutions receiving grants for school construction. Even then, the minimum of 360 rubles put teachers only slightly ahead of factory workers, whose salaries averaged 250 rubles. By comparison, a school inspector earned 2000 rubles per annum; secondary school teachers (also state employees) about 1500 rubles. It took nearly two decades after the revolution before the Soviet state fully centralised financing, a key to protecting teachers from local interests and enhancing their authority in local communities.

Yet for most of this period, teachers remained vulnerable to pressures from both community and state due to their fragile professional identity and class status. Feminisation in primary schools accelerated with the rapid expansion of schools in the 1890s, and by the First World War, 70 percent of teachers were women. Although it failed to gain full control over teacher training, the central state restricted the legal rights of teachers (through prohibitions by local inspectors affecting both professional behaviour and personal life). It also resisted teachers' attempts at professional self-organisation and prevented their participation in the burgeoning co-operative movement and even their involvement in adult education programmes. In fact, if Prussian teachers were responsible for victory at Sedan, and French teachers promoted republican values, as a rule Russian teachers, while sharing the civilising, *Kulturtrager* ethos widespread elsewhere, clearly also subscribed to democratic and moderate socialist beliefs. If not revolutionary, their views hardly coincided with the conservative ethos of the Tsarist state.

However, a vast gulf divided primary and secondary school teachers. The latter were exclusively male, trained at universities, enjoying the status and perquisites of state service (they wore uniforms), and they worked in an exclusively urban milieu, instructing children of educated society. For this reason, both in 1905 and after 1917, secondary school teachers rejected the idea of creating a unified teachers' union and they tended to be both connected to the Tsarist state and more remote from the popular classes. By promoting a unified, state-run teachers' union, the new Soviet state cleverly won grudging support from primary school educators (who had been leftist but anti-Bolshevik), and crushed the more militant opposition of secondary school teachers.

Relations with the local community were often even more complicated than between sectors of the profession and historians are not in agreement about this topic. Generally, teachers fit the classic anthropological definition of 'stranger outsiders' to the village, which disposed peasants to see them as both dangerous and vulnerable. The feminisation of the profession in the primary schools, along with miserably low salaries, only further diminished their status in the eyes of villagers. And yet, teachers also possessed a valued commodity, namely literacy and numeracy, which, as we have seen, by the end of the century were in high demand by peasants. During times of war and instability (for instance, the 1905 and 1917 revolutions, the Russo-Japanese War and the First World War) they everywhere served as 'decoders' of news and information of enormous importance to peasants and helped villagers write petitions to the authorities (which swamped the authorities in St. Petersburg as well as the newly formed State Duma). These roles often earned teachers the trust and respect of peasants. During the first decades of Soviet power, ambiguity persisted. Their obligatory involvement in official literacy campaigns, which carried a militantly anti-religious tone and bore the unfortunate title of *Cheka* (or Extraordinary Commission, the same acronym used for the forerunner of the NKVD and KGB, some of whose characteristics it also shared) promised to incur popular hostility, at a time when the Soviet state was too weak to protect teachers. Stalin's collectivisation only increased the wrath of much of the population, even as a basic education provided enormous social mobility. This promise of advancement (and escape from a traumatised village) along with the comprehensive Stalinist reinstallation of hierarchy, including that of the teacher in the classroom, and the merging of the first eight years of schooling into a unified *obshchee srednee obrazovanie* (general secondary school) finally helped to solidify teachers' status and prestige.

What was achieved: literacy and enrolments

With few exceptions, most historians have long agreed on the 'educational failure' of Tsarist Russia. Most, too, have acknowledged (or trumpeted) the achievement of full literacy and universal enrolment in the Soviet Union within two decades of the revolution. In truth, the Soviet achievement was uneven, if considerable, and Tsarist progress towards those goals was far greater than commonly ascribed. The ideological distortions of the Cold War combined with rather elementary miscalculations and terminological confusion to muddy the picture and exaggerate the 'before' and 'after' (1917) story of mass education in Russia. Ideologically, the tropes of 'backwardness' and inevitable collapse of empires in favour of nation-states in the West dovetailed with the Soviet master narrative of triumphal modernisation once the hopelessly retrograde Tsarist order had been swept aside, are well known. Thus, grand political narratives shaped the picture of Russian schooling. It is the more prosaic errors in counting we must consider here.

It can be easily demonstrated that despite continuing widespread illiteracy in the Russian Empire as late as 1914, the proportion of children who were gaining some schooling was high. The most commonly used index of enrolment in the West was a population ratio, rather than that based on age groups. As a proportion of the entire population, regardless of age, enrolments in European Russia rose between 1880 and 1911 from 1.5 per cent to 2.9 per cent in 1894 and 4.5 per cent on the eve of the First World War. By this yardstick, Russian school enrolments lagged far behind Great Britain (17.4 per cent), Germany (17 per cent), France and Sweden (14.2 per cent) and the United States (19.4 per cent). No wonder the source of these figures was a book (published in Russia itself) entitled *Education in the Civilised World, and in Russia*.

Indeed, given the huge (100 million) gain in population in the Russian countryside in the second half of the nineteenth century, even the increase from 1.5 per cent to 4.5 per cent represented a major effort, and considerable gain. But such figures fail to distinguish between the notion of a proper school age and actual enrolment figures; unless allowance is made for national differences in the age of school entry and school leaving, they hardly demonstrate 'educational failure'.

A better way to determine what proportion of school-age children ever saw the inside of a school is to begin with the school-age cohort. Even here, however, a sense of inferiority deeply coloured the presentation of data. Until the 1890s, most Russian educators, borrowing from the West, used the ages 7–14, or an eight-year span, as the proper school-age base. According to estimates based upon these assumptions, enrolment increased only from 8.7 per cent in 1880 to 15.6 per cent in 1894 and to 23.8 per cent of the age-cohort in 1911. From this, it is often hastily concluded that only one in four children (i.e. 24 per cent) of children had any schooling whatsoever. Yet, as the historian E. G. West showed long ago in his study of schooling in England, such calculations are misplaced; according to him, the Kerry Report of 1833 also arrived at the conclusion that only one in four children actually saw the inside of a school, but since the school-age base was considered to be 6–13 and the average length of stay in school only 2–3, rather than eight years, then in fact 9 in 10 children actually received some schooling at one point between ages 6 and 13.[43]

The same applies for Russia: once educators finally began to regard 8–11 as the proper school age (while allowing children to stay in school up to age 14), they estimated the proportion of the population in that age group at 9–9.5 per cent of the total, and the one-day survey of schools conducted on 18 January 1911, showed that more than one half of all boys in that group were actually in school (for girls, the figure was one-third to one-quarter).

Yet even these figures are an understatement; three-quarters of all schools offered three, not four (that is 8–9–10–11) year programs, so if all children received three years of schooling, on any given day only one quarter of that age cohort would be out of school. Moreover, the average length of stay in school was actually 2.5, not 3 years; and on any given day 7–10 per cent of children were absent (probably much higher in the dead of winter). Finally, demand for a place in the schoolroom far exceeded availability; for that reason, children initially denied a place often enrolled later, staying after the age of 11.[44] For all these reasons, while attendance (measured in terms of pupils present on a given day in the dead of winter!) had officially reached 51 per cent (both boys and girls of children aged 8–11) by 1914, local surveys taking into account all these factors suggest that approximately three-quarters of the child population in European Russia was actually receiving between 2 and 3 years of elementary education on the eve of the First World War. Literacy figures remained dismally low in Russia, but if disaggregated to highlight generational cohorts, better reflecting the advances in schooling, they also demonstrate comparable progress.

Yet, after the revolution, in the early 1920s, many Russians still spoke of their country's 'Asiatic lack of culture'. In 1921 Lenin wrote in disgust of a country vast enough to house several major civilisations, yet dominated by 'patriarchy, 'semi-barbarity – even total barbarity'.[45] Understandably, Soviet progress in promoting literacy and schooling was halting in the first decade after the revolution. The external conditions have been described above, and specialists have estimated that it was only in the middle of the 1920s that a turning point was reached and a decline in enrolments and literacy reversed, though pre-war enrolment levels were reached only in 1927.[46] Policy decisions as well as war had played a role in this decline; initially it was decided to focus scarce resources on the adult literacy campaign, and this came at a loss to expenditures on schooling, which had already suffered from the decision to decentralise financing of schools in 1921. But Stalinism rectified this situation, and even as the era of progressive experimentation in schooling was brought to an abrupt halt by decrees in the early 1930s, in re-establishing traditional discipline and hierarchy, textbooks, and formal learning, unprecedented effort was applied to schooling the entire younger generation.

Indeed, the Stalinist effort was remarkably successful: illiteracy was eradicated and compulsory basic schooling for the ages 8–10 was mandated in 1930 and achieved by 1939. Full secondary education was implemented by the time of Khrushchev, and a vast system of higher education institutions built by the late Soviet era. Moreover, these schools were the platform for remarkable social mobility, for those who ruled the Soviet Union up to its collapse were largely the so-called *vydvyzhentsy* or products of 'affirmative action' policies bringing peasants and workers (both men and women) into all levels of schooling and from there into positions of status and power.[47] Robert Conquest, in reply to those who argued that the enormous sacrifices of the Soviet modernisation project had been justified by its outcome, retorted that 'Stalinism was to industrialisation as cannibalism is to a high-protein diet'. But whatever one feels about the Soviet project, Moshe Lewin was surely right in listing education, along with urbanisation and industrialisation, as one of the key achievements of the Soviet Union, providing both its superpower status and the rise of a huge middle class. Along with victory in the Second World War, this triad of developments also served to legitimate Soviet power in the eyes of the population. Ironically, however, it was this very middle class which helped usher in the age of *perestroika, and whose discontents led to the ultimate collapse of the Soviet Union in 1991.

Learning outcomes: a Russian culture of schooling?

Finally, what did children learn during their stay in school? Here it is more difficult to combine a discussion of Tsarist and Soviet periods, for the differences
abound, not only in length of stay, but also, obviously, in ideological regimes. Yet
it is possible to argue that in the late Imperial period, a distinct Russian culture of
schooling emerged, and that this classroom culture persisted well into the Soviet
period, leaving traces even today. This culture emphasised on the one hand, a
rigorously applied structure and schedule, as well as the unquestioned authority
of the teacher. On the other hand, it cherished a benevolent notion of childhood,
even, during the Soviet period, a cult of childhood, as well as the rejection of
corporal punishment. These characteristics may well explain the marked success
achieved by Russian schools.

But what evidence is there of success? Could the brief, three- to four-year programme really teach children how to read, write, and count? In fact, before the
revolution, many educators despaired of the brevity of the school experience, the
pervasive drop-out rate before completion, and worried about recidivist illiteracy
once pupils departed the school gate. Indeed, while three-quarters of all children
entered school, only one in 10 took the certifying exams marking completion of
the three- or four-year program, and only one in 500 continued on to a secondary school.[48]

Yet was this another example of preconceptions of backwardness distorting
reality, of misleading statistical indicators? It seems so. Surprisingly, there is in
fact much evidence that schools were succeeding in teaching basic skills. This
evidence is in retention studies, commonly conducted a decade or so after pupils
departed the school. Both mathematical tabulations and comments attached to
these studies, conducted around the turn of the century in Voronezh, Simbirsk,
Kursk and other widely dispersed provinces, unfailingly pointed to the same conclusion: former pupils could still read, write, and count.[49]

Consider briefly the results of two typical studies. In Voronezh, the average
reading speed of graduates was 8–13 lines a minute of modern Russian, and 6–12
lines of Church Slavonic. Examiners rated the average comprehension (on a scale
of 1–5) at 3.7, increasing with the length of time since graduation. In Simbirsk,
investigators found that writing skills had slipped, but that the technique of reading was fully intact. Former pupils performed best when tested on the retention of
basic maths skills (the four functions, simple and compound numbers, and basic
fractions, both oral and written calculations). As the school inspector, Krasev, who
conducted this study, commented: 'Truly, the peasant practises his addition, sub-
traction (etc) throughout his life...he counts the strips of land in his field, the
trees in his forest, the money in his pocket'.[50] As for writing, in Kursk, in six to
seven lines of dictation, improper knowledge of word boundaries was observed in
50 per cent of compositions, word distortion in 29 per cent, and omission of hard
and soft signs in 34 per cent. By far, the worst faults were with redundant Church
Slavonic elements in the orthographical system, all of which were eliminated with
the language reforms of 1917, at no cost in meaning. When we look closely at the
deficiencies observed in writing, we see that pupils were properly learning the

mechanics and were transcribing on paper what they heard in speech in daily life; the result was a phonetically correct reproduction of local dialects rather than proper (formal) Russian.

In the schools, too, inspectors generally reported that pupils performed credibly with 'explanatory reading' as well as *pereskaz,* or retelling of passages from an unfamiliar text. Nikolai Bunakov, a prominent educator who often tangled with officialdom, and made sharp criticisms of school policies, at the request of the local school board in the district where he taught, took part in the annual certifying examinations for graduating pupils, and concluded: 'Reading, both in modern Russian and Church Slavonic...was generally confident and intelligent. In almost all schools the weak side of reading was the persistence of gross local pronunciation...when all is said and done, the results in reading...were good in all five schools surveyed.'[51]

Later studies, including a questionnaire sent to more than 11,000 teachers for the Zemstvo Congress of Education in 1911, inquiring of their pupils' prowess during their school years, produced similar results in reading speed, comprehension, ability to reformulate orally what pupils had read and maths skills.[52] Well-respected educators and observers of rural life, who often differed sharply on other issues, all made the same point. Finally, a huge volume of school inspectors' reports, both Holy Synod (Orthodox Church) and Ministry of Education, concurred that similar results were being achieved by pupils by the end of the second, or midway in the third year of attendance. In short, peasant support of school expansion, pressure by parents on schools to enrol their children, combined with their children's successful appropriation of reading and writing and counting skills, despite the high dropout rate, all suggest both successful teaching approaches and a forceful strategy of both promoting and limiting schooling in Russia.[53]

There are striking parallels here to Eugen Weber's observations concerning schools in France in the nineteenth century. Schools began by propagating an artificial language, while peasants drew out what was useful in their own familiar world, with the object of communicating with loved ones in the city (or back home), keeping a record, sending a message; it mattered little whether it was in formal Russian or transcribed vernacular.[54]

How about religion, geography, nature, and history? How did mass elementary education transmit the values and ideals associated with citizenship, nationhood, and social cohesion (both explicitly and implicitly)? At teachers' summer refresher courses in 1900, a questionnaire asked teachers whether geography and history could fairly be tested on exit exams, and virtually unanimously the answer was, 'to the degree that such topics are addressed in explanatory reading hours and provided in the elementary readers used in the schools'.[55] For complicated reasons, the texts and readers available were so diverse that it is hard to generalise from what pupils read in their elementary classes.[56] But two factors militated against transmitting such values. First, the time in school was so limited, and the curriculum so focused upon inculcating basic reading, writing, and computation skills, as well as some elements of knowledge of the natural world, that little time was left over for those domains (history, etc.) where such notions generally reside.

Only in the fourth grade (25 per cent of schools but far fewer proportionally of students) was time specifically allocated to history or geography.

Orthodoxy did play a major role in the curriculum (along with Church Slavonic), and was a major point of friction between the liberal intelligentsia and the state. The Orthodox Church also played a significant role in the borderland zones where other faiths were strong. The issue of church schools and religious studies was so contentious it resulted in the momentous School Bill of 1908 being hung up in the Duma and failing to pass. In general, for educators, the claims made by Orthodoxy often conflicted with the aspirations of state and empire, but especially of Russian nationalism.[57] It is noteworthy too that extracurricular activities such as scouts or paramilitary training made little headway in early twentieth-century Russia.

The second obstacle to such 'transmission' was the teaching profession, which, as we have seen, differed in its ethos from that of Germany and France. Teachers in Russia saw themselves as cultural missionaries and believed strongly in the Enlightenment project (a common trope in their memoirs was that of bringing 'light' to the 'dark' masses). Many too were patriots in that they revered both Russian high and folk culture, and believed along with the famous educator *Konstantin Ushinsky that all knowledge should begin with the cultivation of one's native language. Yet the *Populist tendencies of many teachers, as well as state reluctance to grant corporate autonomy (to any profession, not only teachers) made many teachers reluctant propagandists of official ideology. How about the village priests who taught in church parish schools but were also obliged to provide Bible lessons in the secular zemstvo schools? Promoting 'God and Tsar' was a large part of their mission, and conservative priests often tangled with secular teachers. The conflict, though, should not be exaggerated: many teachers were themselves from clerical families, and in fact many priests were themselves sympathetic to socialist ideologies. The three most recent Western studies of village teachers differ in their conclusions about their impact on village culture.[58] A generation later, however, when Stalin launched collectivisation, many of these teachers were seen as emissaries of the loathed state, and were raped, had acid thrown in their faces, or were even murdered.[59] Yet it is impossible to ignore the important role Soviet teachers came to play in many children's lives, possibly because of the caretaker role many assumed during the difficult times of the Stalin era. An echo of this can be heard even today: when elementary school pupils form the traditional 'lineup' to meet their teacher on the first day of class, she will often say, 'Now listen to me; your mother is number one in your life... and I am number two!'

Moving beyond textbooks, subjects such as geography, history, and religion, and even the role of the teacher, and turning to the 'hidden curriculum' one might well argue that the restructuring of daily life accompanying schooling contributed to promoting the 'industrious revolution' that Bayly, following Jan de Vries, argues was key to the origins of 'modernity'.[60] Above, I argued that a 'distinct culture of schooling' emerged in Russia in the second half of the nineteenth century (which perhaps was passed on to the Soviet school).[61] What I have in mind was the unusual combination of 'frontal approaches' or the top down, highly structured, even regimented scheduling and organisation of learning in the school with a markedly humane, child-centred set of beliefs originating of course in the Enlightenment, but given added impulse by the teachings of *Tolstoy and the Populist leanings of the teaching profession. Perhaps the best indicator of the latter was the virtual exclusion of corporal punishment from the Russian primary school by the turn of the century. As to the structure, one has only to turn to reports of teachers' summer courses, inspectors' reports on the schools, memoirs, and handbooks by educators, to see how pervasive the concern was for the minute organisation of every moment of the school day. After all, most teachers were dealing simultaneously with two or three classes of children, and had to keep them engaged for five to six hours daily. This required commitment, skill, and above all planning. It is difficult to extract proof that such routines and scheduling changed children internally, but it is also noteworthy that educators persistently remarked at the joy with which children first came to school. Many also commented that this love of schooling only increased over time.[62] And in some areas of the empire, especially the Russian north, where distance to schools and severe winters made travel hazardous, a large proportion of children spent the entire week at the school, sleeping in the classroom, or in specially built dormitories, or renting a space in a cottage near the school.

Finally, while above I noted that only a tiny fraction of Russian children continued their education beyond primary school, the peasant population was so vast that despite the very low 'access percentage'[63] by 1914 peasants made up nearly half of all the students in Russia's rapidly growing secondary school system. Doing some rough calculations, this means that by that time there were perhaps a half a million Russian peasants who had gained at least some secondary schooling.[64] Anecdotal evidence supports the notion of a rise of the 'peasant intellectual,' a socially mobile class of peasantry (becoming for instance, book publishers, military officers, merchant millionaires, or writers such as *Maxim Gorky). But this potentially rich topic remains unexplored.

Nationhood and citizenship

In relation to Tsarist Russia, it is more relevant to discuss community ties and class identities and the long-standing gap between popular and educated culture than differing notions of nationhood (Russia's famous 'dual culture' separated the traditionalist and common people from the educated and Westernised). Moreover, the central core of Soviet ideology repudiated, of course, the nation as an object of loyalty in favour of a 'Soviet federation', which itself was to be a temporary structure until the world revolution would bring about a confederation of socialist communities, however defined. The sad history of the *Comintern (Communist International) informs us that virtually from the start loyalty to socialism meant loyalty to the Soviet state, and the interests of the Soviet state soon came to be defined in ways which had an eerie resemblance to the *Realpolitik* of the autocratic policy makers, that is, the pursuit of Russian great power interests. The

Second World War brought the re-emergence of the colonising mission of Russian culture and suppression of local languages in schools as well as the expansion of the already large network of 'total institutions' for children, both boarding schools and orphanages.

Did the Soviet school contribute to modernisation, national identity, or notions of citizenship? Certainly the link between education, economic growth, and social transformation is a strong one, even if difficult to pin down. The social mobility ensuing from educational expansion, as noted earlier, created a huge middle class which, some have argued, demanded more autonomy, status, and reward, and in so doing fuelled *Gorbachev's reforms. Whether or not this new middle class had developed notions of citizenship is a thorny issue, for more than two-thirds worked in closed cities in the defence industry), and had little of the geographical mobility or horizontal connections normally associated with middle classes and civil society.[65]

With the collapse of the Soviet Union, the virtual elimination of funding for schooling, and the emigration of over 200,000 highly trained specialists, many policy makers have been worried about the decline of 'human capital' and the irreplaceable loss caused by a generational rupture in continuity in education levels. The collapse of the Soviet Union also sparked Western fears that a wave of 'radical, xenophobic nationalism' would be unleashed, appealing to a society enduring great hardship and humiliation. But, as Stephen Lovell points out, these fears were not borne out.[66] As Lovell wryly notes, 'National identity was a muddle in post-Soviet Russia, which was almost certainly a good thing'. In other words, while the 'iron law of post-communism' that in conditions of uncertainty over boundaries and institutions, 'all politicians try to use nationalism in their interests,' might have applied to Russia, it has so far had little resonance there. Despite enormous hardship, levels of xenophobia and anti-Semitism were not much higher than in a much more stable Western Europe. How much all of this can be traced back to schooling and to its beginnings in the period 1870–1930 is a matter of speculation, but certainly of interest.

Conclusion

In short, the story of the arrival of mass schooling and literacy in Russia both informs and further complicates the larger narrative of modern Russia as a latecomer and modernising empire, then nation. Indeed, a tragic irony informs the story of national literacy. This story began with the emancipation of the serfs in 1861, with the hopes born in the period of Russia's sweeping Great Reforms, and the village and city schools built upon these hopes. The story continues with elite intervention, both state and societal in the 1890s; an intervention prompted by a faith in the liberating potential of schooling, by the concern to discipline the work force, and by the sense that the proliferating 'wild' popular literacy needed to be regulated. However, the story of national literacy continues with the creation of a massively interventionist state in the 1930s, the establishment of universal compulsory schooling, and a rigidly centralised curriculum. Popular response to Stalinist schools was ambiguous; teachers were sometimes associated with the hated collectivisation campaign and viciously attacked for that reason; yet the population also eagerly pursued schooling that promoted unheard of opportunities for economic advancement. A huge middle class emerged as Soviet society evolved, but no civil society with intricate horizontal ties followed upon this development. The peasant state vanished in the early twentieth century, but the modernisation paradigm contributes little to understanding the type of state, society or school that emerged from war and revolution. Agency in the form of societal inputs in building a school system certainly existed before the revolution, but with the coming to power of Stalin, it took the form mainly of contestation, resistance, and 'collaboration' rather than initiative and creativity. Citizenship and national consciousness, too, took on distorted forms. But it might also be argued that the collapse of the Soviet Union, and onset of an economic depression, some estimate was roughly three times the scale of the Great Depression in the West, resulted in very little turmoil and violence and this was due at least partly to the successes of a school system that expanded and flourished during, but especially after the Stalinist period. But that is another story entirely.

Timeline

1861: Emancipation of the Serfs – the 'Great Reforms'

1864: School Statute establishes tuition-free three year schools (but without state funding)

1872: Establishment of municipal schools offering an extended elementary education

1897: Promulgation of a model curriculum for public elementary schools

1905: Russo-Japanese War and Revolution

1908: School Bill (not passed by legislature, but nevertheless funded by the state: goal set to achieve universal 3- to 4-year elementary education by 1922)

1912: Establishment of higher elementary schools which offered some peasant children the chance to access secondary education

1917: February Revolution – Provisional Government

October Revolution – Bolshevik Government

1918–21: Civil War

1918: Bolshevik decree establishing three to four year schools for all children irrespective of social class with a secular curriculum

1921–9: NEP period

1924: death of Lenin

1927–1929: Stalin established in sole leadership position

1931: curriculum restored along traditional lines

Glossary

Comintern: The Communist International, abbreviated as Comintern, (1919–1943) was an international communist organisation founded in Moscow and aiming to establish an international Soviet Republic as a transition stage towards the complete abolition of the state.

cypher schools: schools set up by Tsar Peter the Great to provide mathematical training for army and navy officers.

Gorbachev: Mikhail Gorbachev (b. 1931) was the last head of state of the USSR from 1988 to 1991. Gorbachev's attempts at reform as well as summit conferences with United States President Ronald Reagan, and his reorientation of Soviet strategic aims contributed to the end of the Cold War and led to the dissolution of the Soviet Union. He was awarded the Nobel Peace Prize in 1990.

Gorky: Maxim Gorky (1868–1936), Russian writer and political activist. Orphaned in childhood, he was raised by his grandmother. His writings focused on the sufferings of the poor and he was a fervent advocate of Russia's social, political, and cultural transformation.

***Kulturtrager* ethos:** the Enlightenment civilising mission pervasive among the Russian intelligentsia in the late nineteenth century.

NEP (New Economic Policy): The term describing the interval between the end of the Civil War (1918–1921) and the onset of Stalinism (1929). Despite the retention of the single-party state, the period was marked by a mixed economy, progressive social legislation, cultural and artistic experimentation, and affirmative action policies for the borderland minorities. During *perestroika*, Gorbachev and other reformers often pointed to the NEP period as a model of the 'socialism with a human face' they were trying to create.

normal schools: term used widely on the continent of Europe for teacher training colleges.

Pan-Slavism: emerged in the 1860s. It wedded an early Slavophilism with an aggressive social Darwinism to produce an ideology of imperialism justifying Russian intervention in the Balkans in defence of 'Slavic brothers'.

Perestroika: refers to the policy of 'restructuring' the Soviet political and economic systems during the Gorbachev era.

Populists: or *Narodniks*, were a political movement which emerged in the 1860s following the emancipation of Russia's serfs. They believed the peasantry were the potential revolutionary class and saw the village community as the embryo socialist unit.

post-Petrine: the Russian state in the eighteenth and nineteenth centuries that owed its main features to the Tsar Peter 1 (1682–1726).

Sonderweg: a term commonly used to described Germany's (and Russia's) purported 'exceptionalism' or deviation from the classic patterns of modernisation, modelled after Great Britain. 'Ideologies of compensation' describe the romantic nationalist currents which claimed a unique genius to be found in local peasant traditions, and the 'special way' to be pursued historically by such nations. Russian Slavophilism of the 1840s was one such current, arguing the distinctiveness of Russian culture.

Tolstoy: Leo Tolstoy (1828–1910) was the pre-eminent Russian novelist of his day. He was a social and educational reformer who founded schools for the serfs on his estate.

unified schools (1918): established by the Bolsheviks, were so named because they were intended to eliminate any barriers in moving from elementary to secondary education. Russians spoke of 'rungs' on the 'ladder' of education; the Tsarist government had systematically eliminated 'rungs' between elementary and secondary school in order to restrict such movement.

Ushinsky, Konstantin: (1824–71) was a teacher and writer, credited as the founder of modern educational theory and practices in Russia, emphasising the Russian language at the core of the curriculum.

vol'nye shkoly: ('free schools') the name given to peasant-established schools, dating back to the eighteenth century, and gradually incorporated into the official school system towards the end of the nineteenth century. Such schools were funded by local communes, and often employed itinerant teachers, local priests, or even retired soldiers to provide the rudiments of literacy and numeracy.

Zemstvos and Dumas: local self-governing councils set up in the era of the Great Reforms (1860s) in district and provincial towns in European Russia, to provide services (education, road-building, agronomical aid, veterinarian and medical aid), as well as collect statistics on the population. They gradually became platforms for mobilisation of the movement for liberal reform in the 1890s, and contended with the state for control over educational curriculum.

Notes

1. Cited in M. Kort (1985) *The Soviet Colossus: the Rise and Fall of the USSR* (New York: M.E. Sharpe), p. 125.
2. M. Lewin (1985) *The Making of the Soviet System: Essays in the Social History of Inter-War Russia* (New York: Pantheon Books). A good recent overview of this period can be found in T. Weeks (2011) *Across the Revolutionary Divide: Russia and the USSR, 1861–1945* (Malden, MA, and Oxford: Wiley-Blackwell).
3. J. Brooks (1985) *When Russia Learned to Read: Literacy and Popular Literature, 1861–1917* (Princeton: Princeton University Press); B. Eklof (1986) *Russian Peasant Schools: Officialdom, Village Culture and Popular Pedagogy, 1861–1914* (Berkeley, CA: University of California Press). The argument for the creation of a distinctive Russian classroom culture can be found in B. Eklof (Jan. 2010) *'Laska i Poriadok*: The Daily Life of the Rural

School in Late Imperial Russia', *Russian Review*, 69, 7–29. References to a copious literature in Russian as well as to archival sources in Russia can be found in these books and
articles.

4. L. McReynold (2003) *Russia at Play: Leisure Activities at the End of the Tsarist Era* (Ithaca,
   NY: Cornell University Press).
5. Outstanding recent examples emphasising continuity are C. Kelly (2007) *Children's
   World: Growing Up in Russia, 1890–1991* (New Haven, CT: Yale University Press) and, in
   politics, P. Holquist (2002) *Making War, Forging Revolution: Russia's Continuum of Crisis,
   1914–1921* (Cambridge, MA: Harvard University Press); and for this essay, L. Holmes
   (1991) *The Kremlin and the Schoolhouse: Reforming Education in Soviet Russia, 1917–1931*
   (Bloomington, IN: Indiana University Press), in which the author deploys the concept
   of 'slow history' to school politics in the early Soviet period.
6. A persuasive recent attempt to globalise, while modifying the term 'modernisation' is
   by C.A. Bayly (2004) *The Birth of the Modern World, 1780–1914: Global Connections and
   Comparisons* (Malden, MA, and Oxford: Blackwell).
7. B. Eklof (1988) 'Kindertempel or Shack? The School Building in Late Imperial Russia
   (A Case Study of Backwardness)', *The Russian Review*, 47, 117–43; I. Gerasimov (2009)
   *Modernism and Public Reform in Late Imperial Russia: Rural Professionals and Self-
   Organisation, 1905–1930* (Basingstoke: Palgrave Macmillan); B.B. Gorshkov (2009)
   Russia's Factory Children: State, Society and Law, 1800–1917 (Pittsburgh, PA: University
   of Pittsburgh), p. 146. Gorshkov notes, in relation to child labour, that 'contemporary
   overemphasis upon 'backwardness'' seems to have distorted Russian reality.
8. R. Bartlett (2005) *A History of Russia* (Basingstoke: Palgrave Macmillan), pp. 103–5.
9. C. Gaudin (2007) *Ruling Peasants: Village and State in Late Imperial Russia* (DeKalb, IL:
   Northern Illinois University Press).
10. Stolypin's ambitious land reforms, which sought to replace peasant communal by pri-
    vate landholding, have received much attention from historians. His local government
    reforms aimed to extend the reach of St. Petersburg below the district to the canton
    level, and to bring all estates (*sosloviia*) into the same institutions.
11. In addition to Holmes, Holquist, and Kelly, see P. Gatrell (2005) *Russia's First World War:
    A Social and Economic History* (Harlow: Pearson/Longman).
12. A major recent work is by J. Bradley (2009) *From Subjects to Citizens* (Cambridge, MA:
    Harvard University Press). For a survey of historiography on the topic, see also his
    article (2003) 'Subjects into Citizens: Societies, Civil Society, and Autocracy in Tsarist
    Russia', *The American Historical Review*, 107/4, pp. 1094–1123.
13. In 1897 peasants made up 84.2 per cent of the population of European Russia, and
    77 per cent of the population of the entire Empire: (1995) *Rossiia 1913 god. Statistiko-
    dokumental'nyi spravochnik* (St. Petersburg), p. 219.
14. R. F. Hamilton and H. H. Herwig (2003) *The Origins of World War I* (Cambridge:
    Cambridge University Press). In their words, 'the decision is best seen in terms of small
    group dynamics, as opposed to the notions of hierarchy and authority,' (p. 11). As to
    the 'prevalence, intensity and import' of 'mass nationalism,' they argue that the only
    honest answer, given the lack of reliable public opinion surveys, is 'don't know', that is
    indeterminacy (p. 22).
15. This term is used and a comparison between Germany and Russia masterfully exe-
    cuted by A. Walicki in his magisterial work (1989) *The Slavophile Controversy: History
    of a Conservative Utopia in Nineteenth-Century Russian thought* (Oxford: Clarendon
    Press).
16. Michale Confino (1994) 'Present Events and the Representation of the Past: Some
    Current Problems in Russian Historical Writing,' *Cahiers du Monde Russe*, 35/4,
    839–68.
17. The classic essay on the twin fault lines between the Russian state and educated society,
    and between educated society (including the state) and the common people (*narod*),

both worker and peasant, is by L. Haimson (1964–5) 'The Problem of Social Stability in Russia, 1905–1917,' *Slavic Review*, 23/4, 619–42, and 24/1, 1–22.

18. Later modified to allow four-year schools, usually with two teachers. By 1914 roughly one-quarter of all zemstvo schools offered four years of instruction.

19. E.D. Dneprov (ed.) (1981) *Ocherki istorii shkoly i pedagogicheskoi mysli narodov SSSR: konets xix-nachalo xx v.* (Moscow: Akademiia pedagogichikh nauk), pp. 85–99. In 1990 historian Edward Dneprov became Minister of Education of the Russian Federation and launched ambitious reforms, embodied in the 1992 School Statute, emulating the spirit of Ignatiev's project. However, as with the NEP reforms of the 1920s, decentralisation in a period of economic ruin led to financial collapse, dooming these school reforms. See Eklof, B. (2005) 'Russian Education: the Past in the Present' in B. Eklof, L. Holmes and V. Kaplan (eds) *Educational Reform in Post-Soviet Russia: Legacies and Prospects* (Basingstoke: Palgrave), pp. 1–22; Bucur, M. and Eklof, B. (2007) 'Russia and Eastern Europe' in R.F. Arnove and C. A. Torres (eds) *Comparative Education: The Dialectic of the Global and the Local*, 3rd edition (New York: Rowman and Littlefield), pp. 333–56.

20. N.I. Smirnov (1994) *Na perelome: rossiiskoe uchitel'stvo nakanune i v dni revoliutsii 1917 goda* (St. Petersburg:Nauka); Eklof, B. and Seregny, S.J. (2005) 'Teachers in Russia: State, Community and Profession' in Eklof et al., *Educational Reform in Post Soviet Russia*, pp. 197–220.

21. Early Soviet educational policy has been masterfully covered by Holmes, *The Kremlin and the Schoolhouse*.

22. The most recent and detailed work on the topic of conflicting state and societal visions of popular education is by A. P. Romanov (2009) *Nachal'noe obrazovanie russkogo krest'ianstva v poslednei chtverti xix-nachale xx vekov* (Cheliabinsk: Entsikolpediia).

23. N. V. Chekhov (1923), *Tipy russkoi shkoly: v ikh istoricheskom razvitii* (Moscow: Mir).

24. T. Emmons and W.S. Vucinich (eds) (1982) *The Zemstvo in Russia: An Experiment in Local Self-Government* (Cambridge: Cambridge University Press).

25. There is no comprehensive study of minority education policy in the Russian Empire. For the Western regions, see E. Thaden and M.H. Haltzel (eds) (1981) *Russification in the Baltic Provinces and Finland, 1855–1944* (Princeton: Princeton University Press).

26. P. Werth (2002) *At the Margins of Orthodoxy: Mission, Governance, and Confessional Politics in Russia's Volga-Kama Region, 1827–1905* (Ithaca: Cornell University Press); R. Geraci (2002) *Window on the East: National and Imperial Identities in Late Tsarist Russia* (Ithaca, NY: Cornell University Press); S. Duke (1999) 'Educating non-Russians in Late Imperial Russia' (unpublished PhD. Dissertation, Indiana University, Bloomington, IN); W. Dowler (2001) *Classroom and Empire: the Politics of Schooling Russia's Eastern Nationalities, 1860–1917* (Montreal: McGill-Queen's University Press); Dneprov, *Ocherki istorii shkoly*, pp. 313–416.

27. *Natsional'nyi arkhiv Respublika Tatarstan*, f.92, po 2, d. 4797, ll. 32–34 (the Archive of the National Republic of Tatarstan, Russian Federation); the office of the Curator of the Kazan Educational District, Secret Correspondence (1905–1906), pp. 32–34.

28. See Eklof, *Russian Peasant Schools*, 'Intervention: The Transformation of Elite Attitudes', pp. 97–119.

29. A good summary is in N. Charnoluskii (1909), *Osnovnye voprosy obrazovaniia v Rossii* (Moscow: n.p.); O. Anweiler (1964) *Geschichte der Schule und Pädogogik in Russland* (Berlin: On behalf of Quelle & Meyer, Heidelberg).

30. On the impact of popular violence during the 1905 revolution on Russian educated professionals, see the landmark work by L. Engelstein (1992) *The Keys to Happiness: Sex and the Search for Modernity in Fin-de-siècle Russia* (Ithaca, NY: Cornell University Press). But it is clear from teachers' memoirs and diaries as well as other local sources, that the emancipatory, *Kulturtrager* impulse remained strong among 'second tier' intellectuals outside the capital cities. On this, see S. J. Seregny (1989) *Russian Teachers and Peasant Revolution: The Politics of Education in 1905* (Bloomington, IN: Indiana

University Press) as well as his many later articles on the First World War era; also Gerasimov, *Modernism and Public Reform*.

31. Ibid., pp. 115–19; Dneprov, *Ocherki istorii skhol*, pp. 59–134.

32. See Eklof, *'Laska i poriadok'*, for a description of how progressive educational tendencies were modified by external exigencies to create a distinct 'mainstream approach' combining structure with child-centred perspectives and discipline. See also Dneprov, *Ocherki istorii russkoi shkoly*, pp. 173–312.

33. A. Wachtel (1990) *The Battle for Childhood: Creation of a Russian Myth* (Stanford, CA: Stanford University Press).

34. Eklof, *Russian Peasant Schools*, 'Control of the Schools: Zemstvo, Inspector and Local School Board', pp. 120–54.

35. Along with this general consensus, a rich variety of approaches continued to flourish. Leo Tolstoy's 'free education', based upon his schools for peasants on his own estate, and allowing children to follow their own inclinations and natural curiosity rather than a curriculum imposed from above enjoyed enormous popularity. Experimental psychology, Montessori schools, and others also had their proponents. The works of John Dewey and others were widely read in translation. In 1914, there were over 150 periodicals specialising in education issues in the Russian Empire; many provided 'chronicles' of current events in education elsewhere in the world.

36. Evidence for this argument can be found in Eklof, *Russian Peasant Schools*, 'Peasant Pedagogy', pp. 251–82. In brief, peasants sent their boys to school first, but whenever most or all boys in a village were enrolled, peasants began to send their girls to school.

37. I have argued this case at length elsewhere. Russian educators at the time noted peasant support of schooling and willingness to sacrifice for it and many zemstvo opinion surveys confirmed this point. The conclusion that peasants also supported schooling for girls but gave priority to boys, stems from multiple statistical studies demonstrating that demand for schooling far exceeded the number of places available, but that as soon as the number of schools increased and a given region approached universal availability of schooling, once all boys were served the enrolment of girls rapidly increased. This is not to argue that opportunity costs did not play a role, but in most cases peasants seemed to believe that up to the age of 12, the benefits of schooling outweighed its opportunity costs for both sexes. As for limiting the amount of schooling, the same surveys reflected the prevailing peasant view that anything more than functional literacy and numeracy could only stir up generational conflict and risk the loss of children to the city. See Eklof, *Russian Peasant Schools*, especially the chapters on 'Peasant Pedagogy (pp. 251-82) and 'Child Labor and the Schools' (pp. 352–88).

38. E.M. Balashov (2003) *Shkola v rossiiskom obshchestve 1917–1927 gg. : stanovlenie 'novogo cheloveka'* (St. Petersburg: D. Bulanin). This human catastrophe, which reached from 1914 until 1945, and which left many millions of children orphaned, at times overwhelmed the capacity of schools and other institutions to cope. In Catriona Kelly's magisterial recent book, *Children's World*, the author rightly devotes over one-third of the more than 600 pages to the attempts of the party-state to deal with the devastating impact of abandonment and orphanage. Despite the atrocious phenomenon of Stalinist penal camps for 'children of the enemies of the people', Kelly, like Allen Ball in his study, concludes that on balance, and in comparison with other states across the globe dealing with similar phenomena but on a much smaller scale, the Soviet state made a credible effort to provide for such children. I would argue that this effort was a defining one of the history of Soviet childhood and schooling. A. M. Ball (1994) *And Now My Soul is Hardened: Abandoned Children in Soviet Russia, 1918–1930* (Berkeley: University of California Press).

39. The best work on these topics is by Larry Holmes. See his *The Kremlin and the Schoolhouse* as well as his essay 'School and Schooling under Stalin, 1931–1933' in Eklof, Holmes and Kaplan, *Educational Reform in Post-Soviet Russia*, pp. 56–102.

40. However, a progressive, experimental tradition continued to exist at the margins of Soviet schools and pedagogy, enriched by the ideas of Vygotsky, Bakhtin and others and promoted by activists such as Dneprov; see S.T. Kerr, 'The Experimental Tradition in Russian Education,' in Eklof, Holmes and Kaplan, *Educational Reform in Post-Soviet Russia*, pp. 102–28.

41. There has been some interesting work on these topics: see E. Balashov's rich study based on a multitude of surveys conducted in the 1920s (note 38 above); A.E. Gorsuch (2000) *Youth in Revolutionary Russia: Enthusiasts, Bohemians, Delinquents* (Bloomington, IN: Indiana University Press), and J. Bushnell (1990) *Moscow Graffiti: Language and Subculture* (Boston: Unwin Hyman) on graffiti culture in the 1980s.

42. This network of *vneshkolnye* institutions was created largely after 1930. Despite its enormous impact on Soviet youth socialisation, it does not have its historian in any language.

43. E. G. West (1971) 'The Interpretation of Early Nineteenth-Century Education Statistics', *Economic History Review*, 24/4, 633–42.

44. Information contained in the 1911 School Census yields insight into the aspirations and blocked hopes of an anonymous, silent population; in 1910, some 999,852 – very nearly a million – children were denied admission to the elementary school ... this out of an estimated school-age population of 12 million, and an enrolled (8–11) population of 6,600,000.

45. Cited in A. Piskunov and E.D. Dneprov (1978) 'A Short History of the Soviet School and Soviet Pedagogy over Sixty Years', *Soviet Education*, 20/4–5, 6-194, p. 29.

46. Lapidus, G. (1976) 'Socialism and Modernity: Education, Industrialisation and Social Change in the USSR' in P. Cocks, R.V. Daniels and N.W. Heer (eds) *The Dynamics of Soviet Politics* (Cambridge, MA: Harvard University Press), pp. 200–3.

47. On the literacy campaigns, see Eklof, B. (1987) 'Russian Literacy Campaigns' in H. G. Graff (ed.) *National Literacy Campaigns: Historical and Comparative Perspectives* (New York: Plenum Press), pp. 123–144. On *vydvyzhentsy* and in general on the cultural politics of the early Stalin era, see especially the work of Sheila Fitzpatrick, cited in n. 59.

48. B. Eklof, 'Beyond Primary School' in *Russian Peasant Schools*, pp. 438–70.

49. On retention studies, see B. Eklof (1986) 'The Adequacy of Basic Schooling in Rural Russia: Teachers and their Craft, 1880-1914', *History of Education Quarterly*, 26/ 2, 199–223.

50. A. A. Krasev (1887) *Chto daet krest'ianam nachal'naia narodnaia shkola*, No. 1 (no place: no publisher), pp. 67–70. For a survey of retention studies, see E.A. Zviagintsev (1912) *Narodnaia zhizn' i sel'skaia shkola* (2 vols: Moscow: no publisher) Vol. 1, pp. 1–21. For the Voronezh, Kursk and Simbirsk studies, see Eklof, *Russian Peasant Schools*, pp. 389–410.

51. N. Bunakov (1901) *Sel'skaia shkola i narodnaia zhizn'* (St Petersburg: no publisher.), p. 187.

52. With the reservation that five years after completion, pupils were more adept at solving simple maths problems orally than at carrying out written operations; compound composite numbers and basic division seemed to give the most trouble. Biuro pervogo vseobshchego s'ezda po narodnomu obrazovaniiu (1911) *Pervyi vseobshchii zemskii s'ezd po narodomu obrazovaniiu.* Vol. V: *Anketa* (Moscow: no publisher), pp. 63–79.

53. Schools in the Volga region which sometimes enrolled pupils who spoke one of two or three native tongues, alongside Russian children, were much less successful.

54. E. Weber (1976) *Peasants into Frenchmen: The Modernization of Rural France, 1870–1914* (Stanford: Stanford University Press).

55. State Archive of Kirov Region (GAKO) f.616, op. 5, ed. khran. 52–56.

56. Textbooks, and other topics below are covered in my recent article (Jan., 2010) '*Laska i Poriadok*'.

57. First, among liberal educators, who sought to create a unified secular state, but especially in the borderlands, where aggressive proselytising of Orthodoxy conflicted with pan-Turkic, pan-Islamic, Catholic, Lutheran constituencies and ideologies. In Central Asia, especially, the issue was framed in terms of priorities over which should be

promoted first, the Orthodox faith or the Russian language. This was most prominent in the conflict over the doctrines of the missionary Ilminsky: see Dowler *Classroom and Empire*.

58. Apart from my own work, *Russian Peasant Schools*, pp. 179–250, see Seregny, *Russian Teachers and Peasant Revolution*; C. Ruane (1994) *Gender, Class, and the Professionalization of Russian City Teachers, 1864–1917* (Pittsburgh, PA: University of Pittsburgh Press). The differences are over the level of political engagement of teachers, relations with the local community, and the role of gender. Recently published is I. V. Zubkov (2010) *Rossiiskoe uchitel'stvo: povsedevnaia zhizn' prepodavatelei zemskikh shkol, gimnazii i real'nykh uchilishch 1870–1916* (Moscow: Novyi khrongraf).

59. On such violence, see S. Fitzpatrick (1979) *Education and Social Mobility in the Soviet Union, 1921–1934* (Cambridge: Cambridge University Press), pp 161–73. While resented by peasants as agents of the state, teachers were also often 'dekulakized,' deported or forced to register with the collective farm, which deprived them of passports and the right to relocate.

60. See Bayly, *Birth of the Modern World*, pp. 6 and 49–50.

61. Eklof, 'Laska i Poriadok', p. 29.

62. Children's enthusiasm for schooling in the 'southern hemisphere' and the aversion to it in the northern hemisphere, is the subject of a recent inquiry: K. M. Anderson-Levitt (2005) 'The Schoolyard Gate: Schooling and Childhood in Global Perspective', *Journal of Social History*, 38/4, 987–1006.

63. F. K. Ringer (1979) *Education and Society in Modern Europe* (Bloomington, IN: Indiana University Press). The distinction is at the core of this major work on education and social mobility.

64. Peasant admission to secondary schools was greatly facilitated by the establishment of Higher Elementary Schools in 1912 (successors to 1872 Municipal Schools, offering a six-year curriculum). Tuition in secondary schools was generally free, and some stipends were offered; however throughout the Imperial period, Tsarist authorities sought to limit the access of commoners to secondary education by ensuring that the curriculum in lower schools did not match the requirements for admission to most secondary schools. But even before 1912, an amorphous, somewhat ramshackle structure of advanced primary education had been established by a process of accretion, providing a bewildering variety of schools offering vocational training or remedial education for those determined to gain entrance to a secondary school. Study of the question is further complicated by the multiple waves of (largely unsuccessful) attempts to restructure secondary school during the reign of Nicholas II (1894–1917). This topic awaits further study; see Eklof, *Russian Peasant Schools*, pp. 438–70.

65. M. Lewin (1988) *The Gorbachev Phenomenon: A Historical Interpretation* (London: Hutchinson Radius).

66. As S. Lovell (2006) *Destination in Doubt: Russia since 1989* (London: Zed Books) points out, Russian nationalism, especially after the Second World War, and in the Brezhnev era, was a core value of the Soviet state, but it found its allegiance primarily among the administrative elite and intellectuals (especially writers of 'village prose'). The irony was that 'the main card-carrying nationalists in the USSR were people who had prospered... in a system designed to transcend the nation-state and they emerged as an opposition (under Yeltsin) determined to save that state'.

Part III

The Wider World

Introduction

Laurence Brockliss and Nicola Sheldon

As the Europeans colonised the Americas in the course of the early modern period, they established a similar range of educational institutions as existed in their mother countries. By the second half of the eighteenth century, there were institutions of higher education – colleges and universities – in all the major towns and cities of the Spanish, Portuguese, French and British colonies. Most kept abreast of intellectual developments in Europe and a handful, particularly the University of Mexico, offered an education and professional training as good as anything that could be found on the other side of the Atlantic.[1] In Portuguese and Spanish America, elementary education was less developed; until the situation began to improve towards the end of the eighteenth century, most poor whites as well as the abused native Indian majority were illiterate.[2] But in the Protestant British American colonies, where literacy was widely extended throughout the white population and not just the privilege of the ruling elite, there was a network of rural elementary schools sustained by the local communities known as townships. These district schools were supported through a combination of local taxes, payments in kind and fees. Frequently the buildings and teachers were far from ideal; there was no common structure to the curriculum and punishments were harsh. Parents appointed the teachers, determined what was taught, and commonly used the schools as a child-minding service for children too young to work.[3]

After the United States became independent in 1783, a number of individuals called for the establishment of a government-controlled system of elementary education which could be used to bind the former colonies into one people. The most prominent advocate was the Yale-educated Noah Webster, who believed that the new America also needed to create its own independent English language with its own standard spelling and syntax. Few Americans supported Webster's demand for the creation of a federal-run system of education, but several Founding Fathers tried to set up a system at state level even before independence was secure. Jefferson believed not only that all citizens should have the vote but also that all should be able to stand for office. This, though, could only be practicable if everyone had been properly educated. On three occasions, therefore – 1779, the 1790s and 1817 – he presented bills in the Virginia legislature for the erection of a free and universal system of elementary education for whites. In the first decades of the new republic, however, he and other pioneers of a state-run system received little support. Opinions began to change only from the 1820s. In the 40 years before the American Civil War, the north-eastern states in particular changed their character dramatically. Universal male suffrage, urbanisation, industrialisation and the arrival of the first wave of non-Protestant immigrants convinced many that the provision of elementary education should not be left to parents or, in the case of the poor, to voluntary societies of the kind that dominated the English landscape in the first two-thirds of the nineteenth century. A free, universal, structured and homogeneous system controlled by the state was judged to be the only way to prevent social breakdown. Instructing the young was now so important that teachers had to be properly trained and examined. In the words of one of the most popular teaching manuals of the age, 'Society expects that teachers will make children and youth social, honorable and benevolent members'.[4]

As a result, in both the north-eastern and new western states of the Union, state-wide systems of *common schools headed by a superintendent of education had been established by the outbreak of the war. In the south, on the other hand, where the slave-dominated society changed far more slowly, there was far less interest, and only North Carolina had created a state superintendent by 1860. The reformers in the north were also anxious that the new state systems would benefit the individual not just save society. Unlike their European counterparts, they were much more positive about the meritocratic possibilities of education. According to the Michigan superintendent of common schools, John Pierce, in 1837, 'By means of the public schools, the poor boy of today…may be the man of learning and influence of tomorrow; and he may accumulate and die the possessor of tens of thousands; he may even reach the highest station in the republic'.[5] However, the rhetoric far outstripped the reality. Some states, beginning with Massachusetts, did open free *high schools but they were filled with the children of the middle class. Indeed, even the establishment of a working state system of common schools took time. The time-lag in Ohio was typical. A school bill allowing but not compelling local authorities to set up common schools paid for by a local tax was passed by the legislature in 1821. But attempts in the 1830s to set up a state superintendent of education failed. It was not until 1853 that a bill was carried that created free schooling throughout the state and established a system for examining would-be teachers. In Ohio, as in all states, there was a great deal of hostility to the initiative: parents wanted to maintain complete control of the schools, the affluent did not want their offspring sharing a classroom with the children of the poor, and religious minorities did not like the Protestant tone of the common schools.

Spanish and Portuguese America gained their independence in the 1820s, though in their case they became a growing number of separate states, not a single federal union. The new Spanish-speaking states were liberal, theoretically racially egalitarian republics, while Portuguese Brazil was a monarchical state based on slavery. Irrespective of this distinction, the new states from their inception showed a commitment to spreading educational opportunity for ideological as well as practical reasons. Peru was particularly precocious. Article 181 of the constitution of 1823 recognised the right to education of all citizens, and in 1828 the legislature declared primary education free for all boys. The state also wanted education to be kept out of the hands of the church. But in Peru, as in other Latin American states, it proved impossible to turn good intentions into deeds. Everywhere the establishment of elementary schools was left to local councils who had neither the funds nor the will to set up a proper network. Racial and class prejudice ran deep, and the law was simply ignored. As political regimes came and went across the nineteenth century, various attempts were made to kick-start the system, sometimes by introducing an element of central funding and organisation. But little was achieved. There was never enough money, never enough teachers, and too little interest from ordinary citizens.[6]

In the world's non-European literate civilisations, on the other hand, there had been no attempt whatsoever to establish a national network of state-controlled schools before 1870. In most of these societies – be they the Muslim Ottoman Empire and Persia, Buddhist Siam and Burma or pre-British India – schooling was provided by the religious authorities and literacy levels appear to have been low, although reliable statistical information is unavailable.[7] In two far-eastern Confucian cultures, however, access to schooling of some kind seems to have been much more widespread. In socially rigid Japan, in the first part of the nineteenth century, school attendance was encouraged by the authorities but provision was left to private initiative. There were two main types of school. The samurai warrior elite went to special schools that were closed to all but a few outsiders, where they were trained in an austere Confucianism through a range of philosophical, literary and artistic subjects deemed suitable for gentlemen. The rest of the population attended mainly fee-paying *terakoya* or writing schools, which had sprung up in great numbers from the end of the eighteenth century and which were attended by both boys and girls for three to four years. These schools used antiquated texts that belonged to an entirely different era and had a Buddhist rather than Confucian orientation.[8] In the slightly more socially fluid nineteenth-century China, the Ch'ing state encouraged education as an antidote to unorthodoxy and rebellion but equally made no effort to provide funding at the lowest level. Here there were three types of schooling for beginners. The rich and powerful employed private tutors; the urban poor went to charity schools founded and maintained by local leaders, magistrates and provincial governors; while the children of the gentry and the peasants attended the clan or *sushu* schools, exclusive institutions established to provide education for the extended family or lineage, the dominant social force in pre-modern China.[9] All three forms of elementary school taught pupils to read and write Chinese characters, the basics of Chinese history and science, and the fundamental Confucian values of loyalty to the family and filial piety. Such schooling was meant to inculcate discipline rather than knowledge, but it did provide the basics for those who, aspiring to gentry status and a place in the bureaucracy, would later go on to compete in the open Chinese examination system, where memorisation of Chinese classics was the key to success.[10] Both the Japanese and Chinese schools educated to a low level a significant part of the population. In Japan in the late 1860s possibly 43 per cent of boys and 19 per cent of girls aged 6 to 13 were in school. In China across the nineteenth century supposedly (though this is contested), 30 to 45 per cent of men and 2 to 10 per cent of women could read and write to some degree.[11] This though still left the majority of the population illiterate, and it has been estimated that as late as 1908 only 5 per cent of Chinese had a 'politically active' (i.e. reflective) literacy.[12]

At the beginning of the nineteenth century, the only parts of Asia firmly in European hands were modern Indonesia and the Indian sub-continent. As it came to look more and more likely by the second half of the nineteenth century that the rest of Asia would be taken over unless determined countermeasures were adopted, significant sections of the ruling elite of Thailand, Iran and the Ottoman, Japanese and Chinese empires came to the conclusion that their states had to Westernise to survive. In each case, the extension and reform of elementary education was seen as a key to success: provision had to become universal; pupils had to be taught mathematics; and reading and writing had to be introduced through texts that inculcated patriotism and knowledge of the modern world. As in Latin America, however, effecting change on the ground proved very difficult. In Iran, virtually nothing was achieved before Reza Shah seized power and established the Pahlavi autocracy in 1925, and even then progress was slow.[13] In the Ottoman Empire, similarly, the sultanate had laid only the foundations of a national system before the collapse of the state at the end of the First World War. It would only be in the 1920s with the establishment of the new Turkish republic that real strides towards a national system of education would be taken in the old imperial heartland.[14] In China, even though a three-tiered western style education system for both boys and girls was set up on paper between 1898 and 1907, complete with teachers training colleges, it would prove impossible to build a nationwide system of elementary education teaching the three R's before the communist takeover in 1949. For all the enthusiasm of advocates of reform, such as Zhang Zhidong (Education Minister 1907–9), the Chinese, both before and after the Nationalists came to power in 1912, lacked the financial resources and the popular support to push through the necessary changes. Under the reforms of the late imperial period, the creation of elementary schools was left to local communities and private initiative. As initially landowners, big and small, preferred to use the old familial schools, which were never closed, progress was inevitably slow. Forceful provincial governors could encourage change: thanks to the efforts of governor Yuan, the metropolitan province of Zhili boasted 20 public primary schools per county by 1906. But this was still a drop in the ocean. Zhili had a population of 30 million and a school-age population of 2.5 million. In 1909 the province only had 209,668 primary school places.[15]

The big success story was Japan, where advance was eased by the overthrow of the traditionalist Tokugawa shogunate in 1868 and its replacement by the western-leaning Meiji regime.[16] Japan introduced a compulsory education law in 1872: all children were expected to attend public co-educational elementary schools for four years (raised to six in 1907), where from 1881 they would study ethics, the three R's, singing and physical education. The speed with which the new system was realised was extraordinary. Although as late as 1910, 90 per cent of the cost came from local taxes and though there were still only half the anticipated number of public primary schools in 1902, virtually every Japanese child of school age was in school on the eve of the First World War. They emerged from the classroom as ardent and selfless patriots. Initially the Japanese reformers had been influenced by the American common school and had hoped to build a system that would encourage individual social mobility as well as national cohesion. From the 1880s, however, a more stridently nationalist policy was pursued, epitomised by the educationalist, Mori Arinori, who looked to a time when Japan would dominate the world.

> Our country must move from its third-class position to second-class, and from second-class to first; and ultimately to the leading position among all countries of the world. The best way to do this is [by laying] the foundations of elementary education.[17]

Japanese children were turned into fervent patriots through the inculcation of a neo-Confucian ethic, which stressed loyalty to the Imperial House and love of country as much as filial piety and deference. Everyone had a duty to maintain and guard the prosperity of the Imperial throne. The new morality was laid out in the Imperial Rescript of 1890 that had to be learnt off by heart and was recited in class on special days. Citizens had also to be prepared for war, so an increasing emphasis was placed on physical as well as moral development. As the 1900 Law of Educational Administration made clear, the value of education for the individual was pushed into the background.

> Education is not simply the development of the individual's abilities, nor should its main principles be derived in accord with the requirements and demands of the individual: the primary aim is to cultivate imperial subjects for the benefit of the state, citizens who will contribute to its existence and survival.[18]

But the elementary school system did not completely lose sight of its original commitment to social mobility. In theory, anyone with talent could go on to secondary or middle school, and eventually to university, if he or she passed the rigorous entrance examinations. However, schooling was only free at the elementary level, schools were single-sex at the higher level and opportunities for girls were limited, and entry to university was dominated by a handful of prestigious secondary schools. In the 1930s only one out of every 100 entrants to a primary school reached university and only one out of 200 gained a degree.[19] Ultimately, the system was even more closed than in the countries of Western Europe.[20]

The third section of this book examines in detail the history of mass education in three very different independent extra-European states between 1870 and 1930: the United States, Brazil and the Ottoman Empire/Turkey. Besides their size, what they share in common is that at the turn of the twentieth century, they were multicultural societies which were largely controlled by a single racial or ethnic group. Each state was committed to establishing or perfecting a nationwide mass education system. But in each case intra-national divisions and tensions affected how the system developed and operated.

The United States was a white, Protestant Anglo-Saxon democratic federal republic with a black, ex-slave minority and a small segregated native population that post-1870 opened its doors ever wider to wave after wave of Catholic and Jewish immigrants from southern and eastern Europe. In consequence, by 1900 it had become the melting pot of cliché, though the WASPS remained firmly in control. Ellen Berg (Chapter 7) explores how the already well-developed systems of mass education in the north-eastern and mid-western states were extended across the whole of the country in the decades following the Civil War, and the extent to which the establishment of a network of open entry, free high schools at the turn of the twentieth century provided opportunities for individual social mobility unknown elsewhere in the Western world. She also charts the role played by these public educational systems in creating a more inclusive view of American citizenship, a development to which the immigrant population made a positive contribution. Recognising the potential of education for upward mobility, Catholic and Jewish immigrants commonly eschewed confessional schools and used the law to ensure the *public (state) schools lost their hitherto Protestant tone. The blacks and native Americans, on the other hand, were thrust to the edges of the system, and Berg's account of American mass education in the first decades of the twentieth century is far less triumphalist than earlier histories.[21]

Brazil in contrast during most of the period under review was a white, Catholic, Portuguese-speaking, federal liberal republic (the Empire was overthrown in 1889) with a black, ex-slave majority. It too was subject to immigration towards the end of the nineteenth century but never on the scale of the United States. The new Brazilian Republic saw elementary education as a primary agent of modernisation, secularisation and citizenship building, even if, unlike its imperial predecessor, it never made attendance compulsory. However, as Cristina Gouvea and Alesandra Schueller's chapter (Chapter 8) makes clear, the state educational project promoted from the centre suffered from all the problems experienced by other South American states in the era. The system was locally organised, underfunded and underdeveloped. Until Brazil succumbed to a centralising dictatorship in the 1930s, it remained a country of illiterates and economically backward: the liberal oligarchs who ran the country at federal and state level were white racists who were little interested in using education to create a common Brazilian culture.

The Ottoman Empire, on the other hand, at the beginning of the period was a Muslim semi-autocracy of longstanding with large Christian and Jewish minorities that had become the plaything of the great European powers in the nineteenth century, if not before. A wish to establish an inclusive and compulsory system of mass education in order to create a common Ottoman identity was part of the reform programme of the last decades of the century aimed at retaining the empire's independence. As Nazan Cicek (Chapter 9) explains, however, virtually nothing was achieved. It proved impossible to replace the separate school systems run by the different religious groups with a network of secular state schools staffed by dedicated teachers: there was no money and little enthusiasm on the ground. It was only when the Empire imploded that mass education came to the Muslim heartland. The new state of Turkey created following the First World War was a unitary and relatively ethnically and religiously homogeneous republic with a secular ethos that made mass education a priority and found ingenious ways of quickly raising literacy levels and inculcating a Turkish nationalism.[22]

Glossary

common Schools: from the 1840s in the United States, these were public schools established for children of all social classes, funded from local taxes and based on non-sectarian principles

high school: secondary school, usually for ages 13 and over in the United States

public school: (United States and Canada): institutions supported by the government (primarily at the state and local level) and free to attending students

Notes

1. L. A. Cremin (1970) *American Education: The Colonial Experience, 1607–1783* (New York: Harper & Row); A. M. Rodríguez Cruz (1973) *Historia de las universidades hispanoamericanas: periodo hispánico*, 2 vols (Bogotá: Instituto Caro y Cuervo); also M. Peset (prologue) (1987) *Universidades españolas y americanas* (Valencia: Generalitat Valenciana).
2. P. Gonzalbo Aizpuru (1974) *Historia de la educación en la época colonia. El mundo indigena* (Mexico City: Colegió de México); *id.* (1990) *Historia de la educación en la época colonial. La educación de los criollos y la vida urbana* (Mexico City: Colegió de México).
3. K. A. Lockridge (1974) *Literacy in Colonial New England: An Enquiry into the Social Context of Literacy in the Early Modern West* (New York: Norton); C. F. Kaestle (1983) *Pillars of the Republic. Common Schools and American Society, 1780–1860* (New York: Hill and Wang), ch. 2.
4. Cited in Kaestle, *Pillars*, p. 96. Information in this and the following paragraph is based on Kaestle's authoritative study.
5. Ibid., p. 91.
6. Tanzin-Castellanos, I (1984) 'Quelques éléments sur l'éducation au Pérou au XIXe siècle', in *Escolarización y sociedad en la España contemporanea 1808–1970. II coloquio de História de la Educación 1983* (Valenci: Ediciones Rubio Esteban); G. Antonio Espinoza (2010) 'State, Primary Schools and Local Communities in the Region (*Departamento*) of Lima, 1821–1905' (unpublished paper kindly lent to the editors of this volume by the

author). For a similar story in the collection *Escolarización y sociedad en la España contemporanea*, see Berchenko, B. 'Alumnos y maestros: problemas de integración al sistema escuolar en Chile'. For other parts of former Spanish America, see (1986) *L'Enseignement primaire en Espagne et au Amérique latine du XVIIIe siècle à nos jours*: Actes du colloque de Tours 29–30 novembre 1985 [du] C.I.R.E.M.A (Tours: Publications de l'Université de Tours). For Brazil, see below, ch. 8.

7. In India's case the establishment of the British Raj in 1858 seems to have made matters worse: see below, pp. 291–2.

8. R. Dore (1984) *Education in Tokugawa Japan* (London: Athlone). Dore's account of premodern Japanese education is the best available in English.

9. The Ming dynasty (1368–1644) had championed state schools and in the late sixteenth century the official Lü K'un had advocated compulsory education for all children for three years. Only the Yung-Chen Ch'ing Emperor in the second quarter of the eighteenth century had been equally enthusiastic for state involvement in education.

10. B. A. Elman and A. Woodside (eds) (1984) *Education and Society in Late Imperial China, 1600–1900* (Berkeley: University of California Press), esp. Intro., Conclusion and chs 11 and 12. Vietnam also recruited to government service through an open examination. Korea had a similar examination system but it was dominated by a few families.

11. Dore, *Education*, Appendix 1, pp. 317–22; E. S. Rawski (1979) *Education and Popular Literacy in Ch'ing China* (Ann Arbor: University of Michigan Press), p. 140. For a critique of Rawski, see A. Woodside (1983) 'Some Mid-Qing Theorists of Popular Schools: Their Innovations, Inhibitions and Attitudes toward the Poor', *Modern China*, 9, 3–35. S. Borthwick (1983) *Education and Social Change in China. The Beginnings of the Modern Era* (Stanford, Calif.: Hoover Institute Press), p. 25.

12. Elman and Woodside, *Education and Society*, p. 532.

13. R. A. Arasteh (1969), *Education and Social Awakening in Iran, 1850–1968* (Leiden: Brill), ch. 4: as late as the 1960s only 30 per cent of Iranian children were in school (p. 82). .

14. See below, p. 234ff.

15. Borthwick, *Education and Social Change in China*, pp. 87–90, 108 (on Zhili). See also R. Hayhoe (1992) (ed.) *Education and Modernization. The Chinese Experience* (Oxford: Pergamon).

16. Two other Asian countries where there was a largely unsuccessful attempt to promote elementary education at the turn of the twentieth century were Korea before the Japanese take-over in 1910 and Siam in the reign of Rama V (1853–1910): see D. Adams and E. E. Gottlieb (1993) *Education and Social Change in Korea* (London: Garland Publishing), p. 11, and D. K. Wyatt (1969) *The Politics of Reform in Thailand: Education in the Reign of King Chulalongkorn* (New Haven, CT: Yale University Press).

17. Cited in H. Passin (1982) *Society and Education in Japan*, paperback edn (Tokyo: Kodansha International Ltd), p. 68. Part 1 is a good introduction to the new educational system.

18. Cited in T. Horio (1990) *Educational Thought and Ideology in Modern Japan. State Authority and Intellectual Freedom* (Tokyo: Tokyo University Press), p. 80. On patriotic education specifically, see Y. Khan (1997) *Japanese Moral Education. Past and Present* (London: Associated University Presses), ch. 3.

19. Statistics in Passin, *Society*, p. 108, and W. K. Cummings (1980) *Education and Equality in Japan* (Princeton, NJ: Princeton University Press), p. 21.

20. From 2 to 5 per cent of 18- to 21-year-olds in Western Europe were in university education on the eve of the First World War: statistics in P. Flora (1983–7), *State, Economy and Society in Western Europe 1815-1975. A Data Handbook in Two Volumes* (Frankfurt and London: Campus Verlag and Macmillan), vol. 1, ch. 10, *passim*.

21. Esp. L. Cremin (1988) *American Education: The Metropolitan Experience, 1876–1980* (London: Harper & Row); *id.* (1964) *The Transformation of the School: Progressivism in American Education 1876–1957* (New York: Vintage).

22. Gouvea and Schueller's study is the first account of the Brazilian experience. There exists an important recent study in English of educational provision in the last decades of the Ottoman sultanate: see B. Fortna (2002) *Imperial Classroom: Islam, the State and Education in the Late Ottoman Empire* (Oxford: Oxford University Press). Important insights for the whole period can also be gleaned from *id.* (2010) *Learning to Read in the Late Ottoman Empire and Early Turkish Republic* (Basingstoke: Palgrave Macmillan). But Cicek's is the first English account to provide an overview that crosses the Ottoman and Turkish divide.

7

'To Become GOOD MEMBERS OF CIVIL SOCIETY and PATRIOTIC AMERICANS': Mass Education in the United States, 1870–1930

Ellen L. Berg

The desire to educate future citizens stimulated the foundation of public schools in the United States. The resulting American public school system was one of the most extensive in the world during the period from 1870 to 1930, as measured by the proportion of children attending and public funds spent. Yet the transformations in the racial and religious composition of the eligible school population created tensions over the goals of public education and access to it. During this era, the changing national definitions of citizenship, including attempts to integrate African Americans and newer immigrant populations, led to a broadening of the citizenry that was often at odds with some Americans' idealised vision of their country. Debates over American citizenship, while national in scope, were thus played out locally – and overtly – in the public schools. Public schools educated the heterogeneous population for American citizenship, and their uneven and contested rise represented the, at times ambiguous, development of a unified sense of nationhood.

The intimate relationship between American citizenship and public education transformed the nature of both. As citizenship and suffrage expanded, so did education in response, but it did so irregularly, with some jurisdictions expanding enthusiastically and others deliberately lagging or even actively blocking certain eligible students from enrolling. The disparate statuses of religious and racial minorities were reflected in the quality and content of local educational opportunities. Thus, with the vastly increasing scope and coverage of the American public schools during these decades came geographical pockets of increasing disparity that limited access to public education for certain groups. At the same time, changing school curricula reflected school organisers' views of citizenship. Schools worked more to develop moral members of society than to create an educated electorate, for suffrage was not a right of all citizens, nor were the voting rights of all potential voters protected. Teachers in some public schools directly endorsed Protestant religious views, and citizenship education often focused more on citizens' obligations to the country than on their rights. However, such biased educational approaches could not alter the underlying fundamental values of the American political system. As American public education expanded, minority and oppressed groups used their knowledge of American political ideals, obtained both within the public schools and independently, to call for the government to grant them their rights as citizens.

Early formation of public schools

From the days of the early republic, many Americans identified public education as a key component in the development of virtuous citizens for the sake of a well-functioning representative democracy. As new laws widened the circles of potential citizens and voters – two distinct categories – states also expanded the available public educational opportunities. *'Jacksonian Democracy' came to life in the 1810s and 1820s with states' removal of property requirements for suffrage, which had previously limited voting rights to only a minority of men. The newly instituted universal white male suffrage highlighted to political leaders the need not just for education, but for *public* education in particular.[1] These changes in voting laws, as well as regional factors such as migration to the West, and the effects of increased immigration and organised labour in the North, propelled the further spread of the 'common school,' a quasi-public institution that was locally organised and supported both by local and state governments as well as by student fees.[2] Education differed little for boys and girls.[3] Co-education in schools developed quietly and naturally by the mid-nineteenth century, with boys and girls attending school at similar rates.[4] Even though some experts made prescriptions related to gender, such as the separation of boys and girls, local teachers and schools often ignored such advice.[5]

The *Common School Revival, which lasted through the onset of the Civil War in 1860 and set the stage for the free public schools of the later nineteenth century, had the greatest impact in northern and western states with high population densities and well-developed reform traditions. Education leaders such as *Horace Mann, secretary of the new Board of Education for the state of Massachusetts, argued for the social and political importance of providing free public education to all. Schools were expected to prepare children for futures in the American economic and political systems as well as in the dominant Protestant culture.[6] Although these early public schools were ostensibly non-religious, clergymen were among their strong supporters, for in this country dominated by Protestants, the qualities of good citizenship were bound up with a generalised Protestant Christianity, with moral education a key component of both.[7] For the promoters of public education, public schools promised the possibility 'of making the United States literally God's country'.[8] By contrast, conditions in the South – namely low population density and political control by the slave-owning class, who had little interest in educating either slaves or poorer whites – were not conducive to the founding of public schools. Wealthy white southerners largely relied on private academies to educate their children. Furthermore, economic declines in the late 1830s and 1840s weakened the South's prosperity, making public educational reform an even lower priority there.[9]

Where they prevailed, common school reformers argued not only for public elementary education but also for public higher education. Private academies and seminaries had, since the eighteenth century, offered secondary education in the so-called modern subjects (modern languages, history and geography, and mathematics and science), most often in a co-educational setting, though the sexes might be divided for instruction. Although some state governments provided them with financial support in order to increase the pool of potential teachers, academies served wealthier families who could afford the fee. Mann argued that such private institutions reduced community support for public education, while public higher education would increase social cohesiveness across the classes. Boston, Massachusetts organised the first public *high school in 1821, though it excluded girls. The number of public high schools, mostly co-educational, grew gradually in the North, particularly from the 1840s onwards, as advocates won state and local debates about the use of tax dollars for secondary education by convincing their opponents that making higher education available to the academically gifted of all classes (as determined by admissions tests) was a republican virtue.[10]

The early expansion of the common school at all levels was founded on an institutional model that persisted in the public schools of the late nineteenth century as well as in modified form today. Schools were supervised by the various states, but control was local and support came largely from local taxes. Leaders of the common school revival of the nineteenth century depicted 'each local district school as a bulwark of the Republic', a vision that prompted increasingly vigorous educational work by states.[11] The details of how best to create an educated, moral citizenry were considered from multiple angles – according to Mann, even the very design of the schoolhouse should contribute to the children's civic development.[12] By the time the Civil War began in 1860, most states had publicly supported schools. Small towns generally vested authority in the hands of a democratically elected school committee, whereas large cities had boards of education. By giving control to local authorities who were reliant on the support of the people they served, this system placed responsibility with the local public to help shape the political lessons to be taught.[13] Because all social classes of people were eligible for participation in the decisions of the local schools, as they were in the larger American representative democracy, class identities did not provide a major area of conflict in the development of American schools.[14] In fact, the American public school offered the ideal (if not always the reality) of providing all children with the opportunity to become part of a 'leadership cadre' based on both 'the shared experience and the shared curriculum' of the public school.[15] Despite this foundation, however, religious and racial differences proved to be a barrier to the development of a truly common school experience for American children.

American Education, c. 1870–1914

In 1870, the United States was in the midst of its post-Civil War *Reconstruction period. The end of the war and the reunification of the southern and northern states led to a general re-evaluation of the preferred development trajectory of American society. The United States was still primarily an agrarian nation, steeped in the Protestantism of its founders, but nascent trends in technology, politics, demographics and territory hinted that the country was on the cusp of great change. Over the next 60 years, the country would add 11 western states, bringing its total to 48. During these years, it would become highly industrialised, particularly in the Northeast and Midwest, with unprecedented rates of immigration. Furthermore, for the first time, the population would shift from a majority living in rural areas to a majority living in cities. The effects of these dramatic shifts were uneven, however, bringing fewer changes to the South. The civil rights reforms of Reconstruction in the South would be short-lived, with the white planter class maintaining political and economic control. In all regions, the public school was the subject of politicisation, as its students served as a tangible representation of the future of the country.[16]

Along with these broader developments in American society, the period from 1870 to 1930 witnessed a vast expansion of the American educational system. Throughout this period, the propagation of American public schools was not primarily a *federal* project but was very much a *national* one, propelled by elite participants in broad educational movements with specific agendas enacted at the state and local levels. Together, these institutions and individuals made manifest the desire for a united and educated citizenry by creating a relatively uniform system of education within the nation. The federal government did, however, demonstrate explicit interest in the improvement of American education during Reconstruction, primarily through a new focus on educational statistics. The Department of Education, founded in 1867 and variously called the Office of Education or Bureau of Education and Statistics in ensuing years, was authorised to gather statistics that would 'show the condition and progress of education in the several States and Territories' as well as to spread information about school organisation, management and pedagogy that would 'promote the cause of education throughout the country'.[17] One of the bureau's early findings was that 57 per cent of children aged 5 to 18 were enrolled in school in 1870.[18] In addition, Congress required new states during this period to provide public education, and it set aside more land for public schools than for other institutions including universities and hospitals.[19]

Educational programmes grew dramatically after the Civil War, especially during the 1870s, as the youth population both grew and attended school at higher rates.[20] Some of this growth occurred in the public high schools, which had largely dropped the requirement for students to pass an entrance examination in order to attend.[21] For several decades, attendance in public high schools in the North had outstripped that of the private academies.[22] Nevertheless, the theoretical access to public secondary education was not yet enough to make it a universal experience for American youths. At the end of the century, only 7 per cent of American teenagers graduated from high school.[23] Many of these were young women who would become teachers.[24] Girls aged 10–14 had reached higher educational achievements than boys the same age by 1870, and as public co-educational high schools expanded, girls attended at higher rates than boys.[25] Prepared by the public schools, women increasingly entered the education profession, representing 57 per cent of teachers in 1879–80 and 86 per cent by 1919–20.[26]

On the surface, the United States appeared to be achieving the goal of providing a common education for its young people by 1900, when 72 per cent of Americans aged 5 to 18 were enrolled in school.[27] An 1880 study by Michael G. Mulhall found that the United States had 'what was in many respects the most popular system of education in the world'; it had a higher proportion of children in school and more money spent per child than European countries such as England, France, and Germany.[28] Nevertheless, the popularisation of education did not create uniformity in the experiences of all young people. Cities and counties provided over 75 per cent of public school funding through the period of this study, with the remainder coming from the existing 48 state governments rather than the federal government.[29] The states and localities grappled, both individually and collectively, with the task of incorporating disparate religious, racial, and ethnic minorities into the schools and thus into the national fabric.

The effects of immigration and religion on patriotic education

The decades prior to 1920 coincided with unprecedented levels of migration to the United States, with one in seven residents of the United States having been born in another country. This shift in population led both to discussions about the nature of religious education in the public schools and to re-evaluations of the ways in which patriotism and citizenship should be developed in the children of the United States.

Religion was one seemingly intractable problem in American public schools. Throughout much of the early period of schooling in the United States, public education was tied inseparably to the teaching of moral and religious values. Though New England states had begun issuing laws restricting the teaching of sectarian religion in the public schools in the mid-nineteenth century, elements such as prayers and the reading of Bible verses were deemed acceptable and remained in many schools. During the period of renewed Protestant fervour after the Civil War, Protestant ministers maintained an active interest in public school, and they and many other advocates for the public schools re-emphasised the importance of religious education for good citizenship.[30] Rising immigration after the Civil War included large numbers of Catholics, who came to comprise 17 per cent of the population by 1907.[31] This migration, coupled with the strong history of anti-Catholicism in the United States, contributed to an additional advocacy for Protestant religious education in the schools.[32]

Catholics repeatedly protested the ostensibly non-sectarian religious teachings embedded in the public school curricula. They believed, for example, that reading Bible verses, even 'without note or comment' was an unacceptable, sectarian activity.[33] Thus, whereas American children on the whole were becoming increasingly likely to attend public rather than private schools – 47 per cent of all educational spending funded public schools in 1850, rising to 79 per cent in 1890 – the trend towards consolidation of education in the public schools was not entirely true for Catholic children.[34] Conservative Catholics urged the founding of Catholic parochial schools, which were usually organised by the parish. The propensity towards school formation varied by ethnicity of the parish, with Italians, for instance, less likely than some Catholic groups to form their own schools.[35] (It should be noted that ethnic barriers were not absolute, so immigrant children in parochial schools did encounter those of different ethnicities, a situation that probably had some assimilatory effect on them.)[36] Catholic schools became increasingly popular, doubling the percentage of the student population they served between 1870 and 1930, when they taught 9 per cent of primary school students. Contemporary sources estimated that one-third to one-half of all eligible Catholic children attended parochial school.[37] In Providence, Rhode Island, for example, approximately 38 per cent of Catholic students attended Catholic schools in 1880, though that number declined to 28 per cent by 1925.[38]

Not all non-Protestants believed that sending their children to religious schools was the best solution to the conflicts over religion in the schools. Liberal Catholics known as Americanists, who gained influence in American Catholicism in the 1890s, preferred to participate in – and help mould – the public schools rather than be relegated to what they saw as second-class citizenship.[39] For example, in Worcester, Massachusetts, leading Irish-Catholics supported public education rather than building their own parochial schools.[40] Catholics who wanted to send their children to public schools lobbied against the morning religious exercises, including hymns, prayers, and Bible reading, which they felt were sectarian in nature and thus contradicted the separation of church and state.[41]

Jews, like Catholics, were also migrating to the United States in greater numbers by the end of the end of the nineteenth century. Orthodox and Reform Jews joined together to protest religious aspects of public school life, including Christmas celebrations in the classroom.[42] Some school districts adapted to these concerns, in part because they feared that alienated non-Protestants would remove their children from the positive influence of the public schools. For example, Troy, New York, banned all religious exercises in its schools in 1875, 'in order that children of all class's [sic] may share in that education essential to good citizenship'.[43] The need to consider the religious sensibilities of non-Protestants seemed to signify 'the gradual collapse of the *traditional* American public school' for some Americans, who blamed the Catholic minority for a perceived decline in character training in the public schools.[44] As schools modified their curricula to better suit the religious beliefs of their changing populations, some educational leaders began to argue that the religion being taught in schools had become so attenuated as to be meaningless.[45]

In reality, a shift away from the Protestant underpinnings of the public school was not fully achieved during this time period. Education for citizenship clearly still drew on America's Protestant roots. Sociologist Lester F. Ward provided one possible justification for this inclusion of religion in the public schools, despite the antagonism it created, by pronouncing in 1883 that the needs of the state were the most important to consider in providing education to the young – superseding the claims of the church, the family, and the children themselves.[46] The challenges to the teaching of religion in the public sphere strengthened some Protestants' resolve to include religious education in the public schools at what may have been an unprecedented level. After all, the repeated demands for Bible reading in the public schools over the course of the nineteenth century suggest that the practice was not already standard at many schools.[47] Either way, religion remained a regular part of the classroom experience for many American children. In 1912, laws in 14 states (and the Constitution of one state) called for Bible reading in the classroom.[48] Even today, debates over religion in the American public schools persist in many parts of the country.

While non-Protestant immigrants prompted specific debates about the extent of religious education in the public schools, the entire mass migration of the late nineteenth and early twentieth centuries contributed to a rethinking of the public understanding of citizenship in the United States. Public schools were the arena in which Americans contested and negotiated conflicting ideas about patriotism that were developing as they looked back over the course of the nineteenth century.[49] Patriotic education was becoming more prominently incorporated into the curriculum of the public school. From the 1870s, some school leaders required teachers to include citizenship education in their curricula, perhaps because of the 'decline of patriotic fervor' evident in the decades after the Civil War, though they did not explicate the ideal pedagogical methods for doing so.[50] Beginning in the late 1880s, American public schools began to display more uniformity in how they taught patriotism to children. The advocates of the schoolhouse flag movement sought to place an American flag outside every school – thereby emphasising the school's ties to the larger nation – and to institute the daily recitation of a pledge of allegiance.[51] Both the U.S. Commissioner of Education, William Torrey Harris, and teacher members of the *National Education Association supported such moves.[52]

During these years, the United States exhibited what was perhaps the most 'elaborate development' of formal civics training compared to other nations.[53] This instruction began simply as the study of American history, mandated by 23 states in statutes passed between the Civil War and 1900. By the First World War, yet even more states required civics education, which focused on knowledge of 'governmental machinery' with some attention to 'patriots of the past'.[54] Some of the publications in this new movement for civics education served as a sort of secular catechism intended to shape children's thoughts about their country. For example, one asked, '"What is the aim of the Public School?" ... To Train us in such habits of behavior as will best fit us to become GOOD MEMBERS OF CIVIL SOCIETY and PATRIOTIC AMERICANS'.[55]

Although a large part of the renewed interest in national patriotism stemmed from the nation's need to reconcile the North and the South after the Civil War, the daily arrival of large numbers of new immigrants served also to stoke the insecurities of the native white population. Whereas previous migrants originated primarily from northern and western Europe, first- and second-generation immigrants, who now comprised one-third of the country's population, more often traced their origins to southern and eastern Europe after 1880. The increasing industrialisation and urbanisation of the country added to native-born Americans' sense of disorientation. By 1920, the majority of all American residents lived in urban areas. Immigrants were even more likely than average to live in cities – up to 75 per cent of them did – so in the largest cities in the country, first- and second-generation immigrants comprised the majority of the population.[56] The growth of the cities and their changing demographics fuelled such social service efforts as settlement houses, kindergartens, playgrounds, milk stations, institutional churches, and community centres, all of which served children, at least in part.

The major trend in education for citizenship during this period was that of educating children not as future voters – for suffrage was not a right of all citizens – but as moral members of the larger society. Sometimes this goal was discussed in the specific context of Americanisation. Francis Adams wrote in 1875 that the public school 'draws children from all nations together and marks them with the impress of nationality'.[57] For Harris, public school meant encouraging immigrants 'to participate in our best civilization'.[58] But often this goal was used to refer to society in general. Education was both one requirement for active participation 'in the social organism' and a means of obtaining the other skills necessary to be a good member of society.[59] Community civic courses taught children to think about 'community welfare' and their relationships with those around them.[60] Julie Reuben sees this shift as being intended to de-emphasise voting and to restrict individual rights.[61] Certainly, as recognised by social control theory, this approach perpetuated inequalities, such as women's ineligibility to vote despite their citizenship and southern blacks' inability to exercise their voting rights. However, broader conceptions of citizenship could also be used to tie children more firmly to their local communities (through 'civic patriotism' and its focus on local action) as well as encourage them to develop a sense of connectedness that transcended national boundaries.[62] This goal was nevertheless likely not fully realised; as Patricia Graham suggests, in the hands of 'the beleaguered school administrator', school curricula were likely to express a simpler, less expansive view of patriotism.[63] In either case, ideals of citizenship as stated in the early twentieth century emphasised individual behaviour that was not directly tied to voting or traditional modes of political participation but to contributions to the larger society.[64]

Compulsory education was another component of the expansion of the educational system. Starting in 1852 in Massachusetts, a decentralised – but national – compulsory education movement had been progressing among the states. By 1890, about 30 of the 42 states had such laws, usually requiring attendance from age 8 to 14. More states enacted similar laws over the next two decades, with required attendance often dropping to age 7 and ending at age 14 or 15. New Jersey (age 7 to 17) and Idaho (age 8 to 18) adopted the most extensive requirements.[65] In the states of the North and West, 'compulsory school attendance was concrete evidence of their institutional strength; for young territories it was a symbol of their wish to obtain statehood.'[66] In 1912, American William A. Cook argued that in England, compulsory education 'has been regarded as necessary in order to keep the lower classes from wronging themselves.' He contrasted this situation with that of the United States:

> In America the matter has been considered from the social and political point of view instead of from the personal point of view. Americans consider compulsory education as the *sine qua non* of political existence, since the state cannot, for its own sake permit any of its citizens to grow up in ignorance.[67]

Whether for their personal reasons or for their commitment to the American polity, immigrants during this period needed little coaxing to send their children to primary school. While immigrants had typically attended school at rates lower than other groups,[68] school attendance was relatively high for immigrants during this period. For example, school enrolment of 10- to 13-year-olds in 1910 was over 90 per cent for children of British, Irish, Scandinavian, Jewish, Canadian, German, Italian, Polish, and Russian families living in the United States, compared with 92.9 per cent for native whites and strikingly lower rates for American Indians (72.1 per cent) and African Americans (70.1 per cent).[69] Compulsory attendance laws thus remained largely symbolic, as evidenced by a lack of both need and enforcement, though some cities also initiated concerted efforts to counteract truancy by the turn of the twentieth century.[70]

Although compulsory education laws seemed largely unnecessary in the North due to high rates of school participation, their relative absence in the South reflected that region's ambivalence about the citizenship of some of its residents. In 1904, only two states among those in the broad definition of 'the South' had compulsory education laws, West Virginia and Kentucky, while only one state outside the South, Missouri, lacked them.[71] Despite a national movement for such laws, in 1912, seven states, all in the South, still lacked them.[72] The reluctance of southern states to institute compulsory education laws originated, in large part, with whites' concerns about the fitness of non-whites to be full-fledged American citizens. For white inhabitants of these states, compulsory education 'signaled a threat to the traditional means of social control, which the planter class sought to maintain in a racially divided form', for it required the education of all African American children.[73] Finally, all states enacted them in the ensuing years, with the final holdout, Mississippi, succumbing in 1918.[74] A more detailed discussion of race in the history of public education, however, demonstrates that inequalities remained much more persistent.

Race, education, and second-class citizenship

Historians have traditionally downplayed the role of race in the development and refining of the public school system in the United States. In his discussion of the American common schools, Carl F. Kaestle argues that Americans drew on 'republican, Protestant, and capitalist values' in their efforts to develop school systems 'to integrate and assimilate a diverse population into the nation's political, economic, and cultural institutions.'[75] Hilary Moss makes the point, however, that racial ideologies were also central to the values of the early common school: 'as greater numbers of white people availed themselves of public schooling, some white people also sought to deny access to their black neighbours because it was a mark of the very citizenship they sought to withhold from African Americans.'[76] Although the early public schools were known as common schools, children's experiences were often not common at all, depending on their race. Moss's research focuses on the early nineteenth century, and it is clear that racism in public education persisted well into the next century. Between 1870 and 1930, public education opportunities in the United States varied across demographic groups, a reflection of the dominant local cultures' desires to reserve the full rights of citizenship for themselves. In any public school, both the conditions and the curriculum reflected a vision of citizenship that the school organisers saw as desirable for the particular student body. As James Anderson writes, 'Both schooling for democratic citizenship and schooling for second-class citizenship have been basic traditions in American education.'[77] Non-whites, whether Native Americans, Asians, or African Americans, had vastly different educational experiences from their white counterparts. Over the course of these years, and into the mid-twentieth century, however, minority groups in the United States would assert their rights of citizenship, sometimes based on the very lessons they learned in the public schools.

This period saw multiple redefinitions of the rights of citizenship and suffrage for different races, both in principle and in practice. The Fourteenth Amendment to the United States Constitution, adopted in 1868 as part of Reconstruction after the Civil War, declared, 'All persons born or naturalized in the United States, and subject to the jurisdiction thereof, are citizens of the United States and of the State wherein they reside.' As Americans struggled with the consequences of this widened definition of citizenship, they continually reshaped the composition of the public schools to reflect their views of how citizens of different categories should be educated. Though the federal government had an official interest in American public education, the schools themselves remained almost entirely decentralised.[78] Local control resulted in diversity in how schools were conducted. Robert William Dale, a Congregational pastor who visited in 1877 from England, noted that in the United States, 'local educational authorities have a much larger amount of freedom than is permitted to *School Boards in this country.'[79] Even though the federal government had the final say on who was an American citizen (and thus a citizen of his or her state of residence), smaller organisational units such as states and counties often instituted a sort of second-class citizenship for racial minorities. School segregation was a common method of differentiating between citizens of different backgrounds. For example, until the mid-twentieth century, local school boards in Texas isolated Americans of Mexican descent in their own schools, though the state of Texas itself only called for two separate branches of schools, for blacks and whites.[80]

The impact of local conditions and preferences can be seen in the case of Chinese immigrants, who encountered massive discrimination, including limits on immigration beginning in 1882. Chinese immigrants were not eligible for citizenship (and would not be until 1952), but an 1884 U.S. Circuit Court case found that their American-born children were citizens under the Fourteenth Amendment.[81] As a result, San Francisco's Board of Education was compelled to provide public education for Asian children who were birthright citizens. It did so by the establishment of a new, segregated, 'Oriental Public School'.[82] By contrast, due to different local decisions made in New York City, children of Chinese descent attended integrated schools such as P.S. 23, where they studied alongside Italian-American children.[83]

African Americans suffered the consequences of localised and regional prejudice more than any other group. At the beginning of the Civil War, African Americans were enslaved only in the South, but they faced strong prejudice and legalised inequality in the North as well. For example, in 1857 the Supreme Court had ruled in *Dred Scott v. Sandford* that African Americans could not be citizens, and their inequality was perpetuated in conditions such as segregated schools.[84] Education provided a path to the citizenship status that some whites wanted to preserve for their own race.[85] Massachusetts was the first state to abolish school segregation, in 1855, but more widespread desegregation did not occur easily. Northern teachers had little interest in challenging local norms, and only a few whites advocated openly for the importance of African American education in general.[86] Although the Fourteenth Amendment broadened citizenship to include all people born in the United States, African Americans were thereafter treated as second-class citizens, as can be seen in their education in the public schools, particularly in the South. In 1874, the Republican Party responded to segregation not only in the South but also in northern states such as Ohio by attempting to require racially mixed public schools nationwide. Their efforts were politically disastrous, with Republicans across the country losing seats as a result of their party's support for the bill.[87] While other northern states and localities followed suit in integrating schools in the 1870s and 1880s, as in Philadelphia in 1881, the enactment of these laws against school segregation did not guarantee enforcement on the local level.[88] Furthermore, northerners increasingly adopted segregationist views in the 1890s and 1900s, a result both of a growing black migration to the North as well as northern and southern reunification behind *Social Darwinism, which supported 'racialist theories of progress' and allowed for a 'new nationalism' based 'on the unity of Anglo-Saxons'.[89] These ideas were used by supporters of the 1898 Spanish-American War to justify international imperialist expansion of the white-controlled United States beyond the borders of North America.[90] The increased racialist thinking was also visible within the country. Some cities in Illinois, New Jersey, Kansas, and Pennsylvania actually segregated their previously integrated schools.[91]

Of course, public educational opportunities for African Americans in the South were even worse throughout this period. Black children entering public schools had a disadvantage from the start. Because slaves were largely denied education for centuries, approximately 70 per cent of African Americans living in southern states were illiterate in 1870.[92] Furthermore, prior to the Civil War, the southern states (with the exception of North Carolina) had been slow to adopt public education even for white children, and afterwards they resented being required to fund public education for African Americans as a prerequisite to being readmitted to the Union. Southerners associated public schools with the Republican Party, with its history of abolitionism and its post-war efforts to educate African Americans 'to be worthy of the responsibilities of citizenship and suffrage'.[93] To no one's surprise, the South responded to the requirement by providing racially segregated schools, following the pattern of schools in much of the North.[94] New Orleans, Louisiana, was the sole southern city to integrate its schools, but its 1869 experiment was short-lived, ending in 1876 due to whites' extreme opposition.[95] In 1877, the federal government abandoned its policies of Reconstruction in the South, leaving the southern states free to enact so-called 'Jim Crow' laws, which kept African Americans from exercising their rights of citizenship. For example, state and local laws throughout the South deterred African Americans from registering to vote through the use of poll taxes, literacy tests, and other requirements. Public school opportunities for African Americans, too, typically declined in this era. In Maryland, an 1872 law required counties to offer schools for African Americans, but within two decades these institutions were being neglected; 11 of the 23 counties stopped funding the schools open to their large African American populations, leaving them to rely on state and private funds.[96]

The history of the southern states' secession during the Civil War reverberated through the curriculum presented to both black and white Southerners. During Reconstruction, 'black Southerners emerged as the region's patriots, while most Confederates retreated from the public sphere in despair,' according to Cecilia O'Leary. The end of Reconstruction and the introduction of Jim Crow laws tended to have a dampening effect on African-American patriotism, in part because some African Americans lost confidence in the country's ability to guarantee them liberty. For their part, white Southerners resented their loss in the Civil War, and Confederate veterans' organisations succeeded in affirming white Southerners' patriotism while still glorifying the 'Lost Cause' and white supremacy.[97] With the forces opposing displays of national patriotism arrayed against them, southern African Americans kept a low profile in terms of embracing American identity. It was not until 1899 that one African American school located in Calhoun, Alabama, flew the American flag, and an African American teacher on St. John's Island in South Carolina was surprised to find in 1910 that her students had never learned the patriotic song, 'America the Beautiful'.[98]

White Southerners' freedom to discriminate against African Americans grew even stronger at the end of the nineteenth century. An 1896 Supreme Court case, *Plessy v. Ferguson*, upheld the constitutionality of racial segregation, further fuelling the decline of conditions for African Americans in the South. Given the animosity felt by whites towards African Americans, it is no surprise that southern cities and counties tended not to abide by Plessy's mandate for 'separate but

equal' treatment. As Patricia Graham argues, 'when schooling was seen as primarily serving the needs of the society to prepare citizens, few whites wished to
spend much of their limited funds on schooling for their black neighbors, who,
despite the post-Civil War amendments to the U.S. Constitution, still did not
enjoy full rights as citizens.'[99] White northerners tended not to interfere in southern racism during this time. Drawing on their perceived shared racial superiority,
made explicit in Social Darwinist texts, whites in the North and South essentially
made a pact: those in the South would agree to national reunification so long as
they had the authority to control race relations in their own region.

White Southerners were aided in promoting their Confederate heritage in part
by friendly publishers. They could purchase textbooks written and produced in
the South but they could also choose from among textbooks produced in the
North by publishers who avoided passing judgment about the South's culpability
in the Civil War in order to guarantee southern sales.[100] Detesting this collaboration, Union veterans active in the *Grand Army of the Republic fraternal organisation worked to assert the moral superiority of the North in textbook discussions
of the Civil War. This effort began in 1888, and within a decade they felt that their
influence had caused some improvements.[101] However, the reunification of North
and South behind imperialism also translated into 'common ground...in a shared
racism', with northern historians 'softening – even romanticizing – their pictures
of slavery' ever more.[102] One 1911 textbook, *A Birds'-Eye View of American History*,
by Leon C. Prince of Pennsylvania's Dickinson College, received the approbation
of numerous Southerners for its supposed 'impartiality', which might better be
described as support for the southern point of view. Most notable was the praise
of Thomas Dixon, Jr., whose book *The Clansman* helped to reignite national interest in the Ku Klux Klan and who wrote of Prince, 'As a loyal American of loyal
Southern blood, let me thank you for the service you have rendered the cause of
truth in this fearless statement of facts.'[103] Northerners were clearly complicit in
maintaining the system of racial hierarchy entrenched in the South.

The South was a poor region, with a higher population of children than the
North, and maintaining a dual system of separate schools for blacks and whites
was expensive. As a result, southern states earmarked school funds with priority
to whites, particularly between 1900 and 1915, as educational reformers achieved
increased funding for schools.[104] By 1918, African Americans comprised 11 per
cent of the southern population but received only 2 per cent of school funding.[105]
In the state of Alabama, for instance, the legislature passed laws allocating state
funds for education with differential rates according to the races served. Two prior
decades of somewhat equitable teacher pay for whites and blacks were thus ended;
by 1910, salaries of white teachers were more than double those of black teachers.[106] (And those hiring African American teachers for African American schools
preferred 'native southerners who were untainted by northern influences and
amenable to the direction of southern whites', which is to say, African Americans
who would not be expected to challenge the racial hierarchy.)[107] Overall spending could be even more disparate, according to local preferences, because states
allowed local school boards to designate funds as they wished and did not enforce

equality in the programmes offered. In one agricultural county in Alabama, school expenditures per white child were over 30 times those per African American child in 1912.[108]

Public school systems in the South had not yet caught up with those in the rest of the country, and the persistence of poor economic conditions and school segregation perpetuated the inferior educational opportunities for African Americans in those states. While 90 per cent of American children aged 6 to 14 attended schools in 1919, participation lagged in the South, totalling 70 per cent of southern whites and 56 per cent of southern blacks, and both instructional days and average days of school attended were lower than in the North.[109] Public high schools were increasingly established for whites in the South after 1900, but the same was not true for African Americans, who had few public high schools available to them in the South until the 1920s, and those primarily in cities.[110] Rural children, who made up 80 per cent of the southern school-aged population, were generally disadvantaged according to one contemporary who stated that the superiority of the urban schools was 'universally accepted,' with urban dwellers receiving 'nearly 30 per cent more and better education every year'.[111] The low levels of education in the South in general prompted one southern observer in 1904 to insist that illiteracy did not preclude good citizenship – though he did acknowledge that it lead to weaker institutions.[112]

Even if Southern schools had offered equal accommodations for blacks, it would have been difficult for them to overcome the educational handicap derived from generations of enslavement.[113] Nevertheless, African American educational attainment in the South grew dramatically, a testament to the work of African American educators and families.[114] Illiteracy rates dropped to 30 per cent for southern African Americans by 1910, high compared to the 5 per cent for whites but much lower than the post-Civil War years, with higher rates of illiteracy for boys than for girls.[115] However, public schools continued to reflect African Americans' second-class citizenship, and not until 1954 did the *Brown v. Board of Education* Supreme Court ruling lead to the gradual national dismantling of school racial segregation.

In contrast to African Americans, the case of the Native Americans in the United States provides an unusually strong example of publicly supported education for citizenship, perhaps because the federal government rather than the states was the driving force behind the Indian schools. An 1884 Supreme Court case ruled that members of the nation's Indian population, then living on reservations, were not American citizens, but three years later, the Dawes Severalty Act began to provide them with an avenue for gaining citizenship by owning private land and giving up claims to tribal property. As a result of the Dawes Act, the American federal government set up Indian schools with the intention of transforming the youngest Native Americans into potential American citizens by instilling in them new modes of conduct.[116] For example, the Indian schools generally had an English-only language policy; even the one Superintendent of Indian Schools who was more flexible on this point nevertheless held ethnocentric beliefs favouring 'what is good and best in the American civilization, to which the red children of plain and forest are to be led.'[117] To achieve their ends, educators of Native Americans adopted an assimilationist approach, increasingly separating children from their families and challenging parental authority as a way of helping the child to become individualised, in addition to promoting Christian teachings. By 1900, 153 of the 307 Indian schools were boarding schools, and they had a much larger capacity than the day schools, teaching 82 per cent of students served by the Indian Bureau. Over a third of the boarding schools were located off-reservation, further distancing the children from their home communities.[118] Congress tinkered with the rules of citizenship for Native Americans, eventually enacting in 1917 a policy that offered citizenship in exchange for the attainment of 21 years of age and the completion of the Indian Schools' course of study.[119] Now, truly, education directly created new American citizens. However, while education in the Indian schools became a permanent part of the identity of those who attended them, it could not guarantee Native American children and teens that they would find acceptance and happiness in the larger community of the United States.[120] For Native Americans, as for other minority groups, technical citizenship was distinct from cultural acceptance.

The First World War and beyond

During the First World War, the practice of identifying good citizenship as a broad set of specific, personal practices became further exaggerated in the then-dominant 'Americanization movement', whose proponents emphasised what they construed as the mutual benefits of assimilating into the dominant American national identity. In the most extreme cases, Americanisers sought to impose cultural ideals on the immigrant population, claiming that true Americans would eat, dress, and talk as Anglo-Americans did.[121] Although teachers were not primary proponents of Americanisation, they saw its effects in national discussions about public schools and their curricula.[122] Teachers accused of disloyalty, such as not being appropriately pro-war, were dismissed from their positions.[123] The 'English-Only' movement in language education had begun to gain favour during the late nineteenth century, countering a history of bilingual education that naturally developed in areas dominated by diverse immigrant groups. It took off during the war, directed largely against German-language instruction, with English 'elevated to a mythic, sacrosanct status by school officials who sought to immunize immigrants against alleged disloyalty and subversiveness.'[124] Almost half the states in the country banned or limited the use of German language, removing it as a subject from public schools.[125] The war also prompted requirements that schools 'teach for citizenship' in an explicit way; all states had such laws within the decade.[126]

In the immediate post-war period, including the 1919–1920 Red Scare, many Americans questioned the loyalty of immigrant groups. They urged the development of specific Americanisation courses for adults above the age of compulsory education, yet they seemed more sanguine about the children of foreign descent, arguing that the programmes of the public schools would make Americans out of them, for example by providing lessons on the founding of the country and its national heroes. In some schools, too, children participated in experiments of self-government.[127] Experts newly concerned with the 'efficiency' of society urged increased teaching of social studies – up to one-third of students' time in school – in order to help children grow 'to meet the increasingly complex problems of an ever-increasingly complex civilization'.[128]

Those involved in educating for citizenship in the 1920s had structural reasons to argue that their efforts would be more successful than ever. At the turn of the twentieth century, the length of the American school year had been much shorter than the 40 weeks that one observer suggested was standard for schools in Germany, France, and England.[129] However, both the length of the school year and the average attendance rate rose dramatically in the twentieth century, particularly during the 1920s. By 1929–1930, students attended 143 days of school on average compared to 78 days in 1869–1870.[130] For decades, student/teacher ratios had stayed roughly steady at approximately 34–37 students per teacher as had expenditures per pupil (after inflation), but in the 1920s, class sizes grew smaller and expenditures rose.[131]

This period also saw huge growth in attendance at comprehensive high schools, making secondary school part of true mass public education in the United States. By 1940, 49 per cent of American teenagers would graduate from high school, the vast majority of those receiving free public education.[132] In 1918, almost 90 per cent of secondary school students in the United States attended free public schools, with the states paying over twice as much per high school student as they did for elementary school students.[133] These schools tended to draw on the hands-on approach of the *Progressive education movement, offering practical industrial or commercial topics of study in addition to academic preparation for college as well as providing education for citizenship.[134] In the American public high school, teens 'from all sorts and conditions of families' were educated in different tracks within the same institution, an organisational format that ostensibly provided them with a democratic experience, even while some focused on academic and others on vocational training.[135]

However, in addition to a broadening of educational opportunities, the 1920s also had a darker side. The mass immigration of the preceding decades – and, perhaps, the immigrants' successes in becoming part of American life – led to immigration restrictions in 1921 and 1924. Furthermore, nativists from groups such as the Ku Klux Klan fought to preserve the public school from the so-called perils of pluralism.[136] They urged that children be required not merely to attend school but to attend *public* school, in order to emphasise the ideas taught therein, though this movement for compulsory public education ultimately had little traction.[137] Civic education in the 1920s tended to be similarly repressive. In a study of textbooks, historian and former teacher Bessie Pierce had found that 'history and civics texts primarily emphasized the duties and responsibilities citizens owed the government because of the protection it provided'.[138] So citizenship was portrayed as a set of obligations, and those who appeared to be challenging the government were portrayed in an extremely negative light. Sociologist Malcolm

Willey critiqued the provocative language in some high school textbooks, arguing that terms used to describe labour organisers such as *'predatory, hold-up, guerrilla,* and *revolutionary* are certain to raise prejudiced pictures of trade unionism in the minds of immature boys and girls'. Similarly, he decried the contrasting of the International Workers of the World (known as the Wobblies) with 'right-thinking' Americans and 'decent' men.[139] By the 1920s, civic education was not as simple as teaching children about how the government worked; it was also providing a platform for the expression of political ideology as political fact. Children of the 1920s, witnessing that age's political repression, immigration restrictions, and the activities of racially based organisations such as the Ku Klux Klan, received a political education indeed, both within and outside school.

Conclusion

The public school was not alone in working to transform young people into American citizens, but it had the strongest impact. Some other institutions, such as the political parties, focused their attention primarily on adults. The press reached children somewhat more extensively, with activities such as the *Lyceum League of America, organised by the *Youth's Companion* magazine to encourage boys to engage in the tradition of political debate. Better known, of course, are the Boy Scouts of America and analogous organisations for girls, the Girl Scouts and the Camp Fire Girls. These types of societies were intended to supplement the lessons in citizenship that children already received in school, providing them with opportunities for 'character-building with civic interests as incidental and collateral'.[140] Proponents of civic education also advocated the insertion of their message into other 'accessory educational agencies', including 'moving pictures, public libraries, Red Cross service, and the like', although these efforts probably had a less substantive effect on children.[141] Instead, it was the public schools that reached the most children with their long-term emphasis on education for citizenship.

   The effectiveness of programmes for citizenship can be difficult to measure. Educators and reformers were emphatic about the success of their work in providing children with early experiences in citizenship, perhaps even more than they would find in later civic life. Mary Kingsbury Simkhovitch, a social worker and part of the *settlement house movement, wrote, 'The children in the public schools lead more nearly a life of real democracy than any other group. They are instilled with a common point of view.' She claimed, 'The reason is, not because they daily salute the flag, but because there is no strain to which their loyalty is subjected'. While adult immigrants saw native-born Americans receive 'preferment, privileges, great differences in modes of living', Simkhovitch held out hope that their children might have the opportunity to prosper as citizens even after 'the mask of idealism' of public school was removed from their faces, though she acknowledged that native-born Americans' treatment of immigrants and their children often lacked 'a cordial welcome, a practical fraternalism and democracy'.[142] Michael Olneck notes the acculturative effects of schools and extracurricular programs but is sceptical about the success of their 'attempts to intensify patriotic sentiments and to develop American attitudes and beliefs'.[143] Research by Reed Ueda suggests how this education might have had an impact, if not exactly how its proponents intended. Studying second-generation Japanese immigrants living in Hawaii in the 1920s and 1930s, Ueda described the 'progressive education program aimed at cultivating democratic citizenship' in their schools: '[e]ssay and elocution contests, lectures, student government, and service programs were vehicles for teaching patriotism, citizenship, and democratic values'.[144] He finds that the youth were able to build on their citizenship education to assert their rights. According to one student, 'I am an American citizen so I think I should have equal rights as others'.[145] Ueda argues that citizenship education influenced youth much more than the cultural education emphasising Anglo-conformity, for the youths used their status of American citizenship to assert their right to have an ethnic, Japanese-American identity.[146] While the community civics approach to citizenship may have been intended to teach children to subordinate themselves to public institutions, the end result was often quite different.

The population of citizens in the United States over the decades of 1870 to 1930 grew not only through the immigration of new ethnic groups but also through legal redefinitions. In response, diverse groups of Americans responded by re-envisioning the education for citizenship that was still the basis for the growing public school system. Though they softened some aspects of the curriculum, becoming more sensitive to non-Protestants' concern about possible sectarian teachings, for example, they did not make dramatic alterations. And at times, they responded to requirements for greater inclusion of minority groups in the public schools by providing inferior education, or education intended to subordinate groups. It is impossible to measure exactly how effective American public schools were at instilling any single lesson about citizenship in the hearts of the children they taught. Yet the public school's response to religious and racial difference, changing as it did over these decades to mirror popular opinion, gave children a palpable lesson of how the citizenship of different groups was valued. Opposing these real-life lessons about diversity and inequality were the universalist ideals of American citizenship, whose power is evident in the ways that they were sometimes turned back against the school. By teaching children about the established rights and responsibilities of what it meant to be Americans, educators gave the children the tools and, perhaps, the motivation to assert their own convictions about what American citizenship meant to them.

Timeline

1821: first public high school founded (Massachusetts)

1852: first compulsory education law passed in an American state (Massachusetts)

1855: Massachusetts abolished school segregation

1867: founding of the United States Department of Education

1868: Fourteenth Amendment of the United States Constitution declaring everyone born or naturalised in the United States, including blacks, was a citizen

1877: end of Reconstruction period after the American Civil War

1887: Dawes Act leads to Federal Government setting up schools for native Americans

1896: Supreme Court case, Plessy v. Ferguson, upholds the constitutionality of racial segregation in the United States

1918: Mississippi is last of all American states to pass compulsory education law

1954: *Brown v. Board of Education* Supreme Court ruling ends segregation in schools

Glossary

Common School Movement: from the 1840s, this movement advocated the establishment of public schools for children of all social classes, funded from local taxes and based on non-sectarian principles.

Grand Army of the Republic: a fraternal organisation of veterans of the Union army who had served in the Civil War (1861–5).

high school: secondary school, usually for ages 14 and over in the United States.

Horace Mann: (1796–1859) credited as 'father of the Common School Movement', Mann advocated the provision of universal public schooling as a means of creating responsible US citizens.

Jacksonian Democracy: promoted the strength of the president and executive at the expense of Congress, whilst also seeking to broaden the public's participation in government.

Lyceum League: The Lyceum League was a patriotic society and debating club composed of high school students and recent graduates. The League was intended to supplement the work of the public school and supported the spirit of 'Americanism'.

National Education Association: a professional employee organization and labour union founded in the United States in 1857 as the National Teachers Association. It adopted its current name in 1870 when it became allied with three other existing organizations. Prior to its founding, many states had their own educational associations; today, state associations are affiliated with the NEA.

Progressive Education Movement: an educational reform movement promoting the benefits of experiential and cooperative learning. It emerged in the United States during the late nineteenth century through the early work of Francis Parker and was further disseminated through the work of philosopher John Dewey.

Reconstruction: period in the United States from the end of the Civil War in 1865 until 1877.

school boards: elected school boards have jurisdiction over local school districts, employing the teachers and controlling buildings and curriculum.

Settlement House Movement: a reform movement, most extensive between the 1880s and the 1920s in England and the United States, in which middle-class volunteers moved to poor, urban neighbourhoods in order to improve the lives of residents. In addition to living as neighbours to members of the community, the residents of social settlements also offered services such as day nurseries, kindergartens, and classes and clubs for children and adults.

Social Darwinism: a movement in the late nineteenth century that stressed that life at the individual and national level was a competitive struggle. According to its guru, Herbert Spencer, nations had to use education to maximise the talents of their people if they were to survive.

Notes

1. It should be noted that while the pool of eligible voters grew in general, some states disqualified previous black voters on the basis of their race. C. F. Kaestle (1983) *Pillars of the Republic: Common Schools and American Society, 1780–1860* (New York: Hill and Wang), p. 97; Reuben, J.A. (2005) 'Patriotic Purposes: Public Schools and the Education of Citizens,' in S. Furhman and M. Lazerson (eds) *The Institutions of American Democracy: The Public Schools* (Oxford: Oxford University Press), p. 7; Fuhrman, S., and Lazerson, M. (2005) 'Introduction,' in *id., Institutions of American Democracy*, p. xxix.
2. Russell, W. F. (1918) 'United States,' in P. Sandiford (ed.) *Comparative Education: Studies of the Educational Systems of Six Modern Nations* (London: J. M. Dent and Sons), pp. 8–9; H. J. Moss (2009) *Schooling Citizens: The Struggle for African American Education* (Chicago: University of Chicago Press), p. 158.
3. S. Lassonde (1996) 'Learning and Earning: Schooling, Juvenile Employment, and the Early Life Course in Late Nineteenth-Century New Haven', *Journal of Social History*, 29/4, 839–70.
4. D. B. Tyack and E. Hansot (1992) *Learning Together: A History of Coeducation in American Schools* (New York: Russell Sage Foundation); Snyder, T. D. (1993) 'Education Characteristics of the Population,' in *id.* (ed.) *120 Years of American Education: A Statistical Portrait* (Washington, D.C.: National Center for Education Statistics), p. 6.
5. Tyack and Hansot, *Learning Together*, pp. 69–70.
6. Kaestle, *Pillars of the Republic*, p. x.
7. S. W. Brown (1912) *The Secularization of American Education* (New York: Teachers College), p. 2; B. Justice (2005) *The War That Wasn't: Religious Conflict and Compromise in the Common Schools of New York State, 1865–1900* (Albany: State University of New York Press), p. 23.
8. D. B. Tyack and L. Cuban (1992) *Tinkering toward Utopia: A Century of Public School Reform* (Cambridge: Harvard University Press), p. 2.
9. Reuben, 'Patriotic Purposes', p. 8.
10. W. J. Reese (1995) *The Origins of the American High School* (New Haven, CT: Yale University Press), pp. 29, 43, 256.
11. L. A. Cremin (1961) *The Transformation of the School: Progressivism in American Education, 1876–1957* (New York: Knopf), p. 10.

12. W. W. III Cutler (1989) 'Cathedral of Culture: The Schoolhouse in American Educational Thought and Practice since 1820,' *History of Education Quarterly*, 29/1, 1–40.
13. Cremin, *Transformation of the School*, p. 10.
14. I. Katznelson and M. Weir (1985) *Schooling for All: Class, Race, and the Decline of the Democratic Ideal* (New York: Basic Books), p. 54.
15. Pelikan, J. (2005) 'General Introduction: The Public Schools as an Institution of American Constitutional Democracy,' in Fuhrman and Lazerson, *Institutions of American Democracy*, p. xvii.
16. W. M. McAfee (1998) *Religion, Race, and Reconstruction: The Public School in the Politics of the 1870s* (Albany: State University of New York Press), p. 173.
17. Grant, W. V. (1993) 'Statistics in the U.S. Department of Education: Highlights from the Past 120 Years,' in Snyder, *American Education*, p. 1.
18. Cremin, *Transformation of the School*, p. 13; Reese, *America's Public Schools*, p. 77–8.
19. D. Tyack, T. James, and A. Benavot (eds) (1991) *Law and the Shaping of Public Education, 1785–1954* (Madison: University of Wisconsin Press), p. 22.
20. W. C. Sonnenberg (1993) 'Elementary and Secondary Education,' in Snyder, *American Education*, pp. 25–6.
21. Lassonde, S. (2004) 'High School,' in P. S. Fass (ed.) *Encyclopedia of Children and Childhood*, 3 vols (New York: Thomson Gale), vol. 2, p. 420.
22. Reese, *Origins of the American High School*, p. 57.
23. Lassonde, 'High School', p. 420.
24. W. J. Reese (2005) *America's Public Schools: From the Common School To 'No Child Left Behind'* (Baltimore: Johns Hopkins University Press), p. 62.
25. Ibid., pp. 46, 114.
26. Sonnenberg, 'Elementary and Secondary Education', p. 28.
27. Cremin, *Transformation of the School*, p. 13; Reese, *America's Public Schools*, pp. 77–8.
28. L. A. Cremin (1980) *American Education: The National Experience, 1783–1876* (New York: Harper and Row), pp. 489–90; Tyack, James, and Benavot (eds), *Law and the Shaping of Public Education*, p. 54.
29. Sonnenberg, 'Elementary and Secondary Education', p. 31.
30. Justice, *The War That Wasn't*, pp. 111–2.
31. D. B. Tyack (1974) *The One Best System: A History of American Urban Education* (Cambridge: Harvard University Press), p. 86.
32. R. A. Billington (1964) *The Protestant Crusade, 1800–1860: A Study of the Origins of American Nativism* (Chicago: Quadrangle Books).
33. R. L. Moore (2000) 'Bible Reading and Nonsectarian Schooling: The Failure of Religious Instruction in Nineteenth-Century Public Education', *Journal of American History*, 86/4, 1581–99, at p. 1588.
34. Tyack, James, and Benavot (eds), *Law and the Shaping of Public Education*, p. 54.
35. M. E. Brown (1995) *Churches, Communities, and Children: Italian Immigrants in the Archdiocese of New York, 1880-1945* (Staten Island: Center for Migration Studies), p. 64.
36. L. A. Cremin (1988) *American Education: The Metropolitan Experience, 1876–1980* (New York: Harper and Row), p. 135.
37. Moore, 'Bible Reading and Nonsectarian Schooling', p. 1587; J. A. Burns (1901) 'Catholic Secondary Schools', *The American Catholic Quarterly Review*, 26/103, 485–99, at p. 492.
38. J. Perlmann (1988) *Ethnic Differences: Schooling and Social Structure among the Irish, Italians, Jews, and Blacks in an American City, 1880–1935* (Cambridge: Cambridge University Press), p. 269 n. 41.
39. T. J. Meagher (2001) *Inventing Irish America: Generation, Class, and Ethnic Identity in a New England City, 1880–1928* (Notre Dame: University of Notre Dame Press), p. 205; J. M. Vinyard (1998) *For Faith and Fortune: The Education of Catholic Immigrants in Detroit, 1805–1925* (Urbana: University of Illinois Press), p. 109; Tyack, *The One Best System*, p. 86.

40. Meagher, *Inventing Irish America*, p. 133.
41. L. P. Jorgenson (1987) *The State and the Non-Public School, 1825–1925* (Columbia: University of Missouri Press), p. 155; Justice, *The War That Wasn't*, p. 115.
42. N. W. Cohen (1992) *Jews in Christian America: The Pursuit of Religious Equality* (Oxford University Press), p. 105; Leonard Bloom (1980) 'A Successful Jewish Boycott of the New York City Public Schools', *American Jewish History*, 70/2, 180–5.
43. Justice, *The War That Wasn't*, p. 115.
44. Moore, 'Bible Reading and Nonsectarian Schooling', p. 1596; McAfee, *Religion, Race, and Reconstruction*, p. 191.
45. Moore, 'Bible Reading and Nonsectarian Schooling', p. 1594.
46. Jorgenson, *The State and the Non-Public School*, pp. 151–2.
47. Moore, 'Bible Reading and Nonsectarian Schooling', p. 1585.
48. Brown, *The Secularization of American Education*, p. 156.
49. H. M. Kliebard (2004) *The Struggle for the American Curriculum, 1893–1958* (New York: Routledge Falmer).
50. C. E. O'Leary (1999) *To Die For: The Paradox of American Patriotism* (Princeton, NJ: Princeton University Press), pp. 177–8.
51. R. J. Ellis (2005) *To the Flag: The Unlikely History of the Pledge of Allegiance* (Lawrence: University Press of Kansas); Jorgenson, *The State and the Non-Public School*, p. 1.
52. O'Leary, *To Die For*, p. 177.
53. Charles Edward Merriam (1931) *The Making of Citizens: A Comparative Study of Methods of Civic Training* (Chicago: University of Chicago Press), p. 212.
54. C. H. Wesley (1941) 'Education for Citizenship in a Democracy', *The Journal of Negro Education*, 10/1, 68–78, at pp. 70–1.
55. O'Leary, *To Die For*, p. 152.
56. P. A. Graham (2005) *Schooling America: How the Public Schools Met the Nation's Changing Needs* (Oxford: Oxford University Press), p. 14.
57. Quoted in Reese, *America's Public Schools*, p. 51.
58. Graham, *Schooling America*, p. 11.
59. W. H. Hand (1904) 'Some Arguments for Compulsory Education', in *Proceedings of the Conference for Education in the South: The Seventh Session* (New York), p. 82.
60. Reuben, 'Patriotic Purposes'; M. R. Olneck (1989) 'Americanization and the Education of Immigrants, 1900-1925: An Analysis of Symbolic Action', *American Journal of Education*, 97/4, 398–423, at p. 406.
61. J. A. Reuben (1997) 'Beyond Politics: Community Civics and the Redefinition of Citizenship in the Progressive Era', *History of Education Quarterly*, 37/4, 399–420, at pp. 417–8.
62. E. L. Berg (2004) 'Citizens in the Republic of Childhood: Immigrants and the American Kindergarten, 1880–1920' (unpublished Ph.D. dissertation, University of California, Berkeley).
63. Graham, *Schooling America*, pp. 24–6.
64. Y. K. Pak (2001) *Wherever I Go, I Will Always Be a Loyal American: Seattle's Japanese American Schoolchildren During World War II* (New York: Routledge Falmer).
65. W. A. Cook (1912) 'A Brief Survey of the Development of Compulsory Education in the United States', *The Elementary School Teacher*, 12/ 7, 331-5, at pp. 333–4.
66. Richardson, J. G. (2004) 'Compulsory School Attendance,' in Fass (ed.), *Encyclopedia*, vol. 1, pp. 232–3.
67. Cook, 'A Brief Survey,' pp. 331–2.
68. C. F. Kaestle and M. Vinovskis (1980) *Education and Social Change in Nineteenth-Century Massachusetts* (Cambridge: Cambridge University Press), p. 98.
69. Reese, *America's Public Schools*, p. 126.
70. Reuben, 'Patriotic Purposes', p. 11; R.E. Hughes (1902) *The Making of Citizens: A Study in Comparative Education* (London: Walter Scott Publishing Company), pp. 136–7;

J. G. Richardson (1994) 'Common, Delinquent, and Special: On the Formalization of Common Schooling in the American States', *American Educational Research Journal*, 31/4, 695–723.

71. Hand, 'Some Arguments for Compulsory Education', p. 77.
72. The states were Alabama, Florida, Georgia, Louisiana, Mississippi, South Carolina, and Texas.
73. Richardson, 'Compulsory School Attendance'.
74. Cremin, *Transformation of the School*, p. 128.
75. Kaestle, *Pillars of the Republic*, p. x.
76. Moss, *Schooling Citizens*, p. 9.
77. J. D. Anderson (1988) *The Education of Blacks in the South, 1860–1935* (Chapel Hill: University of North Carolina Press), p. 1.
78. The Indian Schools were an exception.
79. R. W. Dale (1878) 'Impressions of America: III. Popular Education', *The Nineteenth Century*, 3/15, 949–68, at p. 956.
80. J. Spring (2004) *The American School, 1642–2004* (New York: McGraw-Hill Humanities), p. 171; Reese, *America's Public Schools*, p. 54; G. G. Gonzalez (1990) *Chicano Education in the Era of Segregation* (Philadelphia: Balch Institute Press), p. 21.
81. The U.S. Supreme Court later affirmed this finding in 1898. C. J. McClain (1994) *In Search of Equality: The Chinese Struggle against Discrimination in Nineteenth-Century America* (Berkeley: University of California Press), p. 163.
82. J. Yung, *Unbound Feet: A Social History of Chinese Women in San Francisco* (Berkeley: University of California Press), p. 126.
83. X. Wang (2001) *Surviving the City: The Chinese Immigrant Experience in New York City, 1890–1970* (Lanham: Rowman and Littlefield), p. 11; A. Bonner (1997) *Alas! What Brought Thee Hither?: The Chinese in New York, 1800–1950* (Madison: Fairleigh Dickinson University Press), p. 133.
84. M. J. Klarman (2004) *From Jim Crow to Civil Rights: The Supreme Court and the Struggle for Racial Equality* (New York: Oxford University Press), p. 25.
85. Moss, *Schooling Citizens*.
86. Reese, *America's Public Schools*, p. 73; Graham, *Schooling America*, p. 20.
87. McAfee, *Religion, Race, and Reconstruction*.
88. Reuben, 'Patriotic Purposes', pp. 9, 15; Du Bois, W. E. B. (2007) in H. L. Gates, Jr. (ed.) *The Philadelphia Negro: A Social Study* (Oxford: Oxford University Press), p. 63.
89. N. Silber (1997) *The Romance of Reunion: Northerners and the South, 1865–1900* (Chapel Hill: University of North Carolina Press), p. 158.
90. O'Leary, *To Die For*, p. 141.
91. Klarman, *From Jim Crow to Civil Rights*, p. 24.
92. Tyack and Hansot, *Learning Together*, p. 53.
93. McAfee, *Religion, Race, and Reconstruction*, p. 3; Reuben, 'Patriotic Purposes', pp. 8–9; Cremin, *Transformation of the School*, p. 13.
94. Reuben, 'Patriotic Purposes', p. 14; Klarman, *From Jim Crow to Civil Rights*, p. 25.
95. J. W. Blassingame (1976) *Black New Orleans, 1860–1880* (Chicago: University of Chicago Press), pp. 116–22.
96. W. S. Hill (2003) *Before Us Lies the Timber: The Segregated High School of Montgomery County, Maryland, 1927–1960* (Silver Spring, Maryland: Bartleby Press), p. 23.
97. O'Leary, *To Die For*, pp. 123–25.
98. W. A. Blair (2003) *Cities of the Dead: Contesting the Memory of the Civil War in the South, 1865–1914* (Chapel Hill: University of North Carolina Press), pp. 159–60; F. Morgan (2005) *Women and Patriotism in Jim Crow America* (Chapel Hill: University of North Carolina Press), p. 23.
99. Graham, *Schooling America*, pp. 19–20.

100. C. E. O'Leary (1996) '"Blood Brotherhood": The Racialization of Patriotism, 1865–1918', in J. E. Bodnar (ed.) *Bonds of Affection: Americans Define Their Patriotism* (Princeton: Princeton University Press), p. 66.
101. S. McConnell (1992) *Glorious Contentment: The Grand Army of the Republic, 1865–1900* (Chapel Hill: University of North Carolina Press), pp. 224–5.
102. O'Leary, 'Blood Brotherhood', p. 66.
103. (1911) 'Educational' *The Book Buyer: A Monthly Review of American and Foreign Literature*, 36/9, 217–8, at p. 217.
104. Klarman, *From Jim Crow to Civil Rights*, p. 44.
105. Russell, 'United States,' p. 98.
106. Graham, *Schooling America*, p. 22.
107. Adam Fairclough (2007) *A Class of Their Own: Black Teachers in the Segregated South* (Cambridge: Harvard University Press), pp. 151–2.
108. Graham, *Schooling America*, p. 22.
109. Ibid., pp. 20–1.
110. Klarman, *From Jim Crow to Civil Rights*, p. 148. See also Anderson, *The Education of Blacks in the South*, pp. 193–6.
111. E. W. Knight (1922) *Public Education in the South* (Boston: Ginn and Company), p. vi.
112. Hand, 'Some Arguments for Compulsory Education', p. 79.
113. R. A. Margo (1990) *Race and Schooling in the South, 1880–1950: An Economic History* (Chicago: University of Chicago Press), p. 86.
114. Fairclough, *A Class of Their Own*.
115. Tyack and Hansot, *Learning Together*, p. 53.
116. A. Trachtenberg (1982) *The Incorporation of America: Culture and Society in the Gilded Age* (New York: Hill and Wang), p. 33.
117. Quoted in R. Spack (2002) *America's Second Tongue: American Indian Education and the Ownership of English, 1860–1900* (Lincoln: University of Nebraska Press), p. 26.
118. D. W. Adams (1995) *Education for Extinction: American Indians and the Boarding School Experience, 1875–1928* (Lawrence: University Press of Kansas), pp. 24, 58–9.
119. Ibid., p. 146.
120. R. A. Trennert (1988) *The Phoenix Indian School: Forced Assimilation in Arizona, 1891–1935* (Norman: University of Oklahoma Press), p. 206.
121. Olneck, 'Americanization and the Education of Immigrants', pp. 409–10.
122. J. Higham (1994) *Strangers in the Land: Patterns of American Nativism, 1860–1925*, 2nd edn (New Brunswick, NJ: Rutgers University Press), p. 236.
123. F. H. Early (1997) *A World without War: How U.S. Feminists and Pacifists Resisted World War I* (Syracuse: Syracuse University Press), pp. 38, 40–1; H. C. Peterson and G. C. Fite (1957) *Opponents of War, 1917–1918* (Madison: University of Wisconsin Press), p. 110.
124. Blanton, C. K. (2006) 'The Rise of English-Only Pedagogy: Immigrant Children, Progressive Education, and Language Policy in the United States, 1900–1930', in B. Beatty, E. D. Cahan and J. Grant (eds) *When Science Encounters the Child: Education, Parenting, and Child Welfare in 20th Century America* (New York: Teachers College Press), p. 67.
125. R. Schaffer (1991) *America in the Great War: The Rise of the War Welfare State* (New York: Oxford University Press), pp. 20–1.
126. D. Heater (2004) *A History of Education for Citizenship* (London: RoutledgeFalmer), p. 118.
127. H. C. Hill (1919) 'The Americanization Movement', *The American Journal of Sociology*, 24/6, 609–42; Merriam, *Making of Citizens*, p. 97.
128. C. A. Ellwood (1920) 'Education for Citizenship in a Democracy', *The American Journal of Sociology*, 26/1, 73–81, at pp. 74–7; D. Snedden (1919) 'Some New Problems in Education for Citizenship', *International Journal of Ethics*, 30/1, 1–15.
129. Hughes, *The Making of Citizens*, p. 135.

130. Sonnenberg, 'Elementary and Secondary Education', p. 27.
131. Ibid., pp. 28, 32.
132. Lassonde, 'High School', p. 420.
133. N. Beadie and K. Tolley (eds) (2002) *Chartered Schools: Two Hundred Years of Independent Academies in the United States, 1727–1925* (New York: Routledge).
134. K. Graves (1998) *Girls' Schooling During the Progressive Era: From Female Scholar to Domesticated Citizen* (New York: Garland Publishing).
135. Reese, W. J. (2004) 'Education, United States,' in Fass (ed.) *Encyclopedia*, vol. 1, p. 310; Russell, 'United States', p. 63.
136. J. Zimmerman (2002) *Whose America? Culture Wars in the Public Schools* (Cambridge: Harvard University Press), p. 14; Tyack, James, and Benavot (eds) *Law and the Shaping of Public Education*, p. 179.
137. W. Ross (1994) *Forging New Freedoms: Nativism, Education and the Constitution, 1917–1927* (Lincoln: University of Nebraska Press).
138. J. H. Spring (1992) *Images of American Life: A History of Ideological Management in Schools, Movies, Radio, and Television* (Albany: State University of New York Press), p. 46.
139. M. M. Willey (1924) 'Education for Citizenship', *Journal of Social Forces*, 2/5, 676–9.
140. Merriam, *Making of Citizens*, p. 119.
141. Snedden, 'Some New Problems', p. 9.
142. M. M. K. Simkhovitch (1917) *The City Worker's World in America* (New York: Macmillan), pp. 189–91.
143. Olneck, 'Americanization and the Education of Immigrants', pp. 398–9.
144. R. Ueda (1999) 'Second-Generation Civic America: Education, Citizenship, and the Children of Immigrants', *Journal of Interdisciplinary History*, 29/4, 661–81, at pp. 663–5.
145. Ibid., p. 672.
146. Ibid., p. 673.

8
Primary Education and the Construction of Citizenship in Brazil, 1870–1930: Progress and Tensions

Maria Cristina Soares de Gouvea and Alessandra Frota Schueller

In Brazil, the process of educating the next generation can only be understood in the context of the tensions that marked the constitution and consolidation of an independent country, one defined as a geographical, linguistic and historical unit, in which the spread of elementary education played a fundamental role. Over the nineteenth century, the country underwent a huge transformation. From a Portuguese colony, it became the seat of the Lusophone Empire in 1808, when the Portuguese court moved to Rio de Janeiro after the Napoleonic invasion of Portugal, then gained independence in the form of an imperial monarchy built on slavery in 1822. This regime came to an end with the abolition of slavery in 1888 and the overthrow of the monarchy the following year, which led to the establishment of the Brazilian Republic with a constitution closely modelled on that of the United States. Later, this order was again disrupted, and the move towards a representative democracy ended with the Revolution of 1930, which heralded a new political order. Thus, the period that witnessed the growth of elementary education in most Western countries saw in Brazil the fall of the empire, followed by the installation, consolidation, decay and consequent subversion of a liberal federal republic.

To analyse the development of education between 1889 and 1930 we must try to understand the constitution and disintegration of what is known as the *Primeira República* (the First Republic) and its consequences. On one hand, as Lessa points out, it comprised the longest period of political stability in the history of the Brazilian Republic to date (41 years). On the other hand, according to José Murilo de Carvalho, 'it was the high point of the system of oligarchy, when the Republic was furthest from democracy'.[1] This highlights the fact that the regime was a formal democracy but deeply indifferent towards the general population. Brazilian society in this period was hierarchically organised and marked by an inequality that stemmed from its heterogeneous ethno-racial composition. The precarious access to written culture meant that until the end of the nineteenth century, around 85 per cent of the population was illiterate.[2] Only in 1960 did the literate population outnumber the illiterate (respectively 54.3 and 46.7 per cent).[3] While schools in the period were cultural centres that helped to overcome deep socio-economic inequality, at the same time they legitimised the differences. Such contradictions were seen throughout the nineteenth and the first decades of the twentieth century in Brazilian political and administrative life. But they are the key to understanding the historical conditions in which education played a role in turning Brazilian children into citizens.

The constitution of the nation

When independence from Portugal was proclaimed in 1822,[4] a slave-owning Catholic monarchy was formed with a limited role for representative institutions, and the country was divided into provinces whose leaders were chosen by the central power. It was a challenge to constitute a nation from a territory the size of a continent, with its vast differences in lifestyle, economic development and socio-racial make-up. Stability was achieved by installing a conservative centralist government, in which the interests of the different regional groups were balanced by the *poder moderador* (moderating power) of the emperor. The conservative government guaranteed the autonomy of the regional elite, but at the same time subjected it to the state's needs.[5] According to Lessa, the system was a top-down one, with no regional politics as such. Despite this, it was a genuinely federal organisation as the different provinces were responsible for managing their own regions and local private power-holders directly negotiated with the national government. This order became vulnerable from the start of the 1860s when the imperial government was increasingly damaged by internal squabbles and stand-offs over different projects for building the state, nationality and citizenship. These crises in government penetrated downwards to the wider society, all the more because the issues argued over involved redefining the status of citizenship and the extent of political participation of the masses. Of particular significance was the electoral reform introduced in 1881, which brought in new rules for the electoral system. This meant that voters were no longer required to have a salary and property in order to be eligible to vote: they now were required only to be able to read and write. The reform was intended to ensure that the voting population had been enlightened about the political process in school, but it also institutionalised the value and worth of writing in a society with a strong oral tradition.[6] However, according to J. M. de Carvalho, the reforms ended up further restricting voter numbers, which fell significantly in comparison with the 1872 elections.[7] That year 13 per cent of the population had voted. After the reforms of 1881, this percentage fell to around 1 per cent. It was only in 1945 that the country would again have a similar percentage of voters as in 1872.

Despite the quarrels at the top, Brazil slowly modernised in the second half of the nineteenth century, which had a significant impact on its economic organisation and lifestyle of its citizens and contributed to bringing down the monarchic system. Serious social reform immediately led to regime change. Thus, the republic was proclaimed only a year after the abolition of slavery in 1888 by an opposition movement that sought to cut Brazil's ties with the existing system now seen as outdated and to bring the country into the fold of the civilised nations by advancing modernisation more quickly. Those responsible for ushering in the republican regime were members of the elite who themselves embraced differing projects for forging the new nation. While throughout the transition process various political perspectives jostled for supremacy, a liberal regime based on North American federalism where the country was divided into states was eventually adopted as the political model. The federal state's intervention in the lives of its citizens would be minimal, and their interests would be ruled instead by the market.

A new constitution was created in 1891. For Bresciani, this represented the victory of the regional oligarchies, who established a state that facilitated their desire to concentrate political power and liberate the economy.[8] This was a liberal ideal highly influenced by *Social Darwinism. The nation was conceived as a stage for the survival of the fittest, with power in the hands of the strongest, in this case, the regional elite. Throughout the republican period, political stability was founded on what President Campos Sales called 'state governor politics'.[9] Power was not in the hands of citizens of the Republic, but in those of the regional state governors. In turn, regional authority was exercised by the local oligarchs without interference from centralised power.[10] Different states had differing degrees of influence over the direction of national politics. There was an intense concentration of political power in the more economically developed states which were better able to impose their regional interests at a national level, in particular São Paulo and Minas Gerais, which took turns holding power at the centre throughout the period.[11] The economies of states like these were based on agricultural exports, particularly coffee. Agriculture was extremely important at the time, as the country had undergone an intense process of ruralisation. While in 1872, 60 per cent of the population had lived in rural areas, this went up to 64 per cent in 1900 and reached 70 per cent in 1920. At the same time, large landowners dominated the countryside, with 4 per cent of agricultural establishments occupying 63 per cent of rural land. This ratio corresponded to the concentration of political power held by the agricultural oligarchies.[12]

The modernisation programme instigated by this governing elite until the 1930s was characterised by a mutual agreement to exclude or repress participation by the general populace. There was wide-ranging debate about the strengths and weaknesses of the Brazilian population, based on *European racial theories. It was suggested that the lower classes, in particular the ex-slaves and their descendents, represented the imperial social order, and reflected a past that needed to be destroyed at any cost through revoking any sign of it.[13] The approach to integrating the population and constituting a Brazilian citizenship favoured by the new republican regime was centred on the formation of 'regenerating activities' that would enable the population to live in a civilised country. As the referent of civilisation, the regime privileged European and North American cultural customs and ideals, which were associated with modernisation. As Sevcenko put it, the regime sought 'modernisation at any price'.[14] Thus new techniques and approaches were developed for health, housing,[15] urban planning and education, this last through investment in public state education.

While in formal political terms the people were excluded from institutionalised participation in the new state (the franchise at the time was exercised by between 1 and 3.4 per cent of the total population), they increasingly made their voice heard through organised movements like strikes, demonstrations and protests against state action,[16] both in urban and rural areas.[17] The republican regime interpreted these uprisings either as reactions against modernisation, uncultured expressions by a populace whose racial make-up was explanation in itself for its uncouthness, backwardness and ignorance, or as inflammatory insurrections by subversive foreign groups. All these demonstrations were crushed by the state, using police or military action. This ongoing conflict progressively weakened the republic. Eventually the governing elite lost the support not only of the lower classes, but of the regional oligarchies and intellectuals. The last group, unhappy with the course taken by the Brazilian republic and its representatives, demanded a genuine modernisation of the Brazilian social structure and more incisive involvement by the central government.[18] The regional elite for their part were frustrated by the unequal distribution of power, while the lower classes were antagonised by the systematically segregationalist and anti-populist approach of the state.

The dissatisfaction of these groups, together with the return of the army to more decisive political activity, provoked the Revolution of 1930. The initial spark for this was a revolt against fraud and rigging in the presidential elections. A new political alliance was formed, the 'Liberal Alliance', with a heterogeneous base, that united different groups based on the need for social and economic modernisation steered by central government. In 1930, the Liberal Alliance seized power in a military coup supported by the army and led by Getúlio Vargas, a candidate who had been defeated in the presidential elections and was from the landed elite in the south of the country, an area that had historically been looked down upon by the dominant states of São Paulo and Minas Gerais. The government of the time put up very little resistance, which was evidence of its inherent weakness. Getúlio Vargas was at the helm of the country for 15 years, a period which saw radical transformations to the economic, social and political bases of the Brazilian state. Vargas implemented centralist policies for social and economic modernisation, but he trampled over the fragile democratic republican order and instigated a dictatorship from 1937 onwards.[19]

The new president was to become a central player in Brazilian history, creating what is now called the *Era Vargas*, which lasted until 1954. Getúlio Vargas wanted to guide the process of modernisation, reconfigure the political field (on a centralist and authoritarian model), redesign the economy (highlighting investment in the industrialisation of the country) and directly refashion its culture (promoting nationalism and using political propaganda). His first stint as the country's president (1930–1945) introduced an authoritarian regime divided into two distinct phases. The first was between 1930 and 1937 when he presided over a provisional government that restructured the political framework, broke away from the hierarchies of power which had controlled the previous regime, and intervened in the state governments by selecting their leaders. The second began in 1937 when, as dictator, he inaugurated the *Estado Novo* (new state), dissolving congress, abolishing political parties and imposing tight controls over the media and communication. The *Estado Novo* lasted until 1945, when the call for the re-democratisation of the country, together with the authoritarian government's slipping control, forced presidential elections to take place.[20]

The republican education project and primary school organization

During the imperial period, public education was regulated by an imperial act of 1834. This handed the management of primary education to the provinces, while retaining at central government level the responsibility for offering secondary and further education. The different provinces set out to increase access to formal elementary education by promulgating laws making school attendance compulsory. Schooling was declared to be the responsibility of the state, a parental obligation and a child's right. The regulations included a fine for parents who did not enrol their children in public school, and thus created lists of 'errant parents' who risked legal sanctions.[21] In fact, the reality was very different. The extent of schooling available to the new generation was always precarious: elementary schools had little popular support, while the introduction of centralised public accounting from 1850 discouraged investment in education by the provincial governments.

The Brazilian republic sought to modernise the country through government-initiated reform.[22] Modernisation in education was understood to mean adopting the educational agenda and pedagogical vocabulary of the 'civilised' nations (the leading European countries and increasingly the United States). Initially, however, education was low on the new regime's political agenda. In the text of the 1891 Constitution, little attention was given to the subject, although there were some new developments. The constitutional charter broke with the empire's model by taking Catholicism out of the classroom and stipulating that education must be secular. However, it was less progressive, as it back-tracked on compulsory education and allowed individual states to decide on the degree to which free elementary schooling would be provided. The republican line was to forget the empire's experiment. It was only in the text for the 1934 Constitution that the national state again guaranteed compulsory free primary education for every Brazilian citizen.[23] At the same time, in response to the strong lobbying from the Catholic Church, religious education was reintroduced into the primary school curriculum.[24]

In accordance with the liberal model, political rights were not seen as natural, but rather as a reward bestowed on an individual in possession of the requisite marks of eligibility. From 1881, as we have seen, the right to vote was the prerogative of only the literate population. During the early years of the republic, this association between education and citizenship became more accentuated within a society that was predominantly illiterate, the majority of whose members were therefore considered ineligible to influence the political scene. As Bessa points out, a new concept of the potential of the Brazilian population emerged over this period: the idea that the people were incapable of fulfilling their role as citizens was matched by a belief in the regenerating role of education. Primary state education therefore took on the task of breathing a new life into this population that was so unfairly represented. But the role of schooling was double-edged. Illiteracy was combated to a degree, but illiterate people were also stereotyped as incapable of true citizenship. This was not only because they lacked the basic tool necessary to vote, but also because they were usually the black and mulatto descendents of and heirs to the outdated order that the regime wanted to bury.[25]

The Constitution gave each state complete freedom to organise its primary education and entrusted to the federal republic the responsibility for secondary and further education. The decentralised model of the imperial era was once more emphasised. The distribution of funds followed this template of decentralisation, which accentuated the regional differences.[26] Another aspect worth noting is that by removing the obligation of the states to offer education, the new regime paved the way for private initiatives, particularly the establishment of Catholic schools and colleges, aimed at the middle classes. As Cury has realised, whether these initiatives were permitted for ideological or pragmatic reasons, they conflicted with the ethos underlying the state's educational policy. 'The state saw public education as a means of enabling access to political rights, but without segregation, while the private initiatives suggested it was a question of choice and competition.'[27]

The great difficulty historians have in providing an accurate account of the educational situation in the empire or in the republic is precisely due to the high level of inequality and the historically constructed diversity of Brazilian education. The regional divergences are evident from the statistical records on literacy. Thus, in 1922, while the population of the federal capital (which was then Rio de Janeiro) had 61.3 per cent literacy, those from poorer states in the north/north-east of the country further from the nexus of power such as Alagoas and Piauí had only 14.8 and 12 per cent literacy levels respectively.[28] Regarding numbers of children attending school, the data again indicates the tremendous divergences between the states. While in Alagoas and Piauí 95 and 94 per cent of school age children respectively did not attend school, in the capital 56 per cent of children went to school (the highest proportion in the country).[29]

To complicate matters further, the states introduced reforms to reorganise primary education in two distinct but historically contiguous phases. The first, based on the introduction of the *escola graduada* (*graduated school), led to the creation of the *grupos escolares* (schools where pupils were divided into classes according to their level of attainment), which were implemented at the end of the nineteenth and over the first two decades of the twentieth century. The second phase was the introduction of the *escola novista* (or 'progressive' school), based on an interactive pedagogical ideal, which began towards the end of the first republican period and continued after the Revolution of 1930. In both phases the emphasis was on modernisation. Their advocates proclaimed a new era for Brazilian schools and a break with a past associated with tradition and the old order. José Gondra and Ana

Magaldi have talked of an ongoing 'culture of reform' during this period, which was articulated through a continual investment by the states in constructing legal texts that in many cases were more rhetorical than practical.[30] The state of São Paulo pioneered the first cycle of state educational reforms in 1892 when it created the first *grupo escolar* in Brazil, in accordance with the graduated school model. This soon became a reference for other states in the federation. The graduated school model was based on reorganising the available space, constructing buildings that were appropriate for their educational purpose, rationalising the use of time by ensuring school work reflected the correct educational level, promoting pedagogical best practice, particularly the so-called intuitive method, and management rationalisation, which allowed more effective control over school activities.[31]

The concern with public spending, the condition of the school buildings and houses, the construction of new buildings, school graduation rates and the requirement for teachers to be qualified, not to mention the (recurring) insistence on reforming primary education and developing the *normal school, all these aspects show that schooling the population was a central problem tackled by the republican government. The statistics show real improvement. If in 1907 the country had 12,448 schools that gave instruction to 638,378 students, by 1922 it had 23,836 schools that educated 1,783,571. However, this was still a drop in the ocean. In 1927, 71 per cent of the population of school age were not in the classroom and 68 per cent of the population was still illiterate.[32]

In truth, while it is possible to see some enthusiasm amongst republican politicians and sectors of the cultural and economic elite for the expansion of the school system, the structure and composition of the political system imposed restrictions on their effectiveness. State governor politics left its mark. Education found itself subjected to the dominant political actors of the time: the elite oligarchies. These did not always have education as a priority – either they viewed its potential value for the wider population with distrust, or in implementing the republican model adapted it to their own political interests. Thus the construction of schools, the provision of school places, and teacher and headteacher selection were the object of constant local political bartering or were used as tools to control the population.[33] On the one hand, the adoption of the organisational model of the *grupos escolares* was a way of showcasing the republican schooling project with its aim of educating the lower classes. On the other, its implementation showed how the new schools were used as bargaining chips in power struggles within the ruling elite.

As a result, in quantitative terms, the earlier imperial educational system, founded on the so-called *escolas isoladas* (single classroom schools) continued to dominate the educational landscape. It was these schools, generally situated in rural and upstate areas, as well as in some municipalities, that educated the majority of the Brazilian population, under difficult circumstances, in improvised classrooms with untrained teachers and inadequate teaching materials. Even after 1910, when the diffusion of graduated schools and the creation of the *grupos escolares* had been intensified, the old schools were never swept from the field. From the statistics, the predominance of *escolas isoladas* in relation to the *grupos escolares* is clear, even in the states that most invested in the new model. Thus in 1927 in São Paulo, there were 194 *grupos escolares* and 1792 *escolas isoladas*.In national terms, the *grupos escolares* constituted only 5.55 per cent of schools in Brazil, 71 per cent of which were concentrated in the centre of the country (Rio de Janeiro, São Paulo and Minas Gerais). In 1933 the national records reveal little had changed with the revolution. Brazil in that year had 26,950 primary schools, 1635 of which were *grupos escolares*, 968 'reunited' schools (an intermediary model) and 22,630 *escolas isoladas*.[34]

Throughout the entire life of the *Primeira Republica*, the records show that the rural and district *escolas isoladas* were predominant not just in their quantity but in relation to the number of children they enrolled, reflecting the fact that around 70 per cent of the population lived in rural areas. The majority of school children were therefore educated in a *casa de escola* (single-roomed school house) with one teacher looking after a mixed-year class. Yet, with regard to the distribution of resources, these schools competed on unequal terms with the *grupos escolares* for funds. The *grupos* required greater resources for their implementation and running costs. They were also convenient bargaining tools, giving their promoters at state level greater political visibility despite their smaller social reach.

While it is difficult to unravel the states' investment in the area of education, the data suggest that this was far from uniform. In 1922, the state of Santa Catarina (whose population in the twentieth century was basically made up of immigrants) put aside 20 per cent of its resources for primary education (the highest amount nationally at the time), São Paulo put aside 17 per cent and the states of Pernambuco and Bahia (both situated in the north-east of the country) only 3 and 5 per cent respectively. The difference in funding had repercussions on access to schools. While in Bahia, only 13 per cent of the school-age population had access to a school, and Pernambuco 19 per cent, in Santa Catarina 57 per cent of the school-age population went to school and in São Paulo 44 per cent. In national terms, the states together devoted only 11 per cent of their budget to education with the result, as noted above, that 71 per cent of the school age population did not attend school. Investment was also erratic from year to year emphasising a characteristic discontinuity in public educational policies in Brazil.[35]

From 1910 onwards, state governor politics, and hence the approach to education, were under challenge. Increasingly, intellectuals representing the urban middle class began to have an impact on educational policy. They considered an investment in state-driven education to be vital for progress and the dissemination of 'civilised' culture. These intellectuals were active at regional level in promoting a new cycle of reforms under the label of the *escola novista movement, and at federal level in creating a national association which convened congresses and conferences.[36] The reforms, mostly put in place at the end of the 1920s, built on previous reforms, while placing a new emphasis on investment in making classroom teaching more scientific and on seeking to coordinate activities nationally. These reforms were once more trumpeted in the beginning as a break with earlier traditions and were again presented as announcing a new age for the Brazilian school system. There were significant differences between the models adopted by different states, but the reformers shared a belief in promoting schools as spaces to build citizenship through their activities with the children. Schools were to be social units that did not reproduce the inequality of the existing social order but that projected a model for the future. At the same time they sought to make the school experience more meaningful and attractive by incorporating new technology and extending the premises. The *escola novista* movement would dominate the primary education agenda over the following decades.[37]

The nation-building emphasis of the movement was stated with particular clarity in the 1932 publication of the *Manifesto dos Pioneiros da Escola Nova* (the New School Pioneers' Manifesto), which was signed by 25 representatives of the Brazilian intelligentsia. The manifesto emphasised that public education should be the responsibility of the federal government and a national policy formulated whose implementation should be given priority. But this manifesto came out of a new political context that followed the end of the *Primeira Republica*. With the Revolution of 1930, a new age began for schooling: it now became the object of decisive action from the central government, although it continued to be the responsibility of the states. One of the first signs of the attempts to centralise the education system, and also the health system, was the creation of the *Ministério da Educação and Saúde* (MES) (the Ministry of Education and Health) in 1930. This radical shift in approach to education was expressed in the new 1934 constitutional charter, which again confirmed the compulsory and free nature of primary education[38] and outlined a national plan with directives and guidelines for the states to follow, stating that a minimum of 20 per cent of the budget should be spent on education by each federal state.[39] Even though they continued to be responsible for offering primary education, the states were henceforth in thrall to a national policy.

The new directives were the result of negotiations and bickering between the political leaders of the new regime and representatives of the school system, debates in which the Catholic Church, its religious orders and other church or lay private educational providers and interest groups featured prominently. According to Gomes, few real advances in the field of primary education resulted from the federal government's national policy. What it actually achieved was increased centralisation and control over the curriculum, which was an important element in the policy of integrating immigrants into the nation.[40] The statistical data confirms this. Under Vargas, the decentralised model was maintained and there was no significant advance in schooling provision. In 1922, there were 23,826 schools and in 1937 there were 38,829: this was still an insufficient number to provide schooling for the whole school-age population.[41]

Conditions for primary education: between universalisation and inequality

According to data from the first general census in the imperial era (1872), the population consisted of approximately 10 million inhabitants.[42] From the census, it was estimated that of this total only 1,564,981 people knew how to read and write. In other words, 84 per cent of the Brazilian population were illiterate, and the majority of these were women: the percentage of literate men was 19.8 per cent while that of women was only 11.5 per cent. Under the republican regime, the census of 1920 showed a population of 17,318,554 inhabitants, of whom 70% per cent were still illiterate.[43] However, while there had been no significant change in the number of men recorded as literate, there had been considerable growth in the number of literate women.

Children's access to schooling was conditioned by the hierarchies of power and the social distinctions between citizens, as well as by varying historical interpretations of the actual concept of citizenship. During the imperial era, the different provinces had set out to increase access to education by promulgating laws on compulsory education. Despite the fine words that schooling was the responsibility of the state, a parental obligation and a child's right, these initiatives had little effect. The majority of the Brazilian people at the time lived in poverty and hardship, and child labour, whether unpaid in the home or remunerated, was an important factor in the maintenance of the family.[44] Fining parents who failed to send their children to school was clearly not a viable option. Primary schooling in this early period was also ineffective. Before the introduction of graduated schools, pupils of different ages and levels of knowledge sat side by side in sparsely populated classrooms, often set up in teachers' homes, with inadequate resources. The teachers too were poorly trained. Added to this, the sheer size of the country, the dispersal of the population and the precarious infrastructure (of roads and public transport) made it difficult to open new schools and keep fiscal tabs on them.

It is important also to note that the state primary school was not the principal centre for elementary education: the private church schools and tuition at home were just as important. This reflected in part the country's ethno-racial tensions. The state primary school of the imperial era had been conceived as a civilising space for the poor population and for those of African descent. The free Afro-Brazilians, a considerable presence in a country where *miscegenation was common, made up a significant proportion of the state school population, as the most recent studies show.[45] Their presence though led to tension and resistance from teachers and more upwardly mobile families who were afraid of inter-ethnic contact. Several records suggest that the parents of white and socially privileged children opted for home schooling or to send them to private schools for fear of mixing with Afro-Brazilian students.[46]

Under the republican regime, local governments invested in the expansion of primary education for the majority of the population to promote modernisation and to overcome social inequality, describing it as being in the interests of the state.[47] However, this only showed up the contradictions between the republican model and the views of the political elite. Although education was a means to access political citizenship, statements by the governing, intellectual and educator elites of the time showed their distrust of its capacity to actually work. The people were represented as incapable of self-government, either due to their slave heritage or to their ethno-racial composition.[48] Although in order to build the republic it was deemed fundamental to educate the Brazilian people, the elite in its different manifestations cast doubt on the ability of black Brazilians to overcome their supposed deficiencies. For some historians, public schooling in the period of the *Primeira Republica* was marked by a 'whitening', not only of its clientele but also of its pedagogical ideology.[49] Although the Afro-Brazilian population had experienced prejudice in the imperial schools, the new racial theories gave scientific weight to the diffusion of discriminatory practices in the classroom. Consequently the education of the Afro-Brazilian population suffered; there was a high level of absenteeism, failure and having to repeat the school year. The statistics showing levels of schooling for the Brazilian population confirm this analysis, indicating that there is, to this day, a persistent difference in the length of education between the white population and Brazilians of African descent.[50]

In the analysis of the ethnic make-up of the school population of the time, it is important to consider the high level of immigration. In the transition from slave to free labour, the need to fill the positions previously occupied by slaves and to find better qualified workers meant that a programme of welcoming immigrants from Europe and Asia was developed. This altered not only the ethno-racial composition of the Brazilian population in the central-south of the country, but it also reconfigured socio-economic relations as well as cultural practices and property ownership in that part of the country. In addition to rebuilding the workforce, immigration was encouraged as a strategy by the elite to 'whiten' Brazil, through mixing foreigners with the native population.[51] The arrival of immigrants also had an effect on schooling. The foreigners tended to be much more literate (52 per cent of the immigrant population knew how to read and write, as opposed to 23 per cent of the national population).[52] The immigrants demanded that the public authorities increase the number of schools, particularly in the rural areas they colonised in the south. However, due to the inability of state governments to meet such great demand, other forms of schooling were created: community schools (financed by the population and by the home country governments), and Catholic and non-Catholic church schools.[53] The existence of these schools, initially presented as being complementary to or as substitutes for state action, gradually began to threaten the construction of a Brazilian national identity, particularly after Brazil became involved in the First World War in 1917.[54] The schools that served the immigrant population had customised curricula, in which the Portuguese language and the history and geography of Brazil were of secondary importance or were wholly replaced by the language, history and geography of the immigrants' home countries.

The role of education in the development of nationality became more apparent from the 1920s onwards when it was given impetus by new cultural factors. In this period, another vision of national identity took shape, fashioned by Brazilian high culture and social science, in which the ethno-racial composition of the population[55] and its cultural patrimony began to be seen in a more positive light. In addition to this, relationships with and the representation of immigrant populations also began to change. However, it was in the Vargas Government that the affirmation of *brasilidade* (Brazilianess) resulted in the promotion of schools as spaces for spreading a positive image of the Brazilian people and as part of the *política de nacionalização* (nation-building policy). Shortly before the Second World War, this resulted in official steps being taken against the foreign schools connected with the immigrant groups, a clear indication of an authoritarian and violent trend in the central government's educational policy. These schools were to become strategic spaces for imposing national values on this part of the population.[56] It is estimated that approximately 774 foreign schools were closed in the central-south of the country. The headteachers now had to be Brazilian, Portuguese became the official language in the curriculum, and Brazilian history and geography were prioritised (Decree n. 406, 4 May 1938).

A fundamental feature of schooling during the republican era was the different rates of attendance of the urban and rural population. Although, as has already been mentioned, the rural population was numerically dominant, it had greater difficulty accessing education. According to records from 1933, there were 1,305,835 pupils enrolled in urban schools, and 1,160,257 in rural schools.[57] In the rural areas, the lack of a literate social culture coupled with the need to enter the work force early meant that the written language was not considered important, and many parents resisted sending their children to school. The *escolas isoladas* also provided inferior education offering only two years compulsory education compared with four in the *grupos escolares* and providing a narrower curriculum: science teaching for instance was confined to the graded schools.[58] The *escolas isoladas,* moreover, not only suffered from poor buildings and a lack of teaching materials, but their teachers were also paid less, and were even on occasion responsible for paying the rent for the school buildings. All these factors resulted in high absenteeism and unsatisfactory results. Nevertheless, a considerable number of rural parents did invest in education as a means to rise socially, demanding that the state open more public schools, or even raising money to set up and maintain private schools.[59]

Throughout the imperial era, schools were segregated according to gender. Although there was a common curriculum, there were subjects that were gender specific.[60] The aim of primary education for girls was to prepare them for domestic life, and the curricular differentiation reflected the commitment to maintaining patriarchal control. In the republican era, the segregation of the male and female populations in the *grupos escolares* and the *escolas isoladas* continued to be presupposed. The curricular differences were also retained, and teaching materials were focused on maintaining gender differences and asserting the domesticity of the female and the public life of the male world. However, in the republican era, mixed classes became more common, even if some subjects like manual ones were always taught separately (for example, needlework for girls and carpentry for boys), as there were insufficient students for gender-specific schools.

The republican era also witnessed a rapid expansion in the number of girls in school and by 1933 participation rates were almost equal. Of the 2,466,092 students enrolled in that year, 1,307,558 were boys and 1,158,534 were girls. This can be partly explained by the expanding opportunities for female employment in the republican era. In particular, teaching positions at primary level came to be dominated by women. Even in the 1880s in several areas of the empire they were more numerous than men but by 1933 they held the vast majority of teaching positions (48,517 women were primary school teachers against 9,182 men). Perhaps this gender imbalance explains another interesting fact – the higher number of women at this date completing primary school. Entrants to the teaching profession required a school-leaving diploma at the very least. Of the 179,625 who managed to complete their primary education in 1933, a total of 91,165 were women and only 88,460 men.

With regard to the pupils' social background, in republican schools there was initially greater access for the lower classes.[61] In line with the regime's literacy project for the population, primary education was now called *educação popular* (popular education). The graduated schools had been conceived as a way of managing the number of pupils more rationally and increasing the potential for a larger school population in a single space. However, once the graduated schools were confirmed as an ideal type in the field of primary education, other social groups, including the ruling elite and the urban middle classes, started to want to make use of them too.[62] As a lack of such schools was to be a perennial problem for most of the twentieth century, this inevitably meant that places in graduated schools were soon usurped by the middle classes to the detriment of the lower orders.[63] The geographical location of the graduated school also worked against working-class access. The regulations stated that graduated schools should be situated in central areas of a city, which was where the elite and middle-classes tended to settle. These were not the sole factors undermining the working-class presence, however. As we have already mentioned, the value of child labour often made attending school unviable.

The increasing problem in the republican era of truancy and dropping out of school was related to the introduction of the graduated school and blighted the history of Brazilian primary education until the 1980s. Official statistics express this situation eloquently. According to records from 1933, of the 2,466,092 students enrolled in the country's schools, only 1,628,656 attended school regularly, showing the difference between enrolling a child in school and actually sending the child to the institution. Furthermore, little more than 10 per cent of the total year-one intake that year completed their primary education. The proportion who went on to secondary or tertiary schooling was infinitesimal: in 1933 there were only 98,141 students in secondary and 2,842 in further education.[64] This means that of the entire population who started school in year one, only 0.00115 per cent reached further education. Dropping out and truancy were much more frequent among the lower social classes. The working-class parents who did send their children to school saw primary education as a vehicle for gaining the basic skills (reading, writing and counting) needed to hold down a job. After a short two-year stint of schooling, the child was expected to enter the job market. As the numbers enrolled in school testify, attendance dropped drastically from year three. But children from the lower classes (the majority of whom were black or mixed race) were not simply excluded from advancing through the school system from lack of ambition. Arguably, their absence reflected the elitist and alien cultural norms informing education beyond the lower grades and the high standards of excellence that were required of the students.

A further important characteristic of primary education in this period was the growth of the private school sector, which was dominated by the church schools (especially the Catholic schools). These schools had existed from the colonial period and were more often than not set up to educate the ruling classes; their increased presence reinforced the segregation of Brazilian primary education, for their curricula and infrastructure reflected the social background of the students.[65] The private schools threatened to become even more powerful under the Vargas regime when the sector (predominantly the Catholic schools) criticised the condition of public primary education. As a powerful lobby group, the private schools claimed the right to take over responsibility for primary education *tout court* and were aided by the transfer of public resources from the state to do so. In this model, the state schools would only play a supporting role where private educational provision was insufficient. The debate between the supporters of the public schools (particularly the intellectuals and educators linked with the *1932 'Public School Manifesto') and the proponents of a private-school takeover, many of them connected to the Catholic Church, continued until 1956, when the state affirmed that it was to be responsible for providing education through a free public school system.[66]

This critique of the public school was part and parcel of a longer campaign by the Catholic Church to interfere in the state system. From the beginning of the republican era, the schooling of the poorer strata of the population had not been the main educational focus of the Brazilian Catholic Church. Rather the church had focused on offering private primary and secondary education and on schooling the elite and middle classes. On the other hand, the Catholic Church, which under the empire had enjoyed much more authority over state education, was always anxious to shape the public school curriculum by trying to force onto it the introduction (and maintenance) of compulsory religious instruction, and by taking a stand against the secular emphasis of public schooling. This policy was only abandoned after the promulgation of the Constitution of 1988, which affirmed the compulsory, free and lay character of public education.[67]

Before the promulgation of this Constitution, however, the church's attempt to promote religion in the republican classroom was reasonably successful. During the imperial era, the state had a Catholic agenda and there had been a focus in primary education on using Catholic rituals and teaching materials to build up a conformist religious ethos. In the First Republic, the state had adopted a nakedly secularising educational policy, but Catholic influence never disappeared altogether from the public classroom, where it continued to have a presence in the daily routine and in teaching materials. It came back, moreover, with a vengeance under the Vargas government which deliberately intensified the ties between religious teaching, the Catholic Church and primary education. Even before the overthrow of the First Republic, several states (while upholding the secular character of education) had re-introduced compulsory religious instruction. From

1931, this programme was extended to all public schools in the country, in accordance with the centralist approach of the new regime.[68]

A final characteristic of the primary school during the period under review which needs to be discussed is its role in the transmission of civic and patriotic values. Under the empire, teaching patriotism had not been excluded from the school agenda. From the 1860s, the curriculum included new subjects, such as the history and geography of the nation, aimed at developing symbolic ties to the country. Teaching materials were produced to teach these subjects, and this pattern intensified under the republican regime, which gave greater weight to teaching patriotism and also created secular festivals and holidays for its celebration. These holidays were marked by the schools and became a part of the landscape and calendar of urban life, a time when the school children took to the streets on school parades. However, it was under Vargas that the use of schools to spread nationalism and patriotism was fully exploited, at the same time as these concepts were given a new meaning. In the curriculum and teaching materials of the republican period, the point of reference for the people and the nation had been the idea of civilisation represented by the values and habits of Europe and North America. With the Vargas government, the patriotic axis was centred on the valorisation of the national cultural patrimony. Schools took on the task of transmitting and reproducing in a positive fashion popular culture and folklore and fostering a national identity based on the originality of Brazil's cultural legacy, seen as a product of the 'fusion of three races'. Through teaching subjects like history and geography, schools were given the pragmatic role of forming an ideal citizen for the centralised state, part of the purpose of classroom instruction being to neutralise the power of the regional oligarchies and create a truly Brazilian national sensibility founded on territoriality, race, language and religion, where the people were united under one administrative power. The importance of work was also highlighted, a central tenet in the propaganda of the Vargas era, which was seen as necessary to propel national development.[69]

Conclusion

The history of Brazilian education has undergone a significant revision in recent years. Investment in the study of primary sources and a better knowledge of historical theory has contributed to making the field more scientific and the history of Brazilian education being rewritten. From the increasing number of studies and research projects, one can see that the historic inequality of access to education in Brazil is not only the result, but also the cause, of the socio-economic, regional, ethnic and gender inequalities between the different populations. The contradictions within Brazilian society informed the development of schooling. On the one hand, there was real investment in education by the government which reflected the needs of the economy and a growing popular demand. On the other hand, the historical fragility and instability of the Brazilian state and of democratic institutions, as well as the absence of any official channel for popular participation and construction of citizenship imposed limits to the extension of schooling. This was expressed in the restricted access of a significant stratum of the population to formal education, not to mention its limited stay at school and general lack of scholarly success. This also resulted in unequal conditions of access to citizenship. The standard of teacher training only compounded the problem. During the empire, few teachers had had the benefit of studying at a normal school. In the *Primeira Republica* and in the Vargas era, the regional governments made an effort to extend the network. Nevertheless, the normal schools were unable to provide instruction for all teachers, as they were concentrated in the state capitals and required a long period of study from the trainees (three years), something that was not possible for a large number of teachers, who were themselves from the working class. This situation exacerbated the difference between teaching standards in urban and rural schools; the latter were obliged to employ teachers with much weaker qualifications.[70]

However, it is important not to be too deterministic. Recent work on the history of Brazilian education, focusing on the daily life of the school and school organisation, indicates that different social actors, such as teachers, intellectuals, politicians, families and children themselves, invested in formal education in a variety of ways that reflected their needs, aspirations and cultural capital. We must be careful too not to overprivilege the school as an instrument of acculturation. More recent studies of the history of literacy in Brazil point out that there were different ways of relating to the written word that cannot be reduced merely to the opposition of literate versus illiterate. Social groups without access to formal education found different ways of gaining functional literacy, or used alternative strategies to fit in with a culture in which the acquisition of literacy was becoming increasingly important.[71] The Brazilian government in the twentieth century also used other resources besides the schools – such as parades and the mass media – to broaden the people's knowledge and promote civic and patriotic values.

Furthermore we must take into account that in Brazil there have been other spaces in which to affirm citizenship that are not directly linked to formal instruction. In a society in which the presence of the written word has traditionally been precarious, it is worth highlighting the fecundity of Brazil's social movements and oral traditions, which are constitutive parts both of her culture and of the formation of her people. From that perspective, expressions of traditional popular culture, like music, dance and oral literature, are not to be dismissed as forms of leisure. Nor should it be forgotten that social movements such as popular rebellions, strikes and informal community organisations have constituted expressions of political engagement. Taken together, they have been the building blocks of a popular citizenship in a society where the access to formal channels, such as schooling, was usually restricted.

Timeline

1822: Imperial monarchy established on independence from Portugal

1834: Imperial education act making provinces responsible for primary education

1850: Centralised public accounting discourages investment by the provinces in education

1881: electoral reform requiring literacy test for the franchise

1888: abolition of slavery in Brazil

1889: Brazilian First Republic established

1891: new Constitution stipulated secular education

1892: São Paulo state education reforms – established graduated schools

1930: 'Liberal Alliance' seizes power in a military coup under leadership of Vargas.

Ministry of Health and Education established.

1934: Constitution guaranteed compulsory free universal primary education

1937: Dictatorship *Estado Novo* established under Vargas

Glossary

escola novista **movement:** Brazilian version of progressive primary education from the 1920s to 1930s focused on child-centred theories of learning. Mainly affected urban schools.

European racial theories: usually associated with the eugenics movement which advocated practices aimed at improving the genetic composition of a population. These ideas were widely popular in the early twentieth century.

graduated schools: In Brazil, these schools had separate classes for different age groups and levels of attainment.

miscegenation: the inter-breeding of different racial groups.

normal school: teacher training college or similar institution.

1932 Public School Manifesto: related to the *escola novista* movement (see above). A document proposing modernisation of Brazilian schooling, with universal provision and state rather than church funding of education.

Social Darwinism: a movement in the late-nineteenth century that stressed that life at the individual and national level was a competitive struggle. According to its guru, Herbert Spencer, nations had to use education to maximise the talents of their people if they were to survive.

Notes

1. J. M. Carvalho (2003) 'Os três povos da República', *Revista da USP: Dossiê República*, 59, 96–115, at p. 97; R. Lessa (2003) 'As cidades e as oligarquias: do antiurbanismo da elite política na Primeira República Brasileira', *Revista USP. Dossiê República*, 59, 86–95.
2. J. M. Carvalho, 'Os três povos da República'. Historical studies of Brazilian literacy suggest there was no clear-cut distinction between the literate and illiterate. Social groups as well as individuals constructed experiments with written culture that make such a

distinction otiose. Cf. A. M. Galvão *et al.* (2007) *História da cultura escrita: séculos XIX e XX* (Belo Horizonte: Autêntica).

3. For historical records on population and education see: http://www.ibge.gov.br/seculoxx/arquivos_pdf/educacao.shtm

4. Unlike other South American nations, the transition from a colonial regime to an independent country did not involve war, as independence was declared by a member of the royal family. During the Napoleonic occupation of Portugal, the king had taken refuge in Brazil. On his return home, an attempt was made to reimpose colonial authority which was opposed by the Prince Regent, the king's son, left behind to govern Brazil. The country thus became a Brazilian Imperial Monarchy: F. A. Novais and C. G. Mota (1996) *A Independência política do Brasil* (São Paulo: Hucitec).

5. To better understand the conservative government of the time, see I. R de Mattos (1990) *O Tempo Saquarema. A formação do Estado Imperial* (São Paulo: Hucitec).

6. Decree of 06/09/1881. Relatório do Ministro do Império, 1881.

7. J.M. Carvalho (2007) *Nação e cidadania no Império: novos horizontes* (Rio de Janeiro: Ed. Civilização Brasileira).

8. Bresciani, M. S. (2003) 'Brasil: liberalismo, republicanismo e cidadania' in F. Silva (ed.), *República, liberalismo, cidadania* (Piracicaba: Unimep), p. 18.

9. R. Lessa (1999) *Invenção Republicana: Campos Sales, as Bases e a Decadência da Primeira República Brasileira* (Rio de Janeiro: Topbooks), p. 252 (from a statement in 1908). Campos Sales was elected president of Brazil in 1898. He served until 1902, and during that period implemented fiscal reforms.

10. Ibid.

11. As a result of the alliance between São Paulo, an economic coffee hub, and Minas Gerais, a huge producer of milk, the period became known as the *café com leite* (coffee and milk) era. Nowadays several studies show that, although important, the domination by these states was not actually so central. See C. Viscardi (2001) *O teatro das oligarquias: uma revisão da política do café com leite* (Belo Horizonte: C/Arte).

12. Lessa, *Invenção Republicana*, and Carvalho, 'Os três povos da República'.

13. According to H. Matos, during the first half of nineteenth century the idea that Africans and Brazilians of African descent were racially inferior was not entertained. From the 1860s, however, it gained currency as a way of explaining the supposed backwardness of the country, which was related to its racial composition. See Matos, H. (2009) 'Racialização e cidadania no Império do Brasil', in J. M. Carvalho and L. B. Pereira das Neves. (eds) *Repensando o Brasil do Oitocentos. Cidadania, Política e Liberdade* (Rio de Janeiro: Civilização Brasileira), 349–91; also L. Swarcz (1993) *O espetáculo das raças. Cientistas, instituições e pensamento racial no Brasil: 1870–1930* (São Paulo: Companhia das Letras).

14. Sevcenko, N (1998) 'A capital irradiante: técnica, ritmos e ritos do Rio' in N. Sevcenko (ed.) *História da vida privada no Brasil. República: da belle epoque à era do rádio* (São Paulo: Companhia das letras), p. 253.

15. See J. M. Carvalho (1993) *Os bestializados* (São Paulo, Companhia das Letras).

16. Between 1917 and 1919, there were around 200 strikes in the country, some of which extended beyond specific occupational groups and became general strikes. See E. de Decca (1987) *O silêncio dos vencidos* (São Paulo: Brasiliense).

17. There were strong rural movements against the new regime, which developed a messianic tone. The most important was the 'República dos Canudos' in a miserable area of Bahia state that after four years of war (1893–1897) was destroyed by the Brazilian army. See *Os Sertões* (1902), a novel by Euclides da Cunha, one of the greatest works of Brazilian literature; Eng. trans., Euclides Cunha (1957) *Rebellion in the Backlands* (Chicago: University of Chicago Press).

18. In the words of Vicente Licínio Cardoso, an important intellectual of this period: 'The great sadness and surprise of our generation was to find that Brazil had regressed'. See J. M. Carvalho, 'Os três povos da República', p. 109.

19. To better understand this important event, see B. Fausto (1997) *A Revolução de 30: história e historiografia*. (São Paulo: Companhia das letras).
20. Vargas returned to power as president-elect in 1952. He was however faced with increasing opposition from organised groups following a succession of government scandals denounced by the press. Isolated, Vargas committed suicide in 1954 in the presidential palace, and wrote in his suicide note: 'I have left life so as to enter history'. See B. Fausto (2001) *Pensamento nacionalista autoritário* (Rio de Janeiro: Jorge Zahar).
21. The recent historiography of the imperial period has shown the complete non-existence of fines for errant parents, despite the law: see C. Veiga (2005) 'A produção da infância nas operações escriturísticas da administração da instrução elementar no século XIX', *Revista Brasileira de História da Educação*, 9, 73–108. One can see here the characteristic distance throughout Brazilian history between creating laws and implementing them.
22. About the republican project of modernisation in education see M. Carvalho (2001) *A Escola e a República* (Bragança: Ed. São Francisco).
23. C. J. Cury (2007) 'Estado e políticas de financiamento em educaçao', *Educação e Sociedade*, 100, 831–55. As primary education was the remit of the states, there was inevitably a great difference of opinion when compulsory primary education was discussed at regional level.
24. Cury, C. J. (2010) 'Ensino Religioso: retrato histórico de uma polêmica' in C. H. de Carvalho and W. G. Neto (eds) *Estado, Igreja e Educação no mundo ibero-americano nos séculos XIX e XX* (Campinas: Alínea Editora), 11–50.
25. M. Bessa (2005) *Matrizes da modernidade republicana* (São Paulo: Autores Associados).
26. J. S. B. Horta (1998) ' Direito à educação e obrigatoriedade escolar', *Cadernos de Pesquisa*, 104, 57–78; Castro Gomes, A. (2002) 'A escola republicana: entre luzes e sombras' in A. Castro de Gomes (ed) *O Brasil Republicano* (Rio de Janeiro: Fundação Getúlio Vargas), pp. 384–437.
27. C. J. Cury (2009) ' A desoficialização do ensino no Brasil: a Reforma Rivadávia', *Educação & Sociedade*, 30: 108, 717–38.
28. Data produced by J. C. Araujo (2010) *'A escola primária nas mensagens dos presidentes de Estado de Minas Gerais (1891–1930)'* (mimeographed).
29. Ibid.
30. J. Gondra, A. Magaldi and C. Alves (eds) (2003) *Educação no Brasil: história, cultura e política* (Bragança Paulista, São Francisco: EDUSF).
31. For a detailed study of the new model, see L. Faria Filho (2000) *Dos pardieiros aos palácios* (Passo Fundo: Editora da Universidade de Passo Fundo); R. F. Souza (1998) *Templos de civilização: a implantação da escola primária graduada no estado de São Paulo* (São Paulo: Unesp); and D. G. Vidal (ed.) (2006) *Grupos Escolares: Cultura escolar primária e escolarização da infância no Brasil '1893–1971'* (Campinas: Mercado de Letras). In the graduated school model, grades were one of the key organisational principles, and their establishment was directly related to another organisational element of modern schools, the evaluation of students according to expectations based on their age and level in the school. It was the *grupos escolares* that first organised the primary course into three or four grades. On its introduction, it defined a path to be followed by the student throughout their primary years, and created conditions to strengthen the school culture and the school itself within society.
32. See www.ibge.gov.br (n. 3 above).
33. R. F. Souza (1998) *O direito à educação.* (Campinas: Unicamp). A new administrative player also became involved in education: the municipalities. Several states implemented a model that was both federal and municipal. In order to ensure political control, the state government kept its hands on the management of the system, the creation of schools and teacher placement, while the municipalities shared in the heavy costs of the buildings. This multiplication of the powers responsible for offering instruction

resulted in the fraying of responsibility, as well as the subordination of education to local politics.

34. Araujo, 'A escola primária nas mensagens'.
35. For example, statistics for the state of Rio de Janeiro show that the budget attributed to education varied between 6 and 20 per cent. See Araujo, 'A escola primária nas mensagens'.
36. In 1926 the National Association of Education (Associaçao Nacional de Educação/ ANE) was created and the first National Education Conference took place in 1927.
37. For a more detailed study of the Brazilian *escola nova* see M. do Carmo Xavier (ed.) (2002) *Manifesto dos pioneiros da educação: um legado educacional em debate* (Rio de Janeiro: Fundação Getúlio Vargas); and D. G. Vidal (2001) *O exercício disciplinado do olhar: livros, leituras e práticas de formação docente no Instituto de Educação do Distrito Federal (1932–1937)* (Bragança Paulista: EDUSF).
38. Art. 149: 'Education is a right for all and it should be given by the family and by public institutions to Brazilians and foreigners resident in the country'.
39. This changed in 1937 when a new decree declared that a federal state was not obliged to spend that amount.
40. Gomes, A. (2002) 'A escola republicana: entre luzes e sombras', in A. C. Gomes, D. Pandolfi, and V. Alberti, *A República no Brasil* Rio de Janeiro: Nova Fronteira, CPDOC/ FGV).
41. See: www.ibge.gov.br (n. 3 above).
42. This included freemen, ex-slaves and slaves.
43. See: www.ibge.gov.br (n.3 above).
44. This problem has remained throughout the history of Brazilian education. It was only at the end of the twentieth century that 90 per cent of school-age children were attending school. Among other factors, this was achieved as a result of public policies to eradicate child labour and by offering financial rewards to families who enrolled their children in school (*bolsa-escola* and *bolsa-família* grants).
45. C. Veiga (2008) 'Escola pública para os negros e os pobres no Brasil: uma invenção imperial', *Revista Brasileira de Educação*, 13/39, 502–27; A. F. M de Schueler and A. M. B. de Mello Magaldi (2009) 'Educação escolar na Primeira República: memória, história e perspectivas de pesquisa', *Tempo. Revista do Departamento de História da Universidade Federal Fluminense*, 13/26, 43–66.
46. C. Veiga (2010) 'Conflitos e tensões na produção da inclusão escolar de crianças pobres, negras e mestiças, Brasil, século XIX', *Educaçao em Revista*, 26/1, 263–86.
47. Souza, *Templos de civilização*.
48. There is a continuity in this vision of the Brazilian population from Couty who stated in 1872 'Brazil does not have a people', through Gilberto Amado who reiterated in 1916 'We don't have our own people', to Alberto Torres who in 1914, at the same time as he was criticising the republican government, said 'This state is not a nation. This country is not a society. These inhabitants are not a people. Our men are not citizens.' See Carvalho, 'Os três povos da República', p. 98.
49. R. F. Souza (2008) *História da organização do trabalho escolar e do currículo no século XX* (São Paulo: Cortez).
50. According to data from the Instituto Brasileiro de Geografia e Estatistica, in 1999, 8.3 per cent of Brazil's white population was illiterate and 21 per cent of Brazilians of African descent. See Swarcz, *O espetáculo das raças*.
51. In Brazil, racial theories that posited the absolute inferiority of the black race were not prominent. Facing a highly miscegenated population, it became more common to advocate theories of 'whitening' whereby, through mixing distinct races, the most developed genes would win out and be passed on to later generations. Thus, the arrival of foreign immigrants and their miscegenation with the local population would lead to a 'whitening' and to the consequent purification of the racial composition of the Brazilian population. See Swarcz, *O espetáculo das raças*.

52. M. A. Carvalho (2003) 'Vertentes do republicanismo nos oitocentos brasileiro', *Revista da USP: Dossiê República*, 59, 159–87.
53. L. Kreutz (2001) 'Escolas comunitárias de imigrantes no Brasil: instâncias de coordenação e estruturas de apoio', *Revista Brasileira de Educação*, 1/15, 159–77; J. Almeida (2007) 'Missionárias norte- americanas na educação brasileira: vestígios da passagem nas escolas de São Paulo no século XIX', *Revista Brasileira de Educação*, 12/35, 327–42.
54. Although it did not directly send troops as it did later in the Second World War, the bombing of a Brazilian ship by a German submarine led to war being declared in 1917, internally sparking xenophobic attitudes and distrust regarding immigrants. The declaration of war also contributed to the rise of strikes and demonstrations in which immigrants actively participated, particularly those from Italy who were involved in urban strikes between 1917 and 1919.
55. Of note in the field of social science was the 1933 publication of Gilberto Freyre's classic study, *Casa Grande e senzala* [Eng. trans. (1969)] *The Mansions and the Shanties: The Making of Modern Brazil* (New York, Alfred Knopk), in which the author rewrote the history of racial relations in Brazil, emphasising the complexity of African culture and its contribution to the formation of the Brazilian people. In the field of art, a sign of change in the representation of the country was the *Semana de Arte Moderna* (Modern Art week) in 1922 in São Paulo, which in different ways gave expression to *brasilidade* ('Brazilianess') by valorising the culture and racial identity of the Brazilian people. See N. Sevcenko (1992) *Orfeu Extático na Metrópole: São Paulo nos frementes anos 20* (São Paulo: Companhia das Letras).
56. Brazil was involved more decisively in the Second World War in which its troops were engaged. This belligerence accentuated internal tensions with the Japanese, Italian and German populations.
57. See: www.ibge.gov.br (n. 3 above).
58. According to most state legislation, even though one can see regional differences and changes within the same state over the whole period.
59. As mentioned earlier, the immigrant population of the centre-south of the country in particular resorted to private financing for community schools.
60. Although the curriculum had a common foundation centred on religious teaching and on reading and writing, the curriculum for girls included needlework, and for boys the principles of geometry.
61. T. M. Vago (2002) *Cultura escolar, cultivo dos corpos: educação física e ginástica com o práticas constitutivas dos corpos de crianças no ensino público primário de Belo Horizonte* (Bragança: São Francisco); Filho, *Dos pardeiros aos palácios*; R. F. Souza (1998) *O direito à educação* (Campinas: Unicamp).
62. Souza, *O direito à educação*, gives an interesting record of campaigns in the press denouncing the schools for being filled with the middle classes to the detriment of the lower classes.
63. Ibid.
64. See www.ibge.gov.br (n. 3 above).
65. According to records from 1922, 45.7 per cent of primary schools in São Paulo and 31 per cent in Pernambuco were private, showing the strength of the sector.
66. Throughout this period, the church continued to benefit from public funds, from being given public land on which to build schools, from receiving tax breaks and from payments by the state for places for poor students in their religious schools. Cf. Cury, 'Estado e políticas de financiamento'; Horta,' Direito à educação e obrigatoriedade escolar'.
67. Cury, 'Ensino Religioso'. It is important to say that sectors of the Brazilian Catholic Church after the 1950s and predominantly during the military regime played a large part in social movements for popular education. It was especially connected with the radical pedagogical theory of Paulo Freire (1921–97).

68. The popularity of the move, however, was clear. Witness letters from the Secretary of Education for the state of Minas Gerais and later from the Minister of Education Francisco Campos to Presidente Vargas on the subject of the decree that introduced religious education in schools: 'You can be sure that the church will know how to thank your Excellency for this act'. Fundaçao Getúlio Vargas CPDOC: 13/04/1931: cited in Cury, 'Ensino Religioso'.

69. T. N. Fonseca (2002) 'A Inconfidência Mineira e Tiradentes vistos pela imprensa: a vitalização dos mitos (1930-1960)', *Revista Brasileira de História*, 22/44, 439–62; and T. Fonseca (2005)'A exteriorização da escola e a formação do cidadão no Brasil (1930–1960)', *Educação em Revista*, 41, 43–57.

70. Vidal, *O exercício disciplinado do olhar*.

71. This issue has spanned the twentieth century, with Brazil still presenting, albeit in lower numbers, persistent levels of illiteracy, even among children attending school. Cf. n. 2 above.

9
The Role of Mass Education in Nation-Building in the Ottoman Empire and the Turkish Republic, 1870–1930

Nazan Cicek

The backdrop: feeling under attack from inside and out

Throughout the long nineteenth century, the chimera of the Eastern Question never failed to remind the Ottoman statesmen that the empire owed its existence to the dictates of a fragile and temporary balance of power in Europe and that as a 'sick man' whose days were otherwise numbered they should apply some Western-origin remedies to lengthen its life. 'In the Ottoman Empire, as in so many regions of the contemporary globe, the state's educational initiative [was] a part of a larger attempt to reform society in order to render it modern.'[1] As the Ottoman reformist elite fought their way into building a 'modern state with infrastructural power' in Michael Mann's terms,[2] they believed that educating future generations in the 'sciences' would bring about progress, industrial development and 'civilisation', which in turn would save the empire from an untimely death.

Another dimension of the Eastern Question which posed even a greater threat to the existence of the empire than the imperialistically driven ambitions of the Great Powers was the nationalistic aspirations of her large group of ethno-religious minorities. Therefore in her struggle to survive, the Ottoman state unsuccessfully tried to use education, along with promoting industrial development, to create an Ottoman brotherhood and patriotism among her Muslim and non-Muslim subjects and to generate political unity. Nevertheless this did not lead to the development of a secular national elementary education system. The government, observing the ancient rights that ruled the relationships between the state and the communities on the basis of the *'millet' system, continued to let the minority communities educate their own children at the elementary level in their own language and in accordance with the precepts of their religion. Thus left alone, the 'millets' were free throughout the nineteenth and early twentieth century to educate their own as they saw fit with almost no interference from the civil bureaucracy.

From the beginning of the nineteenth century, each Western 'Great' Power fighting for a political and economic hold in the Eastern Mediterranean considered their co-religionists inhabiting the sultan's dominions as their protégés and vigilantly oversaw any supposed encroachments by the Ottoman government on their community rights, including educational ones. In line with this general Western meddling attitude, in the aftermath of the Crimean War, the allies of the Ottoman Empire insisted on the promulgation of a Reform Edict (*Islahat Fermanı*) in which the sultan promised complete equality among his subjects. The Reform Edict of 1856 acknowledged the right of every officially recognised religious community to establish their own public schools on condition that the method of instruction and the selection of the teachers would be controlled by a mixed council of public instruction, the members of which were to be named by the sultan. This official acknowledgment caused a rapid development of educational networks among Armenians, Bulgarians and Greeks. Concurrently a series of foreign private schools mostly founded by the Christian missionaries from different Western countries started proliferating across the Empire.

These developments led the Ottoman government to found the Ministry of Public Education in 1857 with a view to better controlling non-Muslim and foreign schools. They also wanted to promote the development of government schools but these did not acquire any popularity, even among the Muslim population. Nonetheless, the establishment of the ministry was the first step in a plan 'that while the primary level should preserve the culture of the religious community, the secondary level should provide the socialization of non-Muslims into the Ottoman imperial culture.'[3] Any attempt at closing down the primary schools run by non-Muslim communities as well as the foreign missionaries might not only cause havoc in the Ottoman government's tottering relationship with the minorities, many of which had already exhibited their separatist tendencies, but also incur the wrath of the Western Powers.

The reluctance and seeming incapacity of the government to impose uniformity and standardisation in the field of primary education also applied to the Muslim majority in general and the Turkish-speaking Muslim community in particular. Instead of building on or adapting the existing Muslim schools, the state sought to construct a parallel system but without the supports necessary to ensure it superseded existing systems. Throughout the century, no concrete steps were taken to gather the children of the Muslims, who were the core population of the empire, into elementary schools administered and controlled by a central authority with a standardised curriculum and syllabus. Until the final collapse of the empire after the First World War, large numbers of traditional Qur'an schools continued to exist alongside the government-supported public schools. These were sponsored by wealthy local inhabitants or by pious endowments and sought to create devoted Muslims rather than patriotic Ottoman citizens. They functioned as essential elementary schooling institutions where children were taught some religious knowledge as well as to read and memorise the Qur'an, mostly without acquiring any literacy.[4] In this sense, traditional Ottoman primary education lacked the common characteristics of elementary education elsewhere; they were also far from being a uniform educational network with an institutional structure. The instructors were maintained by the foundation and by parental fees and there was no state funding. Alongside the Qur'an, schools were the newly introduced government elementary schools, where literacy and classes of arithmetic, geography and history were introduced to the curriculum. However, secular instruction was not favoured by many parents. As Louis de Salve, the first director of the *Mektebi Sultani*,[5] would comment in an article in 1874, unlike the rest of the world where school was rapidly becoming more of a place to constitute and strengthen the bonding between children of the country, in the Ottoman Empire the school was serving to confine children from different religions and sects to their own separate worlds.[6] When the Regulation of Public Education (*Maarif-i Umumiyye Nizamnamesi*), the first comprehensive Ottoman document that examined primary education in a holistic manner, was promulgated in 1869, there seemed to be no system in the empire that deserved to be called Ottoman 'national' elementary education.

The struggle to meet the 'demands of the present': elementary education in the Ottoman Empire between 1870 and 1920

The Regulation of Public Education, which was prepared under the influence of the French Minister of Education, Jean Victor Duruy, was promulgated on 1 September 1869.[7] This was a document that systematised and stratified education and provided the legal basis to reform the primary school system into a more democratic, universal and national educational network.[8] It announced four-year compulsory elementary education for all Ottoman children stating that all girls aged between 6 and 10 and all boys aged between 7 and 11 were to attend elementary school. In every neighbourhood and every village would be built at least one elementary school building and in places where Muslims and non-Muslims lived together a school would be built for each community. Non-Muslim elementary schools would continue to instruct children in their own religion and give history classes in their own language. Schools were classified as either 'general' or 'private', and the former were placed 'under state control and administration'. The private schools also would be supervised by state although their administration and of course funding was left in private hands. Although this showed that the government was at least cognisant of the necessity for a more active involvement in regulating elementary education, the regulation lacked the necessary qualities to effect a radical transformation in the prevailing system. The government did not seem to think that it was incumbent upon the state to fund or construct the school buildings in every village and neighbourhood as stipulated in the regulation where the Ottoman children complying with the rule of compulsory education would attend. Neither did it take it as the state's responsibility to pay the salaries of the elementary school teachers who, according to the regulation, would be selected, appointed and inspected by the state.

Moreover, although the regulation was 'a part of the Ottomanist project of integrating Muslim, non-Muslim and foreign schools within a legal framework'[9] its contribution to the practice of *Ottomanism did not go beyond this legal realm. Its ambition for national unity rested on the wishful thinking that through efficient inspection and supervision the schools run by the minority communities and foreign missionaries could be incorporated in the ideal of Ottoman nationalism. In March 1886, the Education Minister Münif Paşa complained in a memorandum that 'unlike other states, the Ottoman Empire was completely in the dark about the curricula, textbooks, and moral character and behaviour of the teachers in its non-Muslim schools.'[10] That being the case, to the extent that they did work, the educational reforms undertaken by the Ottoman governments throughout the nineteenth century laid the foundations, not of an Ottoman national education but a separate national education for Muslim Turks and for each of the non-Muslim minorities. The education of Greeks, for example, thanks to the reforms that integrated their ancient rights and measures into the new legal framework, was officially retained as a privilege monopolised by the Patriarchate. Far from collaborating in building up a new consciousness of Ottomanism, the Patriarchate instead co-operated with the Constantinople Society for Hellenic Philology (Sillogos) and worked as a sort of Ministry of Education for the national education of 'Hellenes living in Turkey.'[11] In other words, by maintaining and even strengthening the organisation of pre-existent religion-based divisions within educational provision, the Ottoman state ironically helped the minorities to develop their own national education system. Thus the minority communities gradually came to be seen as 'educational competitors by the state which are also often viewed as political clients of the foreign powers, if not their outright agents.'[12] For this reason, in spite of their de facto openness to all subjects, the Ottoman state schools were largely conceived of as Muslim schools.

Seven years after the promulgation of the Regulation of Public Education, the Ottoman Empire declared itself a constitutional monarchy and the first Ottoman parliament, where the deputies representing all officially recognised communities sat together, opened in Istanbul. Article 18 of the Constitution of 1876 stipulated that all Ottoman subjects who wished to be employed by the empire as state servants had to prove their knowledge of the official language, i.e. Turkish, implying that 'the Ottoman policy of political unity would be guided by the maxim of *cujus regio, ejus lingua.*'[13] Moreover Article 16 declared that all schools operating in the Ottoman Empire were to be controlled strictly by the state and measures to standardise the management and curriculum of all schools other than the religious ones were to be taken without delay. This Article was met with loud protests from Armenian, Greek, Slav, Arab and Albanian deputies who saw it as a threat to the existence and well-being of their communities.[14]

The Ottomanising policy of this, the *Tanzimat* era (1839–76), crystallised in the opening of the Ottoman parliament in 1876, but came to an abrupt end when the Sultan Abdülhamid II suspended the parliament in 1878 and set out to re-consolidate the power of the palace while vigorously working out a monarchist imperialist ideology with strong Islamic-Turkish overtones. The aim of the

Hamidian regime (1876–1909) was to promote public schools as a source of loyal and obedient subjects who would serve the state in troubled times. Almost immediately, the schools content and overall raison d'être were drastically altered.[15] Ottoman educational policies now concentrated on expanding schooling for Muslim Ottomans who were increasingly seen as the bulwark of the state's loyalty base. This implicitly conceded that the discourse of Ottomanism that fashioned the educational approach of the earlier periods had failed to quell the nationalistic aspirations of the minority communities or curb the proliferation of foreign and missionary schools. Although the Hamidian state officially sought to re-emphasise 'Ottomanism' and educational policy continued to uphold the universalistic notion of an educational system open to all the population, in fact the state school system was increasingly seen as de facto Muslim, as the regime attempted to ward off 'educational competition provided by foreign missionaries, neighbouring states and the local minority communities'.[16] This retrenchment did not necessarily mean that the Ottoman statesmen failed to recognise the different path taken by most Western states to unify and standardise their educational systems.[17] However, faced with the Eastern Question, the Ottoman state opted to educate its Muslims to turn them into loyal 'warriors' with sufficient academic skills to confront the external as well as internal 'enemies' of the empire.

'The government placed great faith in the power of moral instruction as a means of safeguarding the Empire's future' and took 'what they saw as the successful examples of centralized state expansion in Western Europe. Thus, such features of Western education as boarding schools, centralized curricular planning, and textbook standardization became common features of late Ottoman education.'[18] Curriculum policy in the state-run schools focused on inculcating key concepts (mostly associated with Islamic morality) such as loyalty, religious observance, patience, forbearance, self-restraint, docility, compassionate and charitable action, obedience and respect.[19] In most elementary school textbooks of the era, the authors wasted no opportunity to instrumentalise the *hadiths and Quranic verses liberally.[20] Textbooks for primary schools acknowledged the necessity of adopting Western technology and science but exhorted children to stay away from what was seen as the Western spiritual and cultural domain as well as its lifestyle.[21] Greed, fear, laziness, extortion, ignorance as well as crying and begging (as indicators of weak character) were regularly denounced in textbooks while the lion's share of the books' content focused on obedience towards authority and piety.[22] As one hornbook of the Hamidian era suggests, apart from the love and respect for God and the Prophet 'it is the most sacred duty of Ottoman children to vigorously obey all the instructions, orders and *fermans* of the Caliph Sultan. What is more, all the officials and state servants regardless of their situations should be obeyed and revered since they follow and implement the orders of the Caliph Sultan.'[23]

In line with this reasoning in the textbooks of the era, the position of the teacher was 'clearly an extension of the Ottoman state' vis-à-vis the student and his authority was supposed to exceed that of parents. Parents could not be trusted to inculcate a well-balanced blend of the regime's political and moral values in their youth but were presented as belonging to a world of ignorance from which the child could be rescued by the teacher. 'The removal of the family from the locus of education, its moral component in particular, cleared the way for the pre-eminence of the relationship between the state and the student. The state, acting through the local bureaucrats employed in each school, stands in *loco parentis*.'[24] However, despite this official discourse about the unrivalled position of the teacher in the student's life, the Ottoman state largely failed to train and supply an adequate number of teachers who could rescue students from the ignorant world of the family. The first teacher training institution for elementary school teachers (*Darülmuallimin-i Sıbyan*) was founded in 1868 in Istanbul but there were no such schools in the provinces until 1875. Likewise it was not until 1870 that a teacher training institution to provide staff for elementary and secondary girls' schools (*Darülmuallimat*) was opened. In addition, finding qualified and willing students who wished to train as elementary school teachers proved to be a tough challenge. The number of students attending the *Darülmuallimin-i Sıbyan* in 1875 did not exceed 25.[25] The Regulation of 1869 held the Ministry of Education responsible for selecting, appointing and inspecting elementary school teachers but their payment was left to the community. The fact that teacher salaries paid by the local community were remarkably low and often irregular only aggravated the problem.

During the Tanzimat era, establishing government-run teachers training institutions was largely motivated by the ruling elite's desire to exclude the teachers who came from the traditional *medrese system and raise a new army of teachers as the conveyors of the larger modernisation project. Nevertheless the student body of the teacher training institutions was overwhelmingly composed of students or graduates of *medrese*s who were the only group sufficiently well-qualified to be accepted to train as elementary school teachers. They mostly proved reluctant to adopt new and modern teaching methods taught during their teacher training and after their appointment, they also tended to refrain from clashing with the local community over what the aim and content of elementary education should be. By contrast, the Hamidian regime with its Islamic and moral agenda turned to *medrese* schools and their graduates *(ulama)* for help in its efforts to prevent the contagion of foreign culture and morality seeping into the public school system. Courses in Islamic morals were mostly taught by *ulama* and because of the increasing number of new schools, '*ulama* were hired to serve as interim instructors while the appropriate personnel could be trained.'[26] In 1891, the Ministry of Education declared that due to the lack of a sufficient number of teachers *imam*s in the villages and neighbourhoods would act as elementary school teachers. Out of 20,000 Muslim elementary schools across the empire in 1892–3, only 3,000 were staffed by non-*ulama*.[27]

In 1900, Istanbul *Darülmuallimin* had only 168 students while the total number of students at 15 teacher training institutions in the provinces did not exceed 500.[28] In order to meet the ever-increasing staffing demands of new state-run schools, training institutions even accepted students who had completed their education only to elementary level. During the Hamidian era, evidence that teachers could offer a strong moral example to their students became as important in their selection and appointment as their educational and pedagogical training. Many elementary school textbooks of the era reinforced the idea that teachers, be they Muslim or non-Muslim, should all be of good moral character.[29] The Regulation for Elementary Schools of Istanbul of 1895 stressed that since the first and most essential duty of a teacher was to raise loyal and obedient Muslims, teachers were expected to relentlessly inculcate in the students sound moral qualities and follow only the authorised textbooks. Those who failed to do so would be sacked.[30]

Although they were designed and vigorously worked to foster Islamic piety and Ottoman loyalty, paradoxically Hamidian schools may well have contributed to ending the regime in which they flourished. Students educated in Abdülhamid II's educational institutions played an active role in the *Young Turk Revolution of 1908 spearheaded by the Committee of Union and Progress (CUP), which was to re-open the suspended parliament and a year later also dethrone the sultan. Through their moral education Hamidian schools seem to have raised a consciousness among their students as to the duties of true Muslim subjects towards the fatherland, which was stricken with poverty, internal conflict and continuous external intervention. Imbued with feelings of loyalty to the empire as well as a distinctive sense of duty to save the fatherland, the educated Muslim youth of the Hamidian regime came up with a new response to the 'demands of the present' – a constitutional monarchy operating through a parliament that would give all subjects of the sultan a say in the decision and policy making process. After the 1908 Revolution the CUP became the most important political force, beginning what is known as the Second Constitutional era (1908–1920) of the Ottoman Empire. In their professed mission of saving the empire, CUP cadres placed great faith in the expansion of a new brand of public education which would promote the idea of Ottoman brotherhood engendered and underpinned by the identity of Ottoman citizenship.

Unlike the Hamidian era, which allowed for a distinctive religious Muslim Ottoman identity and did not pursue a unified school system, the 'Second Constitutional era with its awareness as well as emphasis on the centrality of elementary schooling in the formation of citizen and nation bears resemblance to the Third Republic in France.'[31] Ottoman dissident intellectuals who had been forced to live in exile in Europe during the Hamidian regime had observed the transformation that the French educational system underwent and returned home after the re-opening of the Ottoman parliament with strong convictions that elementary school was the place where the construction of the nation and the production of its law-abiding citizens should start. This awareness also coincided with the percolation of new ideas among Ottoman intellectuals and pedagogues about the modern conception of childhood typified by Rousseau's *Emile*. '[Children] in this Apollonian image were not curbed nor beaten into submission but encouraged, enabled, and facilitated';[32] they were expected to live in the world of childhood, untainted by corruption, the ingredients of which, as

Cunningham remarked, were 'innocence, school, fun, games, friends, nature, and sweets.'[33] This modern notion of childhood that had been sacralised in the West since the beginning of the Victorian era treated children as a sui generis group separate from adults who deserved special treatment and care. Slowly, under the influence of these formerly exiled Ottoman intellectuals, the official discourse on the meaning as well as the value of children for the society and the nation began to change. Whilst, in the eyes of the pioneer Ottoman pedagogues, the elementary school was increasingly becoming a place whereby the socialisation of children was carried out by also preserving childhood 'innocence', the policy-makers eagerly tended to engrave their nationalistic aspirations on the fabric of this promising 'innocence'.

One of the first tasks carried out by the Ministry of Education of the Second Constitutional era was to introduce civics classes in the government-supported elementary schools which would teach children as 'the trustees of the future of the Empire'[34] their 'natural' rights and duties vis-à-vis the state.[35] Echoing Spencer's Social Darwinist approach in education, the Regulation for Elementary Schools of 1915 declared that elementary education would no longer aim at 'taming and chastening' the children or filling their heads with unnecessary information. On the contrary, it would, as in Western world, concentrate on raising enterprising individuals who are well prepared to protect their own as well as the country's interests.[36] In line with the hygienist approach that was gaining strength in Western education, the civics books used in the Ottoman Muslim elementary schools attached primary significance to the duty of each individual to maintain a healthy body and mind. Learning good manners, virtuous behaviour and acceptable forms of contact with other members of society was seen essential to the task of creating a common public sphere where an Ottoman nation united through common conduct could exist and function. Once the forms of *sociabilité* or the standard behaviour codes for use in public were internalised through schooling, it was believed social harmony would ensue.[37]

A series of new national holidays and celebrations as opposed to the traditional religious festivals that had been segmenting the society were invented by the government in order to build up the sense of common Ottoman identity. 'Recitations of patriotic and religious songs at schools, encouragement of the students to enrol in youth clubs such as *Power, Youth and Scouts and teaching the civilian students applied military classes'[38] became an integral part of the educational system. Elementary schools also were charged with the mission of teaching children not only about the 'evils' of the previous despotic Hamidian regime but also to love, support and protect the constitutional system as well as sacrifice their lives for the fatherland. The concept of brotherhood was at the crux of the process of envisioning and imagining an Ottoman nation who shared a common identity largely derived from having lived in the same territory under the reign of the same state for centuries and who were now equally endowed with the same rights and duties towards the fatherland, the state and their fellow citizens, including the duty of doing military service from which previously non-Muslims had been excluded. In line with the policy of compulsory and universal military service introduced by the CUP, civics books presented the different ethnic groups serving in the same army side by side and fighting against a common enemy as one of the most distinctive common denominators that bonded all Ottomans regardless of their religious, ethnic, linguistic as well as class-based identities.[39]

The 'necessity' for a gender-based differentiation in the curriculum of the elementary school was also 'discovered' by the ruling elite of the Second Constitutional era, as confirmed in a Ministry of Education circular in 1913. In civics classes at girls' schools, the importance of charitable and compassionate conduct and worship of family would be emphasised and girls would be encouraged to learn frugality, thriftiness, tidiness and attentiveness – the qualities that would prepare them for their future roles as housewives and mothers, who would be responsible for the reproduction of the nation. The CUP policy makers believed that unless the girls received basic primary education it would be impossible to construct a well-functioning family built on companionship, mutual respect and labour division that would guarantee healthy and well-mannered children. The civics books written for girls during this era clearly show that the female role was 'to provide logistical support from the private sphere to the state's project of transforming males into politically and economically active citizens in the public sphere.'[40] As a primary school textbook of the era suggests 'the first obligation of mothers is to whisper the words "homeland", "citizenship", "nation" and "patriotism" to their children while they are in their cradles, and tell of their sanctity and importance in order to raise trustworthy, useful children.'[41] A good citizen could be brought up only by a good mother and the first requirement of being a good mother was to acquire knowledge in modern child-care and housekeeping methods along with literacy and basic information on the rights and duties of citizens.

Before the Balkan Wars of 1912–1913 during which the Empire lost almost all her remaining territory in Europe to the Balkan League (Serbia, Montenegro, Greece and Bulgaria) the definition of the nation in elementary school civics books was largely inspired by French-style civic nationalism. Students were asked to imagine the fatherland as a big house accommodating all Ottoman citizens who had common interests that superseded their differences.[42] After the territorial losses, however, Ottoman civics books gradually began to accentuate the principal position and 'superiority' of the Turks as the founding element within the Ottoman nation. There was even more stress by the Ottoman ruling elite and intelligentsia on the role that elementary education could play in nation-building and citizenship formation. Muslim Turkish educated opinion was bitterly aware of the role elementary education had played in the Balkan states' successful mobilisation of their populations for the nationalist cause.

In this atmosphere, the Provisory Elementary Education Law (*Tedrisat-ı İptidaiye Kanun-ı Muvakkatı*) was promulgated in 1913. This increased compulsory free elementary education to six years in all state schools. The primary school curriculum, which followed the norms set by the Provisory Law, was thoroughly inspired and informed by a (Turkish) nationalistic perspective. The curricular booklet not only delineated the pedagogical methods that would nourish nationalist feelings and ideas in pupils but also set the norms for the physical appearance of the schools. Accordingly, all primary school buildings were to be decorated with national and religious symbols in order to enable children to internalise the principles of the Constitutional regime and Turkish nationalism.

> Ottoman flags, the portrait of the sultan, 'long live the sultan' banners, various verses from the Quran as well as some *hadith* banners on the walls, banners with the formula of *Bismillahirrahmanirrahim*, the verses of the Ottoman national anthem and songs hung near the teacher's desk, the pictures of the capital city and the previous sultans, a map displaying the Ottoman territory, illustrations of some moral stories and of nationally significant events were the compulsory materials that had to be present in all classrooms in the primary schools.[43]

Students would read stories about the glorious Ottoman Turkish-Islamic cultural inheritance in the Quran and in their own language and reading lessons while the history classes would teach about Ottoman military victories and narrate the life of prominent Ottoman Turkish officers, statesmen and thinkers.[44] The government also moved to regulate private schools in 1915, making courses in Turkish, Ottoman History and Ottoman Geography compulsory in all minority and foreign schools operating across the sultan's dominions.[45]

As ever, the Ottoman state was quick to respond to the 'demands of the present' as perceived through the paradigm of 'saving the Empire'. What was missing was not the ability to diagnose the malady and decide on the remedy but the capacity to carry out the treatment as prescribed. In other words, the Ottoman state had neither bureaucratic nor financial resources to achieve such a 'quantum leap' in elementary education. A disastrous external borrowing policy, which had been pursued from the mid-nineteenth century onwards coupled with the inherent structural weakness of the Ottoman administrative and tax system, had culminated in financial bankruptcy in 1875 and in 1881, with the establishment of the Public Debt Administration, the best revenue sources of the country were snatched by the former creditors of the empire. Thus at the turn of the century the bankrupt Ottoman finances offered no hope for funding the educational mobilisation campaign on which both the CUP and the Ottoman intellectuals alike set their hopes for the salvage of the empire.

Despite an increase in the number as well as quality of teacher training institutions during the Second Constitutional era, elementary schools in large parts continued to be staffed by imams or other members of the *ulama* who used traditional teaching methods, memorising and reciting the Qur'an being their primary goal for the children in their care. Education Minister Emrullah Efendi confessed in 1910 that at least 70,000 teachers, with the required pedagogical qualifications, were needed to staff the elementary schools in the provinces and the existing number of qualified teachers did not even amount to 1 per cent of this figure.[46] In the school year 1913–1914, the total number of students attending the 16 teacher training institutions in the provinces was only 1,550.[47] In order to meet the vast demand for elementary school teachers in the short term the Provisory

Law of 1913 resorted to an extraordinary and temporary solution, which allowed the elementary education councils headed by the governors in the provinces to hand out teaching certificates to those who successfully passed exams specifically held for this purpose. Before long the Ministry of Education declared that the only qualification the candidates would have to prove in these exams would be their literacy. The training institutions were also subject to scathing criticism for what was seen as an extremely academic curriculum cut off from the reality of ordinary school life in the rural areas. Trained teachers from these institutions, mostly born and raised in big cities, found it hard to connect with the local population in the provinces they served and win them to the government's cause of creating an Ottoman nation via public education. Owing to the low and irregular salaries they received, elementary school teachers' prestige within the local community they worked for was remarkably low. Many male teachers could not afford to marry and hence as bachelors appeared to be suspicious and unreliable personalities whose close contact or involvement with local families was frowned upon.[48] From their urban accents to their Western style outfits, they were seen as foreign and alien by the religious, conservative and poverty-stricken provincial Muslim communities who were quite ready to project their distaste of the novelties introduced by the central government on to its teachers.

While the Ottoman Empire was rapidly approaching its final collapse which would be provoked by the First World War towards the end of 1918, the Muslim elementary education system in the country reflected all the shortcomings of a society that had been in turmoil for longer than a century. It was disorganised, poorly funded, under-staffed, insufficient in number and disappointing and discouraging in quality. The literacy rate among the Muslim Turkish population was below 10 per cent. For the educated strata and intelligentsia, the dramatic state of elementary education came to represent the Olympian failure of the Ottoman Empire in keeping up with the advanced and 'civilised' countries in the contemporary world. The words uttered in 1914 by İsmayıl Hakkı (Baltacıoğlu), who would later come to be referred as the 'father' of Republican Turkish educational thought and practice, leave no room for doubt that the construction of a national mass elementary education would be the first priority in the minds of the founding elite of the Turkish Republic in 1920s. 'It is the un-national quality of our education system that should be held responsible for all the disasters that befall us', Baltacıoğlu cried out. 'We failed to construct and operate a mass elementary education informed by nationalist feelings and ideas and have now ended up with a weak-willed, cowardly and soulless young generation who do not know how to worship the flag and respect their ancestors' graves.'[49]

Learning the lesson by heart: elementary education in early Republican Turkey (1923–1930)

The eventful and traumatic final years of the Ottoman Empire terminated in its ultimate defeat in the First World War, followed by the military invasion of the Turkish heartland, Anatolia, by the Allied powers. This sparked the Turkish resistance movement (1920–1922), which was organised and led by Mustafa Kemal and his followers. After ensuring through a series of treaties and agreements, the retreat of French and Italian forces from Anatolian soil, the Turkish nationalists concentrated on fighting the Greek forces, who were largely armed and supported by the British government under the leadership of Lloyd George. The ultimate defeat of the Greeks came in late 1922. As the victorious commanders of the resistance movement, the Turkish nationalists announced the abolition of the Ottoman Sultanate in November 1922 and the foundation of the Turkish Republic in October 1923.

The founding politico-bureaucratic elite, or the Kemalists as they came widely to be known, were determined to create a culturally and linguistically homogenised socio-political body, to be called the Turkish nation, out of an extremely diverse ethnic and linguistic amalgam, as part of their nation and state-building strategy. Thus the definition of 'Turkishness' in the 1924 Constitution of the Republic, which was informed by French-style civic nationalism stated: 'The People of Turkey, regardless of religion and race are Turks as regards citizenship' (Article 88).

School, elementary school in particular, had a central place in the socialisation of these new Turkish citizens as well as in their integration in the new nation-building project. In the process of 'inventing' and 'imagining' the Turkish nation, only formal and secular schooling, it was believed, could turn the young generation into ideal Turkish citizens and lead them to internalise the norms and values of the new regime. Elementary school with its standardised curriculum, strictly controlled by the central government and taught in Turkish as the official language, would help construct a close-knit national society whose members spoke and read in the same language and acted on the same values. Ziya Gökalp, whose ideas largely inspired the nation-building process in the republic, stated that the 'nation [was] not a racial, ethnic, geographical, political, or voluntary group or association. The nation [was] a group composed of men and women who have gone through the same education, who have received the same acquisition in language, morality, religion, and aesthetics.'[50] The basic education of the Turkish child must be according to Turkish culture which now was to be redefined by the Turkish nationalists.

Even in the eventful days of the Turkish Independence War and the foundation of the Turkish National Assembly (TBMM) in Ankara (23 April 1920), Mustafa Kemal never missed any opportunity to talk about his government's future plans for the establishment of a Turkish national education.[51] After the abolition of the Caliphate on 3 March 1924, one of the first actions taken by the National Assembly was to pass the Law of Unification of Education (*Tevhid-i Tedrisat Kanunu*) (3 March 1924) by which the *medreses* and other religious schools were abolished. Funds used by the *Evkaf* (pious foundations) for educational purposes were taken over by the Ministry of Education. Private schools run by minorities, missionaries or Turkish citizens alike also came under the purview of the Ministry of Education, which granted permission for their opening, approved their curricula and regulations governing their operation and periodically inspected them. Private schools were no longer allowed to propagate any religion and use any kind of religious symbols – all crosses and crucifixes were banned except in the churches of the schools.[52] In Mustafa Kemal's own words, unification of education was a requirement to 'become an honourable member of the world's family of civilisations.'[53] Nevertheless, throughout the 1920s and into the 1930s, various sections of society opposed Kemalist nation-building as well as its habitus-transforming practices on ethnic, religious, and political grounds.

Elementary Education Law No. 430 of the new Republic and subsequent modifications guaranteed free elementary schooling lasting five years which was compulsory for all Turkish children aged between 7 and 11. The principle of co-education would also be observed, girls and boys attending the same elementary schools and being taught in the same classrooms.

> The policy targets stipulated that compulsory school attendance be held as close to 100 per cent of the respective age-group and that allocating scarce resources to elementary education was essential for assuring the political socialization of the population which in turn would ensure the survival of the new nation-state as well as the gainful participation of the population in economic activity.[54]

The main objectives of the new Turkish national elementary education would be to raise 'useful, practical and productive people who will make great farmers, shoemakers, factory owners and workers, businessmen and trades people'[55] and who will also be ready to 'altruistically fight against everything that threatens the independence of the Republic as well as the character and existence of the Turkish nation.'[56]

The emphasis on the modernising role of educated youth beginning in the *Tanzimat* period had culminated in the 1920s in a veritable cult of youth initiated by the new Turkish state in an attempt to build a national consciousness and a modern nation state.[57] The Kemalists went further than their late nineteenth century predecessors and embarked on a mission of creating a child-centred society where child-rearing was seen as a political and national duty. The activities of the Children's Protection Society (CPS/*Himaye-i Etfal*), one of the most publicly visible institutions of the republican regime which fronted large-scale state-run campaigns to increase the quality of life of children, indicate that the Kemalist-nationalist cadres regarded children as a group whose needs were to be prioritised.[58] They regarded the nation's children as a prospective devoted army who in the future would defend and reproduce the ideals of the state. In this respect, Turkey was now modernising in the fashion of a Western state.[59] The first three decades of the republican regime could be called the 'age of elementary schools' because of the unprecedented push to increase the quantity as well as quality of the elementary instruction. Despite the dire state of the country's finances and the extreme poverty in the society as a result of years of war, the republican government nevertheless mobilised its scarce resources for the expansion of elementary education. During the early years of the republic, the Ministry of Education had the third largest share in the general budget following National Defence and the Home Office. The number of elementary schools increased from 4,894 in 1923 to 6,713 by 1932. During this period the number of elementary school students also increased from 341,941 to 523,611.[60]

In official discourse, the rapidly implemented co-education policy was often cast in terms of democracy, equality and modern civilisation. Since education was a human right, 'the existence of differences in rights between men and women violated the true principle of equality', and educating girls in the same classrooms with boys was 'a natural, required component of the new socio-political programme pursued by the nationalist, egalitarian republic.'[61] Civics courses from the Second Constitutional Era were reintroduced under the new name of 'Instruction of Citizenship' and were now designed to inculcate the 'benefits of the republican regime' into Turkish elementary school pupils.[62] The first attempt of the new regime to reorganise the curricula of the elementary schools came in 1926 with the promulgation of the Programme for the Elementary School Curriculum. As the programme made clear, the elementary education system of the new republic aimed to transform young pupils into 'civilised' and 'patriotic' Turkish citizens by incorporating them into the national polity. Accordingly, the main objective of elementary schooling was to raise 'good and useful citizens' by facilitating their integration into their social environment, which was now defined as the Turkish nation.[63] With its emphasis on the necessity of 'integration', elementary education in the new republic planned to rehabilitate young people to fit the demands of the nation-state.

For most children, formal schooling did not extend past their elementary education. In order to optimise the indoctrination of young Turkish citizens during their rather short formal education period, elementary schools were used to foster 'militant' citizens whose national identity was constructed on the axis of loyalty, sacrifice and obedience to the republican regime. Elementary school pupils wearing black uniforms started each school day by repeating an oath in which they promised to be industrious and truthful as an ideal Turkish child should be, and also swearing that they would love those younger than themselves, respect their elders and happily sacrifice their lives for their nation and fatherland if necessary. Mustafa Kemal's 'Address to the Turkish Youth', one of the cult texts of Kemalism in which the youth is exhorted to be ready for duty in times of danger was expressed in hyperbolic language, was reproduced in almost all course material and was regularly repeated by students. On every Monday and Friday, flag ceremonies were held in school yards and the national anthem was recited collectively. Several national festivals were invented and pupils wore special costumes for the occasion and performed in pageants to celebrate them.[64] Likewise the collective praying rituals carried out at the Ottoman schools were replaced by collective physical training and gymnastics classes undertaken by mixed gender groups. Once keeping one's body fit was perceived as the duty and responsibility of a good citizen, the terrain of physical education and sports became the primary peacetime outlet for young citizens to prove their patriotism as well as their loyalty to the regime.[65]

The curriculum in these schools was designed so that, along with basic skills in literacy and numeracy, children would be taught 'the greatness and distinguished character of the Turkish nation'; 'the superiority of the republican parliamentary regime over the other types of political regime as well as the crucial place it assumes in the survival of the Turkish nation'; 'the mechanics of the state machinery'; and the 'civilised' manners and etiquette that are observed in advanced Western societies.[66] As we have seen from the less radically charged modernisation efforts of the Second Constitutional era, the task of creating the new individual who conducted himself in the public sphere according to the dictates of civility was not the invention of the republican regime, although the republican founding elite sought to legitimise and consolidate the new nation-state mainly by denying agency to its Ottoman predecessors. It formulated an official narrative of institutional and ontological fracture between the empire and the republic, but the continuities between the late Ottoman and early Republican periods in the realm of education appear much stronger than the republican elite would have liked us to believe. The 'civilised' manners that should be adopted in the street, in theatres, in public transport, in restaurants as well as at home were repeatedly explained in civics text books and imposed upon children with the overt aim of re-constructing the public and private spheres and the fabric of the society along Western lines.

Although the ultimate modernising aim remained the same as in earlier regimes, the republic was nevertheless insistent on employing a new set of pedagogical methods to obtain the desired results.

> In the 1924 curriculum, officials counselled teachers that school life required open discussion of daily events and a co-operative approach to learning. In this formulation, modern socio-political conduct entailed joint activity, co-operation, and self-imposed discipline – all considered different from the late Ottoman approach in school and society.[67]

The republican citizenship promoted in elementary school textbooks was formulated on the basis of duties rather than rights and freedoms. Rights, it was reiterated, only existed in order to allow citizens to perform their duties. The new regime aimed to construct social homogeneity, solidarity and cultural commonality by 'cultivating adherence to a social whole as well as devotion to serving the collective entity which would secure spiritual density and organic solidarity in the society'.[68] This became the most urgent aim of Turkish elementary schooling.

The government ensured that no textbook that was not inspected and authorised by the Ministry of Education found its way to the classrooms. A committee in the ministry carefully examined all textbooks and censored any 'improper' statements and assertions that did not comply with the principles of the republican regime. Teachers were allowed to choose from among the textbooks that passed state inspection. These had been published by privately owned publishing houses since Ottoman times, but the Republican state decided to involve itself in the textbook publishing and distributing business more directly. Every year, the Ministry of Education organised textbook writing competitions. Winning books were published by the state for use in schools throughout the country and were distributed through the book stores it had established for this particular purpose. Between 1933 and 1945, all history and citizenship textbooks that the regime considered essential in nation-building were chosen and published in this way.[69]

As the cultural and political consolidation of the republican regime gained impetus in the 1930s, the definition of the Turkish nation in elementary school textbooks underwent a transformation and took on an increasingly cultural-ethnicist tone. The Turkish language, Turkish blood as well as Turkish history rather than the legal bond between the Turkish nation state and the Turkish citizen gradually became the primary signifiers of national identity.[70] At the same time, Islam, which had been called on to establish bonds of social cohesion and political unity during the Independence War and the establishment of the new state, began to lose its determining role in the construction of Turkish identity.[71] 'Kemalist modernization based its will to civilize on populism, nationalism, and secularism – in the process producing new boundaries and excluding and marginalizing Islamic identity.'[72] Thus, the republican regime not only redefined the position of religion in Turkish society 'by assigning a threatening role to the public assertion of Islam that must always be kept under control'[73] but also used an extremely secularised and 'Turkified' version of 'official' Islam to further and consolidate the nationalistic ideals. Religion (Islam) classes in elementary schools taught after second grade were reduced to only an hour a week in 1926. The aim of the religion classes was to teach a unifying form of Islam which supported the assertion of the nation and to refute superstitions and fallacious beliefs. Bigotry was to be strictly condemned and children would learn that fatalism, which had been hailed as an Islamic virtue, was in fact a sin. Inertia and lethargy had no place in true Islam.[74] The textbooks for elementary schools published in the 1920s prescribed that a 'true Muslim has to love his country, pay his taxes regularly, respect the laws of the Republic, submit to the progressive guidance of the state officials, apply scrupulously the principles of good hygiene and work energetically for the development of the country.'[75] In 1930, religion classes for elementary schools became optional, being allowed in the fifth grade (the oldest class) for half an hour a week only, at the request of parents.

In line with the process of the 'disestablishment' and 're-establishment' of Islam in the Republican period, mosques and imams were completely removed from any role in state education. In order to fill the void, the government allocated a large part of the already scarce resources for teacher training for forming secular teachers. Before long, however, it became obvious that filling the void by means of traditional teacher-training methods would take a very long time. In 1923, there were 10,102 elementary school teachers (9,021 male and 1,081 female) working in Turkish elementary schools. In 1936 this figure had increased to only 13,934 (9,343 male and 4,591 female) while there were still 35,000 villages waiting for a teacher to be appointed. The Law for Elementary School Teachers of 1926 did not designate the profession of teaching as a career exclusively for the graduates of teacher training institutions, but instead allowed the graduates of secondary and high schools to enter the profession after successfully completing the pedagogy classes on the training course.[76] Nevertheless, the demand for elementary school teachers remained higher than the supply by a decisive margin. As the Ministry of Education of the time, Saffet Arıkan, remarked in 1936, with this slow increase rate it would take at least a century to supply staff for all the elementary schools in the country.[77] Very low salaries for elementary school teachers and delays in paying wages were additional hindrances. The republican government, despite being urged to tackle this by the American educationalist *John Dewey on a visit in 1924, waited until 1948 to take over the payment of teachers from poverty-stricken provincial administrations. As İsmet İnönü, the staunch comrade of Mustafa Kemal and his successor as president of the republic from 1938, commented in 1925, 'teachers were expected to work with ultimate public spirit, self-denial and devotion without expecting much in return in the short run.'[78] Education inspectors sent out by the central government paid visits to teachers annually and assessed their work and success in schools. From the late 1920s onwards, teachers were encouraged to join the Republican People's Party (CHP) founded by Mustafa Kemal, which was rapidly becoming the sole legal political organisation in the country. Before long registering with the party became a requisite for the teachers to prove their commitment to the regime as well as to its large-scale modernisation project.[79]

John Dewey was not the only famous pedagogue or educationalist that the republic consulted on the educational problems of the country. *Kühne in 1925, *Omar Buyse in 1926 and a group of American educationalists in 1930 visited Turkey and left lengthy reports behind them for the bureaucrats and pedagogues of the Ministry of Education to examine, mostly with frustration. Most of their suggestions such as substantial increases in teachers' salaries, establishment and expansion of vocational schools and sending teachers abroad for training etc. were simply beyond the economic means of the young and poor republic. Other suggestions that mainly aimed to lighten the burden of the state such as abandonment of free boarding schools and introducing new taxes for educational purposes also seemed simply unacceptable for a new regime which needed to bolster its popularity amongst an already over-taxed public.[80]

Five years after the foundation of the republic and despite the self-sacrifice displayed by all quarters of society, the government did not seem close to achieving its target of universal literacy – the literacy rate of the population was still only 10.6 per cent in 1928. This strengthened the hands of the champions of language reform who had long been entertaining the idea of an alphabet switch. Since the time of the *Tanzimat* (1839–76), the challenges of learning to read Turkish in Arabic script had been discussed in *extenso* among the Turkish-speaking intelligentsia and the new republic was eager to add another radical change to its political repertoire in the way of 'modernisation'. It was believed that a new Turkish alphabet, based on Latin, and also excising a profusion of Arabic and Persian words from the vocabulary by replacing them with Turkish neologisms, would contribute enormously not only to the educational mobilisation campaign but also to the nation-building and secularisation processes. From the Turkish nation-alists' vantage point, Arabic script as well as Arabic and Persian vocabulary and nomenclature linked the Muslim population of the republic to their Ottoman-imperial past and accentuated the Islamic and oriental roots that the Kemalist regime opted to forget. It was hoped that the new alphabet by facilitating literacy among the masses would enable the Turkish Republic to 'reclaim its place in the civilized world.'[81] The Turkish Grand National Assembly passed the Law for the New Turkish Alphabet on 1 November 1928 announcing that from 1 January 1929 onwards all publications in the country would be in the new alphabet.

The government synchronized the preparations for a new alphabet with the establishment of elementary schools for adults named National Schools (*Millet Mektepleri*). In the early years following the alphabet reform, over two and a half million people attended these schools. Along with the elementary schools, National Schools were the instruments of a massive literacy campaign standing as proof of the state's commitment to create secular, Westernised and patriotic Turkish citizens as well as to transform the outlook of the people through mass education.

Conclusion

What one historian of education suggests for the Ottoman Empire also applies to the Turkish republican case in the broadest sense: 'The setting up of a modern public school network as an alternative to the religious school system was initi-ated from the top, without a noticeable civil movement asking for educational modernisation.'[82] From the mid-nineteenth century onwards, the state issued numerous orders and regulations in order to rehabilitate and 'nationalise' the educational system but these mostly remained on paper and failed to materialise. The stated aspirations of the Ottoman administrations did not correspond to the political and especially financial reality of the empire. The state was not oblivi-ous to the necessity of raising new funds to meet the educational challenges but devising new taxes for this purpose only contributed to the distaste felt by the poverty-stricken and already overtaxed Muslim masses for the Porte's reforms. The contrast between rhetoric and reality found its expression most potently in the field of teacher training. The state expected (in fact ordered) teachers to rescue children from a world of ignorance built upon a set of traditional values and non-scientific knowledge that were sneered at by the modernising elites. At the same time, it asked the 'ignorant' parents to uphold and sponsor this service of cardinal importance. What is more, unlike the republican state during its first decades, the Ottoman state failed to create a vanguard group of teachers as its staunchest sup-porters, who would embody and reproduce its principles with a spirit bordering on 'martyrdom'.[83] By and large, the Ottoman state was not successful in activat-ing grassroots support or incorporating the masses in its modernisation project for education. Nationally awakened minorities eagerly clung to their ancient rights for educating their own children and loudly protested at most attempts to co-opt them into any national scheme for education. The Ottoman state's hands were also fettered by the political constraints of the 'Eastern Question', which rendered Ottoman educational efforts towards 'nationalisation' a Sisyphean task.

The Kemalist founding elite inherited from the Ottoman Empire a smaller territory and a population that was much less diverse in ethnic, religious and linguistic terms, and hence more conducive for 'imagining' a Turkish nation. Drawing lessons from the Ottoman case, the republican elite wasted no time in building a centrally controlled and standardised elementary education system, developing it rather skilfully as an instrument of nation-building. Nevertheless the republican elite's ambitious plans to reach universal literacy in the country in only one or two decades proved utopian. Despite all the vigorous efforts by the new republic, the literacy rate increased from 10.6 per cent in 1927 to only 20.4 per cent in 1935.[84] By mid-1930s, overall educational expenses took up 5.44 per cent of the general budget but given the evident poor state of the finances this sum was by no means adequate to create a magic wand out of education that would, as hoped by the founding elite, turn an 'ignorant, superstitious, un-national and unproductive' population into a 'civilised', enterprising, national-istic and republic-loving society. Even the strongest and staunchest political will operating from the top with a professed aim of spreading elementary education in a large territory with scarce resources was bound to be disappointed. No mat-ter how impeccably constructed the discourse of self-denial and devotedness, intertwined with the ideals of patriotism and progress, without school buildings, trained teachers and a child population whose labour was not needed by the family, the ideals of national education and universal literacy still lay beyond reach for the Turkish republic.

Timeline

1839: Promulgation of the *Tanzimat* Reform Edict which started the era of Ottoman reorganization

1856: Promulgation of the *Islahat* Reform Edict: every officially recognised reli-gious community could establish its own schools

1857: Establishment of the Ottoman Ministry of Public Education

1868: Foundation of the First Teachers School to train elementary education teachers (*Darülmuallimin-i Sıbyan*)

1869: Promulgation of the Regulation of Public Education (*Maarif-i Umumiyye Nizamnamesi*). Announced four years compulsory education for all Ottoman children

1870: Foundation of the First Teachers School for Girls (*Darülmuallimat*)

1876: Beginning of the First Constitutional Era (Hamidian Era) and Opening of the First Ottoman Parliament. All state servants to know Turkish

1878: The Ottoman Parliament was suspended

1908: Beginning of the Second Constitutional Era and re-opening of the Ottoman Parliament

1912–1913: Balkan Wars

1913: The Provisory Elementary Education Law was issued: compulsory free education for six years. Elementary schools to promote Turkish nationalism

1918: Final defeat of the Ottoman Empire in the First World War and invasion of Anatolia by Allied Powers

1919: Turkish resistance movement started

1920: Treaty of Sevrès was signed/ Grand Turkish National Assembly was opened in Ankara

1921: Himaye-i Etfal Cemiyeti (Turkey Children's Protection Society) was founded in Ankara

1919–1922: Turkish Independence War in Anatolia

1923: Establishment of the Turkish Republic

1924: Law of Unification of Education (*Tevhid-i Tedrisat Kanunu*) was passed. Religious schools abolished. Free and compulsory schooling for five years

1926: Programme for the Elementary School Curriculum. To create 'civilised' and patriotic citizens

1926: Law for Elementary School Teachers: allowed graduates of secondary and high schools to teach uncertificated

1928: New (Latin) Turkish Alphabet was accepted

1929: Opening of National Schools (*Millet Mektepleri*) to teach literacy to adults

1938: Mustafa Kemal Atatürk died

Glossary

Bismillahirrahmanirrahim: An adjuration or exclamation commonly used by Muslims to ask for God's blessings on any conduct. In Arabic it means 'in the name of Allah, most gracious and most merciful'. With one exception all *Qur'anic surahs* also start with this exclamation.

Buyse, Omar: Buyse was an Egyptian born pedagogue who built his academic career in the United States and wrote about the American educational system and pedagogical methods. He was serving as Belgian Vocational Training General Coordinator when he was invited to Turkey by the Minister of Education, Necati Bey, in order to examine the deficiencies of Turkish vocational schools and draw up a report for their rehabilitation. Buyse conducted his research and also completed his report in 1927, which was published by the Ministry of Education in 1939 under the title of 'Teknik Öğretim Hakkında Rapor' (Report on the Technical-Vocational Education).

Dewey, John: American educational reformer, philosopher and psychologist (1859–1952). Author inter alia of *Democracy and Education* (1916). Dewey stressed the importance of the school as a site for socialisation and advocated interactive learning.

Emile: Educational novel published by Jean-Jacques Rousseau in 1762. The first educational text to lay out an educational programme that followed the psychological, physical and emotional development of the child.

ferman: refers to the imperial edicts, imperial orders promulgated by the Ottoman Sultan and regarded as binding for all subjects of the Ottoman Empire.

Hadith (hadis): Hadiths refer to a collection of narratives which contain the Islamic Prophet Muhammad's sayings, deeds and statements mostly directed to elaborating on Islamic verses as well as exemplifying the proper Islamic way of thinking and acting to the masses of followers. By traditional Islamic schools of jurisprudence Hadiths are esteemed as an essential source to understanding and interpreting the Qur'an.

İmam: In Sunni Islam, the word 'imam' refers to the person who leads congregational Islamic worship and prayers in the mosque. In the Ottoman Empire, owing to their literacy and religious knowledge, imams also acted as elementary school teachers in traditional Qur'an schools (*sıbyan mekteps*).

Kühne, Alfred: Kühne was a German pedagogue who worked as an adviser to the German Ministry of Industry and Commerce when he was invited to the Turkish Republic by the Ministry of Education. He visited a range of elementary and vocational schools across Turkey in 1925 and submitted his report to the government the same year. In the report, Kühne suggested that Turkish elementary and secondary education system should work towards vocational rather than academic training. His report 'Mesleki Terbiyenin İnkışafına Dair Rapor' ('Report for the Improvement of Vocational Training') was published by the Ministry of Education in 1939.

medrese: Literally translated the Arabic word *madrasah* means the place of learning. In Islamic countries, it refers to the schools where mostly religious studies are taught. In the Ottoman context, *medrese* refers to the school where traditional style higher education, which covered religious teachings as well as styles of writing, syntax, poetry, natural and political sciences and etiquette was carried out. After the *Tanzimat* era started the Ottoman Empire set out to establish new and Western style higher education institutions in order to train the politico-bureaucratic staff demanded by the modernisation project. This brought about a dualism in the higher education system, which in time caused the graduates of *medreses* to lose their claim to be the sole representatives of knowledge in the empire as well as their former prestige and power in the state.

'millet' system: In the Ottoman Empire, the subjects of the sultan were classified and grouped on the basis of their religious identity. Each religious group was acknowledged as a separate community and regarded as a *millet*. The *millet* system regulated the relationships between the state and the religious communities and defined the rights and duties of each community vis-à-vis the state. As part of their *millet* status, each acknowledged community acquired the authority to govern their own religious affairs, settle the civil cases between their own members and establish and run their own schools. Following the Muslim *millet*, the largest millets were the Christian *millet* (inwardly divided on the basis of denominational identity, such as Orthodox and Catholic) and Jewish *millet*.

Ottomanism (*Osmanlıcılık*) refers to the concept as well as the policy which was gradually developed during the *Tanzimat* era (1839–1876) and manifested itself in the introduction of the Ottoman constitution (*Kanun-i Esasi*) and opening of the first Ottoman parliament in 1876. The champions of Ottomanism believed that largely dismantling the *millet* system and replacing it with the principle of equality before the law for all Ottoman subjects regardless of their ethno-religious identity would promote harmony and solidarity in Ottoman society, which in turn would quell the separatist tendencies of non-Muslim subjects and help maintain the political independence and territorial integrity of the empire.

Power, Youth and Scouts: an Ottoman version of the scouting movement: the Scouts organisation (*Keşşaflık Cemiyeti İzci Ocağı*) was first established in İstanbul in April 1914 under the supervision of Harold Parfitt, the founder of the English Scouts, who had been invited to the country by the Committee of Union and Progress (CUP). As part of the CUP's nation-building strategies, the Scouts' organisation was meant to raise a 'skilful, brave, shrewd, selfless and patriotic' youth imbued with the feelings of solidarity and responsibility. Activities of the Scouts mostly concentrated on the high schools in the capital and in some other big cities such as Bursa, İzmir and Beirut. In June 1914 with a view to reach and attract a larger audience another youth organization named Power (*Güç Dernekleri*) was established in İstanbul. This time the CUP avoided directly intermingling with the organisation but secretly controlled and administered it. This organisation was based on similar principles and aims as the Scouts. As the First World War progressed, the CUP, with the help of its German ally, founded a new youth organisation called Youth (*Genç Dernekleri*) in 1916 with the aim of preparing the Ottoman youth for active duty at the front. The organisation which was overtly paramilitary was directly ruled by the Ministry of War and rapidly spread across the Empire opening branches in a large area that sprawled from Edirne (Adrianople) to Kudüs (Jerusalem). It had two sections designed for different age groups. Muslim as well as non-Muslim children aged between 12 and 17 were encouraged to enrol in the Sturdy (*Gürbüz*) section while the Spry/Vigorous (*Dinç*) section admitted those older than 17. In 1917, all members of the *Dinç* section were conscripted in the Ottoman army and sent to the war front.

ulama (ulema): refers to the graduates of the *medrese* school system as opposed to the graduates of higher education institutions modelled on European examples.

Young Turk Revolution: refers to the movement spearheaded by the Committee of Union and Progress (CUP) in 1908, which culminated in the restoration of the constitutional monarchy and re-opening of the Ottoman parliament that had been suspended by the Sultan Abdülhamid II in 1878. The Young Turk Revolution heralded the Second Constitutional era (1908–1920).

Notes

1. B. C. Fortna (2000) *Imperial Classroom: Islam, The State and Education in the Late Ottoman Empire* (Oxford: Oxford University Press), p. 90.
2. M. Mann (1984) 'The Autonomous Power of the State, Its Origins, Mechanisms and Results', *Archives européennes de sociologie*, XXV, 185–213.
3. S. A. Somel (2001) *The Modernization of Public Education in the Ottoman Empire 1839–1908* (Leiden & Boston & Köln: Brill), pp. 43–4. In the Ottoman Empire before the *Tanzimat* era (1839–76) started there was no secular institutions that would serve as secondary or high schools. Muslim pupils who proved their academic skills in elementary school (*sıbyan/Quran mektebi*) proceeded to the **medrese* and carried on their education in those religious institutions. In 1846 owing to the increasing demand of the bureaucracy for civil servants as well as the need of military schools for qualified students the *Tanzimat* regime started opening secondary schools called *rüşdiye*. The *Regulation of Public Education of 1869* (see below) announced that towns larger than 500 households would be entitled to have a *rüşdiye* school. Accordingly expenses for the erection of school buildings and the *rüşdiye* teachers' salaries would be paid out of a town's budget for educational purposes. Graduates of the *sıbyan mektep*s would be accepted to the *rüşdiye*s without an entrance exam. *Rüşdiye* education would last 4 years. The Regulation of 1869 also introduced high schools to the Ottoman education system under the name of *idadi*. *Idadi*s, which would last three years, were designed to gather the students from Muslim and non-Muslim communities together in the same classroom in order to indoctrinate them with the ideals of Ottomanism. Both *rüşdiye* and *idadi* schools proliferated during the Hamidian era (1876–1908). Graduates of *rüşdiye*s were admitted to the *idadi*s after they successfully passed an entrance exam and paid the enrolment fee (12 Ottoman liras). During the Second Constitutional era (1908–20), the secondary education system was re-structured and *idadi*s were constructed as quasi-vocational schools where the syllabus for the last two grades concentrated on industrial, commercial or agricultural courses. In 1909, *idadi*s became fee charging schools and from 1910 onwards uniforms were introduced for *idadi* students. Expenses for the erection and maintenance of the *idadi* school buildings as well as the salaries of the *idadi* school teachers were paid out of the educational budget of the town where they were located.
4. Somel, *Modernization*, p. 18.
5. *Mektebi Sultani* (Galatasaray Lisesi or *Lycée Impérial Ottoman de Galata-Sérai*) was the first Ottoman high school which was modelled on the French lycée institution and opened in September 1868 with 341 pupils. The establishment of the Mektebi Sultani came as a part of the larger reform programme urged by France in late 1860s, which aimed to incorporate the non-Muslim subjects of the sultan into the mainstream and improve their conditions in society. As a first experiment in inter-denominational education in the Ottoman Empire which brought Muslim and non-Muslim pupils together in the same classrooms and dormitories, Mektebi Sultani was regarded as a test for the success of the Ottomanism policy of the *Tanzimat* regime. The classes were taught in French mostly by French teachers and not only curriculum and syllabus but also textbooks were imported from France. As Fortna points out 'from the perspective of the Ottoman state, the justification for mixed education centered on the assumption that communal education would foster a common allegiance to the Ottoman state' and hence[...] Mektebi Sultani 'took a radical step toward dismantling the formal barriers that separated the empire's subjects according to confessional affiliation'. Fortna, *Imperial Classroom*, pp. 102–3.
6. Y. Akyüz (1997) *Türk Eğitim Tarihi Başlangıçtan 1997'e*, 6th edn (İstanbul: İstanbul Kültür Üniversitesi Yayınları), p. 153.

7. The regulation was part of a larger reform package that had been pressed upon the Porte by the French government, and Duruy, who had previously examined the Ottoman educational system and ascertained its deficiencies, was personally involved in constructing the regulation. See C. Y. Bilim (2002) *Türkiye'de Çağdaş Eğitim Tarihi 1734–1876* (Eskişehir: Anadolu Üniversitesi Yayınları), pp. 165–6.
8. Alkan, M. Ö. (2000) 'Modernization from Empire to Republic and Education in the Process of Nationalism' in K. Karpat (ed.) *Ottoman Past and Today's Turkey* (Leiden & Boston & Köln: Brill), pp. 47–132, at p. 61.
9. Somel, *Modernization*, p. 8.
10. Fortna, *Imperial Classroom*, pp. 96–7.
11. Anagnostopulu, A. (2003) 'Tanzimat ve Rum Milletinin Kurumsal Çerçevesi Patrikhane, Cemaat Kurumları, Eğitim' in P. Stathis (ed.), *19. Yüzyıl İstanbul'unda Gayrimüslimler*, 2nd edn, trans. F. and S. Benlisoy (İstanbul: Tarih Vakfı Yurt Yayınları), pp. 1–35, at pp. 17–29.
12. Fortna, *Imperial Classroom*, p. 49.
13. F. Üstel (2005) *Makbul Vatandaşın Peşinde II. Meşrutiyetten Bugüne Vatandaşlık Eğitimi*, 2nd edn (İstanbul: İletişim Yayınları) p. 27.
14. Hastaoğlu, V. (2003) 'Anastasios Adosidis'e Ait Metinlerden Anadolu Rumlarına Dair Bilgiler' in Stathis (ed.), *19. Yüzyıl İstanbul'unda Gayrimüslimler*, pp. 52–64, at p. 62.
15. Fortna, *Imperial Classroom*, p. 15.
16. Ibid., pp. 19,61.
17. For the examples of such awareness among Ottoman statesmen see Fortna , *Imperial Classroom*, pp. 63–4.
18. Ibid., pp. 206, 241. Boarding schools in the Ottoman Empire catered for both elementary and secondary education. They were mostly established and run by missionaries and non-Muslim communities, although the Ottoman government also opened several for Muslim and non-Muslim pupils. For further information, see Özlem Yaktı (2008) '1908–1913 Arası Dönemde Osmanlı İmparatorluğu'nda Kurulan Yatılı Okullar ve Özellikleri' (The Makings of the Boarding Schools in the Ottoman Empire 1908–1913) (unpublished MA thesis, Çukurova Üniversitesi).
19. The Ottoman Empire was not alone in her attempt to blend the Western educational system with a moral content appropriate to the Islamic-Ottoman context. As Fortna asserts, 'a moral agenda of one sort or another lay at the heart of state educational projects unfolding in disparate parts of the late-19th-century globe.' B. C. Fortna (2000) 'Islamic Morality in Late Ottoman 'Secular' Schools', *IJMES*, XXXII, 369–93, at pp. 370–1.
20. N. Doğan (1994) *Ders Kitapları ve Sosyalleşme (1876–1918)* (İstanbul: Bağlam Yayıncılık), pp. 35–8.
21. Ibid., 39–41.
22. Ibid., pp. 52–68.
23. Ibid., pp. 32–4.
24. Fortna, *Imperial Classroom*, p. 234, and Fortna, 'Islamic Morality', p. 388.
25. Y. Akyüz (1978) *Türkiye'de Öğretmenlerin Toplumsal Değişmedeki Etkileri 1848–1940* (Ankara: no publisher), p. 39.
26. Fortna, *Imperial Classroom*, p. 137.
27. Akyüz, *Türkiye'de Öğretmenlerin*, p. 53.
28. Ibid., p. 52.
29. Doğan, *Ders Kitapları*, p. 49.
30. Akyüz, *Türkiye'de Öğretmenlerin*, p. 61.
31. Üstel, *Makbul Vatandaşın Peşinde*, p. 30.
32. C. Jenks (1996) *Childhood* (London and New York: Routledge), p. 73.
33. H. Cunningham (1995) *Children & Childhood In Western Society Since 1500* (London and New York: Longman), p. 1.

248   *Nazan Cicek*

34. A. Duben and C. Behar (1991) *İstanbul Households, Marriage, Family and Fertility 1880– 1940* (Cambridge and New York: Cambridge University Press), p. 229.
35. Üstel, *Makbul Vatandaşın Peşinde*, pp. 23–4.
36. Ibid., p. 40.
37. Ibid., pp. 73–83.
38. Alkan, 'Modernization from Empire to Republic', p. 113.
39. Üstel, *Makbul Vatandaşın Peşinde*, p. 88.
40. Ibid., p. 120.
41. Hakkı Behiç (1327 [1911]) *Malumat-ı Medeniye ve Ahlakiye* (Dersaadet: İkdam Matbaası), p. 118, quoted in E. Enacar (2007) 'Education, Nationalism and Gender in the Young Turk Era', Unpublished MA Thesis (Ankara: Bilkent University), p. 130.
42. Üstel, *Makbul Vatandaşın Peşinde*, pp. 73–4.
43. Maarif Nezareti Mekatib-i İbtidaiye Ders Müfredatı (1329 [1913]) *Bir ve İki Dershane ve Muallimli Mekteblere Mahsus* (İstanbul: Matbaa-ı Amire), p. 100, quoted in Enacar, *Education*, p. 99.
44. Enacar, *Education*, pp. 99–100.
45. H. Aytekin (1991) *İttihat ve Terakki Dönemi Eğitim Yönetimi* (Ankara: Gazi Üniversitesi B.Y.Y.O.) pp. 153–4.
46. Akyüz, *Türkiye'de Öğretmenlerin*, p. 76.
47. Ibid., p. 84.
48. Ibid., p. 94.
49. Akyüz, *Türk Eğitim Tarihi*, p. 274.
50. M.T Özelli (1974) 'The Evolution of the Formal Educational System and Its Relation to Economic Growth Policies in the First Turkish Republic', *IJMES*, V, 77-92, at pp. 78–9.
51. E.g. Mustafa Kemal's speech in the Education Congress held in Ankara on 21 Jul. 1921. This clearly indicated that the Turkish nationalists blamed the backwardness of the country on the lack of a national education system 'informed by an authentic national culture and suitable to national character.' (1989) *Atatürk'ün Söylev ve Demeçleri*, 3 vols (Ankara: Türk İnkılap Tarihi Enstitüsü Yayınları), vol. II, p. 16.
52. İ. Başgöz (2005) *Türkiye'nin Eğitim Çıkmazı ve Atatürk* (İstanbul: Pan), pp. 95–6.
53. S. Akgün and M. Uluğtekin (1989) 'Misak-ı Maarif,' *Atatürk Yolu*, II (3), 285–349, at p. 343. Also see *Atatürk'ün Söylev*, vol. 1, p. 210 and *Atatürk'ün Söylev*, vol. 2, p. 94. For the republican cadres, a 'civilised' nation meant a nation which belonged to the Western world. This approach manifested itself in a circular issued in September 1924 and sent to the teachers by the Minister of Education, Vasıf Bey (Çınar): 'Our educational policy is built on two main pillars: the requirements of our national life and culture and the requirements of contemporary civilisation which has been dominated and represented by the Western world.' Maarif Vekili Vasıf Çınar, Tamim No: 10602-63, in 'Tamimler', *Maarif Vekâleti Mecmuası*, 1 Mart 1341 [1925], No: 1, pp. 48–60. [Vasıf Çınar, Minister of Education, Circular No: 10602-63, in 'Circulars', *Journal of the Ministry of Education*, 1 March 1341 [1925], no. 1, pp. 48–60.]
54. Özelli, 'Evolution of the Educational System', p. 83.
55. A. B. Palazoğlu (1999) *Atatürk'ün Eğitim ile İlgili Düşünceleri* (Ankara: Milli Eğitim Bakanlığı Yayınları), p. 161.
56. *Atatürk'ün Söylev*, vol. 1, p. 223.
57. L. Neyzi (2001) 'Object or Subject? Paradox of Youth in Turkey', *IJMES*, XXXIII, 411–32, at pp. 413–16.
58. Himaye-i Etfal Cemiyeti or the Children's Protection Society was first founded in 1917 as a civil initiative with the professed aim of providing war orphans with shelter, food and education. It was later reorganized by the Kemalist cadres in Ankara in 1921 under the name of Türkiye Himaye-i Etfal Cemiyeti. Although the priority of the society remained the welfare of orphans, in line with the republican elite's focus on children as the new generation who would reproduce and protect the ideals of the regime, a series of new objectives were also incorporated into the society's mission. Among these

were the opening of dispensaries and milk stations as well as libraries and recreation facilities for children, doling out food, clothing, books and stationery to children in need, finding foster families for abandoned, orphaned or poor children, and supplying counselling services to the public with respect to legal, educational and health problems affecting children's lives in the country. For further information on the society's activities see K. Libal (2000) 'The Children's Protection Society: Nationalizing Child Welfare in Early Republican Turkey', *New Perspectives on Turkey*, XXIII, 53–78, and M. Sarıkaya (2007) 'Cumhuriyetin İlk Yıllarında Bir Sosyal Hizmet Kurumu: Türkiye Himaye-i Etfal Cemiyeti', *A.Ü, Türkiye Araştırmaları Dergisi*, XXXIV, 321–38.

59. Üstel, *Makbul Vatandaşın Peşinde*, p. 128.
60. Başgöz, *Türkiye'nin Eğitim Çıkmazı ve Atatürk*, p. 88; Akyüz, *Türk Eğitim Tarihi*, p. 304.
61. Barak A. Salmoni (2004) 'Ordered Liberty and Disciplined Freedom: Turkish Education and Republican Democracy, 1923–50,' *Middle Eastern Studies*, 40, no. 2, March, 80–110.
62. Üstel, *Makbul Vatandaşın Peşinde*, pp. 129, 135.
63. H. Cicioğlu (1983) *Türkiye Cumhuriyeti'nde İlk ve Orta Öğretim, Tarihi Gelişim* (Ankara: Ankara Üniversitesi Basım evi), p. 80, citing from (1926) *İlk Mekteplerin Müfredat Programı* (İstanbul: Maarif Vekaleti Yayınları) pp. 4–17.
64. For a selection of biographies and autobiographies that reflect the indoctrination campaign of the early republican regime in schools see B. Onur (2005) *Türkiye'de Çocukluğun Tarihi* (Ankara: İmge Yayınları) pp. 376–83. A work of oral history which dwells on the perceptions of children around the time of the foundation of the Republic and includes several accounts of school life is M. G. Tan (ed.) (2007) *Cumhuriyette Çocuktular* (İstanbul: Boğaziçi Üniversitesi Yayınları).
65. Y. Akın (2005) 'Ana Hatları ile Cumhuriyet Döneminde Beden Terbiyesi ve Spor Politikaları', *Toplum ve Bilim*, 103, 53–92. and E. G. Ersoy (2001) '1930'ların Kültür ve Eğitim Anlayışının Çocuk Esirgeme Kurumu Neşriyatı Çocuk Dergisindeki Yansımaları', *Kebikeç*, XIX, 373–87.
66. Üstel, *Makbul Vatandaşın Peşinde*, p. 137.
67. Salmoni, 'Ordered Liberty' p. 92.
68. Ibid., p. 87.
69. İlhan Başgöz (2005) *Türkiye'nin Eğitim Çıkmazı ve Atatürk* (İstanbul: Pan), p. 126.
70. Üstel, *Makbul Vatandaşın Peşinde*, p. 166.
71. During the War of Independence (1920–1922) Turkish nationalists actively co-operated with the members of the *ulama* as well as with pro-Sultanate/pro-Caliphate groups in order to strengthen the hands of the resistance movement in Anatolia. There were times when the majority in the National Assembly acted under the influence of *ulamas* and demanded implementation of more Islamic and conservative policies especially in education. Kemalists more than once tactfully gave in to these demands and religion classes in schools enjoyed a renaissance during the war years. See Başgöz, *Türkiye'nin Eğitim*, pp. 71–2.
72. F. Keyman (1995) 'On the Relation Between Global Modernity and Nationalism: The Crisis of Hegemony and the Rise of Islamic Identity in Turkey', *New Perspectives On Turkey*, VIII, 93–120.
73. Ibid, at p. 89.
74. Akyüz, *Türk Eğitim Tarihi*, pp. 302–3.
75. Dumont, P. (1987) 'Islam as a Factor of Change and Revival in Modern Turkey' in S. Akural (ed.) *Turkic Culture: Continuity and Change* (Bloomington, IND: Indiana University Press), p. 3, quoted in Heper, M. (1993) 'Political Culture as a Dimension of Compatibility' in M. Heper, A. Öncü, H. Kramer (eds) (1993) *Turkey and the West: Changing Political and Cultural Identities* (London & New York: I.B.Tauris,) pp. 1–18, at p. 8.
76. After the foundation of the Turkish Republic secondary education was seen essential to train the craftsmen and traders that a young and backward economy like the Turkish one needed. Hence the general tone that shaped the construction of both secondary schools known as *ortaokuls* (literally: middle schools) and high schools called *lises*

was preparing the youth of the country for work. Of these two institutions the latter was also devised to provide the students with the necessary academic skills which would enable them to attend the university. Both *ortaokuls* and *lises* would last 3 years and were free of charge. Graduates of the elementary schools were entitled to enrol in *ortaokuls* with their diplomas and the graduates of *ortaokuls* were eligible to enrol in *lises*.

77. Akyüz, *Türk Eğitim Tarihi*, p. 223.
78. İsmet İnönü (2002) *Eğitim-Öğretim Üzerine* [On Education]', ed. İ. Turan (Ankara: Türk Eğitim Derneği İnönü Vakfı) pp. 19–20.
79. Akyüz, *Türk Eğitim Tarihi*, pp. 270–1.
80. Başgöz, *Türkiye'nin Eğitim*, pp. 151–61.
81. For Mustafa Kemal's own words on the subject see *Atatürk'ün Söylev*, vol. II, p. 251.
82. Somel, *Modernization*, p. 11.
83. For an account of how teachers in the early Republican era perceived themselves as 'embodiments of the public and future-oriented nature of the Republican Project', see ee E. Özyürek (2006) *Nostalgia for the Modern: State, Secularism and Everyday Politics in Turkey* (Durham & London: Duke University Press).
84. N. Sakaoğlu (2003) *Osmanlıdan Günümüze Eğitim Tarihi* (İstanbul: İstanbul Bilgi Üniversitesi Yayınları), p. 202.

Part IV

The Colonial Empires

Introduction

Laurence Brockliss and Nicola Sheldon

The overseas colonial possessions of the Western European powers on the eve of the First World War can be divided into two types. British Canada, Australia and New Zealand were settlement colonies where wave after wave of white immigration had quickly overwhelmed the small indigenous populations and eventually led to the establishment of self-governing but dependent clones of the mother country.[1] Elsewhere in the world – in India, South-East Asia, Africa and the Caribbean – European immigration had generally been very limited, and a minuscule colonial elite, ultimately taking orders from the metropolitan government, was in charge of large swathes of territory occupied by native peoples who were seldom ethnically or linguistically homogeneous. The obvious exceptions were semi-autonomous French Algeria and British South Africa where there had been significant white immigration by the end of the nineteenth century. Even there, though, inhabitants of European stock formed only a small minority of the total population.

The development of elementary education in Britain's three white dominions was inevitably affected by the debate about mass schooling in the mother country. In the first part of the nineteenth century when these territories were beginning to be opened up, the colonial administrations, like the British government, only paid lip service to the need to provide the young with education. In some cases, land was set aside to support an elementary school as each new community was founded; more usually enabling acts were promulgated by the colonial authorities allowing groups of residents to establish their own schools.[2]

Unsurprisingly, these initiatives had a limited effect and most functioning schools in the middle of the century were run, as in England, by the churches or educational charities, albeit, again as in England, with some government support. In the small maritime colony of Newfoundland, for instance, the dominant educational force in the 1840s was the Newfoundland School Society, an evangelical charity set up in 1823 to bring literacy and the 'Word of God' to the children of the province's fishermen.[3] Even sooner than in nineteenth-century

251

Britain, however, it became clear that the voluntary societies with their limited funds could only achieve so much, and by the middle of the century, there were demands that the colonial administrations become more proactive. In Australia and New Zealand, there was concern that schools were chiefly to be found in the towns, while most of the population was made up of farmers. In Canada, there was the more pressing problem of mass discontent. Uprisings in the 1830s against the colonial governments in both Upper and Lower Canada (now the provinces of Ontario and Quebec respectively) convinced the elite that only an effective system of mass education could save the new country from anarchy. What was needed it was felt was a system of government-controlled national or public schools with a common curriculum and properly trained teachers, which would provide instruction for all children of the settler population.[4] The model drawn on was the system that had been set up in Ireland in the 1830s, which was embraced so wholeheartedly that even the textbooks published by Ireland's *National Board of Commissioners were sanctioned for use.[5]

In Canada, the first significant step to creating a system of public schools occurred in 1841 when the first Parliament of the newly united Upper and Lower Canada passed an education act which established a Superintendent of Education with powers to improve and extend the existing provision of elementary schooling. Over the next 10 years under the tutelage of Canada's first educationalist of note, *Egerton Ryerson, the nascent system gradually took shape and was given its definitive form in 1852 when the province established free *common schooling throughout its jurisdiction, paid for and controlled by local taxpayers.[6] Over the next 20 years, the other provinces followed suit, culminating in 1871 with the foundation of a system of free *public schools in the new province of British Columbia. Canada, on the other hand, moved more slowly to make schooling compulsory. Ontario was once more in the van passing an act in 1871 that stipulated all children between 7 and 12 had to spend four months of the year in school. But there were still several provinces where attendance was voluntary as late as 1914, and Quebec and Newfoundland only passed a compulsory law in 1942. However, there seems to have been little need to force Canadians into school: Quebec in 1900, for instance, had a larger proportion of school-age children in the classroom than any other province.[7] Initially the public schools, thanks to local control, had been sensitive to the linguistic and religious divisions of the new country, even if there was a predisposition among their first promoters to non-denominational schooling. Ethnic and confessional sensibilities were always honoured in French and Catholic Quebec, but in other parts of Canada, especially with the growing number of immigrants from outside the British Isles in the years before the First World War, the school system became more aggressively Anglophone and imperialistic. Ryerson had always believed that representative government was imperilled by ignorance, so that the purpose of common schooling was to inculcate the right predispositions, loyalties and sentiments to ensure the stability of the state. His successors were much more jingoistic. The schools were to turn immigrant children into Canadians by teaching the four cornerstones of British Canadian citizenship: imperial patriotism, Protestantism, the English language and cleanliness.[8]

The colonies of Australia and New Zealand set up 'national' systems of education at the same time as their Canadian counterparts. New South Wales, the first Australian 'state' to enjoy a measure of self-government, laid down the administrative foundations for a system of state schools in 1848; the other antipodian colonies had done so by the early 1870s. But the Australians and New Zealanders were slower to establish a free and universal system. None had done so before Victoria took the plunge in 1872, and it would be 1885 before Tasmania followed suit. When they did decide to 'open up' their systems, on the other hand, they also introduced compulsion. Under the Victoria legislation, all children between 5 and 15 years had to be in school for at least 60 days in every half year. At the same time, most states created universal systems that were stolidly secular. Religious instruction, even of a non-denominational kind, was excluded from the school day. The most that was allowed was out of hours non-compulsory Bible reading and religious instruction. The New Zealand education law of 1877 was so strict that clergy were banned from school buildings. When in 1897 the town of Nelson agreed that religion might be taught for half an hour one day a week in its schools in the early morning, it got round the law by pretending that schools on that day did not officially open until the class was finished.[9]

The expulsion of religion from the classroom brought to an end a debate that had raged from the middle of the nineteenth century. When New South Wales set up a 'state-wide' system of education in 1848, it was initially envisaged as a dual system, antedating the one that would be set up in Britain in 1870–1 by more than 20 years: the state's new Board of Education would both administer the new non-denominational state elementary schools and subsidise and oversee the existing schools run by Anglicans, Presbyterians, Methodists and Catholics.[10] When the other Australian states set up their own state-wide systems in the following years, however, they were far less willing to accommodate denominational interests. South Australia ended state aid to denominational schools as early as 1852, Tasmania in 1853. Their withdrawal sparked a trend. From 1880 when Queensland ended its subsidy, church schools were cut adrift.[11] The decision ostensibly reflected a belief that denominational schools were divisive in a confessionally mixed country, although it also masked deep-seated anti-Catholic prejudice among Protestant elites who wanted to make Catholic schools uneconomic. There was also a fear that the newly enfranchised working classes would not use their vote wisely unless they had been suitably groomed in a state institution.[12] Whatever the reasons behind the decision, the creation of a secular school system in Australia did not help to heal the divisions between the Catholic and Protestant communities. The Catholic Archbishop Vaughan in 1879 insisted that Catholic children must be sent to Catholic schools and used the Catholic teaching orders to staff an alternative system. Secular schools were denounced as 'seed-plots of future immorality, infidelity and lawlessness'.[13]

For all the influence of the Irish experiment, the inclusiveness of Canada's elementary school system had much in common with the American system described in an earlier chapter.[14] Australia and New Zealand, on the other hand, ended up with a system that was neither Irish nor British but a hybrid. All three dominions, moreover, showed a greater enthusiasm than the mother country for opening up secondary education to the masses, especially in Australia after 1910, when parties representing the working classes became dominant in state politics. Although the primary purpose of education, it was understood, was to develop hardworking and law abiding citizen patriots – in the Australian case, good Australians rather than Australian Britons[15] – it also came to be accepted that educational opportunity needed to be widened as much as possible. In the early twentieth century, each dominion possessed a mix of private and state-run academic and technical secondary schools, analogous to the system in Britain, but they catered for a much larger proportion of the post-school age population.[16] As early as 1900, 10 per cent of 15- to 19-year-olds in English Canada were attending high school. In New South Wales, Australia's most educationally progressive state, 20 per cent of children leaving elementary school in 1915 went on to some form of secondary school; in 1925 this figure had risen to 41 per cent.[17] Admittedly, access to secondary education was not automatic – the British dominions did not fully go down the American road during the period under review. Even in meritocratic Australia, the passport in most states, following Scotland's example, was a qualifying exam.[18] But much was done to encourage staying on by the state governments. Queensland set up a generous bursary scheme for gifted children as early as 1864; others followed suit. More importantly, the accession to power at the state level of Labour in the second half of the period usually led to the abolition of fees in state-run secondary schools.[19]

The establishment of universal, free and compulsory systems of elementary education in Britain's three white dominions was not matched by a comparable development in Europe's many other colonies where whites were in a decided minority. This is not to say that the metropolitan governments were uninterested in schooling their black and brown subjects. Simply on a practical level, putting children to school, whatever their race, was the obvious way to create docile imperial subjects who would accept the permanent presence of European overlords and work for the good of the mother country. As the governor-general of Algeria put it in 1847, 'one school will replace two batallions'.[20] But both the British and the French were not simply interested in controlling their subject peoples: in Africa especially, they believed that they were benevolent not exploitative colonisers engaged in a mission *civilisatrice*, which could only be effected through education. As early as 1832, the French government's representative in Algiers, Pierre Genty de Bussy, declared that the French were in North Africa to bring enlightenment to an Arab people then living in darkness.

> Called to the beautiful role of colonizing one of the Babary kingdoms, France has taken as an aid in her programs the most powerful means of civilization, education ... To pacify and enlighten these countries in turn, and extend again the benefits of science that have been lost for so many centuries, that is the noble mission which she has proposed for herself and which she will accomplish.[21]

The British may seldom have risen to such flights of rhetoric but they broadly shared De Bussy's conviction of the nobility of their cause. As the report sent by the education committee of the Privy Council to the Colonial Office in 1847 makes clear, the British imperial project was a work of improvement. Through the spread of elementary education, the British overseas were to inculcate Christianity and habits of self-control and moral discipline, teach hygiene, offer practical instruction in common handicrafts and husbandry, and give the peasants sufficient literacy to be able to farm more efficiently and make contracts. Additionally, the natives were to be instructed in the basic structure of capitalism, the benefits of Western governmental structures, and the value of personal independence and security. Finally schools were 'to diffuse a grammatical knowledge of English' as an important agent of civilisation.[22]

The trick was how to turn these dreams of 'reforming' the natives into reality. The British approach, understandably, was to favour voluntary action by encouraging overseas mission societies to combine teaching the three R's with spreading the word. Colonial governments would only step in directly and found state schools to plug perceived gaps: even the limited number of secondary schools for the native population was frequently run by religious charities and orders. The educational profile of the Gold Coast (modern Ghana) at the end of the period was typical. The small cocoa colony in 1930 contained some 600 schools dotted around the territory run by religious organisations, chiefly the Methodists in the towns and the Basel Mission Society in the countryside; only another 30, both elementary and secondary schools, were directly financed and administered by the state.[23] The French, on the other hand, just as understandably given the Third Republic's secularist outlook and its running battle with the Catholic Church, preferred their colonial schools to be state institutions. Algeria was in some respects a peculiar colony because the territory was officially part of metropolitan France from 1848. But it was always the testing ground for French colonial policy *tout court*, so the educational initiatives taken there are a good indication of the state's thinking.[24] Initially, in the 1860s and 1870s the state was content to establish a small network of bilingual schools for both Arab- and French-speaking children primarily in urban areas. This policy was replaced in 1883 by a much more ambitious one that mirrored the reforms carried out in France a few years before. Thereafter every commune in the department was to have a state-run school which would provide free education given in French alone for the whole school-age population: attendance for both boys and girls was made compulsory. The policy was modified in subsequent years to meet Muslim objections to schooling girls but the 1883 law remained the basis of French educational policy in the colony until Algeria gained its independence in 1962.[25]

Inevitably, neither approach was very successful. Forcing dependent peoples to subsidise mass education at a realistic level was politically and practically impossible, especially in Sub-Saharan Africa where the population largely consisted of economically backward, self-sufficient farmers with little or no historic contact with literate civilisations. Nor was it feasible, given the general high financial cost of running an empire, to provide large-scale funding for educational initiatives overseas from the metropolitan budget.

The indigenous populations, furthermore, do not seem to have been highly enthusiastic about the elementary education on offer. In regions of the world with indigenous literate cultures of long-standing, such as North Africa, parents who sought schooling for their children usually preferred to send them to existing or newly founded religious schools lest they be lured from the faith of their fathers and/or Gallicised.[26] In Sub-Saharan Africa, on the other hand, few people, especially those living in the countryside, saw the point of literacy, so European schools were boycotted from indifference. Even the leaders of rural society were reluctant to educate their children: despite the fact that Britain actively 'encouraged' tribal leaders to send their sons away to be schooled, it was estimated that less than half the chiefs in the Gold Coast were literate in 1927.[27] Moreover, the limited number of parents who did use the colonial schools seldom shared their masters' vision of their purpose. Colonial authorities embraced the British belief that through schooling their native subjects could become healthier, more efficient and more productive farmers, artisans and mine workers. The elementary school curriculum therefore was intended to have a practical slant. For the brightest, it was not to be the gateway for a conventional secondary education but for more advanced training in agronomy and engineering given in a handful of 'higher' technical schools. Parents who invested in schooling for any length of time, however, did not want their sons to return to the farm, workshop or mine, even in a managerial or supervisorial capacity. Recognising that Europeans accorded a higher status to those who worked with their head rather than hands and that the key to social advancement in the British and French colonial society was to become a lower grade civil servant or policeman, ambitious parents wanted an academic rather than a practical education for their children. The British from the mid-1920s, following the *Phelps-Stokes reports, began to place an even greater emphasis on practical instruction in their African schools, suggested that greater use should be made of tribal languages in the classroom, and called for more attention to be paid to teaching pupils about their local history and geography. As a consequence, they only alienated the one constituency for western education that actually existed. This was demonstrated graphically in Kenya, when the representatives of the new native elite who filled the colonial African council, set up in 1924, immediately made clear their preference for an academic and Anglophone education.[28]

It is also evident that the representatives of the imperial government on the ground were often less than enthusiastic about pushing the sanguine educational schemes of their metropolitan masters. This was particularly the case in colonies where there was a significant European presence. White settlers wanted the lion's share of any funding provided for education to be used primarily to support their own children and usually got what they wanted. In 1934, the Kenyan government spent 14 shillings per head on African pupils but over 24 shillings per head on financing the education of the children of Europeans; it was 1948 before even half of the educational budget was devoted to African schools. The settlers in

Algeria attempted to close down native schools altogether. In 1908, the Algerian *colon* congress called for primary education for the natives to be suppressed, however practically orientated the curriculum of the state's schools. Particular objection was made to the fact that the Muslim children were taught in French by teachers largely from metropolitan France: this, it was feared, would give the natives ideas above their station, rather than turn them into pliant agricultural workers.[29]

As a result even on the eve of the Second World War, the proportion of the school-age population receiving an education in Europe's non-white colonies, especially in Africa, was still very small. In Algeria, for all the efforts of French educational bureaucrats, a mere 6 per cent of school-age Muslim children were in school in 1931; by 1954 this had risen but only to 13 per cent.[30] In the Gold Coast, supposedly the most educationally developed of Britain's African colonies, at most 25,000 children were in school in 1920 out of a population of one million; 30 years later, functional literacy was still below 20 per cent.[31] Paradoxically, it was the Belgians in the Congo who appear to have been the most successful in schooling the natives: in 1950, a half of the school-age children in the colony were under instruction. The Belgians too built elementary schools where the emphasis was on teaching the natives useful and practical skills but their efforts did not meet with the same indifference. This was partly because, unlike the French and the British to a smaller extent, the Belgians concentrated totally on teaching pupils to read and write in their own language. They may have been happy to see their colonial subjects embrace Christianity but they were not intent on 'civilising' them. More importantly, Belgium had a purely pragmatic attitude towards empire; there was never any suggestion that a black elite might be formed that in time would share or take over the mantle of government. As there was no chance of natives using education as a vehicle of social mobility, they seem to have been much more ready to accept the limited fare on offer.[32]

The final section of this book is devoted to exploring the educational history of two very different colonial societies. It begins with a chapter by Sarah Duff on Britain's fourth dominion – South Africa – where the black population was always the great majority (Chapter 10). While much has been written about educational developments in the three white dominions, South Africa has been largely neglected. In many ways, though, it is the most interesting, given the important rivalries and tensions between the English and Dutch-speaking settler communities, the presence of an Indian as well as a white immigrant population, and the existence of a sizable mixed-race minority, not to mention the considerable ethnic and linguistic divisions within the black population itself. Duff's chapter concentrates principally on the schooling of the white population in Cape Province before South African union in 1910. The narrative she presents has nothing in common with the coming of mass education to Britain's other white dominions. While Australia, Canada and New Zealand had largely set up systems of public education by the final quarter of the nineteenth century, the Cape legislature seemed little inclined to follow suit. A compulsory system was established only in 1905, and even then the Cape was in advance of its neighbouring territories. It would be 1930 before all white children throughout the Union were compelled to go to school. In the Cape itself, the white farming community, largely Dutch-speaking, had apparently no interest in schooling, despite its Bible-centric Calvinist culture. Nor was there any fear in government circles that the colony might fall apart or succumb to Catholicism that might have goaded the legislators into earlier action. The move to introduce a system of public education when it finally came at the turn of the century was principally the work of the Dutch Calvinist church. On the one hand, there was a concern that the colony would not develop economically unless the white population was educated; on the other, there was a worry that blacks who had taken advantage of the opportunities offered by missionary educators would begin to take economic power from white hands. Deep down, too, reform was inspired by a very European concern about degeneration, which was given a specific South African twist: the white population would lose its legitimacy to rule unless it started to demonstrate its moral superiority.

Chapter 11 by Nita Kumar reviews the British effort to educate the inhabitants of its most populous and culturally complex native colony: the Indian Raj. She accepts that, as in other parts of the empire, the British had a commitment to schooling the mass of the sub-continent's population. As elsewhere, however, the colonial government lacked the resources and the will and was content to leave the task on the ground to the missionary societies. At the end of the day, the government saw its primary task to be the creation of an Indian elite who would help the British in their task of running the vast state. In consequence, the state helped fund directly or indirectly secondary and higher education but turned its back on the ordinary Indian. The missionary effort, moreover, seems to have been less successful than even in many African states, for their schools too seem to have catered for the children of the existing social elite. It would appear then that in the century before 1930, the majority of Indians, if they received any formal education, did so through the network of traditional religious schools that existed all over the country. Thereafter the British passed the torch to the Indians themselves. The Indian nationalists were themselves the product of Western education and were as convinced of its civilising potential as any European. Once Indians gained control of state legislatures in the decade before the Second World War, they moved quickly to establish systems of mass education on paper. Kumar is highly critical of their endeavours. It was not simply that they too lacked the resources to carry through the initiative. It was rather that the nationalists had made no effort to reflect on the value of Western education in the Indian context, a problem, she believes, that continues to bedevil Indian education today.

Glossary

common schools: see public schools below.

National Board of Commissioners (Ireland): produced detailed annual reports including data on schools, enrolments and attendance, books and materials, and the training and payment of teachers.

Phelps-Stokes reports: The Phelps-Stokes Fund is an American voluntary body and charitable fund which convened several commissions in the 1920s to report on the educational conditions and needs of black Africans, and made recommendations for improving access and quality.

public school: (United States and Canada): institutions supported by the government (primarily at the state and local level) and free to attending students.

Ryerson, Egerson: (1803–82) Canadian educationalist who advocated non-denominational schools, school libraries and teacher training. Had a major impact on Canadian schooling by sponsoring three pieces of major educational legislation.

Notes

1. Australia and Canada were initially a series of separate colonies with their own legislatures. Hence they eventually became federated states. Canada was formed in 1867 out of Ontario, Quebec, Nova Scotia and New Brunswik. Australia became a federation in 1901.
2. A. Barcan (1980) *A History of Australian Education* (Oxford: Oxford University Press), p. 8; P. Axelrod (1997) *The Promise of Schooling. Education in Canada, 1800–1914* (Toronto: University of Toronto Press), pp. 11–5; B. Curtis (1988) *Building the Educational State: Canada West 1836–71* (London: The Falmer Press), p. 22.
3. McCann, P. (1988) 'The Newfoundland School Society 1823–55: Missionary Enterprise or Cultural Imperialism?' in J. A. Mangan (ed.), *'Benefits Bestowed'? Education and British Imperialism* (Manchester: Manchester University Press), ch. 5.
4. The educational needs of the children of the indigenous populations were largely overlooked. In the second half of the nineteenth century, native Canadian children were taught in mission schools on the reservations; some, following a practice already adopted for some tribes in the United States, were boarded away from their parents in 'industrial schools' where they were taught manual and domestic skills: see Axelrod, *Promise of Schooling*, ch. 4.
5. See above, ch. 3.
6. Curtis, *Building the Educational State*, esp. ch. 3.
7. Axelrod, *Promise of Schooling*, pp. 32–6.
8. Ibid., pp. 85–95. Canada's population in 1841 was 1.6 million and in 1913, 7.2 million.
9. J. J. Small (1965) 'Religion and the Schools in New Zealand 1877–1963', *Comparative Education Review*, 9, pp. 53–62, at p. 55. For a general history of education in New Zealand during the period, see A. G. Butchers (1934) *The Education System. A Concise History of the New Zealand Education System* (Auckland: The National Printing Company).
10. Barcan, *History of Australian Education*, p. 40.
11. Ibid., pp. 88, 135–6.
12. Universal manhood suffrage came early to Australia. In New South Wales, Victoria and Southern Australia all adult males were given the vote in 1856–8.
13. Barcan, *History of Australian Education*, pp. 141–4. In 1864, in his encyclical, *The Syllabus of Errors*, Pope Pius IX had denounced mixed schools.
14. See Chapter 7.
15. Barcan, *History of Australian Education*, p. 234. An emphasis on fostering a common Australian identity within the school system reflected its dual structure: Catholic schools were largely Irish institutions and were unwilling to promote Britishness.
16. The private schools were gendered and confessional. What brought boys of different ethnic and religious backgrounds together was sport: see G. Sherrington and

M. Connellan, 'Socialisation, Imperialism and War: Ideology and Ethnicity in Australian Corporate Schools 1880–1918', in Mangan (ed.), *'Benefits Bestowed'*, ch. 7.

17. Axelrod, *Promise of Schooling*, p. 62; Barcan, *Australian Education*, p. 269, n. 9. For a detailed study of the development of the Canadian high school, see R. D. Gidney and W. P. J. Millar (1991) *Inventing Secondary Education: The Rise of the High School in Nineteenth-Century Ontario* (Montreal: McGill-Queen's University Press).

18. Barcan, *Australian Education*, pp. 205 and 210. For the Scottish 'Qualy', see above, p. 18, n. 11.

19. Barcan, *Australian Education*, pp. 121 and 185, 210 and 217. From 1874 a Queensland bursary provided three years free tuition and a bursary of £50 per annum.

20. Cited in E. M. Harik and D. G. Schilling (1984) *The Politics of Education in Colonial Algeria and Kenya*, Papers in International Studies, Africa series, no. 43 (Athens, Ohio: Centre for International Studies, Ohio University), p. 4.

21. Ibid., pp. 2–3.

22. The full text of the report is published in H. S. Scott (1938) 'The Development of the Education of the African in Relation to Western Culture', *Yearbook of Education* (London: Evans Bros), pp. 693–739.

23. P. Foster (1998) *Education and Social Change in Ghana* (London: Routledge & Kegan Paul), pp. 112–3. For the development of education in neighbouring colonies, see F. H. Hilliard (1957) *A Short History of Education in British West Africa* (London: Thomas Nelson & Sons).

24. S. H. Roberts (1929) *History of French Colonial Policy, 1870–1925*, 2 vols. (London: P. S. King & Son). The French state did not have the same desire to evangelise its subject peoples as its British counterparts. Christian missionaries were active in French sub-Saharan Africa and set up schools, but it was only after the First World War that vernacular mission schools began to be established in significant numbers in French Indo-China. For the debate about the content of the *mission civilisatrice*, see R. F. Betts (1961) *Assimilation and Association in French Colonial Theory 1880–1914* (New York: Columbia University Press).

25. Harik and Schilling, *Politics of Education*, esp. pp. 6–12.

26. The small number of North African Muslims who did go through the French educational system and ultimately spent time in metropolitan France frequently suffered crises of cultural identity when they returned home even in the post-independence period: see Y. Abdelkader (2000) 'Guérir la folie? Les enjeux de la thématique médicale dans le roman maghrebin des années soixante-dix', in J. L. Cabanès (ed.), *Littérature et medicine* II: *Eidôlon* (Cahiers du laboratoire pluridisciplinaire de Recherches sur l'Imaginaire appliqués à la Littérature, vol. 55: Université de Michel de Montaigne: Bordeaux, pp. 401–12.

27. Foster, *Education and Social Change*, pp. 60–1 and 141. The French did the same. Senegal had a notorious 'école des hôtages' from 1854 where the future leaders of rural society were compulsorily turned into French citizens (hence its nickname).

28. Foster, *Education and Social Change*, pp. 156–60; Harik and Schilling, *Politics of Education*, pp. 54–8 and 67–74.

29. Ibid., pp. 24–5. The French-born teachers in Algeria were usually young idealists: see F. Colonna (1975) *Instituteurs algériens 1883–1939* (Paris: Presses de la Fondation nationale des sciences politiques).

30. Harik and Schilling, *Politics of Education*, pp. 17 and 62.

31. Foster, *Education and Social Change*, p.36, fn. 46, and p. 121.

32. Ibid., pp. 152–3 and 172, n. 19.

10

'Education for Every Son and Daughter of South Africa': Race, Class, and the Compulsory Education Debate in the Cape Colony

S. E. Duff

In 1855, Robert Grey, the Church of England's Bishop of Cape Town, commented to the Cape Parliament's Select Committee on Education that he 'should not wish to see a compulsory system of education introduced into this colony' because it would benefit those 'who least require[d] it' and would, then, be 'a very needless expense to the Government'.[1] Grey's point was uncontroversial. Most witnesses called before the committee argued that even if they wished to see the introduction of compulsory education in the future, it was an excessive and financially ruinous response to the problems faced by the Cape's Department of Education. Even in 1872, when the Cape was gripped by concerns about a 'crisis' in colonial education, the Department of Education declined to investigate the potential for introducing free, compulsory elementary schooling, as suggested by a report submitted by the Dutch Reformed Church (DRC). Yet, by 1896, the Select Committee on Education argued that 'evidence... conclusively proves that in consequence of irregular attendance at school such a very large number of children are allowed to grow up in ignorance and vice'. As a result, 'we have come to the conclusion that a law to provide for compulsory school attendance has become not only desirable but necessary if Education is to be extended in an adequate manner in this Colony.'[2]

In the space of only 40 years, compulsory education shifted from being thought of as a disproportionate remedy to the colony's educational woes, to being held up as the best and only way to improve the provision of schooling throughout the colony. This chapter principally focuses on this shift in thinking about the value of compulsory elementary in the Cape Colony between 1870, when colonial commentators began to express concern about the apparently dire state of the Cape's education system, to 1896, when the Select Committee on Education formally recommended the introduction of compulsory elementary education for white children between the ages of 7 and 14. The chapter begins with a brief overview of the introduction of formal education in the Cape during the mid-nineteenth century, and then looks more closely at the education 'crisis' of the 1870s. It argues that interest in education – and specifically the education of white children – was linked to the colony's industrialisation and economic expansion as a result of the 'mineral revolution' (the discovery of diamonds in 1868 in Kimberley, and gold on the Witwatersrand in 1886) and the emergence of colonial nationalisms during the 1870s and 1880s. The second section of the essay looks at the significance of compulsory education to Afrikaner politicians in the 1890s, and it concludes with a brief overview of the introduction of compulsory education for white children between 1910 and 1930.

The focus of this chapter is on the Cape Colony. Before the declaration of Union in 1910, the term 'South Africa' referred to a region, rather than a single political entity, despite the strong social, economic, and, to some extent, political ties which bound together the two British colonies and two Boer Republics which constituted it. The Dutch East India Company established a settlement in the Cape in 1652 to provide fresh produce to ships en route to Dutch possessions in south-east Asia. The Cape became a British colony in 1814 mainly because of its strategic importance for British access to India. The colony of Natal was annexed by the British in 1843, and the two Boer Republics, the South African Republic and the Orange Free State, were founded in 1851 and 1854, respectively. Each colony and republic developed its own, separate system of education during the nineteenth century, and these were consolidated in 1910. The rise of political Afrikaner and African nationalism – the future African National Congress was founded in 1912 and the National Party in 1915 – occurred within a context of the introduction of a system of segregation in most areas of public life in South Africa.

The Cape was geographically the largest polity in the region. In 1875, it had a total population of 720,984, over half of whom were Africans resident in the eastern districts of the colony. The Cape's white population numbered 236,783 and were settled mainly in the colony's urban centres, the most important of which was its seat of government, Cape Town, and on rural farms scattered throughout the sparsely populated interior. About three-quarters of whites spoke a form of Dutch, usually dubbed 'Cape Dutch', and were descended from Dutch, French, and German settlers. These Dutch-Afrikaners[3] were predominantly rural farmers, although a wealthy, highly educated, and bilingual middle-class lived in Cape Town and the surrounding Boland towns of Paarl, Stellenbosch, Wellington, and Malmesbury. Most were members of the Dutch Reformed Church (DRC). English speakers comprised the bulk of the Cape's middle class. Most were settled in Cape Town, as well as Port Elizabeth in the colony's eastern districts. Roughly 100,000 'coloured' and Malay, or Muslim, people lived in the colony's western districts, in and around Cape Town. These were the descendents of slaves imported from South-East Asia (slavery was abolished in 1834), and relationships between white colonists and indigenous people. By 1891, partly as a result of the economic boom brought about by the discovery of diamonds and gold, the colony's population had swelled to 1,525,739 people. Aided by immigration from Britain, Eastern Europe, and St Helena Island, Cape Town's population almost doubled from 45,000 in 1875 to 79,000 in 1891. It increased to 170,000 between 1891 and 1904.

In 1875, slightly less than a quarter of the Cape's total population belonged to the DRC, more than to any other church in the colony. Eighty-five per cent of the DRC's members were white, representing at least 60 per cent of the Cape's total white population.[4] By 1891, around 64 per cent of whites and slightly more than 20 per cent of the total African and coloured population were members of the DRC. The church represented the vast majority of whites (the next biggest church was the Church of England, with slightly fewer than 20 per cent of the white population), and only the Methodist Church had more African and coloured members (23 per cent of the African and coloured population). In 1891, most of the colony's Sunday schools, baptisms, and marriages were conducted by the DRC.[5] Simply in terms of numbers, the DRC was by far the most influential church in the colony.

Before the 1850s, the Cape's value to the empire had lain entirely in its position on the sea route to India, but revenues from the export of wool and, after 1868, diamonds, transformed the Cape from a colonial backwater into a prosperous and significant settler colony located firmly within imperial networks of trade and administration. Industrialisation and economic growth fuelled the founding of towns throughout the colony's interior during the 1850s; the extension of hard roads and the railway across South Africa in the 1860s and 1870s; and the improvement of colonial infrastructure. The Cape gained its own Parliament in 1854, and was granted self-government in 1872. The second half of the nineteenth century witnessed the rise of a more 'modern' and industrialised state in the Cape. Concerns about colonial education must be understood within this context of rapid social, economic, and political change.

Cape education in crisis

In March 1873, Langham Dale, the Superintendent of Education in the Cape, asked the white, middle-class readers of the *Cape Monthly Magazine*

> if they realise the fact of the children of Dutch-speaking, European parentage growing up with less care bestowed upon them than upon the beasts of the field; – without the ability to read or write even their mother tongue; without any instruction in the knowledge of the God that made them; having at their command no language at all, but a limited vocabulary of semi-Dutch, semi-Hottentot words, and these only concerning the wants and doings of themselves and the animals which they tend?[6]

The purpose of Dale's article was to bring to light the apparently dire state of education available to white children in the Cape Colony's rural interior. Titled 'Our Agricultural Population', Dale appealed to the DRC, the Cape's established church, for assistance.[7] The organisation which exercised the greatest impact on Cape education after the Department of Education was the DRC. Indeed, as noted above, the DRC's influence on colonial society was unparalleled. Although other churches were also involved in the provision of education to colonial children, and the Church of England, Wesleyan Church, and Free Church of Scotland were instrumental in providing African children with schooling, no other church exercised the same influence over white and coloured children's education as the DRC.

The vast majority of rural whites belonged to the DRC, and it was the only major colonial institution with a strong presence and influence in the Cape's vast and sparsely population interior. The DRC was the sole organisation which could both mobilise Dutch-Afrikaners in these districts to send their children to school, and also build, run, and inspect schools in the interior. The DRC responded to Dale's appeal with alacrity. As an evangelical church, its ministers saw teaching and missionary work as fulfilling much the same purpose: the conversion of children, and also the shaping of a new generation of pious Christians. Since the middle of the century, when the DRC had transformed into an evangelical church partly as a result of a 'Great Revival' which swept its congregations in 1860, its involvement in the provision of education had increased. Considering that at least 85 per cent of its congregants were white and living mainly in rural areas,[8] it had focussed on founding schools on farms and in small villages for at least a decade before Dale's appeal.[9] However, from 1873 onwards, the church stepped up its involvement in education, and created what was, effectively, a parallel Department of Education of its own. This was headed by the DRC's own superintendent, staffed by a group of inspectors, and funded by the church's congregations. DRC inspectors visited government-funded schools and, unlike their colonial counterparts, were charged with collecting statistics and other valuable information about rural schooling.[10] The DRC also opened a *normal school in Cape Town in response to the dearth of teachers in the Cape, and founded a network of girls' schools to train Dutch-Afrikaner young women to be teacher-missionaries.[11]

In 1873, the DRC organised a special *synod on education, and issued a set of recommendations, chief of which was the introduction of a system of free and compulsory elementary education for white children.[12] Educationalists, clergymen, politicians, and other commentators in the Cape were certainly aware of the introduction of compulsory elementary education in England in 1870. The enactment of similar legislation in settler colonies such as Victoria (1872) and New Zealand (1877) was the cause of much discussion in the colony.[13] Nevertheless, Dale rejected the DRC's suggestion on the grounds that it would be too expensive and too complicated to implement. Yet his unwillingness even to countenance the idea that white children, at least, should be compelled to attend elementary school also stemmed from his – and others' – understanding of the nature of the education 'crisis' in the 1870s. Education in the Cape had been in 'crisis' long before the early 1870s. Rural white children, in particular, had had very limited access to schools since the founding of the Cape's Department of Education in 1839. So why the apparently sudden interest during this decade?

Ostensibly, the provision of education improved from the 1840s onwards. The Department of Education was headed by a superintendent, and the three men who were appointed to the position during the nineteenth century – James Rose-Innes (1839–1859), Langham Dale (1859–1892), and Thomas Muir (1892–1915) – were among the most powerful civil servants in the colony, in terms of the influence they wielded over the Cape government, and also the resources they commanded. Rose-Innes instituted a system of secular (or 'undenominational') public schools, all of which taught a curriculum approved of by the department, and were, theoretically, open to any child, regardless of race or gender. Elementary education was free or very cheap, while secondary schools charged higher fees.[14] The numbers of children attending school – and the numbers of schools themselves – did certainly increase from the middle of the nineteenth century onwards. By 1853 there were a dozen state schools in the Cape, mainly in towns and villages, and six years later there were more than 50.[15] But those who attended school regularly were still a fraction of the total number of children of school-going age in the Cape (between 7 and 14 years). There was also an enormous disparity between the numbers of children enrolled in schools and those who actually attended. In 1843, 5,318 black, coloured, and white children were enrolled in state-aided schools, and by 1860 this number had jumped to 18,757. In 1878, of a total of 60,000 white children of school-going age in the colony, only about a third – or 21,000 – were enrolled in state-funded schools, and fewer than 8000 were estimated to be attending private schools, which were not obliged to furnish the Education Department with information regarding their enrolment figures. In other words, in 1878, more than half of the colony's white children were not attending school.[16] The figures were even more alarming for black and coloured children, most of whom attended schools run by missionary societies: in 1875, there were approximately 171,581 black and coloured children under the age of 15 in the Cape, but only 31,322 – or fewer than 20 per cent – of these were in school.[17] In the same year, 5 per cent of black and coloured people reported that they could read and write, in comparison to 62 per cent of whites.[18]

Standards of education were also very low. Of those white children in school at the end of the 1870s, only 17 per cent were above Standard II level (that is, were reading and writing fluently, and receiving instruction in subjects other than the three R's). In 1883, the inspector-general, Donald Ross, suggested that 80 per cent of poor and rural children were in Standard I or below, meaning that they could barely read or write. The first significant enquiry into the state of Cape education, the Watermeyer Commission (1861–1863), noted

> the lamentable state of gross ignorance in which the white children in the back districts ... are growing up ... The standard of education reached in the elementary schools of the Cape Colony appears from the evidence to be very low. Though the attendance averages only 65% and is irregular, it is almost incredible that not more than 5% leave school with the capacity of reading with tolerable fluency, writing a plain hand, and working correctly examples in the simple rules of arithmetic.[19]

The Department of Education introduced a range of measures during the 1870s and 1880s to increase white children's access to schools in the colony's interior. From 1841, the department funded mission schools by paying the salary of the teacher as a supplement to the money raised by churches and mission societies.[20] Farm schools required only five pupils to receive state funding, and the department hoped that this would encourage farmers to found schools for their children, and those of their (white) labourers. Circuit – or itinerant – teachers were introduced in 1887 to travel rural districts, providing schooling at very distant schools. Poor schools provided a free education to impoverished white children and replaced circuit teachers in 1893.[21] Why, then, did so few white children from rural areas attend school? Firstly, it was difficult to open schools in rural areas. Rural farmers had to provide accommodation for the pupils attending their schools and also hire and house the teachers employed in these schools. School rooms had to conform to stringent standards set by the department,[22] and the farmer was responsible for the initial financial outlay and the voluminous administrative work required by the department. Even those farm schools which were successful frequently excluded the children of poor farmers or white labourers.[23] Moreover, most education was in English and although Dutch became an official medium of instruction from 1882, all textbooks remained in English.[24] The Cape's levels of literacy among adults remained low throughout the century. In 1860, only 60 per cent of whites could read and write, and this increased to only 62 percent by 1875.[25] The likelihood of barely literate parents sending their children to school was not high.

Most importantly, though, the model of schooling implemented by the Department of Education was antithetical to the rhythms of rural life, as reports from the 1890s made clear. Many rural farmers lived a semi-nomadic existence, and would 'trek away' from their farms during times of drought or pestilence.[26] One inspector explained: 'The nature of the country and the circumstances of the people are unfavourable to the spread of education among the farming population. The farmers are poor. They live in tents or "Matjes" houses (houses made of twigs and reeds), or in their wagons. Their circumstances compel them to lead a wandering life. Owing to the scarcity of native labour their own children herd their flocks.'[27] Even those parents who could afford to employ labourers believed that their children should contribute to the upkeep of the farm.[28] School attendance was sporadic, and linked to the seasonal nature of farm work.[29] Teachers complained that rural parents refused to defer to their authority. One inspector reported that 'more than one' school in his district had been closed during the year because of 'improper interference' from parents. Parents, he wrote, were quick to remove children for a variety reasons: one pupil was withdrawn 'because he was not allowed to have a light in his bed-room', while others were taken away from school because their parents objected to them being punished or not being promoted to the next standard.[30] The Cape's system of education was designed to suit a relatively affluent population which was settled for long periods of time, in or near urban centres. This was a model suited for middle-class living – to middle-class parents who were deferential to the authority of civil servants, and who saw the education of their children, and particularly their sons, as absolutely crucial for preparing them for middle-class occupations. This education system did not cater to the needs or lifestyle of a rural population, which was poor, widely scattered, frequently nomadic, and occasionally suspicious of the motives of the colonial government.

Travellers and journalists had described rural whites in the Cape in deeply unflattering terms since well before the last quarter of the nineteenth century. They depicted these Dutch Afrikaners as ignorant, lazy, dirty, and entirely indifferent to the apparent progress of the Cape's towns and villages.[31] Remarks, like Dale's, about rural whites during the 1870s were part of this broader discourse which positioned rural dwellers – white or not – as lacking in all the characteristics which constituted 'civilised', 'rational', and 'progressive' behaviour.[32] But during the 1870s, commentators began to focus increasingly on rural white youth: the concern was now for the impact of rural life on children. Not only did it deny them an adequate education, but, according to Dale, '*Jan* and *Piet*, as soon as they can toddle, slouch about the homestead, or lie about in the veld, in charge of a few goats or head of cattle... they drift on to puberty.' It was 'a long dull, monotonous youth'.[33] These were childhoods which lacked guidance from parents and other adults and as a result did not prepare children adequately for adulthood. The education which the majority of white rural children had once received at home, and from their parents, was no longer deemed adequate, as a specialist in agriculture wrote for the *Cape Monthly*:

> But who can tell whether in a similar manner [to the Industrial Revolution in Europe] the discovery of diamond and gold-mines may not produce capital, directly and indirectly, which, by the additional influx of consumers may spur on enterprise, cause large and extended irrigation works to be erected to supply the additional mouths, and gradually turn many a barren desert into a land flowing with milk and honey? But without education, – without those higher qualities which the morality of the New Testament tends to foster, the most fruitful countries... may become a howling wilderness instead of life to other lands.[34]

The granting of responsible government in 1872, and the expansion of the Cape's economy during the early 1870s, positioned South Africa as a significant territory within the British imperial network. For the members of the colony's English- and Dutch-speaking middle class, these developments were signs of the strength of the Cape's political structures and also its economic promise: a colonial nationalist discourse which had been in the making since the 1830s and 1840s 'reached maturity in the 1870s'. Colonial nationalism promoted the interests and prosperity of the Cape over that of the empire. Colonial nationalists 'were people who, by birth or adoption, came to identify not only with the metropole but also with the country in which they lived.'[35] As the century progressed, colonial nationalism became increasingly racially exclusive, partly because of a growing interest in discourses around scientific racism: the future prosperity of the Cape – and South Africa – needed to be in white hands.

As a result, white children needed to be educated in order for the colony's future prosperity and social and political stability to be ensured. The large number of white children out of school meant that white control over the Cape was in jeopardy. Furthermore, white commentators were also deeply anxious about an increase in numbers of impoverished *bywoners* (tenant farmers) and rural petit-bourgeoisie as a result of the Cape's industrialisation. While a wealthier and larger middle class had benefited from the Cape's new-found prosperity, short economic downturns during the 1870s and 1880s had had a disproportionate effect on rural farmers, most of whom were Dutch-Afrikaans.[36] The existence of impoverished, uneducated white children performing the manual labour increasingly associated with black and coloured employment undermined notions of whiteness and mastery. White children were to be raised as masters and employers of labourers, and not as unskilled workers.

F. W. Reitz, an expert on colonial agriculture recommended: 'What we want is to get the lads away for two or three years from the unobservant, listless existence of a back-country farm, and to train them where all their faculties will be awakened and kept awake.'[37] According to Dale, boys needed to be removed from their homes altogether:

[A]n agency…is necessary to bring the boys away from the farm and train them in the order and discipline of a well-regulated home; where by mutual contact, and by the daily intercourse with superior minds, they may develop those qualities which are not wanting to their race, – truthfulness, self-reliance, emulation. A boarding-school is required in every district…where farmers' sons could be maintained and fairly educated at a rate not exceeding £20 each per annum.[38]

Dale went on to point out that should Dutch-Afrikaner youth remain on their parents' farms, a generation would be left with 'their minds a blank, their powers of observation undeveloped, their life a mere animal existence, listless, objectless, and without any aspiration after or thought of a life to come.'[39] Education became, then, a means not only of producing a new generation of politicians, farmers, businessmen, and other professionals who would exploit the Cape's own 'industrial revolution' and would lead it as an increasingly politically and socially independent entity within the empire, but also as a way of moulding and forming white young men into the kinds of leaders, educationalists and colonial commentators who would be beneficial to the Cape. Removed from the apparently disorganised households of their rural, white, and impoverished parents, they could be transformed into respectable, progressive, conscientious, and middle-class male citizens of the future. A 'progressive' and 'scientific' movement emerged during the late 1870s and 1880s around the better management of sheep and cattle stocks, water reservoirs, soil erosion, and plant and animal disease. Dutch-Afrikaner farmers were often described as being deeply resistant to many of these 'modern' and 'improving' measures, and were, thus, figured as 'backward' and 'anti-modern'.[40] Educators argued that by removing white boys from rural areas and educating them in the Cape's urban centres, they could be 'civilised': they could become part of the colony's progressive movement. Within this context, rural domesticity became a site where boundaries between civilised and unciv-ilised – between coloniser and colonised – were dangerously fluid. Boarding schools, on the other hand, were able to maintain these distinctions.

What the Education Department – and, indeed, the DRC – required parents to do was to rethink the ways in which they organised labour, and also about the relationship between their families and their livelihood. Urban, middle-class families in the Cape – in common with middle-class families in the rest of the industrialising world – had succeeded, largely, in separating the functions of work and home, meaning that the labour of wives and children was no longer required to support the household. On rural farms, or in impoverished rural areas, poor families – of all races – relied on the contributions of both parents and children. The successful extension of education into the colony's interior was, thus, reliant as much on training teachers and building schools as it was on altering the ways in which parents thought about their children's childhood: it was now to be a period of education away from the home, instead of training within its bounds.

It was partly for this reason that, although suggested, compulsory education was not held up as the best means of ensuring that white children would attend school. Dale and others were concerned primarily with the education and train-ing of white adolescent boys, and not necessarily with the schooling of white girls and younger children. Having appealed to the DRC for assistance in improving the provision of schools in the Cape's rural districts, the Department of Education believed that it had done all that was possible to make schooling more easily available to rural white children. Secondly, Dale and other politicians balked at the thought of allowing the state to intervene in the relationship between parents and children. Through the church's long tradition of *huisbesoek* (home visiting), DRC ministers were accustomed to monitoring the ways in which their congre-gants raised and educated their children. The DRC did not distinguish between private and public spheres, but – at least during the 1870s – the colonial govern-ment did. The reason this changed was because of a shift in the political land-scape, and the 'discovery' of a social 'problem'.

Children and 'poor whiteism'

During the 1890s, the Cape's political class 'discovered poor whiteism'. There had been a substantial population of impoverished whites long before the 1890s, but attitudes towards white poverty shifted at the end of the century for a number of reasons: decades of poor education meant that a generation of impoverished whites was unemployable. Those who moved to Cape Town and other urban centres in search of work found that employers favoured better-trained coloured and black labourers, whose wages were lower, or newly arrived immigrants from Europe.[41] Secondly, both in South Africa and in the rest of the world, poverty was racialised during the 1880s and 1890s. The existence of unemployed and unemployable poor whites challenged the association of 'natural' supremacy and the exercise of power with whiteness. The term 'poor white' no longer simply referred to white people who lived in poverty, but, rather, invoked a set of fears around racial mixing and white superiority.[42] Finally, and connected to this, the emergence of an early Afrikaner nationalism and the entry of middle-class Dutch-Afrikaners into Cape politics contributed to the shaping of a new, distinct 'Afrikaner' ethnic identity towards the end of the century. The majority of poor whites were Dutch – or, rather, Afrikaans – speaking, and had been viewed with a certain amount of disdain by middle-class Dutch-Afrikaners in the 1860s and 1870s. By the end of the century, the middle-class expressed a sense of responsibility for this poor underclass on the grounds that they were all 'Afrikaners'. Addressing the Afrikaner Bond (AB), the first political party representing the interests of Afrikaners in politics, in 1893, Rev. A. J. L. Hofmeyr suggested that 'we must take these poor people by the hand' to 'save Africa for the Afrikanders [sic]'.[43]

The concerted colonial response to 'poor whiteism' of the 1890s came from three sides. The Department of Education, now under the energetic leadership of Thomas Muir, was overhauled and made more efficient: Muir appointed 13 inspectors – one for each of the colony's magistracies – in place of the original two inspectors general, and streamlined the organisation of the department. Inspectors were now responsible for collecting statistics, assisting their districts to establish schools, and identifying the reasons for low school attendance. Mimicking the DRC, the department began to compile detailed reports about the condition of poor white children in each magistracy. The primary goal of the Department of Education during the 1890s was on educating poor white children, and this was reflected by the department's efforts to segregate children at school.[44] In 1894, the department began to publish attendance statistics 'arranged according to the colour of the pupils', and reserved all state-funded secondary schools for white children.[45]

But the department acknowledged that it was still heavily reliant on DRC ministers' involvement in running rural schools and encouraging parents to send their children to school.[46] The DRC was the second colonial organisation which became involved in 'solving' the poor white problem in the 1890s. After John X. Merriman, the colony's Minister for Agriculture, appealed directly to Andrew Murray jnr., the influential moderator of the DRC, the church convened a special conference on 'poor whiteism' in 1893, and resolved to institute industrial schools in the Cape's major urban centres.[47] The Cape government had made grants available for industrial schools for white children earlier that year, and the DRC agreed to become responsible for establishing and running the schools.[48] Industrial schools in the Cape had a complicated history, but it worth noting that South African industrial schools were not reformatories – although reformatories in the Cape did certainly provide similar training – but provided purely vocational schooling. The first industrial schools originated in 1855 and were designed to provide high-quality vocational training to African children. There were 48 of these schools by 1870, and they assisted in the creation of an African artisan class. Within the first five years of their existence these schools trained 151 skilled workers, including 59 agriculturalists, and 47 women for 'household work'. Although run by churches and missionary societies, the schools were funded directly by the Colonial Office: between 1855 and 1861, the Colonial Office granted them £46,000. In 1856, they received £10,000 – about the same as that given towards white education by the colonial government.[49]

Industrial schools for white children were a feature of the 1890s and beyond. Those established before 1910 were run exclusively by churches. The Salesian Institute and the network of orphanages established by the Catholic Church were all aimed at alleviating the poverty of destitute white children, and provided some technical training alongside elementary schooling.[50] All the remaining industrial schools were run by the DRC, and the first of these were founded in Cape Town (1894) and Uitenhage, near Port Elizabeth, and Stellenbosch in 1895 (the latter was an agricultural school). Its schools for girls followed later in the decade.[51] These schools did not survive long, despite the fact that they were run along the lines of the very successful pre-existing model for African children. Why this failure? The instruction was described as 'amateurish'; they proved to be difficult to fund; and the railway and mining industries were also beginning to establish their own schools, such as the South African School of Mines in Kimberley in 1895.[52] These schools, wrote one educationalist, were 'instituted ... as means for solving the poor white problem. They were conceived in charity and with the idea of redemption.'[53] The DRC saw the industrial schools as *'liefdadig werk'* (charitable work), and not – as the Department of Education intended – as a means of supplying colonial industry and business with trained white workers. It is telling that the industrial school for girls established in Wellington was transformed into an orphanage for impoverished white girls by the end of the nineteenth century.[54] The Cape's small number of industrial schools produced only a very small group of white carpenters, blacksmiths, agricultural workers, printers, tailors, and other craftsmen during the 1890s.

There was, then, a certain amount of similarity between the responses to the education 'crisis' of the 1870s and the poor white 'problem' of the 1890s: neither 'crisis' nor 'problem' were new to these decades, and the first response of the colonial government in both cases was to call on the DRC for assistance. As during the 1870s, all parties concerned about poor whiteism agreed that the best way to eradicate the 'problem' was to focus on children. Haldane Murray, an inspector in the Department of Education and the son of Andrew Murray jnr., summed up the colonial response when he wrote: 'The hope lies with the children; a thorough elementary education will enlarge their mental horizon and help to create that divine discontent so absolutely necessary for the progress for any individual or class, while industrial training ... will enable them to find new openings for their present dormant energies.'[55] Through compulsory education and the introduction of industrial schools, impoverished white children could be transformed into hardworking and productive adults.

The difference between the responses during these two decades was the involvement of the AB. The same forces which invigorated colonial nationalism – responsible government, and the economic boom caused by the early years of the mineral revolution – were also behind the emergence of the first manifestations of an Afrikaner nationalism in the Cape. Unlike colonial nationalism, which was a predominantly urban phenomenon, the first Afrikaner nationalists were drawn from the educated, middle-class Dutch-Afrikaners of the districts around Cape Town, whose participation in colonial politics had been, before the 1870s, very limited. Responsible government now made political representation possible, and competition over the control of increasing state revenues made political involvement ever more desirable. Throughout the 1870s and 1880s they coalesced into a collection of organisations representing the interests of farmers, which merged in 1881 to form the Afrikaner Bond under the leadership of the prominent politician J.H. Hofmeyr.[56]

Having entered politics almost as soon as it was formed in 1881, the Bond formed a coalition with arch-imperialist Cecil John Rhodes between 1890 and 1895. It was this odd pairing that led to poor whiteism becoming a key political issue during this period. Although the Bond's definition of an 'Afrikaner' was inclusive to the extent that it referred to whites whose political and social loyalties were to South Africa, it represented the interests of a group of people who were increasingly aware of themselves as 'Afrikaners' who spoke Dutch, or Afrikaans, and who were white. Its interest in 'poor whiteism' – as a hindrance to the future of Afrikaners, and as a threat to white supremacy in the colony more generally – led to the introduction of the Destitute Children Relief Bill in 1894.

The Destitute Children Relief Act of 1895 was formulated explicitly 'to benefit the poor whites'.[57] The Act required clergymen and justices of the peace to report cases of destitute white children to magistrates, who were authorised to take custody of these children and then place them in public schools. This legislation was not unprecedented.[58] The Act complemented existing laws regulating the apprenticeship of poor and orphaned white children, and reflected the Department of Education's concerted attempts to eradicate 'poor whiteism' through the better provision of elementary education in rural areas. There were, though, significant differences between the responses of the 1870s and the 1890s. The Act was passed within a broader context of growing state involvement in private life. For example, the creation of a Department of Public Health in 1891 allowed the state to prosecute parents who did not vaccinate their children during epidemics.[59] In 1895, The Deserted Wives and Children Protection Act forced husbands who deserted their wives to maintain their families financially.[60] The colonial government was willing during the 1890s to limit the powers of parents over their children, and to take on responsibility for destitute and neglected children. In 1894, when Sir Thomas Scanlen, Member of Parliament for Cradock and former Prime Minister of the Cape, was asked by the Committee on the Destitute Children Relief Bill if he thought it 'a very hard case for a poor European if his child were forcibly taken away from him to a school for three years', he responded for many when he said:

> There you have to consider and come to a determination between what you call a hardship to the parent and the interests of society. I take it it is not in the interests of society that any children should grow up uneducated, and

probably swell the criminal classes. ... When a parent neglects that duty I think the State is quite justified in stepping in, and that the inconvenience, or supposed inconvenience, to the parent ought not to stand in the way of the interests of the State and the interests of the child.[61]

Although Scanlen was not a member of the Bond, he was a supporter of Rhodes and the coalition, and shared the AB's belief that the existence of poor, white, uneducated, and unemployed children posed an existential threat to the maintenance of white power in the Cape. A distinction can be drawn here with the views of the DRC. Ministers of the DRC saw it as their duty to educate and improve the lives of impoverished whites and thought of the schools they established for poor white children as *'liefdadig werk'* (charitable work).[62] There is little evidence to suggest that the church was concerned by the maintenance of white power.[63] In contrast, one supporter of the Bond urged other members to 'Reflect for a moment [on] the danger to the State to have such an army of what might be termed "White Barbarians"'.[64] Bond politicians and activists were now willing to empower the state to remove children from their parents. The Act also defined what should constitute a white childhood. In doing so, the Act linked the upbringings of white children more closely to the interests of the state. According to the Act, white children should expect to have financially solvent parents who would educate their children until, at least, their fifteenth birthday, and would raise them to be productive, hardworking citizens. Like the DRC, the colonial state came to realise that the 'proper' upbringing and education of white children was absolutely vital to the future prosperity of the state, and used school attendance and the law as ways of enforcing the kind of white childhood which it believed would produce good colonial citizens. This was, clearly, a middle-class childhood: white, middle-class parents could afford to provide their children with the prolonged childhoods spent mainly at school and in other 'improving' activities. As in the 1870s, the colonial government 'normalised' middle-class family life and held it up as the only – the 'natural' – way in which to raise children.

Politicians argued that rural children who worked on their parents' farms and were raised without schooling experienced 'unnatural' childhoods. They risked becoming perpetually 'idle' adults. J.M. Coetzee argues that since the seventeenth century, colonial commentators had been obsessed by the idea of 'idleness'. Allegations of 'Hottentot' idleness were used partly as justification for European conquest: idleness, cited usually along with a set of characteristics which included not washing, living in impermanent structures, and being nomadic, were provided as examples of indigenous 'uncivilisation'. Later concerns about white idleness were seen as a betrayal of the civilising mission – as a retreat from 'European' values.[65] Witnesses called before the commission of inquiry into the Destitute Children Relief Bill were anxious to ensure that poor white children in the colony's rural areas were not allowed to continue being idle. Haldane Murray said that the 'idle' poor whites in his district married too early, and married their cousins. Rev. Christoffel Muller of the DRC who had previously worked among the poor white woodcutters in Knysna suggested that some were so 'lazy, indigent and slovenly' they 'even refuse[d] to wash themselves'.[66] Fears around rural idleness were connected to the discourse around the 'backwardness' of the colony's rural white farmers. Their unwillingness to implement new 'scientific' farming methods was frequently characterised as a kind of idleness. Poor white adults lacked the skills and the will to work, and were in grave danger of becoming racially 'degenerate'. They operated wilfully on the fringes of colonial society and economy, and needed to be brought within the Cape's developing capitalist system. Poor white adults, believed inspectors, could not be saved – or pulled back from this retreat – but children certainly could. One Cape industrialist spoke for many when he argued 'that the adults are irreclaimable. You must let them die off, and teach the young ones to work.'[67] Indeed, poor white adults were characterised largely as 'careless' and incompetent parents: Thomas te Water, a Bond MP, agreed that poor white children needed to be 'rescued' from their parents.[68] All the inspectors recommended that compulsory elementary education be introduced, and that rural white children attend industrial schools to train them to be skilled artisans and productive farmers. They had to be removed from their parents to learn 'working habits' and to become integrated into white, middle-class colonial society.

White childhood was, thus, to be productive. White children were not to be destitute, neglected, abused, or idle. The Act empowered the state to remove white children found 'habitually begging', 'wandering and not having any home or settled place of abode', or without 'possible means of subsistence' from their parents or guardians. Children would only be returned to their parents if they could prove that they were able to educate and support their children.[69] The Act enforced this particular understanding of white childhood by allowing the state to intervene in what was formerly considered to be the wholly 'sanctified' space of the white home. When parents were unable to fulfil their 'parental duty of maintenance', the law was allowed to step in.[70] Also, the Destitute Children Relief Act effectively instituted compulsory education for white children whose parents were either neglectful or very poor. In 1896, an Education Commission recommended that compulsory elementary education be implemented for white children, but before then, regional meetings of the Bond had alluded repeatedly to the need to educate poor white children, and even to introduce compulsory education.[71] At one such meeting a member of the AB announced that 'We must have education for every son and daughter of South Africa.'[72] By this he meant that the Cape should institute compulsory education for every white boy and girl in the colony, but this argument showed up the extent to which education had become linked to the political aims of the Bond, and, more broadly, to the future prosperity of the Cape.

Mass education for white children?

In 1905, the Cape's Education Act introduced compulsory education for white children between the ages of 7 and 14. Coloured and black parents were encouraged to send their children to school, but the Education Act did not compel them to do so.[73] Natal and the two former Boer Republics enacted similar legislation, and along with a greater availability of bursaries and boarding schools for poor children, caused an increase in the numbers of white children attending school after the South African War. Nevertheless, when the Union was declared in 1910, only slightly more than half of all white children between the ages of 7 and 15 years were enrolled in school.[74] The 1895 Destitute Children Relief Act made the legislation passed by the Cape in 1905, possible. But the concerns which informed this Act – a profound fear of the social, political, and economic implications of white poverty – did not disappear after 1910. If anything, they were amplified. Education in South Africa after Union was, as in the Cape during the final decades of the nineteenth century, organised around the needs of white children, and specifically those who were poor. This shaped education policy during the 1920s and 1930s. The declaration of Union, as well as the emergence of a stronger Afrikaner nationalist movement, connected the education of white children more closely to the future fortunes of South Africa.

Even after 1910, each of the four provinces – the two former British colonies and Boer Republics – which constituted South Africa retained autonomy over education policy. The national Department of Education was responsible for the provision of higher education, which will be discussed in greater detail below, and, after the passing of the 1913 Children's Protection Act, for the education of destitute and neglected children.[75] Between 1910 and 1930, the numbers of white children enrolled in school almost doubled, from 179,000 to 384,000. By 1930, 88 per cent of all white children between the ages of 7 and 15 were enrolled in full-time education. This success over a relatively short period of time was due to two main factors. Firstly, government spending on education grew from 14 per cent of the national budget in 1910, to almost 28 per cent in 1930.[76] Secondly, South Africa witnessed massive urbanisation during the first half of the twentieth century. Industrialisation, drought, and two devastating depressions at the beginning and end of the 1920s had a disproportionate impact on the country's agricultural population. Former farmers and agricultural workers of all races streamed to the country's cities. Urbanisation of impoverished whites was particularly noticeable: in 1926, half of all whites lived in cities, and within a decade this rose to more than 65 per cent.[77] As a result of this, more white children than ever before were living near schools.

As in the Cape at the end of the nineteenth century, industrialisation and economic expansion in the 1920s and 1930s increased the numbers of impoverished whites. In 1929, the South African government devoted 13 per cent of its budget to the eradication of white poverty. By the end of the 1920s, it was estimated that out of a total of 1,800,000 whites, 300,000 were 'very poor', and nearly all of these were Afrikaans. The *Carnegie Commission of Investigation on the Poor White Question (1929–1932) concluded that an inability to adapt to a changing economic climate, outdated farming methods, and poor education were to blame for the existence of such a large proportion of impoverished whites. It recommended that access to schooling be improved for these white children.[78] African poverty was as acute and even more widespread, but the existence of this group of poor whites was seen to hamper South Africa's economic and political growth, and to undermine the country's growing international stature. South African politicians saw the South African state as representing the interests of its white population, and, as a result, it was the education of its white population which concerned its government.[79]

From 1910 onwards, in their attempts to improve the quality of white education and to boost the numbers of white children at school both the national and provincial departments of education focussed on two aspects of education policy: language and vocational training. The Carnegie Commission (as late as 1932) and others blamed predominantly English-medium education for the low proportion of impoverished Afrikaners who attended school. Since the 1909 South Africa Act, Dutch and English had been placed on an equal footing. By 1920, Dutch had been replaced by Afrikaans, and all four provinces had enacted legislation which allowed for mother tongue education. The introduction of Afrikaans-medium schooling was, though, a very slow process, and particularly so for schools in rural areas.[80] Vocational education was rolled out more quickly. From the early 1920s, domestic and agricultural science, and woodwork were added to the elementary school curriculum. The state also took over responsibility for industrial education, though this was always small beer despite its rapid expansion. In the Cape, there were almost 400 pupils in these institutions by 1910, and nationally, this number swelled to 3,479 pupils in 43 industrial schools by 1930. As the Department of Education noted, this was hardly an adequate response to 'poor whiteism'.[81]

Yet the extension of higher education meant that vocational training for older adolescents was increasingly available. In 1916, the University Act established a new national university, the University of South Africa, and gave two university colleges, in Cape Town and Stellenbosch, full university status. The Universities of the Witwatersrand and Pretoria followed in 1921 and 1930, respectively. This legislation, greater financial aid, and the increasing numbers of white pupils finishing secondary school meant that after 1920 the numbers of whites attending university soared. In 1920, around 3,000 white students were enrolled at university. Twenty years later, this number jumped to over 13,000.[82] The 1923 Higher Education Act legislated for the introduction of vocational high schools offering technical, commercial, and domestic training. These proved to be particularly successful. They were well funded by the Union government, and also permitted students to enrol on a part-time basis. This meant that by 1926, they had 2,484 full-time and 13,184 part-time students.[83]

These developments in state-organised schooling, though, only benefited white and, in the Cape, coloured children. For African children, education remained in the hands of mission societies and churches, although these mission schools did receive some state aid. In the Cape, all elementary education, regardless of race, was made free in 1920. Each of the provinces supported the principle of mother tongue education for African children, and contributed to industrial and agricultural training for African children. All curricula emphasised vocational over academic education. Those schools which were run efficiently provided a small number of African children with a good quality elementary and secondary education. The children of the tiny African middle-class received schooling which was of an equal quality with the best education on offer to their white counterparts at well-established mission schools like Lovedale, Blythswood, and Healdtown. The 1923 Higher Education Act also made provision for a university specifically for African students, the University of Fort Hare. But the overwhelming majority of African children received little or no education. By the mid-1930s, at least 70 per cent of African children were not in school, and that schooling which was available was badly funded, chaotic, and overcrowded. This was largely because of fears that educated Africans would pose a threat to the employment prospects of whites.[84]

As at the end of the nineteenth century, education was 'raced' in early twentieth-century South Africa. White children were educated to become skilled workers and employers of labour, while African children were prepared for lives as manual and unskilled labourers. Nevertheless, even though the majority of white children were in full-time education by 1930, providing white children with good quality education, with a particular focus on vocational training which was believed to be particularly crucial to South Africa's economic development, was by no means a smooth and uncomplicated process. Importantly, it was now widely accepted that elementary education for whites should be compulsory, that this education should be provided by the state, and that the state had a right and a duty to ensure that all white children were enrolled in school.

Conclusion

The purpose of this chapter has been to seek the origins of the discourse around compulsory education in South Africa and, particularly, the Cape Colony. The idea of compulsory education for white children was first mooted during the 1870s, at a moment when colonial nationalism 'reached maturity', the Cape's economy began to expand as a result of the mineral revolution, and responsible government was granted. White children – and particularly white boys – needed to be educated to become the next generation of colonial politicians, businessmen, and professionals. In addition to this, commentators worried that the Cape's rural interior – and its white rural population – was being left behind by the colony's economic and political progress. Removing white boys from their homes to be educated in urban boarding schools seemed to be one way of gradually bringing rural whites into the Cape's white, middle class mainstream. However, the Department of Education balked at the idea of making education compulsory for white children: it was an excessive remedy to the problem, Superintendent Dale argued, and the state had no right to intervene in the 'sanctified' space of the home.

Yet by the 1890s, with the emergence of a strong Afrikaner nationalist movement in Cape politics and in the midst of growing concerns about 'poor whiteism', nationalist politicians began to agitate for the introduction of compulsory education for all white children as the best means of ensuring the maintenance of political and economic power in white hands. The Destitute Children Relief Act not only linked the upbringing and education of white children to the well-being of the state by defining what should constitute a white childhood, but it instituted a form of compulsory education for those children whose parents, it was believed, were most guilty of ignoring their instruction. It was aimed at the poorest white families. While the DRC had long been willing to intervene in relationships between parents and children in the name of spreading the Gospel, the AB and the Cape government enacted legislation in the 1890s which made the colonial state ultimately responsible for the care and education of poor and neglected white children.

Between 1910 and 1930, compulsory elementary education was introduced for South Africa's white children. Because these children were seen as being significant to the maintenance of white power over South Africa's politics and economy, their education was privileged above that of their black and coloured counterparts. Indeed, South African citizenship was conceived in racial terms, meaning that white children – whose citizenship was never in doubt – received a better funded and organised education than their black and coloured counterparts. It was only in 1996, exactly a century after a commission of enquiry into education first recommended that compulsory education be implemented in the Cape, that education became compulsory for all South African children between the ages of 7 and 15, regardless of race. The South African Schools Act effectively introduced mass education. As in the nineteenth century, education was highly politicised in twentieth-century South Africa. After 1948, the Apartheid state instituted discrete departments of education for each race group, and systematically and deliberately underfunded the education of coloured and, especially, black children, who were intended – as in the nineteenth century – only to be prepared to become manual or semi-skilled labourers. The idea of mass education in South Africa was, then, 'raced' throughout most of the nineteenth and twentieth centuries. Mass education, as it was experienced in the West during the nineteenth and twentieth centuries, was only implemented in South Africa in the 1990s.

Timeline

1839: Cape Colony's Department of Education founded

1861–63: Watermeyer Commission. First significant enquiry into the state of education in the Cape Colony

1873: The Dutch Reformed Church in the Cape Colony calls for the introduction of free and compulsory education for white children

1895: The Destitute Children Relief Act. Allowed magistrates in the Cape Colony to take children away from their parents and place them in school

1896: Cape Colony's Select Committee on Education calls for compulsory schooling

1905: Cape Colony instituted compulsory education for white children from 7 to 15

1916: Establishment of the University of South Africa

1923: Higher Education Act: introduced vocational high schools in the Union of South Africa and made provision for a university for African students, Fort Hare

1996: compulsory education for all children in South Africa from seven to 15, regardless of race

Glossary

Carnegie Commission: in 1932 the Carnegie Corporation produced a report on the 'poor white' problem in South Africa. It made recommendations about segregation that some have seen as a blueprint for Apartheid.

normal school: teacher training college or similar institution.

synod: clerical congress with authority over church matters.

Notes

1. Annexures to the Votes and Proceedings of the House of Assembly. *Report of a Select Committee on Public Education, 1855* (Cape Town: Saul Solomon & Co.), p. 7, Cape Archives (hereafter CA), CCP1/2/1/2, A3.
2. *Report of the Select Committee of the Legislative Council. Education, 1896* (Cape Town: W. A. Richards & Sons, 1896), p. iv, CA, CCP2/2/2/2/31 C1.
3. I take the term 'Dutch-Afrikaner' from M. du Toit (1996) 'Women, Welfare and the Nurturing of Afrikaner Nationalism: A Social History of the Afrikaanse Christelike Vroue Vereniging, c. 1870–1939' (D.Phil. thesis, University of Cape Town) to refer to the Cape's 'Dutch' population as it negotiated an identity that was no longer exclusively European, yet distinct from the English-speaking and indigenous inhabitants of the colony during the latter half of the nineteenth century.
4. Annexures to the Votes and Proceedings of the House of Assembly. *Census of 1875* (Cape Town: Saul Solomon & Co.), pp. 17, 140, CA, CCP1/2/1/30, G42.
5. Annexures to the Votes and Proceedings of the House of Assembly. *Census of 1891* (Cape Town: W. A. Richards & Sons, 1891), pp. xli, xliii, CA, CCP1/2/1/81, G6.
6. L. Dale (1873) 'Our Agricultural Population (1),' *Cape Monthly Magazine* (hereafter *CMM*), Mar., 130.
7. J. W. de Gruchy (1979) *The Church Struggle in South Africa*, 2nd edn (London: Collins), pp. 2–3.
8. *Census of 1875* (Cape Town: Saul Solomon & Co.), pp. 17, 140.
9. M. Du Toit Potgieter (1961) 'Die NGK en die Onderwys van Blankes in Kaapland sedert die Eerste Sinode (1824)' (D.Ed. thesis, University of Stellenbosch), pp. 67–70; (1860) 'De Toestand der Kerk: I. Het Onderwijs', *De Kerkbode*, 16 June, 179.
10. E. G. Malherbe (1925) *Education in South Africa*, vol. I (Cape Town: Juta), pp. 109–10, 117; Potgieter 'Die NGK en die Onderwys van Blankes,' pp. 74–102.
11. Potgieter, 'Die DRC en die Onderwys van Blankes', p. 154; *Report of the Select Committee of the Legislative Council. Education, 1896* (Cape Town: W. A. Richards & Sons), pp. 23–4, CCP2/2/2/2/31 C1.
12. A. Hofmeyr (3 May 1873) 'Scholen voor de Buitendistrikten,' *De Kerkbode*, 131–9.
13. R. Griffiths (1987) 'A Tale of 804,573 Horses: Arithmetic Teaching in Victoria 1860–1914,' *Educational Studies in Mathematics*, XVIII, 191–2; J.J. Small (1965) 'Religion and Schools in New Zealand 1877–1963,' *Comparative Education Review*, IX, 53.

14. A. L. Behr and R. G. Macmillan (1971) *Education in South Africa*, 2nd edn (Pretoria: J.L. van Schaik), p. 112; *Report of the Select Committee of the House of Assembly. Education Bill, 1883* (Cape Town: W. A. Richards & Sons), p. 20, CA, CCP1/2/2/1/31, A21.
15. Behr and Macmillan, *Education in South Africa*, pp. 112–3.
16. E. G. Malherbe (1932) *Report of the Carnegie Commission of Investigation on the Poor White Question in South Africa*, 3 vols (Stellenbosch: Pro Ecclesia-Drukkery), vol. III, p. 34.
17. *Census, 1875*, pp. 22–3; Malherbe, *Education in South Africa*, vol. I, p. 99.
18. *Census, 1875*, p. 55.
19. Malherbe, *Report of the Carnegie Commission*, vol. III, pp. 34–8.
20. The sum granted to mission schools varied between £15 and £75 per annum depending on the needs of the school. Unfortunately, no statistics regarding government funding of mission schools were kept.
21. Malherbe, *Report of the Carnegie Commission*, vol. III, p. 26.
22. *Select Committee on Education, 1896*, pp. 32–3.
23. *Select Committee on Education, 1896*, pp. 11, 21.
24. Malherbe, *Report of the Carnegie Commission*, vol. III, pp. 28–33; H. Giliomee (2003) *The Afrikaners: Biography of a People* (Cape Town: Tafeberg), pp. 211–2; D. R. (1873), 'Our Pastoral Population,' *CMM*, July, 53.
25. *Census, 1875*, p. 55.
26. *Select Committee on Education, 1896*, p. 36.
27. Annexures to the Votes and Proceedings of the House of Assembly. *Report of the Superintendent-General of Education, 1893* (W. A. Richards & Sons: Cape Town), p. xxxii, CA, CCP1/2/1/88, G7.
28. F. W. Reitz (1870) 'The Rural Population,' *CMM*, Sept., 130; D.R., 'Our Pastoral Population,' p. 50; F. H. E. (1875) 'The Difficulties of a Country Schoolmaster,' *CMM*, Aug., 82; (1870) 'Correspondence: Genadendal and Mission Stations', *CMM*, Nov., 313; *Select Committee on Education, 1896*, pp. 34, 48.
29. *Report of the Superintendent-General of Education, 1893*, pp. 7–8, 11, vi, xxxii, xli–xlii.
30. Ibid., p. 25.
31. S. Dubow (2006) *A Commonwealth of Knowledge: Science, Sensibility and White South Africa 1820–2000* (Oxford: Oxford University Press), pp. 113–4.
32. Cape of Good Hope (1894) *Debates in the House of Assembly in the First Session of the Ninth Parliament of the Cape of Good Hope, 1894* (Cape Town), pp. 346–7.
33. 'Our Agricultural Population (I),' p. 130. Emphasis in the original.
34. F. W. Reitz (1871) 'South African Agriculture,' *CMM*, Oct., 241.
35. Dubow, *A Commonwealth of Knowledge*, p. 5.
36. Bundy, C. (1986) 'Vagabond Hollanders and Runaway Englishmen: White Poverty in the Cape Before Poor Whiteism,' in W. Beinart, P. Delius, and S. Trapido (eds) *Putting a Plough to the Ground: Accumulation and Dispossession in Rural South Africa 1880–1930* (Johannesburg: Ravan Press), p. 120.
37. Reitz, 'The Rural Population,' p. 159.
38. L. Dale (1873) 'Our Agricultural Population (II),' *CMM*, Apr., 202–3.
39. Id. (1873) 'Our Agricultural Population (III),' *CMM*, May, 274.
40. W. Beinart (2003) *The Rise of Conservation in South Africa: Settlers, Livestock, and the Environment 1770–1950* (Oxford: Oxford University Press), pp. 21–22; Nell, D. (2000) '"For the Public Benefit": Livestock Statistics and Expertise in the Late Nineteenth-Century Cape Colony, 1850–1900,' in S. Dubow (ed.) *Science and Society in Southern Africa* (Manchester: Manchester University Press), pp. 100–12.
41. Giliomee, *The Afrikaners*, p. 319.
42. (1893) 'Arme Blanken,' *De Zuid Afrikaan* (hereafter *ZA*), 14 Feb., 4.
43. (1893) 'Poor Whites,' *Cape Argus*, 27 Feb., 6.
44. Malherbe, *Education in South Africa*, vol. 1, p. 98; *Report of the Superintendent-General of Education, 1893*, pp. 4–5.

45. *Report of the Select Committee of the Legislative Council. Destitute Children Relief Bill* (Cape Town: W. A. Richards & Sons), pp. 2, 6, 9, CA, CCP2/2/2/29, C1.
46. *Report of the Superintendent-General of Education, 1893*, p. 7.
47. P. Lewsen (ed.) (1963) *Selections from the Correspondence of John X. Merriman, 1890–1898* vol. II (Cape Town: Van Riebeeck Society, 1963), pp. 115–6.
48. A. Murray jnr (1893) 'Arme Blanken,' *De Kerkbode*, 16 June, 187–8; (1894) 'Inrichting voor Arme Blanken,' *De Kerkbode*, 10 Aug., 697; P. F. Greyling (1939) *Die Nederduitse Gereformeerde Kerk en Armesorg* (Cape Town: Nasionale Pers), pp. 127–31; *Select Committee on Education, 1896*, p. 77; Malherbe, *Report of the Carnegie Commission*, vol. III, pp. 50, 55, 60; (1894) 'Arme Blanken: De Inrichtingen te Kaapstag en te Uitenhage,' *De Kerkbode*, 6 Jul., 657; (1894) 'De Synode,' *De Kerkbode*, 9 Nov., 805.
49. Malherbe, *Report of the Carnegie Commission*, vol. III, pp. 52–3.
50. *Destitute Children Relief Bill*, pp. 75–81.
51. Malherbe, *Report of the Carnegie Commission*, vol. III, p. 50.
52. Greyling, *Armesorg*, pp. 130–1; Malherbe, *Report of the Carnegie Commission*, vol. III, pp. 55, 60.
53. Malherbe, *Report of the Carnegie Commission*, vol. III, p. 55.
54. 'De Synode,' *De Kerkbode*, p. 805.
55. *Report of the Superintendent-General of Education, 1893*, p. xlv.
56. H. Giliomee (1987) 'The Beginnings of Afrikaner Nationalism, 1870–1915,' *South African Historical Journal*, XIX, 129–30; J. C. Kannemeyer (1984) *Geskiedenis van die Afrikaanse Literatuur*, vol. I, 2nd edn (Pretoria and Cape Town: Academica), pp. 42–3; Hofmeyr, I. (1987) 'Building a Nation from Words: Afrikaans Language, Literature and Ethnic Identity, 1902–1924,' in S. Marks and S. Trapido (eds) *The Politics of Race, Class and Nationalism in Twentieth-Century South Africa* (London: Longman), pp. 96–8.
57. Cape of Good Hope (1895) *Debates in the House of Assembly in the First Session of the Tenth Parliament of the Cape of Good Hope, 1895* (Cape Town), p. 384.
58. L. Chisholm (1986) 'The Pedagogy of Porter: The Origins of the Reformatory in the Cape Colony, 1882–1910,' *The Journal of African History*, XXVII, 483–5; Bundy, 'Vagabond Hollanders and Runaway Englishmen,' p. 121; Vivian Bickford-Smith (1995) *Ethnic Pride and Racial Prejudice in Victorian Cape Town* (Johannesburg: Wits University Press), p. 142.
59. (1893) 'Compulsory Vaccination,' *Cape Argus*, 20 Feb., 5; Van Heyningen, E. (2004) '"Regularly Licensed and Properly Educated Practitioners": Professionalisation, 1860–1910,' in H. Deacon, H. Philips, and E. van Heyningen (eds) *A Social History of the Cape Doctor in the Nineteenth Century* (Amsterdam and New York: Rodopi), pp. 206–11; C. Ilbert (1899) 'South Africa, 1897' *Journal of the Society of Comparative Legislation*, I, 125.
60. C. Ilbert (1896–1897) 'South Africa, 1895,' *Journal of the Society of Comparative Legislation*, I, 90; *Debates in the House of Assembly, 1895*, pp. 189–91.
61. *Destitute Children Relief Bill*, p. 11.
62. 'De Synode,' p. 805.
63. (1892) 'Ons Verarmde Blanke,' *Di Afrikaanse Patriot*, 22 Dec., 5.
64. 'Poor Whites,' p. 6.
65. J. M. Coetzee (1988) 'Idleness in South Africa,' in *White Writing: On the Culture of Letters in South Africa* (New Haven: Yale University Press), pp. 22, 28–9.
66. Annexures to the Votes and Proceedings of the House of Assembly. *Report of the Labour Commission* (Cape Town: W.A. Richards & Sons, 1894), p. 125, CA, CCP1/2/1/8, A1.
67. *Labour Commission*, p. 101.
68. *Destitute Children Relief Bill*, p. 40.
69. Ilbert, 'South Africa, 1895,' 91–2.
70. *Destitute Children Relief Bill*, p. 70.
71. 'Poor Whites'; (1893) 'Bond Congress,' *Cape Argus*, 5 Mar., 5; (1893) 'Schooldwang,' *ZA*, 4 Mar., 4.

72. 'Poor Whites', 6.
73. V. Sampson, E. Manson, and W. R. Bisschop (1906) 'South Africa, 1904,' *Journal of the Society of Comparative Legislation*, VII, 160–2.
74. Malherbe, *Report of the Carnegie Commission*, vol. III, p. 43; E.G. Malherbe (1977) *Education in South Africa*, vol. II (Cape Town: Juta), pp. 155–6.
75. Behr and Macmillan, *Education in South Africa*, pp. 8–10.
76. Malherbe, *Report of the Carnegie Commission*, vol. III, p. 43.
77. Brits, J. P. (1993) 'Political Developments and the Depression of 1929–1934,' in B.J. Liebenberg and S.B. Spies (eds.) *South Africa in the Twentieth Century* (Pretoria: J.L. van Schaik), p. 244.
78. Brits, 'Political Developments,' p. 244.
79. Giliomee, *The Afrikaners*, pp. 344–7.
80. Malherbe, *Education in South Africa*, vol. II, pp. 6–17.
81. Malherbe, *Report of the Carnegie Commission*, vol. III, pp. 50–1.
82. Malherbe, *Education in South Africa*, vol. II, p. 307.
83. Behr and Macmillan, *Education in South Africa*, pp. 203–8; Malherbe, *Education in South Africa*, vol. II, pp. 178–81.
84. Behr and Macmillan, *Education in South Africa*, pp. 388–94.

11
India's Trials with Citizenship, Modernisation and Nationhood

Nita Kumar

A succession of governors-general of the East India Company, from Warren Hastings to Lord Dalhousie, expanded and consolidated the company's territories in India between 1772 and 1857. The officials put new revenue and legal structures in place, based, as they surmised, on some continuing legacies of Mughal and provincial rule. They intervened in the technological processes of the subcontinent, introducing new transport, communication, irrigation, and banking measures. Then, beginning in the 1830s, escalating into the 1850s, they intervened in the educational structures in a formal and deliberate way.

The educational policy of the East India Company was expressed in the Dispatch of 1854, called 'the Magna Charta [sic] of the Education Department:'[1] '...the main object of the educational system...is to diffuse widely among the people European knowledge...' This European knowledge would teach the natives

> the marvellous results of the employment of labour and capital, rouse them to emulate us in the development of the vast resources of the country...; and at the same time, secure to us a large and more certain supply of many articles necessary for our manufactures and extensively consumed by all classes of our population, as well as an almost inexhaustible demand for the products of British labour.[2]

Most radically, the East India Company set up in 1857 three universities in their so-called three presidency towns of Calcutta, Bombay, and Madras, on the model of the University of London. That is, they affiliated and examined the new colleges. The models for the new colleges were the Hindu College, Calcutta (founded [hereafter f.] 1816), and the Elphinstone College, Bombay (f. 1827), both set up in temporary locations by committees of local gentlemen, then moved to their permanent sites and aided and co-administered by the government. By the 1850s, there were 11 English colleges and 40 high schools in British India being run by the government. Additionally there were 92 English-language missionary schools. These, with their 9,000 and 13,000 students respectively, comprised the new 'system.' The system consisted of a new education, characterised by a new *technology,* of buildings, spaces, furniture, textbooks, languages, teaching methods, routines and rituals; by a new *philosophy*, of the relationships between student, teacher, text, and the world; and by a new *politics*, of control by a central power, not only over purpose but over definitions of truth and meaning.

This history is characterised by Syed Nurullah and J.P. Naik, the most succinct commentators on Indian education, as 'a great drama,' where,

> The *setting*...is provided, not only by the social, political, and constitutional history of India, but also by the social, political, and educational developments in contemporary England...The *conflict* of the drama lies in the struggle between the Old and the New, between the effort – however well-intentioned it might have been – by non-Indians to impose a cheap imitation of the British educational system on India and the desire of the people of the country to create a new system to meet their own peculiar needs and problems.[3]

This characterisation of Indian education by terms such as 'impose,' 'imitation,' 'foreign,' and 'conflict,' is reflected in the figures of speech, sometimes the very titles, used by other authors of Indian education; for instance: 'Reversing the gaze;' 'Alternative sciences;' 'Masks of conquest;' 'Dominance without hegemony;' and 'the colonial construction of knowledge.'[4]

This sense of conflict apart, a narrative of Indian education may be shadowed by another sense of doom. We know that today, in 2010, mass education has still not been successfully implemented in India and as many as 40 per cent of Indian people are outside its reach. There is a curious parallel between the sense of failure today and that of the contemporary educators and observers in the period 1870–1930:

> ... it is probable that no government has *ever before* had an educational problem of *such* magnitude and difficulty. The problem of the education of the Filipinos or of the Japanese or even of the Africans, is *not to be compared* with the task of providing India with an education which will develop her people and help them contribute to her national uplift. Only China furnishes a parallel, and *even China* is not hampered so greatly as India by *racial, social, and religious cleavages*.[5]

My submission is that the narrative of Indian education, and the sense of failure that characterises it at every stage is produced by parallel, related, but also unrelated developments that may best be called 'multiple narratives'.

The narrative of missionary education

We proceed then with our narratives. By 'education' we mean here 'colonial education' as introduced formally into India in the nineteenth century by the East India Company, then the British Crown. 'Education' here does not mean indigenous education, education in pre-colonial systems or formats, education of the arts or sciences in the *guru–shishya parampara* (the master–student relationship), vocational training or apprenticeship.

In this usage, we would say that the pioneers in 'mass education' were Christian missionaries and printers, as far back as in the Malabar in the sixteenth century, in Tamil Nadu in the seventeenth century and in Trichnopoly and Tanjore in the eighteenth century. The Serampore trio – William Carey (1761–1834), Joshua Marshman (1768–1837) and William Ward (1769–1823) – were a spectacular example of pioneering work in education in Bengal. Marshman's *Hints Relative to Native Schools* (Serampore, 1816) was followed by fund-raising efforts that enabled them to set up 103 schools in 1816–17. Serampore College, the peak of their educational effort, was founded in 1818. Observations on the culture of the people, often closer than what government would produce in succeeding years, led to an emphasis on teaching in the vernaculars.

But even more, missionary education deserves high marks for its emphasis on the quality of the teaching of English. Individual missionaries put emphasis on *explanation* and could get disturbed by the failure of a foreign tongue and distant ideas to reach the mind of the student, leaving him to simply regurgitate words and passages. It was the missionaries' intention, whatever the individual differences between the Baptist, the Methodist, the Church and the London Missionary Societies – and they could be great – to build up a church in India. For this, they reasoned, they needed to reach the minds of students. The tension between the desirability and the difficulty of doing this, as well as the attendant tension between the distaste for indigenous culture, and the recognition of the dignity of human beings, is well demonstrated in the career of the Scottish missionary Alexander Duff (1806–1878), who arguably created the model for English education in India. The irrelevance of the educator's ideological position becomes clear when we examine how Duff was unabashedly one of the most vitriolic of all missionaries in his attitude towards Hinduism, and on principle opposed to Sanskrit or Hindi. He argued, in his *Recollections*, that it was the very act of learning English that taught new terms, new ideas, and new truths. By learning English, according to Duff, a student learnt to be Christian rather than Hindu.[6]

The Duff thesis was correct to an extent, and missionary education succeeded in producing classes of natives who were proud of their rationalism. The Madras Christian College, (f. 1837), Wilson College, Bombay (f. 1829, renamed in 1843), St John's College, Agra (f. 1853), and the Christian College, Lucknow (f. 1877) were a few of the many examples of the quality of missionary education. While missionaries believed that quality English-learning testified to the superiority of Christianity and that, once learnt, the leaven of Christian ideas would work to fatally rupture the Hindu mould of thought, Indians felt that the value of English could be appropriated without the discourses of Christianity impinging on their everyday life. Indeed, groups of natives followed the example of Christian missionaries in setting up English-language schools. In Calcutta, the School Book Society and the School Society were founded in 1817 and 1819, with grants from the government, which was the first, early acknowledgement by the government of the need for the education of the people.[7]

But the trajectory of missionary schools in India, after their initial leadership, was a troubled one. They were not given, as they saw it, sufficient patronage, or even autonomy to function, by the state. The several Christian associations in England and Scotland which had missions and educational institutions in India, formed one body called the 'General Council on Education in India' that made, in 1881, a set of comparisons between India and Britain. They made the following points:

(1) While in England one twentieth of the revenue was devoted to the education of the people, or 2s. 6d. a head, in India it was only one eightieth, or less than 1d. a head.
(2) In India only nine pupils per 1,000 of the population were in school, whereas in England about 160 in the thousand were.
(3) The department for elementary instruction in India did not keep pace with the natural increase of the population, so that there were millions more of uneducated children than when the Dispatch of 1854 was first promulgated. While the natural increase of the population was 200,000 children of school-age, the increase in the number of children going to school was not even 50,000.[8]

Nothing happened after the 1880s to change this lack of balance between India and Britain. The state and the missionaries both vied for the position of saviour to the Indian people and were not happy with each other. Government schools did not flourish for a variety of reasons that we discuss later. Missionary schools could not flourish because government was partial to its own schools and only nurtured those. Most of all missionary schools could not flourish *as they origi-nally intended* because it was very tedious a process to convert significant numbers through education. Although missionary educators had almost infinite patience, it was clear that by the nineteenth century they had resigned themselves to socialise and influence a relatively small number of upper caste, upper class men, instead of the vast population of India, as had been the original hope. Missionary education's narrative, then, is one of elite and not mass education, although its beginnings had been in the reverse direction.

The education of elite Indians in missionary schools, however, had a direct bearing on the state of the education of the masses. The missionary schools of the elite were at one extreme in the spectrum of schools, with their resources of buildings, teachers, and facilities, at the other extreme of which lay the under-staffed, underprovided village and municipal schools. In the elite missionary schools, the quality of the teaching of the curriculum, with its English and European history, science, philosophy, and literature, and of course the English language, was so superior to the teaching of the same subjects in the schools for the masses that a different breed of Indian person was produced in each school. Secondly, apart from the direct curriculum, and as attested by many school songs, the thrust of the new education was to produce 'gentlemen' who could be counted upon to be always true to the Victorian ideals of manliness, uprightness, sportsmanship, and honour. The hidden curriculum was to produce a distance between elite Indians and the masses of their countrymen, who were ignorant heathens, and definitely not potential gentlemen with the virtues of manliness and truthfulness.

The new educated Indians gradually developed a consciousness of having to explain and defend themselves vis-à-vis the West, of being placed between two worlds, of belonging, in different degrees, to both, and also fully to neither. Their view of the past and future of their societies was shaped by this hyper-consciousness of the West as omnipresent, as something normative and authoritarian, 'watching them'. This colonial consciousness was exacerbated by the use of English professionally and for pleasure. The colonial consciousness, the use of English, the conflicts of identity, and the new art forms and politics this generated, were not shared by the uneducated or those educated in schools different from missionary schools. We may thus be justified in saying about missionary education that, insofar as it was the education of elites in India, and judging from the role in history played by elites, it was the most important narrative in the history of modern Indian education.

The narrative of state education

There was an early impasse between the government and the missionaries, with the latter forbidden until 1823 to enter the East India Company's (EIC) dominions (thus Serampore College, in the EIC's domains, had to ask the king of Denmark for authorisation to give degrees). Close on the heels of the missionary initiative in schooling was that by the East India Company itself, replaced in 1858 by the British Crown. The Dispatch of the Court of Directors dated 19 July 1854 created an officer with the title of Director of Public Instruction, appointed to each of the presidencies[9] and lieutenant-governorships, to whom the superintendence of the work of education was entrusted; and under these officers, a staff of inspectors and sub-inspectors was organised, who were in effect to act in their several spheres as the local representatives of the director. This directive was in line with the efforts being made to construct a system of public instruction back home in England. The principles laid down in the Dispatch of 1854 were considered applicable up to the 1880s, when a commission was appointed on 3 February 1882 to invite suggestions for carrying out still further the policy of that Dispatch.

The comparison made by the missionaries the year before the commission was set up between educational expenditure by the state in England and that in India, cited above, was dismissed by the government as being 'thoroughly European, and not at all Indian'.[10] It was using a European standard to view critically the fact that of the total expenditure of the Indian government in 1877–78 of over £58 million, while over £15 million was spent on the army and £7 million on the collection of revenue, only £730,000 was spent on the entire education of about 200 million people. Similarly, that there were 46 colleges with a total of less than

5,000 pupils in all the colleges of India was a statistic that should not be weighed in comparison with Europe.[11] Yet, if the system of education in India was not to be compared to England's in the sense of expecting a certain amount of government expenditure, government planning, and success in recruiting students, what *was* to be its model? If asked this question, the government would have had to admit this to be its domestic system. The contradiction would then have stared it in the face.

The state's educational policy of spreading Westernisation, claimed government officials in their evidence to this enquiry, could be thwarted in two ways. One was the helplessness of sheer distance from England, the location of the colony in tropical conditions, and the deleterious effects of this on everything, such as school buildings:

> [The architectural styles of educational buildings] were all, like the empire builders themselves, slightly mutated *en voyage* ... The architectural styles got cruder, looser, wider and very often larger. They were making the sea change from a highly advanced Western country, whose art stood in the direct line of descent from Greece, Rome, the Gothic master-masons and the Renaissance, to a country whose educated architecture sprang from different roots altogether, and whose vernacular styles were evolved to meet the demands of extreme poverty and simplicity of material ... Throughout the long building period of British India, the constructions were, so to speak, roughened by their setting. It was inevitable.[12]

The other major undermining of the new policy occurred because of inadequate funding (even when comparisons with England were ignored). The resources available for education were meagre, and it was consensually agreed that almost no school could be properly housed or staffed. The problem lay partly in a structure of distribution, with less going to the provincial than to the presidency towns. But it lay largely in the size of the total outlay. The distance between the amounts needed, say Rs 337 lakhs, and the amount available, Rs 42 lakhs, was incommensurable.[13] The 'filtration theory' favoured in different parts of the subcontinent at different times, but influential everywhere for a large part of the time, advocated concentration on higher education. A major cause of its advocacy was the realisation that the funds government was willing to part with were quite inadequate for mass education.[14]

Apart from directly setting up schools, funds were needed for giving grants-in-aid to the schools set up by concerned individuals and bodies, in line with the top-heavy philosophy of downward filtration. Local taxes were used for this purpose, and they could not be raised above a point. There were differences between the three presidencies and then the North-Western Provinces and Punjab,[15] but two things were in common. Very few of the vernacular schools came to be aided, and these were not the provincial ones. Second, the criteria for receiving grants-in-aid were made progressively more stringent, which was then followed by observations about the inadequacies of the schools. People simply failed to run them according to the new norms, and their failure was then characterised by the state as 'the want of enlightenment in Native communities'.[16]

The recommendation of Thomas Munro in Madras, Thomas Thomason in the Northwestern provinces, and William Adam in Bengal, as well as of Wood's dispatch in 1854 and the Indian Education Commission of 1882, that existing indigenous elementary schools, strengthened and improved by guidance and financial aid, be adopted as the foundation of a national system of education, came to nothing. The policy that was popular was that of 'downward filtration' and the claim most commonly made was of paucity of financial resources. This kept the new education an elite monopoly. The government directed its interest at its universities, even when the Indian Education Commission of 1882 emphasised elementary education and the Government Resolution on Educational Policy of 1904 pointed out that the rate of growth of elementary schools was *not* keeping pace with that of secondary schools. Even while funding gradually increased from both central and state government and numbers rose steadily, the percentage of literacy remained only 5.2 in 1921–22, not appreciably better than the 4.4 per cent calculated on the basis of Adam's figures for 1821–22.

Who attended the schools financed by the government? As with the missionary schools, it was largely the upper classes, and more than with missionary schools, this could be seen as the deliberate policy of the state. The new education catered to those who could be counted upon to be good colonial subjects, who would act as interpreters and middlemen between the state and the masses, who would fulfil all the tasks of imperialism that could not be performed directly by the British. Even the policy of encouraging private enterprise in education led to a result where the urban upper and middle classes had to choose between their own facilities for English learning – the main means of income and respectability open to them – and support for mass education. They certainly demonstrated that they had the will and the resources for educating *their* children. They failed to take leadership of the masses to the extent the government imagined they should. The rural masses had themselves neither the leadership, nor the will, nor the resources. The government, arguably, needed to take the initiative instead of leaving it to private enterprise, and once it had dismissed indigenous education as worthless, to establish an efficient system of mass primary education, as countries like France and England were beginning to do.

Bengal, as the earliest and most intimate contact point of the British, first experienced the emergence of the new educated *comprador class, interested in the new education and seeking it for its children. Drawn from various regions, social strata and histories, its formation was in the new schools, its professions were all directly related to the colonial government, and its lifestyles were definable as 'sahib-like' or anglicised. The 'bhadralok' was the name given to this class in Bengal: a useful term because it combined within it some of the complexities of the situation of the 'middle class,' the 'educated classes,' 'regional elites,' and so on. *Bhadra* means cultured or civil, *lok* means people.

Bhadralok families were sincere about desiring an English and modern education for their children. They could make sacrifices, such as separation, with the son studying in the city supported by his mother while the father and grand-parents continued to be based in the village; or channelling sizeable resources to education rather than other types of consumption. They were mostly high and middle caste families, already in professions that had a continuity with the emerging 'new professions,' such as the legal, medical, administrative, journal-istic and teaching professions. These were also the same professions chosen by the graduates of missionary schools. The difference between the missionary and state schools was that they both did the same thing – educate the new elite of the country – but the missionary schools did it better.

In both cases, we should be clear, there was an upper and a lower end type of school. But the model of this new schooling – a certain school building, printed textbooks, centralised curricula, fixed schedules and examinations – was one that could work better the higher up in society the school was placed. The poorer, rural schools were 'poor' not only with reference to the student body they catered to, but in their facilities and quality of the education they provided.

There were two other major limitations in a possible state plan to educate the masses in India. One was that state schools failed to suggest an alternative to the literary and book-oriented instruction that was established as the norm, by intro-ducing any kind of vocational training. The schemes for this, from Sir Richard Temple's recommendations to the *Famine Commission in 1881, to Abbott and Wood's *Report on Vocational Education in India* in 1937, remained on paper and could not overcome the dominant prejudice that vocational education stood far lower than liberal education. But this 'prejudice' arose only after the modern lib-eral system of non-utilitarian, book-based learning had become entrenched well enough to seem normative to those successful in it or those anticipating success. For peasants and workers, and for pre-colonial professionals as well, the old indig-enous education had been understood as basically 'vocational,' in that it trained differentially according to the career prospect of the student. People made per-iodic demands, such as during the Education Commission Enquiry of 1882, for more 'relevant' subjects such as *mahajani accounts and Indian mathematics that relied on oral tables of fractions. We may speculate that had 'vocational train-ing' been developed as an integral part of the school curriculum, there would have been a positive response to it and not a prejudice, as government claimed it foresaw.

We may further argue that the liberal, book-based education provided by the state was itself a vocational education, in that it prepared students for strictly a certain number of jobs, and rendered them totally incapable of any other work, in skills, but also culturally and psychologically. To spend years in mastering English meant that the student would only ever aim for a career in which English was the requirement. Such jobs were numbered. The circularity of a type of curriculum and school, the production of a type of student, and the natural limitation of the kind of work that such students could then seek to do, was complete – making mass education problematic in principle.

The other limitation of the new education was its lack of appeal to certain com-munities: occupational communities such as artisans, merchants, and farmers, and religious 'communities' such as Muslims. After 1857 the British attitude changed to a more pragmatic and cynical approach: from seeing Indians as backward but amenable to reason and enlightenment, the subcontinent was seen as populated not by persons at all but by communities who had their religious interests in the forefront. They had to be manipulated, not enlightened. The interests of the state demanded that their religious, 'primordial' identities be, if not transformed, rendered private and non-threatening, and one of the means of control was colonial education. Muslims, in fact, were not one 'community' and had a variety of responses to the prospects of colonial schooling. Some turned their backs on it fully and set up Islamic *madrasas*, claiming that the colonial model lacked ethics. Others adopted some part of the model and set up schools that attempted a synthesis between the Western and the domestic traditions. Still other reformers, as we shall see in the narrative of nationalist education, wanted to reform and uplift their brethren by reinterpreting native religion and tradition as amenable to science and rationality, as did Syed Ahmad Khan. Nevertheless, the 'backwardness' of Muslims remained a fact all through our period and was due to the inability of the state to develop a strategy to woo them over to liberal education.

The narrative of indigenous education

What about the indigenous schools, then? These were ambiguous institutions, of which there were reported in the nineteenth century to be thousands in every province, ranging across some 26 different types of schools, that already served as a national education in India, and whose gradual disappearance few seemed to notice, and even fewer mourn. There were different opinions on indigenous schools, some of which were neutral and accepting.

The Director of Public Instruction in the North-Western Provinces, M. Kempson, in his *Reports of the Local Education Committees for 1871*, described indigenous teaching positively. 'Poor as these schools are, they are the national schools of the country and there can be no doubt that without any undue pressure they are capable of being improved and expanded into most prosperous and useful schools.'[17] This opinion had prevailed as far back as 1850: 'it can hardly be doubted, but that it is this class of schools, ill-remunerated, uncertain of their duration, and narrow in their space as they at present are, to which we must look for the basis of any improved system of education for the people.'[18]

The methods of instruction of indigenous schools were called 'rude and primitive' with colonial forthrightness. But Bell and Lancaster were also evoked, who imitated the indigenous *monitorial system in their schools, considering it an improvement on other prevailing systems. The method of reading aloud as the student wrote was similarly praised. Every *Pestalozzian, it was claimed, 'must admit that the system which makes the learner use his fingers and his eyes, at the same time that he employs his vocal muscles and his sense of hearing is more scientific, because capable of making stronger and more diverse nervous impressions, than that of quietly looking at letters in a printed book in order to learn their shapes.'[19]

There were scores of kinds of schools in the indigenous system, with three main kinds of schools: *tols*, for higher education in Sanskrit; *pathshalas* that taught the vernaculars, and *maktabs*, teaching a combination of vernaculars, Urdu, and the Qur'an Sharif. The subjects of instruction in the *pathshalas* were writing, reading, arithmetic and accounts, *zamindari* papers, letter writing, versified *Puranic tales and versified 'heroic legends.'[20] In *maktabs* the students learnt by rote parts of the Qur'an Sharif, and parts of the Persian classics: the Alif Laila (*Thousand Nights*), the Chahar Darvesh (*Tale of the Four Dervishes*), the Gulistan (*The Rose Garden* – a book of Persian Prose from 1259) and Bostan (a book of Persian poetry by Saadi from 1257). In both kinds of schools children entered at about 5 years of age and stayed for about five years.

There was a shift in the understanding of indigenous schools from the 1870s to the turn of the century. The ideas of expansion and improvement were replaced by a different notion of interference, one which understood it as the only 'means by which alone the masses of this country can be raised from their present state of mental degradation.'[21]

> Any patient observer of the indigenous schools will, as a simple matter of fact, be struck by seeing in their 'customary ways' the relics of much deep thought and of many nice adaptations to circumstances...But that which in present circumstances tells most against such patient observation of the indigenous schools is the stark inferiority of their teachers, and also the wretchedness of their poverty, and of all their belongings.[22]

But in the different narratives we have been considering so far, if the missionary school fails because of a lack of state support and its own inner contradictions, and the state school fails because of a lack of funds and political will, it is the indigenous school whose narrative seems to be a total tragedy. It simply becomes reformed out of existence until at the turn of the century, there *are* no more indigenous schools to inspect. It could have survived had there been social capital associated with its patronage. Economic capital, even when forthcoming, was not enough. Any school that continued as a *tol*, *pathshala*, or *maktab*, and did not teach English or adopt the new disciplining, was marginalised and shunned, and gradually did adapt. We know from the Surveys of Education that the number of indigenous schools dropped markedly after the 1870s and that they had almost become extinct by 1900.[23]

But over the whole century, while formal indigenous education declined, it continued informally for the intelligentsia at home. All those who grew up to be active in state bureaucracies; who were at different levels of the professions of law, medicine and teaching; who wrote, spoke, and led from different platforms, had a vernacular education in early childhood. To mention only a few cases at random among India's native intellectual elite: Bankim Chandra (b. 1838) learnt Sanskrit as a child; Kali Prosunno Singh (b. 1841) had Bengali and Sanskrit lessons in his childhood; U. Ve. Caminataiyar (b. 1855) began learning Tamil at seven or eight; Pandit Ajudhianath (b. 1840) studied Arabic and Persian; Surendranath

Banerjea (b. 1848) learnt Bengali in his childhood; Kashinath Trimbak Telang (b. 1850) learnt Marathi very well; Shankaran Nair (b. 1857) learnt Sanskrit as a child; and Motilal Nehru (b. 1861) read only Arabic and Persian till 12. Apart from language(s), some proceeded to a more advanced level of literature, grammar or philosophy in Sanskrit, Arabic or Persian. Initially, knowledge of Sanskrit and especially Persian continued to remain important because of their use in law. But over the nineteenth century, they came to be seen as no long directly related to jobs with the monopoly gradually established by English. Sanskrit, Persian and the mother tongue became non-utilitarian choices: not good for careers, and progressively as of little or no use in the development of the mind.

It can be shown, I think, that the continuity of vernacular and classical education was an amateur, non-ideologised, attempt by the older intelligentsia and elite to reproduce themselves culturally in the face of the ambiguous threat of the colonial school. Here, while we are speaking literally of the language, we must remember that a language can never be divorced from its discourse, its mode of teaching, its power. English schools were at first taken by the older intelligentsia to be shops where the child merely mastered the craft of a new language and an associated science. They were only gradually understood to be educational in a wider sense, as including an ideology and an ethics in their training, therefore acculturating children into worlds that were alien to surrounding ones. We may speculate, and in part document, that the reason for the continuity of indigenous education was this new understanding. The documentation would come from the scores of caste journals and caste association papers that emerged all over India from the end of the nineteenth century onwards, all with the common theme of losing something valuable – that is, both precious, and also something possessed and regarded as inalienable – and speculating on how to protect it.

The results of this continuity may likewise be speculated on and in part documented, and divided, for heuristic convenience, into the conscious and unconscious. Its most evident conscious result was to generate a continuing interest in the languages, literatures and philosophies of India among the intelligentsia. Old languages were revamped, new technologies of print and journalism used, older literary models were refined, new ambitions for the self and the public developed. What did not exist in formal articulation in the language, such as 'history', was freshly expressed or composed. The act was a deliberately constructive one. The construction of 'new' as opposed to 'traditional' was not intellectually problematic, particularly as the activities of the intelligentsia of the 'upcountry' provinces show us. It was logical to use a new epistemology to reinterpret familiar facts, or to fit in new facts into a familiar epistemology. Syed Ahmad Khan (b. 1817) remained a product of Delhi's pre-colonial cultural and intellectual milieu, in spite of serving the British government for some 20 years. As late as 1846–54, when posted in Delhi as *munsif* (district judge for civil cases), he took again to his studies of the intellectual traditions of the two great eighteenth-century Indian Muslim scholars, Shah Waliullah and Shah Abdul Aziz. Other examples were Zakaullah (b. 1832), Nazir Ahmad (b.1830), and Altaf Hussain 'Hali' (b. 1837).

In the Northwestern Provinces, the vernaculars remained the most important medium right through for all those who were in traditional occupations, such as the Kayasthas (scribes), Brahmins (priests) or various trading and commercial castes, even while all the boys learnt English. Bharatendu Harishchandra (b. 1850), father of modern Hindi literature, epitomizes some of these complex trends in his use of the new print technology, his literati creativity, and ambitions for a new nation, all in vernacular language and idioms.[24]

In the presidency capitals, and especially in Calcutta, this re-discovery typically took place in later years, after an adolescent and youthful reception and digestion of Western learning had had its time. Then the memories of childhood training leavened with an urge of creativity, led to a re-learning, re-discovery, and re-cognition, of the 'traditions' of India. Interests might include an extreme of near worship of language or motherland, or language as motherland, such as of Tamil by U.Ve. Caminataiyar, for whom the love of Tamil was a veritable marker of moral character. At the other extreme was a merely practical belief about the necessity and commercial efficacy of English, and the cultural value of the mother tongue or indigenous classical language.

The other, less conscious, more resounding result was that the possible absolute rule of 'Reason' in India was postponed. That is, although children were learning *only* languages, what they were actually learning, as already mentioned, were *discourses*. The less than perfect reproduction of the Western models of history, society and truth were not due to any failure of capacity on the part of educated Indians, or in the very nature of imitation, or due to an inherent conflict between modern and pre-modern or West and East. It was due to the other education that Indians had also received.

We are familiar with another version of this plural learning in the notion of the 'renaissance'. Directly the product of two streams of learning, the renaissance worked at two levels. At one level was the new creativity in languages, genres and media that has come down to us as the achievement of the nineteenth century. The creativity arose from the workings of new Western knowledge not on some abstract 'past', but on other bodies of knowledge encountered in quasi-formal and informal settings outside the school. The same creativity may be seen in everyday life, in average careers and their pragmatic adjustment to domestic milieus, in answers to private/public questions, without any of this reaching the stage of publishing, lecturing, or demonstrating. In this sense, all the first and even later generations of the Western-educated participated in the 'renaissance' because they were all brought up in two worlds, socialised by other teachers, elders, and women-folk as well as by their new teachers and new work experience. These two streams of learning did not stay discrete in their lives but were actively amalgamated in ways that may not necessarily seem compatible to us in our search for some elusive holism and are certainly not sufficiently known by us.

We are further familiar with this in discussion of nationalism. The 'progress' of the nationalist movement from a 'moderate' to an 'extremist' phase was due, of course, to large changes in politics, economics, and ideology. But it matched a similar process within the life span of single individuals who seemed to discover the missing dimension in their lives. Surendranath Benerjee (b. 1848) thundered when he was about 30 years old,

> We are an astute people. We are not as wholly devoid of sagacity and common sense as some people take us to be. Well, then, our fathers, with the astuteness characteristics of our race, at once saw that England's greatness was, to certain extent at least, due to her noble literature, to the immortal truths taught by her science, and to the sublime morality which breathes through the burning words of her great writers and thinkers... Might not Bengal freely grope about, in the same direction, and under the same guidance?[25]

On the occasion of the inauguration of the Banaras Hindu University, when he was about 70 years old, he spoke – together with all the other speakers on the day – about the importance of incorporating 'Indian culture' into the modern curriculum:

> We who have profited by experience are not going to make such mistakes. In our curriculum, Hindu ethics and metaphysics will occupy a foremost place, the Western system being used only for purposes of contrast or illustration. Special attention will also be paid to a knowledge of the country, its literature, its history, and its philosophy.[26]

Again, both the father, but more typically the mother, taught the child a fund of stories, views, and images. An excellent instance is the continuing popularity of the *Ramayana* and *Mahabharata* corpus of stories, which have never been part of the formal school curriculum, and which are not taught in Hindu homes through any formal religious teaching, and are not to be confused with 'religion' in any institutionalised sense. These corpuses of stories went into the making of the Indian intelligentsia in the nineteenth and twentieth centuries and were learnt through their parents, both biological and surrogate. Importantly, they were the same stories learnt and taught by the masses who either went to low-quality schools or to no schools at all.

The narrative of indigenous education becomes over our period, from some kind of a stream of schooling, to countless trickles of knowledge, privatised, invisible, seemingly powerless. The challenge for us is to see how to integrate the home-based education in almost every Indian family into a mainstream narrative of Indian education. If there was no state-based, missionary-led, or formal indigenous mass education, our data tells us that there was a difficult-to-categorize 'education' based in homes, that can only be called 'indigenous', that cut across classes and included teaching in languages, ethics, and local and community histories.

The narrative of nationalist education

This leads directly to our fourth narrative, that of nationalist education. The nationalist movement in India may be dated from 1885, the founding of the Indian

National Congress, although there were other displays of anti-colonial and quasi-nationalist endeavour before that date. The nationalist movement is popularly described as going through three phases: the Moderate (1895–1905), the Extremist (1905–1920) and the Gandhian (1920–1947). In the first phase, Indian nationalists, while swearing loyalty to the Crown, discovered the difference in the state's treatment back home in Britain and in India. Elementary Education Acts were passed in England between 1870 and 1880, and acting as good colonial citizens, an echo of these were first put forward before the Indian Education Commission of 1882 by 'a few enlightened Indians'.[27] 'The Grand Old Man of India, Dadabhai Naoroji, was one of them. He contrasted the 'British policy towards elementary education in England…' with the 'un-British' policy in India. He described it as a 'sad, sad tale' which allowed 'nearly 25 million children to grow up in ignorance'. But, at this early period, the commission would not even entertain the concept of universal and compulsory education and all his eloquent pleading was in vain.[28]

A generation later, the nationalist Gopal Krishna Gokhale, still a loyalist and a Moderate, moved a resolution in 1910 and then a Bill in the Imperial Legislative Council in 1911 for the permissive and gradual introduction of compulsory education through local bodies. The Bill was defeated because the government claimed that the concept of compulsory education was ruled out by 'administrative and financial considerations of decisive weight'.[29] However, the concept came to be accepted in the British Indian provinces, led by Maharaja Sayajirao Gaekwar of Baroda, and once accepted, it was incorporated in the laws of the land after the transfer of education to Indian control in 1921.

One of the most strident nationalist complaints was about the shortage of schools. The government retorted that it placed an emphasis on quality, not quantity, which developed into a major impasse between Lord Curzon's government (1898–1905), accused of a hidden agenda of restricting education for Indians, and all brands of nationalists who had previously called Western education the greatest gift of the British to India. To the complaint of restriction and whittling down was added the growing recognition that indigenous schools had been treated with arrogant superiority and violently rooted out. The climax came much later in 1931 when Gandhi claimed that India in that year had more illiterates than it had 50 or a 100 years earlier.

Together with the criticism of the quantitative shortcomings of education grew a complaint of its qualitative problems. These were manifold:

> … it has made men mercenary and does not build character; its aims have been secular and leave no room for godliness; it has neglected physical, moral and religious training; it has made men unpractical and has neglected vocational education…; it imparts education through a foreign tongue and has made sound education impossible; it has estranged the masses from the educated classes…and lastly, it has utterly ignored India's past culture, traditions, philosophy, arts, learning and history and has bred in the youth no love for their country.[30]

The complaints fell in two categories: colonial education had failed to be the instrument of modernity, as had been promised; and it had produced an active de-nationalisation of the educated, distanced from their culture and the masses of the country. Not only had the profound transformation in Indian life promised not been achieved, but a great harm had been done by making the educational system one 'that has ignored or despised almost every ideal informing the national culture' and educated people to be 'stranger[s] in their own lands'.[31]

There had already been attempts from the beginning of the nineteenth century to create institutions that would be more congenial to the national spirit or soul. Indeed the Hindu *pathshala*, later the Hindu College, later still the Presidency College, had thus been set up by orthodox Hindus who wished to keep it a-religious but did believe that by christening it 'Hindu' (pun intended), they would guarantee against contamination from Western religion and culture. Throughout, nationalist institutions showed a combination of emulation and resistance.[32] This was epitomised by the name used for themselves by Bal Gangadhar Tilak, Gopal Ganesh Agarkar, Vishnu Krishna Chiplunkar, and the group who set up the New English School in 1880: 'the New Jesuits.' They began the New Education Society and founded Fergusson College in 1884 to produce young men who would serve India. Based on the model of the presidencies, schools and colleges were set up by Hindu and Muslim associations representing various castes or caste-like groups, all defining themselves as anti-colonial and – reading the state as Christian – anti-Christian. Kayastha, Agarwal, Khatri, Rajput, and Nair schools were at the forefront, followed at various paces by the Ahirs, Kaseras, Jats, Nadars, Ezhavas, Mahars, and Lingayats. They all called themselves 'nationalists', but their concern was for a long time primarily for their caste or regional group, and their institutions were therefore limited in nationalist imagination and exclusive of other castes and communities.

The second wave of nationalists included both the older ones of the earlier generation and new, so-called Extremist nationalists. Their distinguishing characteristic was their resistance to working within the system, and their preference to step out of it and to find alternatives. In this there was continuity from the Extremist through the Gandhian period of nationalism. Thus, one of the planks of Rabindranath Tagore in 1905, and Mohandas Gandhi in 1920 and 1930, was precisely to boycott government schools, and both of these leaders, together with dozens of others, proposed their own alternative, preferred styles of schooling. Dayanand Saraswati's Arya Samaj, a Vedic reform movement, set up its own schools in 1889, as did the English-born Annie Besant in 1901, the Nobel literary laureate Rabindranath Tagore in 1919, and Syed Ahmad Khan in 1920. They, and many others less famous but equally fierce in their nationalism, did not aim at quantity, and saw the problem of Indian illiteracy as fundamentally a qualitative one. Schools had to be closer to the 'soul' or 'spirit' of the people to be successful, and they sought to provide a model of what an 'Indian' school should ideally be.

While some nationalist schools worked within the government system, such as the Anglo-Vedic Colleges of the Arya Samaj, others, such as Munshi Ram's *gurukul* at Kangri, sought to be more radical and re-create a school that was located in the *kula* or family of the guru, with the child completely in the care of the teacher, practising **brahmacharya*, austerities, and **tapasya*. Less esoteric, but with the same ideology, were the *Vidyapiths*, of Gujarat, Maharashtra, Bihar, and Kashi (U.P.), and the Jamia Millia Islamia in Delhi. They all wanted to sensitise their students to their environments which they claimed the colonial schools had subverted, and chose as their tools: independence from government, teaching strictly by Indians, the use of vernaculars, an emphasis on Indian art and sciences, social service, and political commitment to the nationalist struggle.

Nationalist education continued to aim at this ideal for most of the twentieth century, and one may say, up to today. To oppose colonial values in every form is of course good politics. If their politics were so on the mark, why did they fail to construct a viable Indian system of education? To understand this failure, we have to see what the nationalists actually did. The educational schemes of the new educated elite were idealistic, but also personalised. Starting from Ishvarchandra Vidyasagar, the Sanskrit scholar, going on to Jyoti Rao Phule's work in educating girls, and including many such as the New Jesuits above, they laboured with impressive intensity and set up schools for the masses. Awareness of the need for education provoked scores of others to open at least a school in their native village, and to subsidise relatives and poor children in their studies. But all this action never took on the force of a movement, or even an ideology. No united voice was heard, or consolidated vision put forward. With the growing force of nationalism, the field of 'education' took a seat further back and fell lower in the agenda of demands.

One could argue that when the nationalists wished to broaden their appeal to include the masses, they could have chosen an approach that included constructive programmes such as education. Instead, one of the main planks chosen early on was that of religion. Bal Gangadhar Tilak, Lala Lajpat Rai, and Bepin Chandra Pal were all enterprising in this, with the first achieving fame with his dramatic organisation of the Ganapati (in honour of Ganesh, the elephant God) and Shivaji (in honour of a seventeenth-century Maratha king) festivals in 1893 and 1896, respectively. They did succeed in mobilising the masses, but as we know, with the unfortunate effect of alienating non-Hindus, and for our purposes, with the unfortunate choice of putting at the forefront issues other than education.

To understand the nationalist failure in educating the masses, we must be crystal clear also that, wider as their political base became, the nationalists *were* based in the landowning and privileged classes. The colonial education designed by the British was aimed specifically at making such classes loyal collaborators of the Raj. The modern, liberal education certainly succeeded in making them also reflexive, questioning, and challenging of authority – the epitome of modernity. A good example is the new middle class educated person produced in the Aligarh Muslim University, initially established as a higher educational school in 1875. But there can be no doubt that its founder, Syed Ahmad Khan's solution of a modern, liberal, Muslim middle class educated in both the **shariat* and European science was not one shared by Muslim peasants or artisans. Nor did the Aligarh style of education fail in producing those gentlemanly virtues that increased this distance further. The best graduates of this institution, and of all other similar new institutions, chose to become lawyers, doctors and administrators. It would have been an anomaly for any of them to have chosen to enter the low-ranked, low-paying profession of the teacher or school administrator.

A third reason for the failure of nationalist education to have a mass base was that there was a conflict-ridden reasoning regarding the kind of education that was in fact desirable. Almost all nationalists proposed that the masses should be educated in the vernaculars. Almost all nationalists were themselves educated in English. Admittedly, hard-core nationalist institutions, such as the above-mentioned *gurukuls*, the Anglo-Vedic colleges, the *vidyapiths*, and Besant's schools, used the vernacular as the means of instruction to the end. Other schools and colleges that were caste- or community-based, switched over to teaching English, such as the Agrawal, Gujarati, and Khatri schools, justifying it as the call of their community in changing times. Unfortunately, in either case, the schools failed the masses. In none but the elite schools, whether missionary or privately managed 'public' schools, could a child hope to acquire skills that equipped him for material success in life.

In other words, the level of teaching of the schools for the masses – schools that were apparently well endowed, with good campuses and buildings, dedicated teachers and idealistic managers – remained deceptively weak. In their social capital they were, and are, second-rate, seedy-looking institutions with none of the glamour of elite schools. In their pedagogic strategies and success, they have confirmed this symbolic second-class status. Nationalists in India have never, apparently, understood the pedagogic needs of the country and successfully addressed them.

As I have argued above, this is partly because the nationalist struggle for independence monopolised their energies and left very little to be spent on causes such as education, gender equality, or economic planning. Nationalists did not prove themselves to be good educationists. They were not merely busy fighting the oppressive colonial master, they threw out, as it were, the baby with the bathwater. Because the philosophies of education they were familiar with were grounded in the West, they felt bound to eschew them. Indian pre-colonial philosophies had become erased for all practical purposes, and when resurrected, became irrelevant and even grotesque in the changed circumstances. The nature of learning was lost sight of by the nationalist movement. No grand new educational movement emerged, and not a single leader – sincere as Gandhi, Tagore, and Azad were about education – stood forth as a committed educational philosopher.

The failure has a less tangible, ideological dimension also. The nationalists were coloured by their own colonial education in two subconscious ways that were debilitating to true educational change in India. First, their own education had been successful either because of their own families, or individual English teachers and specific schools. That is, there was not a successful colonial *model* of schooling that produced the impressive nationalist elite that emerged. There were only isolated families and schools and teachers. This connection did not get made by them, and thus the steps taken to move forward from their own experience to a mass education system was not taken. No new prototype was developed and the colonial (non) model was kept. If nationalists failed to perceive where an alternative possible system lay, it was *because* there had already been a break with the indigenous schools and no alternatives were imaginable. They had to re-invent tradition, as in the *gurukuls* and *vidyapiths*. And they *could have* invented or re-invented anything, except that their colonial education was at least good enough for them to be satisfied with the intellectual, ideological, and discursive worlds they now inhabited. This very satisfaction stifled their inventiveness.

Second, the nationalists became colonised enough to think that the masses were predefined to be different from them, a message taught very subtly by the colonial elite. The new education that was to produce the modernity of equality, mobility and progress, produced a *self-definition* of modernity that is built upon a distancing and dis-engagement with the masses. To be a modern person in India came to mean to not be what the masses were: ignorant, superstitious, passive – and uneducated.

Conclusion

The technique of using multiple narratives is meant to highlight the point that the failure of mass education in India was not a simple or transparent one. In the colonial state narrative we have one story of failure. The colonial state, like modernising states elsewhere, could have pushed for mass education, but did not, and gave many justifications why. Another narrative shows how missionary education was popular, not so much with the masses, as with elites, and produced a class of global Indian citizens. Indian elites, however, whether nurtured in missionary schools or in the few colonial state schools that were of quality, continued to be rooted in Indian languages and value systems, thanks to the politics of the family and its agenda of social-cultural reproduction. I would like to propose this as an informal indigenous education that also needs to be brought into the story. At the same time, as narrative three describes, formal indigenous education was purposefully destroyed, leaving the masses between a past and a future with nothing in the present, even as the elite was living successfully in two enriching worlds. The most complicated question comes in the fourth and last narrative, that of the nationalist failure. This, the narrative suggests, arises from the *success* of the state and missionary schools in producing elite proto-colonials who were satisfied with their status. It arises equally from the *failure* of these schools to produce an educated Indian who could identify with the masses.

Timeline

1816: Foundation of the Hindu College, Calcutta. Set up by local gentlemen
1817/1819: Foundation of the Calcutta School Book Society and School Society

1823: Missionary Societies allowed to enter the East India Company's territories

1854: 'Dispatch' of the East India Company outlining its educational policy. This stressed the purpose of education should be to disseminate European values

1857: The East India Company sets up three universities in Calcutta, Bombay and Madras

1882–4: Commission on Education in British India. Report stressed the need to emphasise primary education

1884: Foundation of Fergusson College by the New Education Society as an institution to produce Indian patriots

1885: Foundation of the Indian National Congress

1904: Government Resolution on Educational Policy. Pointed out that secondary education was expanding more quickly than primary

1911: Gokhale's bill in India's Central Legislature to allow local bodies to introduce compulsory education. Failed

1916: establishment of Banaras Hindu University to promote Hindu culture

1921: Education transferred to Indian control. The concept of compulsory education is thereafter given legal sanction

1937: Report on Vocational Education in India. Stressed the need to provide Indians with more than a good liberal education

Glossary

brahmacharya: a way of learning physical and mental discipline through a lengthy education in the Indian traditional sciences combined with sexual abstinence.

comprador: native manager of European business.

Famine Commission 1881: set up in 1880 to report on the Great Indian Famine of 1876–8. Temple was Famine Commissioner for the Government of India.

madrasas: Muslim schools dedicated to studying the Qur'an and Islamic law, culture and history.

mahajani: script used to record the Punjabi and Marwari languages.

maktabs: schools teaching Indian vernaculars, Urdu and the Qur'an.

monitorial system or **the mutual method of teaching**: refers to systems of classroom teaching inspired by the practice of Joseph Lancaster and Andrew Bell in early nineteenth-century England that allowed large numbers of children to be taught in a disciplined fashion by a single teacher. Andrew Bell developed the system while running an orphanage in Madras and appears to have built on a system of instruction used in Indian native schools. Essentially each of the three R's would be broken down into levels of difficulty: a boy or girl who had mastered a particular skill, such as the ability to read two-letter words would be given the task of imparting this knowledge by rote to others.

pathshalas: schools teaching Indian vernaculars, arithmetic and accounting, and indigenous narratives.

Pestalozzian: after the Swiss educationalist, Johann Heinrich Pestalozzi (1746–1827) who emphasised learning by doing.

Puranic: relating to the Puranas: Hindu, Jain and Buddhist historical texts.

Ramayana and Mahabharata: the two great Sanskrit epics. The first depicts ideal characters such as kings, husbands, and servants; the second contains an account of the Kurukshetra war and includes a discussion of the four goals of life.

shariat: the body of doctrines that regulate the lives of those who profess Islam.

tapasya: spiritual enlightenment through self-purification and mortification.

tols: Sanskrit schools.

zamindari: Hindu landowning class.

Notes

1. M. Kempson (1868) *Report on the Progress of Education in North-Western Provinces for the Year 1867–68* (Allahabad), p. 30.
2. Para 7 of the Educational Dispatch of 1854, quoted in Education Commission (1884) *Report by the Bengal Provincial Committee with Evidence taken before the Committee and Memorials addressed to the Education Commission* (Calcutta: The Superintendent of Government Printing, India), p. 74.
3. S. Nurullah and J.P. Naik (1970) *A Students' History of Education in India (1800–1965)* (Bombay: Macmillan and Co).p. v.
4. S. H. Rudolph and L. I. Rudolph (eds) (2000) *Reversing the Gaze: Amar Singh's Diary, A Colonial Subject's Narrative of Imperial India* (Delhi: Oxford University Press); A. Nandy (1995) *Alternative Sciences: Creativity and Authenticity in Two Indian Scientists* (Delhi: Oxford University Press); G. Viswanathan (1989) *Masks of Conquest: Literary Study and British Rule in India* (New York: Columbia University Press); R. Guha (1997) *Dominance without Hegemony* (Cambridge: Harvard University Press); and B. Cohn (1996) *Colonialism and its Forms of Knowledge* (Princeton: Princeton University Press).
5. W. J. McKee (1930) *New Schools for Young India: A Survey of Educational, Economic and Social Conditions in India with Special Reference to More Effective Education* (Chapel Hill: The University of North Carolina Press), p. xii. Author's italics.
6. L. B. Day (1879) *Recollections of Alexander Duff, D.D., Ll.D., and of the Mission College Which he Founded in Calcutta.* (London: Nelson).
7. A. P. Howell (1872) *Education in British India prior to 1854 and in 1870–71* (Calcutta: Government Press).
8. *Report by the Bengal Provincial Committee*, p. 57.
9. There were at this time eight Presidencies and Provinces with organized Departments of Education: Bengal, North-western Provinces, Punjab, Madras, Bombay, Oude, Central Provinces, and Mysore.
10. *Report by the Bengal Provincial Committee*, p. 57.
11. The size of the main provinces under the British government was as follows: Bengal: over 187,000 square miles, population 70 million. If this is taken as 100, Madras was

89 in area and 52 in population; Bombay and Sind was 79 and 27, respectively; Punjab was 67 and 29; and the North-Western Provinces and Oudh were 68 and 69. The United Kingdom, on this scale, was 77 in area and 51 in population.

12. J. Morris (text), and S. Winchester (photographs and captions) (1983) *Stones of Empire: The Buildings of the Raj* (Oxford: Oxford University Press), p. 14.

13. Nurullah and Naik, *History of Education*, p. 155. A lakh is 100,000 rupees.

14. Education Commission (1884) *Report by the Bombay Provincial Committee* (Calcutta: The Superintendent of Government Printing, India), p. 12; S. P. Chaube (1965) *A History of Education in India* (Allahabad: Ram Narain Lal Beni Madho), pp. 307–11.

15. See differences in *Report by the Bengal Provincial Committee*, pp. 168–71 and *Report by the Bombay Provincial Committee*, pp. 18–21.

16. *Report by the Bombay Provincial Committee*, p. 34.

17. M. Kempson (1872) *Reports of the Local Education Committees for 1871* (Allahabad: Government Press), pp. 34–5.

18. R. Thornton (1850) *Memoir on the Statistics of Indigenous Education within the North-Western Provinces of the Bengal Presidency* (Calcutta: Baptist Mission Press), p. 5.

19. *Report by the Bengal Provincial Committee*, p. 72.

20. Ibid., p. 69.

21. Thornton, *Memoir on the Statistics of Indigenous Education*, p. 6.

22. *Report by the Bengal Provincial Committee*, pp. 72–3.

23. Dharmapal (1983) *The Beautiful Tree: Indigenous Education in the Eighteenth Century* (Delhi: Biblia Impex); A. Basu (1981), *Essays in the History of Indian Education* (Delhi: Concept); M. Kempson, (1873) *Report on the Progress of Education in the Northwestern Provinces for 1872–73* (Allahabad: Government Press, 1873); R.T.H. Griffith (1878) *Report on the Progress of Education in the Northwestern Provinces for 1877–78* (Allahabad: Government Press, 1878); A. P. Howell (1872) *Education in British India prior to 1854 and in 1870–71* (Calcutta: Government Press); A. M. Monteath (1867) *Selections from Records of Government of India (State of Education in India)* (Calcutta: Government Press).

24. Minault, G. (1986) 'Sayyid Ahmad Dehlavi and the "Delhi Renaissance"' in R.E.Frykenberg (ed.) *Delhi Through the Ages: Essays in Urban History, Culture and Society.* (Delhi: Oxford University Press), pp. 290–1.

25. S. Banerjea (1878) *Lord Macaulay and Higher Education in India* (Calcutta: n.p.), pp. 6–7.

26. V. A. Sundaram (1956) *Golden Jubilee of the Banaras Hindu University* (Varanasi: n.p.), p. 147.

27. J. P.Naik (1966) *Elementary Education in India: The Unfinished Business* (New York: Asia Publishing House), p. 1.

28. Ibid.

29. Ibid., p. 2.

30. Wanchoo, quoted in S. Seth (2007) *Subject Lessons: The Western Education of Colonial India* (Durham: Duke University Press), p. 161.

31. Coomaraswamy 1917, quoted in Seth, *Subject Lessons*, p. 162.

32. The folowing discussion on nationalist education is based on the large literature on the subject of nationalism in India, of which the following works were especially useful: S. C. Basu (1925) *Problems of Primary Education in India: A Study* (Calcutta: Sen Brothers & Co.); L. Chatterjee and S. Mookerjee (1931) *Representative Indians* (Calcutta: A.C. Dhar, The Popular Agency); F. Chand (1978) *Lajpat Rai: Life and Work* (Government of India: Publications Division, Ministry of Information and Broadcasting); H. Mukherjee and U. Mukherjee (1957) *The Origins of the National Education Movement (1905–1910)* (Jadavpur, Calcutta: Jadavpur University); L. Rai (n.d.) *The Call to Young India* (Madras: S. Ganesan & Co.); L. Rai (1924) *Ideals of Non-Co-operation* (Madras: S. Ganesan); L. Rai (1965) *Young India: An Interpretation and a History of the Nationalist Movement from Within*, with an introduction by V.C. Joshi (Government of India: Publications Division Ministry of Information and Broadcasting); L. Rai (1966) *The Problem of National*

Education in India (Government of India: Publications Division, Ministry of Information and Broadcasting); L. Rai (1967) *A History of the Arya Samaj [An Account of its Origins, Doctrines and Activties with a Biographical Sketch of the Founder]*, revised, expanded and edited by Sri Ram Sharma. (Bombay: Orient Longman); S. Sastri (1972) *A History of the Renaissance in Bengal: Ramtanu Lahiri: Brahman and Reformer*, from the Bengali of P. S. Sastri, edited by Sir R. Lethbridge (Calcutta: Editions Indian); S. Shyamnandan (1986) *Lala Lajpat Rai: His Life and Thought* (Delhi: Chanakya Publications); V. Venkateswarulu (1922) *All about Lok. Tilak*, with a foreword by J. Baptista (Madras: V. Ramaswamy Sastrulu & Sons).

Index